The String Quartets of Joseph Haydn

The String Quartets of Joseph Haydn

Floyd Grave and Margaret Grave

OXFORD
UNIVERSITY PRESS

OXFORD
UNIVERSITY PRESS

Oxford University Press, Inc., publishes works that further
Oxford University's objective of excellence
in research, scholarship, and education.

Oxford   New York
Auckland   Cape Town   Dar es Salaam   Hong Kong   Karachi
Kuala Lumpur   Madrid   Melbourne   Mexico City   Nairobi
New Delhi   Shanghai   Taipei   Toronto

With offices in
Argentina   Austria   Brazil   Chile   Czech Republic   France   Greece
Guatemala   Hungary   Italy   Japan   Poland   Portugal   Singapore
South Korea   Switzerland   Thailand   Turkey   Ukraine   Vietnam

Published by Oxford University Press, Inc.
198 Madison Avenue, New York, New York 10016
www.oup.com

First issued as an Oxford University Press paperback, 2008

Library of Congress Cataloging-in-Publication Data
Grave, Floyd K. (Floyd Kersey), 1945–
The string quartets of Joseph Haydn / Floyd and Margaret Grave.
p. cm.
Includes bibliographical references (p.) and index.
ISBN: 978-0-19-538295-2
1. Haydn, Joseph, 1732–1809. Quartets, strings. 2. String quartet.
I. Grave, Margaret G., 1943–   II. Title.
ML410.H4G69 2006
785′.7194′092—dc22   2005047784

Printed in the United States of America
on acid-free paper

For Jean Bonin

Acknowledgments

Our research, which in its late stages was assisted by a Rutgers University Faculty Academic Study Program Award (2002), was guided from its inception by an unlimited supply of encouragement and advice from Jan LaRue. His methods provided a foundation for our critical approach, and his fine-tuned sensitivity to the stylistic nuances of Haydn's music was an ongoing source of inspiration. To Bathia Churgin we likewise owe a debt of deepest gratitude. Her musicological expertise and analytical insights, not to mention tireless moral support, have aided our work in more ways than can possibly be enumerated. Thanks also are due to the Rutgers University music librarians past and present—Roger Tarman, Harriet Hemmasi, Cynthia Levy, and John Shepard—for their invaluable assistance over the years; to Georg Feder, Armin Raab, and Denis McCaldin for their prompt and helpful responses to our inquiries; to James Webster for kindly supplying detailed information on the autograph manuscripts of the Op. 50 quartets; and to the editors and editorial staff at Oxford University Press—Kim Robinson, Suzanne Ryan, Christine Dahlin, Eve Bachrach, and Norm Hirschy—whose enthusiasm, patience, and guidance proved essential at every step of the process. Others who have supported our work in less concrete but nonetheless important ways include Channan Willner, always a source of shrewd and timely assistance, by no means exclusively in theoretical and bibliographical matters, and Alex Szögyi and Philip Thompson, whose interest and professional wisdom have heartened the journey toward this book's completion.

Contents

The String Quartets of Joseph Haydn

Introduction

To undertake a study of Haydn's string quartets is to enter a domain of music scholarship whose byways far exceed the scope of a single book. The quartets' complexities of texture, thematic process, form, and topical allusion are perennial tests of acuity on the part of critics and interpreters, and explorations of the works have followed many paths. By any measure, the quartets enjoy preeminent stature in the canon of later-eighteenth-century chamber music, and it is easy to imagine that Haydn regarded them as a congenial medium of expression. Widely disseminated through manuscripts and printed editions, and judged favorably for the most part by contemporaries, they helped define the terms of the genre as a touchstone of taste, as a true medium for connoisseurs, and as a type of work whose exacting standards required "a composer who lacks neither genius nor the broadest knowledge of harmony."[1]

Later commentators came to understand the quartets as quintessential reflections of Haydn's artistic personality and, by extension, as emblems of a larger historical process. In this view, the allegedly undistinguished, mid-century Viennese idiom from which the earliest quartets sprang was a starting point, and tendencies witnessed in subsequent opus groups arose either as hindrances or as signs of progress toward the eventual achievement of a mature Classical style.

Recent scholarly writings have tended to view such teleologically driven narratives with skepticism, and in fact the very notion of Viennese Classicism as a coherent, period-defining concept has been vigorously challenged.[2] It is not our purpose to support or repudiate particular claims with respect to the quartets' historical role. However, we do question any method that allows our evaluation of the quartets to become enmeshed in assumptions about stylistic progression. To be sure, patterns of development may be traced in the quartets as in other instrumental repertories from the period. But to argue from a notion of ineluctable progress is to run the risk of suppressing contrary evidence, skewing the analyses to support the thesis, and awarding privileged status to certain works at the expense of other, not necessarily less deserving, compositions. Are we justified in attributing the flaw of stylistic immaturity to music that may well have delighted contemporary listeners and performers with what they may have perceived to be its fashionably up-to-date character and fluent technique? Or in consigning certain works to a kind of stylistic limbo as tokens of transition—shedding the past, looking to the future, but all the while deprived of their own present?

Seeking to minimize such hazards, our own approach asks suitably broad questions of the repertory as a whole while addressing the individual opus groups on their own terms, so to speak, rather than obliging them to represent specific stages of advancement. Which conventions of movement form and cyclic design did Haydn prefer, and under what conditions did he most often digress from his own norms? What were his predilections with regard to string quartet sonority and ensemble play? Which *topoi* and modes of expression did he favor for a quartet's different movements? What are the most telling points of similarity and difference from one opus group to the next? What constraints, motivating circumstances, or other external factors may have impinged on the composition of a given opus group? The issues we raise often do in fact highlight patterns of change as well as lines of continuity between one phase of Haydn's career and the next. But by maintaining a respectful distance from predetermined evolutionary paths, we can better appreciate the possible range of Haydn's compositional choices at a given time in his career and thereby facilitate an inclusive, detailed portrayal of the oeuvre.

How can such a study best be organized? An ostensibly simple, direct approach would have been to arrange the works in chronological order and explicate them one by one. Such a method has the merit of easy reference for a reader in search of thumbnail descriptions, and yet many considerations argue against such a plan. To begin with, an appropriately detailed analysis of each composition would easily have resulted in an unwieldy tome several times the size of this book. But a still more basic concern has to do with the nature of the repertory itself: although Haydn may in a certain sense be described as a composer who seldom repeats himself, the fact is that he relies on a variety of models and habitual strategies that not only recur from one work or opus group to the next but that do so in ways that can yield important stylistic insights. To detach a particular passage or movement design from others to which it bears resemblance is to lose touch with a web of significant interopus relationships, whereas to address such points of connection within a straight, work-by-work account would lead to a hopelessly complex tangle of cross-references.

Our solution has been to divide the book into several discrete yet interrelated parts, each viewing the oeuvre from a different perspective, and each designed to accommodate outstanding and representative details without losing sight of a larger, illuminating context, namely, the common ground of procedures and techniques that underlies a given opus group or that informs the oeuvre in its entirety. We begin with a chronological survey that places Haydn's creation of the quartets within the framework of his career. From there, we proceed to a consideration of the works' distinguishing features as manifestations of a string quartet genre and to an examination of the string quartet ensemble as a medium of performance that invites specialized, idiomatic usage with regard to texture, timbre, and the interaction among parts.

The second part of our book examines Haydn's structural models for the quartets, including sonata, dance, variation, fugue, and rondo, as well as several hybrids and unclassifiable designs. The final section draws on the arguments of earlier chapters as it traverses the opus groups, appraising each as a reflection of the composer's circumstances at a particular juncture in his life. Topics discussed include the immediate stimulus for the undertaking in question; sources, dating, and early publication history; the phenomenon of opus character as manifested in various signs of stylistic unity, diversity, or idiosyncrasy; instances of characteristic or novel usage with regard to cyclic profile, movement design, and the like; and Haydn's recurrent tendency to recall or elaborate on a previous group's prominent features or techniques.

Our project has been assisted by a distinguished body of research on music of the late eighteenth century and on the quartets in particular. Numerous studies are referred to in the notes that accompany the text, and we have drawn on many others as models or as sources of background information. Writings whose guiding influence merits special recognition at the outset include a wealth of books and articles on late-eighteenth-century musical style by Daniel Heartz, Jan LaRue, Leonard Ratner, Charles Rosen, and James Webster; the insightful accounts of eighteenth-century correspondences between music and rhetoric in studies by Elaine Sisman and Mark Evan Bonds; and Gretchen Wheelock's close examination of Haydn's wit and humor. H. C. Robbins Landon's five-volume *Chronicle and Works* has served as an essential reference at practically every turn, and Webster's numerous studies covering aspects of Haydn biography, style, and chronology have proved indispensable. Several important books concerned specifically with quartets also must be mentioned: Ludwig Finscher's groundbreaking study of the origins of the genre and Haydn's contributions through Op. 33; a general survey by Reginald Barrett-Ayres, and the more recent, concise overview by Georg Feder; Hans Keller's book, whose emphasis falls on performance-related issues; and two excellent, detailed accounts of individual opus groups, William Drabkin's examination of Op. 20, and W. Dean Sutcliffe's monograph on the quartets of Op. 50. With regard to these two sets of quartets, our own presentation may be understood as a complementary effort rather than a competing or opposing view.

The most basic resources of all for a study such as ours, Anthony van Hoboken's catalogue of Haydn's works and the *Joseph Haydn Werke* (abbreviated *JHW*) together encompass a veritable treasure of documentary information. (For citations in the text, reference is made to Hoboken only when the information in question is not also given in the *JHW*.)

As of the time of writing, the *JHW* volume encompassing Opp. 42, 50, and 54/55 was not yet available. For music examples and other references to the musical texts of these works, we have relied principally on the readings of the Doblinger edition edited by Barrett-Ayres and Landon. Otherwise, the *JHW* is our principal source.

For various discussions of musical forms in parts II and III, we have incorporated analytical sketches that employ the method made familiar by LaRue: structural proportions, themes, changes of key, and points of articulation are represented on a timeline that corresponds to the order of events in the score. For sonata-related forms, themes are given functional labels wherever appropriate: P (= primary, referring to ideas expounded in tonic at the outset); T (= transition, encompassing unstable, goal-directed motion prior to the establishment of a secondary key); S (= secondary, comprising one or more thematic strands first presented in the latter part of an exposition, once the secondary key has been secured); K (= closing, for the repetitive, punctuating phrases that signal an imminent conclusion to the exposition).

Multiple themes within a given functional area are designated numerically (*1P*, *2P*, etc.); principal subdivisions within themes are designated with lowercase letters (*1Pa*, *b*, etc.); and derivations are indicated by theme-function labels in parentheses, for example, $\frac{(2Pb)}{1Ta}$, to show that the first phrase of *1T* derives from the second phrase of *2P*. Although the use of such labels generally promotes clarity in describing the logic of a particular order of events, certain limitations must be acknowledged. Haydn's thematic functions are often fluid, and the choice of which label to use can sometimes be arbitrary (for example, *2P* as opposed to *1T* to designate a theme that begins by sustaining the home key but that ends with an inflected half cadence that points in the direction of the dominant). Capital and lowercase letters below the timeline distinguish major and minor keys, respectively, whereas horizontal arrows call attention to goal-directed harmonic activity that leads to a change in key. Capital letters are used in the text to designate pitch-classes; and on occasions when reference is made to a specific register, usually in connection with Haydn's high first violin passages, we have adopted the Helmholtz system to make the appropriate distinctions: c^1 represents middle C, and higher superscript numbers signify higher octaves accordingly.

Part I: Points of Departure

I

The Repertory

Haydn's lifelong engagement with the string quartet began in the 1750s with a series of works that proved to be among the most promising fruits of his early maturity. As recounted by his friend and biographer Georg August Griesinger (1769–1845), foundations for this effort may be traced to Haydn's childhood: the early recognition of his talent, the instruction he received in voice and musical instruments as a schoolboy in Hainburg, and subsequent experiences at the choir school of St. Stephen's cathedral in Vienna.[1] Haydn himself explained in an autobiographical sketch from 1776[2] that he had enjoyed success as a singer at the cathedral and at court until his eighteenth year, but from that time on he was obliged to fend for himself as a freelance teacher and musician. Struggling by day to earn a living and teaching himself to compose "well into the night," he had the good fortune to meet the great poet and librettist Metastasio (1698–1782), who happened to reside in the building where he had found lodging. Metastasio introduced him to the Italian opera composer Nicola Porpora (1686–1768), who had arrived in Vienna in 1752 or early 1753, and it was from Porpora that Haydn finally learned "the true fundamentals of composition."

As the occasion arose, Haydn tried his hand in a variety of musical genres, composing sacred works, music for a lost Singspiel (*Der krumme Teufel*), and pieces of instrumental music, such as ballroom dances, keyboard sonatas, keyboard trios, string trios, and quartets. He attracted the attention of music-loving patrons; and by 1761, he had earned his permanent appointment in the court of the Hungarian prince Paul Anton Esterházy (1711–62). But for several years before that time, he served as music director to Count Karl Joseph Franz Morzin (1717–83), possibly beginning in 1757 or 1758; still earlier (specific dates are elusive for this period) he worked for the family of Baron Carl Joseph Fürnberg (ca. 1720–67), and it was allegedly in connection with Fürnberg, sometime around the mid 1750s, that Haydn's first quartet was heard.[3]

We learn from Griesinger that the event took place at Weinzirl castle, Fürnberg's turreted retreat near the Austrian town of Wieselburg, some sixty miles west of Vienna. The baron, who had engaged Haydn to teach music to his children, is said to have asked him to supply music for private performances there. Responding to the request, he furnished a composition for four available string players: Fürnberg's pastor, his steward, Haydn, and a cellist identified by Griesinger as a brother of the composer and theorist Albrechtsberger.[4]

This initial attempt was followed by others; and eventually there were ten such works of similar design (listed in table 1.1). Recognized today under the opus numbers 0, 1, and 2, they circulated as handwritten copies before being taken up by foreign publishers in the 1760s. Exactly where the ten fit chronologically has not been determined with certainty, although for various reasons it seems likely that they were composed within a short time of one another, with perhaps no more than a few years elapsing between first and last.[5]

On the basis of this achievement, is it proper to regard Haydn as the creator of a new genre, or, as he has often been called, the "father of the string quartet"? The account transmitted by Griesinger makes no reference to precedents, yet it appears that at least two contemporaries wrote comparable works for four string parts at around the same time. A group of six such pieces by Franz Xaver Richter (1709–89), eventually published as his Op. 5, may well have predated Haydn's works,[6] and *Partite a 4* by Ignaz Holzbauer (1711–83) could likewise have been written earlier, perhaps by 1751. If claims of paternal rights on Haydn's behalf are dubious in a literal sense, his works nonetheless stand out by virtue of their technical polish, structural control, and sure grasp of the medium's possibilities. The available documentary evidence attests to their popular appeal; and the eventual publication of these works by firms in Paris, Amsterdam, and London (an initiative in which the composer himself apparently played no part) helped ensure their enduring prominence as models of their type.

Meanwhile, Haydn had begun his Esterházy service as vice kapellmeister under a contract that may be described as daunting, to say the least. Peppered with injunctions about deportment and protocol, it specified an array of administrative and musical responsibilities and warned of more open-ended requirements that might arise in the future.[7] Conspicuously placed as fourth in the contract's fourteen clauses was a requirement that music Haydn composed for the court must not be copied or distributed to anyone, but was to be retained for the prince's exclusive use. Whether or not this stipulation seemed irksome to the composer at the time, it would become a matter of consequence as his career progressed.

Doubtless of greater immediate concern, along with everyday business, was the job of meeting local needs for new compositions. In addition to symphonies (Haydn appears to have written more than thirty between 1761 and the end of the decade), keyboard sonatas (perhaps a dozen or so during the 1760s), solo concertos, and other miscellaneous instrumental pieces, there was music to be written for performance by the composer's employer, Prince Nicolaus I (1714–90), who had succeeded his brother in 1762 and was a passionate enthusiast of that large, unusual string instrument, the baryton. There also was much to do in the domain of vocal music, especially after the death of the aging kapellmeister, Gregor Joseph Werner (1693–1766). In addition to several masses, the *Applausus* cantata, and the *Stabat Mater*, the latter part of the decade saw the production of three major comic operas (*La canterina*, 1766; *Lo speziale*, 1768; and *Le pescatrici*, 1769).

For string quartets, however, there appears to have been no demand within the Esterházy milieu, so that further development of the genre (whether directly inspired by Haydn's example or not) was now left to his contemporaries, several of whom made significant contributions during the 1760s. Luigi Boccherini (1743–1805), for example, had sojourned in Vienna during the years 1760–61, and it is possible that he encountered copies of some of the early Haydn quartets there. His own Op. 2 quartets of 1761 (published as Op. 1 by the Parisian publisher Venier in 1767) bear a general resemblance to Haydn's in their attention to ensemble play, although in other respects, notably the prominent part they sometimes give to the composer's instrument, the cello, they are quite different.[8] Composers within the Viennese orbit whose works now helped expand the repertory included Franz Asplmayr (1728–86), whose career intersected briefly with Haydn's during the time when both worked at the court of Count Morzin, Florian Leopold Gassmann (1729–74), Carlo d'Ordonez (1734–86), Johann Georg Albrechtsberger (1736–1809), Leopold Hofmann (1738–93), and Johann Baptist Wanhal (1739–1813). Quartets by several of these musicians betray the influence of a conservative, sonata da chiesa tradition, with imitative fabric in a slow opening movement or fugal procedure in second or fourth place,[9] for example, traits not evident in Haydn's earliest quartets. Also different from Haydn are works by composers in this group that seem more orchestral than soloistic in conception.[10] But resemblances to Haydn's approach are also apparent, notably among certain slow-movement violin solos in Asplmayr's early quartets (for instance, his Op. 2/1/iii), as well as in the lively ensemble writing in his finales. (Asplmayr's Op. 2 was published in Paris ca. 1769; the quartets were probably written no later than 1768.)[11]

Circumstances that prompted Haydn's eventual return to the quartet are not fully clear, although it has been noted that between *Le pescatrici* in 1769 and *L'infedeltà delusa* in 1773 there were no new operas, and that also around this time there was a lull in his production of works for the baryton.[12] The opportunity was thus at hand for turning to that neglected medium in which he had formerly displayed such insight. It also has been proposed, or at least implied, that the stimulus may have come from the prince himself and the Esterházy concertmaster Luigi Tomasini (1741–1808). Tomasini had been part of Nicolaus's retinue on a trip to Paris in the fall of 1767. At the time, Boccherini was performing in Parisian salons, where the two visitors are likely to have heard such newly

published works as the Italian composer's Op. 2 quartets. Assuming their interest had been aroused, they are not likely to have kept their enthusiasm to themselves on their return from the journey.[13]

In any case, Haydn now went about his new task with gusto, altering, mod-
ernizing, and building on the earlier accomplishment. He completed a group of
six quartets, known as Op. 9, by 1770, and a companion set, Op. 17, followed in
short order. Technically demanding, especially for the first violin, and generally
serious in character, although not without a healthy measure of wit, these works
position the quartet as an exemplary genre for connoisseurs. And yet no connoisseur familiar with either set could have anticipated what was to come in 1772: a
third group, Op. 20, that far exceeded its immediate predecessors in matters of
thematic process, ensemble technique, and artful deviations from familiar models
of rhetoric and structure.

The string quartet gained in popularity throughout Europe as the new decade
progressed, and large quantities of such works, many of them tailored to a thriv-
ing amateur market, were being published in Paris. Composers who contributed
significantly to this trend included, among others, Jean-Baptiste Davaux (1742–
1822), Giuseppe Cambini (?1746–1825), and Jean-Baptiste Bréval (1753–1823).[14]
Meanwhile, with the help of ongoing efforts by Haydn's compatriots, the genre
continued to thrive as a predominant form of instrumental chamber music within
the Viennese circle. But once again Haydn himself withdrew. Whatever stimulus had led him to undertake Opp. 9, 17, and 20 had simply expired or was overtaken by other commitments. The demands of his post were formidable, and
they became especially intense from 1776, with the institution of regular, full-
scale theater seasons at his employer's princely estate of Eszterháza. In 1778, for
example, there were no fewer than fifty opera performances, and the numbers
were destined to grow far higher in the coming decade. Operatic works presented
were chiefly those of other composers, although Haydn contributed some himself, among them *Il mondo della luna*, 1777; *La vera costanza*, by 1779; *L'isola dis-
abitata*, 1779; and *La fedeltà premiata*, 1780. It is easy to imagine that insufficient
time and opportunity were principal reasons for his silence.

Haydn's next set of quartets, the famous and well-loved Op. 33, finally came
about in 1781, some nine years after Op. 20. This time, the motivating circumstances can be specified with a degree of certainty: Haydn's fame had grown considerably in the intervening years, and it was at least partially in response to this
fact that in 1779 his contract was redrawn in terms more favorable to his personal and professional interests. Most important, the new agreement omitted the
original clause that had given the prince rights of ownership to his kapellmeister's music. Haydn was now free to produce compositions as he wished, and to
negotiate their sale to publishers or else offer them by subscription directly to the
public.[15]

Before long, Haydn entered into relationships with the firm of Artaria, which had recently begun a music-publishing business in Vienna, and with the publisher William Forster in London. His work with the Eszterháza theater remained a central concern, yet the prospect of writing compositions on his own initiative, targeting local and international markets for their sale, was evidently an irresistible attraction. As it pertained to the Op. 33 quartets, the new arrangement was a rewarding exercise in professional independence. Artistically, it was perhaps also an escape from the public realm of opera production to a musically more intimate environment.

Haydn's apparent plan for Op. 33 was to garner financial reward and prestige by offering manuscript copies on a subscription basis to patrons and connoisseurs, and then to have the works distributed more widely in published form. His claim to have composed them in a "new, quite special way"[16] was obviously intended to pique the curiosity of potential subscribers. But it may have been more than a slogan: in contrast to the more esoteric challenges of Op. 20, the new works are marked not only by technical sophistication but also by a disarming veneer of familiarity and natural sentiment. Suffused with wit and humor, and designed to please a heterogeneous market of amateurs as well as connoisseurs, the set came to epitomize both a classical string quartet ideal and the aspirations of the period as a whole.[17]

The evident success of Op. 33 notwithstanding, its completion was followed by yet another hiatus, this one perhaps harder to understand than the previous lapse. Why did Haydn not choose to capitalize on the recent venture by proceeding to write another, comparably attractive group of quartets? There were, to be sure, competing demands and commitments. The opera season was becoming increasingly long and taxing. There were more than 100 performances in 1783, for example, and in 1786 some 125. But there were new developments as well, arising from the ever-increasing recognition of Haydn's music abroad. A planned 1783 excursion to London did not materialize but nevertheless yielded a group of three symphonies, Nos. 76, 77, and 78; and not long afterward came the commission from a leading French patron, Count d'Ogny (1757–90), for the "Paris" symphonies (Nos. 82–87), written in 1785–86 for performance by the Concert de la Loge Olympique. At around this time, Haydn responded to a request from Cádiz for a group of sacred pieces for orchestra, the *Seven Last Words*, intended for a Holy Week ceremony, and a commission from the King of Naples resulted in a group of concertos for two *lire organizzate*.

Actually, Haydn did write at least one additional quartet by the middle of the decade: a diminutive work in D minor, whose melancholy character seems to reflect its forlorn status as a quartet without companions. It was issued by the composer and publisher Franz Anton Hoffmeister (1754–1812) in 1786 as Op. 42, and it may have been commissioned by him as part of a series of individual quartets by various composers.[18] Other evidence points to a different stimulus, a commission from Spain to which Haydn refers in a letter from 5 April 1784,[19] but about which little else is known.

Op. 42 notwithstanding, Haydn's latest retreat may be viewed from a different perspective altogether. During the year in which the Op. 33 quartets were written, Mozart had come to live in Vienna, and before long the two composers met and became friends. Just when their first meeting occurred is not known. An early documented encounter, allegedly in 1784, involved a quartet party in which an illustrious foursome participated: Haydn and the violinist-composer Carl Ditters von Dittersdorf (1739–99) took the upper parts, while Mozart and Wanhal played the viola and cello, respectively.[20]

Mozart, no less fickle in his attention to the medium than Haydn, had written a total of thirteen quartets between 1770 and 1773, but he then also stopped composing such works until the next decade. Doubtless prompted by Haydn's recent accomplishment, he began in late 1782 to undertake a corresponding new set of his own, comprising K. 387, 421, 428, 458, 464, and 465. When they were published by Artaria in 1785, an accompanying letter of dedication to Haydn described them as "the fruit of a long and laborious study,"[21] a confession borne out by the unusual amounts of crosshatching and alteration observable in the autograph manuscripts.[22] Ambitious technically, superbly original, yet nevertheless steeped in Haydn's idiom, they must have made a deep impression on the older composer, who is likely to have felt challenged to reconsider, reflect, and absorb. Might he have heard Mozart's legato phrases, his mastery of chromaticism, or the streamlined pace of his common-time Allegros as signs of a newly enriched quartet style with which he must come to terms? And if so, might a certain amount of time have been required for him to assimilate before responding?

Whether influenced by Mozart's enterprise or not, Haydn's next group of quartets was a departure from the more easygoing Op. 33. Completed in 1787 and now known as Op. 50, these works seem specially designed for connoisseurs. Informed by a degree of technical complexity recalling that of Op. 20, they represent a renewed commitment to the genre's patrician stature. Apart from their artistic aspirations, they merit notice as a chronological watershed in Haydn's engagement with the medium. Rather than composing quartets in spurts, interrupted by long periods of silence, Haydn now chose to award them a central place in his work as a composer of instrumental music.

It was just one year later, then, that the next set of quartets appeared, those of Op. 54/55. (The double opus number resulted from a practice that began around this time of dividing a set of six works into two separate prints of three each.)[23] Although these works are scarcely deficient in formal novelty or intricate ensemble play, they seem more intent on making an immediate impact than drawing us into a private realm of motivic nuance and textural refinement. Packed with memorable themes, rhythmic vitality, and colorful harmony, they give the impression of striving to compete for attention in a burgeoning market of string quartet publications.[24]

True to Haydn's practice of changing direction in response to practical concerns as well as altered artistic goals, the set of quartets that now followed, Op. 64 (1790), proved markedly different from either of the previous ones. An advertisement for the set, published in the *Wiener Zeitung* of 23 February 1791, concedes that there had been complaints about the extraordinary difficulty of Haydn's works, but claims that with these newest quartets, "the performer as well as the mere amateur will be completely satisfied."[25] In 1788, Haydn's friend Dittersdorf had published a set of colorful, richly diversified quartets to which this description might also apply, and it may well have been the current fashion reflected in such works—for an engaging, not overly challenging idiom—that persuaded Haydn to alter his own approach. Displaying less brilliance and energy than Op. 54/55 and placing less emphasis than Op. 50 on sheer compositional rigor, the new quartets look back to the more intimate, conversational manner of Op. 33, and in keeping with the apparent goal of pleasing both amateurs and connoisseurs, Haydn makes a point of leavening these works (as he had in that earlier set) with tokens of popular style.

With the benefit of hindsight, we can regard Op. 64 as a culmination of sorts, crowning a late Esterházy phase of Haydn's career that had included such memorable instrumental works as the keyboard sonatas in C and E♭ (Hob. XVI:48 and 49), the five symphonies that followed the "Paris" set (Nos. 88–92), seven keyboard trios (Hob. XV:11–17), and the quartets of Opp. 50 and 54/55. By 1790, Haydn had been in Esterházy service for close to thirty years. Although nothing in his recent music could be said to reflect exhaustion or waning resolve, the burdensome duties and social isolation of his position must have been weighing on his spirits. Writing to his close friend Maria Anna von Genzinger in Vienna, he complains of hard work, melancholy, nasty weather, professional vexation, and miserable food.[26] Doubtless he felt ready for a change, and when his longtime patron died in September of that year, any grief he experienced must have been tempered by a feeling of relief that his state of captivity had come to an end.

Fresh opportunities soon beckoned: the London violinist and concert producer Johann Peter Salomon (1745–1815) happened to be traveling in Germany at around the time of the prince's death. When he heard the news, he journeyed from Cologne to Vienna to see Haydn and try to entice him (not for the first time) to come to London. Feeling free now to accept, Haydn signed an agreement on 8 December and took leave of Vienna by the end of the year.[27] (In the publicity that preceded Haydn's arrival in England, Salomon took full credit for the invitation, but the publisher John Bland, who issued the Op. 64 quartets in London, also may have played a role. Apparently he had acted as Salomon's agent in a visit with Haydn the previous year, and he appears to have been the author of a letter to the British ambassador that had proved crucial to the agreement.)[28]

Oddly, in light of the Op. 64 quartets' accent on chamber style rather than brilliance or showmanship, Haydn took pains to have works from this group presented publicly in London. Did his apparent eagerness mean that he believed his quartets could readily accommodate a concert environment? Was he merely curious to see how a public audience would react to these works? Whatever his intentions with Op. 64, the adoption of a public façade is unmistakable in the quartets that followed, those of Op. 71/74,[29] dedicated to Count Anton Georg Apponyi (1751–1817). Completed in 1793 during the interim between the end of his first visit to England (July 1792) and the start of the second (early 1794), these works display such concert-style traits as bold introductory gestures, declamatory unisons, and concertante passages that engage the ensemble in brilliant figuration. At the same time, they recommend themselves to performance in the traditional manner of chamber music, although to experience their special energy to the fullest, performers and listeners should perhaps at least try to imagine the dynamic energy of a public setting.

Haydn returned to Vienna in the summer of 1795, and in the year that followed, he began work on the monumental compositions for vocal soloists, chorus, and orchestra that dominated the final stage of his career: the two late oratorios, *The Creation* (1796–98) and *The Seasons* (1799–1801), and the large-scale concerted masses written principally for the nameday of Princess Maria Hermenegild Esterházy (1768–1845) between 1796 and 1802. Meanwhile, the output of major instrumental works nearly ceased, the second London visit having marked the end of Haydn's contribution as a symphonist. His last piano sonatas were composed by the end of that sojourn, with the last piano trios and the trumpet concerto not long thereafter.[30]

The case was different with the string quartet, however, a domain in which there was still much to be accomplished. A commission from Count Joseph Erdödy (1754–1824) resulted in the six quartets of Op. 76, completed in 1797, whose extraordinary novelty and variety bear no simple comparison with any of the previous opus groups. It is almost as if the creative energies that Haydn might previously have distributed among works in other instrumental genres were now channeled into quartets, whose natural resiliency proved more than sufficient to accommodate those energies without strain.

The technical and stylistic richness of Op. 76 may be seen from another perspective as well, as an effort to stand out with special distinction among the numerous Viennese quartets now being written and published.[31] Many such works were inspired by the Parisian *quatour concertant*, with its emphasis on accessibility, textural transparency, and ease of performance. Popular quartets of this type by Ignaz Pleyel (1757–1831) were in circulation, and there were new contributions by such composers as Hoffmeister, Paul Wranitzky (1756–1808), and Adalbert Gyrowetz (1763–1850). Technically more challenging works also were being composed, including examples of what Hickman has identified as a Viennese *quatuor brilliant,* as seen in works by Paul Wranitzky, Gyrowetz, and Franz Krommer (1759–1831) from the 1790s, which featured the distribution of thematic lines and soloistic figuration among different instruments. Mozart's late "Prussian" quartets (K. 575, 589, and 590) show signs of such a tendency, given their many passages in which the cello vies with the first violin for prominence. Quartets whose attention to motivic development and textural complexity prove closer to Haydn's customary practices include those by Anton Wranitzky (1761–1820), Emanuel Aloys Förster (1748–1823), and Joseph Wölfl (1773–1812).[32]

Before the end of the decade, Haydn himself had another chance to contribute to the genre, this time in response to a 1799 commission from Prince Franz Joseph Maximilian Lobkowitz (1772–1816). Two quartets were finished within the year, but the composer was ailing and pressed by other responsibilities. The project was eventually curtailed, and the two works were published as an incomplete set with the opus number 77. Comparable in size and complexity to those of Op. 76, these last complete quartets may, like them, be heard as worthy instrumental counterparts to the late vocal masterpieces.

There remains the unfinished Op. 103, Haydn's final effort in this field (indeed the final composition altogether, apart from the last folksong arrangements, which may have been largely, if not entirely, the work of pupils):[33] two interior movements for a quartet in D minor that was evidently supposed to have been a third member of the set for Lobkowitz. Why was the piece never finished? As early as 1799, Haydn had described alarming symptoms of mental exhaustion in a letter of 12 June to the Leipzig firm of Breitkopf & Härtel.[34] As reported by Griesinger, the strain of composing *The Seasons* proved to be too much for him. Seized by "brain fever" and undone by the pain of incessant mental effort, he became increasingly weak from this time on.[35] It was not until 1803 that the two middle movements were finished; and as prospects for further work on the quartet grew dim, Haydn consented to having them printed (by Breitkopf & Härtel) as a fragment. Griesinger sent the manuscript to the publisher in April 1806, and accompanied it with a letter in which he described the item as Haydn's swan song.[36] By way of apology for this sad circumstance, he included a copy of the composer's famous visiting card, which quotes from his setting of a text by J. W. L. Gleim, "Der Greis" (Hob. XXVc:5, for four voices and keyboard; see ex. 1.1).[37] Noting that Haydn still hoped he might be able to add a concluding rondo, but recognizing that this was not likely, he suggested that the visiting-card motto be added to the print instead, so that "wherever this quartet sounds, one will see immediately, from these few words, why it is not complete, and one will thus be filled with sad emotions." It was thus left for the performer or listener to imagine the scope and magnitude originally intended for this work.

As summarized in table 1.1, the oeuvre as a whole encompasses sixty-eight quartets: nine works from Opp. 1 and 2, plus the stray Op. 0, yields a total of ten early, five-movement compositions. The subsequent nine opus groups of six quar-

EXAMPLE 1.1 Haydn's visiting-card motto

(Gone is all my strength,
old and weak am I)

tets each add up to an additional fifty-four, and to these are added the lone Op. 42, the two quartets of Op. 77, and finally Op. 103.

A monumental endeavor by the composer and publisher Ignaz Pleyel, a former pupil of Haydn's, sought to acknowledge the epochal importance of the quartets by compiling a complete edition, the *Collection complette des quatuors d'Haydn*, duly issued in 1801 with a dedication to Napoleon. (The 1801 edition encompassed eighty works. A second edition, ca. 1803–4, added the two quartets of Op. 77, and the expanded edition of 1806 included Op. 103.)[38] Pleyel's own prominent stature, added to the fact of his personal association with Haydn, endowed this edition with authority, and the impression of authenticity was enhanced by the claim "attested to by the composer" (avoués par l'Auteur) attached to the thematic catalogue that accompanied the edition. (There are grounds for questioning the veracity of the claim, however: in a letter of 11 July 1801, Hoffmeister reports that Haydn has assured him that he in fact had not written eighty quartets.)[39] In any event, Pleyel's construction of the oeuvre persisted well into the twentieth century and was inscribed, for example, in the widely circulated Eulenburg edition overseen by Wilhelm Altmann.

To reconcile the outdated compilation of an alleged eighty-three quartets with the authentic total of sixty-eight, as portrayed in table 1.1, we may begin by weeding out three items from among the earliest two groups—Op. 1/5 (actually a symphony, Hob. I:107), and Op. 2/3 and 5, both of which originated as sextets for strings plus a pair of horns (Hob. II:21, 22)—then adding the so-called Op. 0, which had not been included in the printed sources on which Pleyel relied for his Opp. 1 and 2. The one-movement sacred pieces comprising *The Seven Last Words*, mentioned earlier in connection with commissions from Spain, must also be subtracted from Pleyel's count. Not only do they have little in common with the multimovement format and secular orientation by which the genre is most reasonably defined, but the string quartet arrangement, adapted from the original orchestral score in 1787, is merely one of several versions: a transcription for keyboard not actually by Haydn also appeared in 1787, and Haydn himself later refashioned the work as a Lenten oratorio with chorus.

TABLE 1.1 An overview of Haydn's string quartets

Opus	Date	Number							
		–	1	2	3	4	5	6	
0	ca 1755–60	E♭							1
1			B♭	E♭	D	G		C	5
2			A	E		F		B♭	4
9	ca 1768–70		C	E♭	G	Dm	B♭	A	6
17	1771		E	F	E♭	Cm	G	D	6
20	1772		E♭	C	Gm	D	Fm	A	6
33	1781		Bm	E♭	C	B♭	G	D	6
42	[?1784–] 1785	Dm							1
50	1787		B♭	C	E♭	F♯m	F	D	6
54/55	1788		G	C	E	A	Fm	B♭	6
64	1790		C	Bm	B♭	G	D	E♭	6
71/74	[?1792–] 1793		B♭	D	E♭	C	F	Gm	6
76	[?1796–] 1797		G	Dm	C	B♭	D	E♭	6
77	1799		G	F					2
103	[?1802–] 1803	Dm							1

Total: 68

Our total, whittled down thus far from eighty-three to seventy-four, may now be further reduced by excising Op. 3, a group of six quartets long thought to be Haydn's but now recognized as unauthentic. Commentators had long been baffled by these pieces, whose place in the canon proved hard to explain in terms of any theory of chronological development: by comparison with the earliest works, on the one hand, and the presumably later quartets of Opp. 9 and 17, on the other, they seemed an anomaly, an unaccountable stylistic detour. (They were in fact first published in 1777, and they may have originated later than Opp. 9, 17, and 20.)

In the 1960s, an important piece of detective work led Haydn scholars to conclude that Op. 3 was not by Haydn at all but was most likely the work of Roman Hofstetter (1742–1815), a Benedictine monk who served as music director of the monastery at Amorbach.[40] That Hofstetter's music might have been mistaken for Haydn's is not surprising. There are other works of Hofstetter's known to have been misattributed to his better-known contemporary, and the two composers' idioms are not unrelated: an 1802 letter from Hofstetter to the music-loving Swedish diplomat and friend of Haydn's, Fredrik Samuel Silverstolpe (1769–1851), bestowed praise on Haydn's music in these terms: "Every-

EXAMPLE 1.2 Roman Hofstetter [?], String Quartet in F, falsely attributed to Haydn as Op. 3/5: ii ("Serenade"), mm. 1–4 (violin 1 only)

thing that flows from Haydn's pen seems to me so beautiful and remains so deeply imprinted on my memory that I cannot prevent myself now and again from imitating something as well as I can."[41]

The discovery of concrete evidence for the misattribution of Op. 3 was a welcome development. It removed a stumbling block that had long confounded attempts to understand basic issues of chronology and stylistic development, and it helped cast the entire oeuvre—its overall scope and its characteristic mix of consistency and diversity—in a clearer light than had previously been thought possible. But at the same time, it had the disturbing result of banishing from the canon a veritable gem: the so-called Serenade of Op. 3/5, quoted in example 1.2. Endowed with melodic charm and the captivating sonority of muted violin with pizzicato accompaniment, this little movement has been cherished with special affection by generations of listeners and amateur performers.

2

Genre and Character

Explaining the origins of the string quartet has proven to be a complex endeavor. Historians have paid due attention to the influence of the Baroque trio sonata,[1] whereas other ingredients of the quartet's prehistory have been sought among early- to mid-eighteenth-century genres whose textural premise of four notated string parts was significant to later developments. As identified in Finscher's groundbreaking study, forerunners from different regions of Europe included the Italian symphony and sonata *a 4*, works identified by the labels "concerto" or "concertino" *a 4* in France as well as Italy, sonatas and symphonies *a 4* in France, the symphony *a 4* in Central Europe, and the North German quartet-sonata.[2]

Of more immediate relevance to the emergence of the quartet are the musical practices of Haydn's own milieu and the colorful array of instrumental chamber-music types prevalent in mid-eighteenth-century Vienna. Embraced within this repertory are works for strings ranging from duets to quintets; mixed-ensemble pieces, many of which are scored for strings and a pair of horns; and compositions for wind band, most often for pairs of oboes, horns, and bassoons. Some of this music is light in tone, perhaps intended for casual outdoor performance, whereas other works are more serious and more demanding of listeners' attention. The number and order of movements are variable, the most common patterns including three-movement sequences (some beginning fast, others starting with a slow movement, with or without a minuet in second or third place); four-movement designs with fast outer movements and a minuet placed second or third; and five-movement cycles with two minuets and a central slow movement. Crucially important is the fact that most of these pieces were performed soloistically (one player to a part) and did not involve the apparatus of a basso continuo accompaniment.[3]

Haydn's own early contributions included that group of expertly crafted works, ten in all, which may be recognized as his earliest string quartets. They were generally not designated as quartets by the composer and his contemporaries, however. Haydn appears to have identified them with the terms "cassatio" and "divertimento a quatro," while early manuscript sources assign such labels as "divertimento," "cassatio," "nottorno," "sonata a quattro," or "quadro," indicating no consensus whatsoever as to what they should be called. In fact, the label "divertimento," standing alone or combined with some modifier, was applied commonly and indiscriminately to many different kinds of composition. Later in the century, the word would acquire more specific connotations, but at this time and place it bore no particular meaning with regard to instrumentation, movement sequence, or character.[4]

To what extent can we be sure of the intended scoring for these early quartets? Specifically, are there grounds for assuming that the lowest part was indeed played solely by a cello, without the presence of a contrabass instrument sounding an octave lower? Early sources tend to follow the custom of labeling the bottom line "basso" (i.e., bass part), no matter what the intended scoring. (The practice of specifying "violoncello," even in works for which that instrument is clearly intended, did not become common until well after this time.) Exhaustive research by Webster has shown that although alternative possibilities cannot be excluded, the only option well supported either by internal evidence or surviving documents is that of our soloistic, string quartet ensemble with cello.[5]

The Customary Profile of a Haydn Quartet

Although the early quartets' instrumentation may be viewed as merely one of numerous choices within a constellation of eighteenth-century Viennese chamber music, it proved to be a truly felicitous one with respect to timbre, registral diversity, and technical agility. The ensemble's homogeneous sonority helped promote unity, and yet the instruments' ability to project as solo voices allowed for a multiplicity of separate strands in the musical fabric. The strings' wide, overlapping compass permitted many gradations between high and low tessitura, and hence a corresponding breadth of color, despite the general timbral consistency. Most important, perhaps, was the ensemble's expressive versatility, its ability to traverse different styles, ranging from virtuosic display to song-like spontaneity, with relative ease and conviction.

Taking advantage of the medium's capacities, Haydn's early quartets represent a veritable playground of contrasts in character and expression, and yet there is nothing haphazard or freewheeling about the controlling parameters of structure and style. On the contrary, the individual works appear to be carefully worked out realizations of a model, as if Haydn were striving to put the genre on a secure footing, methodically defining its standard traits as a foil for the pursuit of compositional ingenuity (involving thematic elaboration, textural complication, rhythmic surprise, and the like) within clearly defined boundaries. Signs of generic consistency are pervasive: all ten quartets are approximately comparable in proportion and tonal range, each comprises a sequence of five movements, with minuet-trio complexes in second and fourth place, and all make use of a similar mix of tempos, formal stereotypes, sources of rhythmic continuity, and modes of expression.

With Haydn's next set of quartets, Op. 9, the reconfiguration of the model from five movements to four was a watershed, a permanent change in his concept of the genre and an occasion to revise some of its stylistic norms and premises. To be sure, important elements remained, notably a dance movement in second place, a soloistic slow movement, and an exuberant, very fast finale, most often in $\frac{2}{4}$ time. But in other respects the new plan differed markedly from its predecessor. Jettisoning the second minuet-trio deprived the slow movement of its stature as the centerpiece of a symmetrical design, as in all but two of the earliest quartets. A further shift of balance was occasioned by the expanded role of the opening movement, now fashioned to compete with the internal slow movement as a forum for solo display and expressive intensity. Distinctions in spirit and function between first and last movements were consequently more sharply drawn, the latter favoring velocity and momentum in the interest of reaffirming the home key and bringing the cycle to an uplifting conclusion.

Haydn's chosen order for the interior movements, which has precedents among his earlier four-movement compositions,[6] may be understood as a variant of the five-movement plan in which a second (arguably redundant) minuet-trio complex gets trimmed before the finale, whereas the expected dance movement in second place is preserved as a buffer between the opening movement and a contemplative soliloquy. But whatever the origin or rationale for the scheme, it was not to endure as a preferred choice. The alternative order, locating the dance movement third rather than second, arises as early as Op. 20 (Nos. 2, 4, and 6). And whereas only two quartets of Op. 33 adopt this approach (Nos. 5 and 6), it becomes standard thereafter, with only four exceptions: Opp. 42, 64/1 and 4, and 77/2.

Apart from the variable order of interior movements, Haydn allowed himself few digressions from the basic model from Op. 9 on: relatively fast outer movements, the first in sonata form, and a slow interior movement either before or after the mandatory minuet-trio scheme. Opp. 9/5, 17/3, and the late 76/6 all contradict the model by featuring variation forms in first place; Op. 55/2 likewise begins with variations, although here Haydn chooses to shift the large-scale opening Allegro to second place rather than to omit it altogether, as he does with the others. Another late quartet, Op. 76/5, opens with a nonstandard opening movement, which (like that of Op. 76/6) progresses from an allegretto pace at the outset to an exhilarating allegro near the close. Op. 54/2 is an exception of a different sort, with an odd finale that begins and ends slowly, confining fast-tempo action to a whirlwind middle section.

The predominant cyclic design may thus be described as one in which a principal, large-scale movement (almost always in first place, usually moderate to fast in tempo, and cast in sonata form) is joined by three other, more or less standard portions that unfold within its orbit. Of the three, the minuet-trio complex proves least susceptible to change in overall design, although the dance forms do exhibit much diversity in proportion, character, and tempo. They also differ in terms of the trio's degree of independence from the minuet proper: some trios derive thematic material from the minuet, some connect to the repeat of the minuet without a full close, and there are cases in which the beginning of the trio elides with the end of the minuet.

The finales exhibit considerable variety of character and form as Haydn explores possibilities for winding up with impressions of whimsy, brilliance, climactic energy, or cumulative rhetorical eloquence. In every set from Op. 20 on, at least one last movement stands out as a showcase for formal innovation, as in the dual-tempo, composite design of Op. 54/2, or the transformative, minor-to-major schemes encountered in two major-key works, Op. 76/1 and 3. Interior slow movements are likewise diverse, although there are some distinctive, recurrent types, notably the variations found with particular frequency from Op. 50 on, and the soloistic, sonata-related designs featured throughout much of the repertory.

Can we speak of an ideal or normal size for a Haydn quartet? Several of the medium's defining features, including timbral uniformity, soloistic scoring, and the attendant connotations of concentration and intimacy, effectively impose upper limits on duration, and none of the quartets reach the dimensions, say, of Haydn's own late symphonies, at least in their outer movements. And yet only one work, the lone Op. 42, may be truly described as a miniature. Outer fast movements of the earliest quartets tend to be rather short, but their concision is balanced by the substantial-size dance movements with da capo repeats (not to mention the fact that there are two of them) and by the verbosity that characterizes most of the Adagios: that of Op. 2/4, for example, with ninety-two measures in $\frac{3}{4}$ time, is longer than many slow movements to be found in subsequent quartets. From Op. 9 on, there are indications of a trend toward increasing quartet size, but the tendency is neither pronounced nor uniformly pervasive. Although the very longest outer movements tend to be concentrated among late works, some of the earlier first movements are remarkably large. (Op. 33/5/i has one of the highest measure counts of any of the quartets' movements in $\frac{2}{4}$ time, its 305 measures exceeded only by the 315 of Op. 71/3/i.) Moreover, there are late examples of more modest proportions, like the common-time opening movement of Op. 71/2, which extends only to 125 measures. (By comparison, Op. 17/4/i, likewise in common time, has 130.) Also worth noting is the fact that in some works with long opening or closing movements, this expansiveness is balanced by smaller proportions elsewhere in the cycle, as in Op. 33/5, whose second, third, and fourth movements are all of moderate size.

The Opus Groups

In surveying the constant elements, variables, and miscellaneous norms that collectively define our concept of Haydn's quartets, it is well to remember that virtually all were intended as part of a set of six works (the earliest quartets and Op. 42 are the only apparent exceptions). This means that although we can certainly appreciate a given quartet as an autonomous piece, capable of standing on its own, the opus group must be recognized as something more than an arbitrary assemblage of unrelated compositions. To begin with, each may be understood to reflect the circumstances of its origin: a patron's request, for example, or a particular segment of the chamber-music market to be addressed. But a more basic consideration is the simple fact of Haydn's habit of conceiving quartets in groups, with all the elements of procedural consistency, balanced diversity, or topical contrast that such a practice is likely to entail. In this view, the opus group is not so much a *musical* entity (even though ambitious performers might choose to read through an entire opus in one sitting) as an immediate environment or larger artistic inspiration from which an individual quartet may be understood to spring.

Several principles of opus-group character and profile may be discerned: every set from Op. 9 on gives each quartet a different home key; minor tonality is always represented (by one work in each case except Op. 20, which has two); and on balance, flat home keys outweigh those with sharps. Within almost any opus, works that display novel, atypical features complement those that adhere more closely to conventional formats and procedures. Often Haydn chooses two or more quartets to embody different perspectives on a certain topic or structural problem—an intraopus theme, in effect, to be explored from different angles: three fugues in Op. 20, three rondos in Op. 33, a concentration of ternary and variation forms in Op. 64, and a startling array of introductory gestures for the first movements of Op. 71/74. Also significant is Haydn's practice of calling on one opus group as a procedural model for another. Resemblances between Opp. 9 and 17 prove especially close, but other pairs may be identified as well: Opp. 20 and 50 (serious tone, fugal polyphony), Opp. 33 and 64 (both relatively light and intimate in character; the same choice of home keys), and Opp. 54/55 and 71/74 (relatively extroverted, with emphasis on solo display). Op. 76 and the abbreviated Op. 77 stand alone in this regard: certain individual movements explicitly recall ones from earlier sets, but neither opus as a whole bears any singular relationship to a previous group.

The Quartet's Voices

To the extent that quartets of Haydn's time were intended for private performance, with amateurs, connoisseurs, and professional musicians taking part, it would
seem desirable for the music to gratify the performers by giving each a measure
of thematic importance. Only rarely is there true equality, however: inevitably,
the first violin predominates as group leader and principal bearer of melodic responsibility. For Haydn, this holds true among later as well as earlier works, and
it seems only natural to hear the top part as a surrogate for the composer's own
voice, a controlling presence that guides the progress of the music.

Nevertheless, there are many situations that enable the performers—the
first violin especially, but others as well—to convey a sense of their own person-
alities and to be perceived as agents in the musical discourse: passages of taxing
figural display, tossed off with spontaneous abandon; ascents to a very high register, riveting attention to the spectacle of precarious fingerings high on the first
violin's E string; and even possibilities for real extemporization (most notably
the cadenzas required in several of the earlier slow movements, but also some opportunities for *Eingänge* in various finales).[7] In addition, there are times when
Haydn mimics the daring expressivity of improvisation without actually yielding
control to the performers, as in his notated cadenzas (e.g., the slow movement of
Op. 55/1, mm. 28–33, 61–67), his richly decorated repeats in certain varied-
reprise structures, the quasi-extemporized manner sometimes featured in strophic
variation movements, and one especially memorable case, the chromatically inflected, rhythmically elastic solo line of Op. 54/2/ii, which seems to imitate a folk
musician's untrammeled outpouring of emotion.

Members of the group often engage in thematic dialogues that assign them
the roles of speaker and listener in alternation, and situations in which individual lines coalesce for a moment of blended harmony or unison declamation may
give the impression that the ensemble has reached full agreement and is speaking as a single, unanimous voice.

Idiomatic Elements and Stylistic Allusions

The integral engagement of ensemble members is assisted by the timbral similarity of the instruments and their capacity for dynamic shadings. But with these
virtues come limitations. The quartet is obviously less well suited than an orchestra for gaining momentum through sheer mass of sound, for generating suspense by a gradual increase in volume and density, or for marking a point of contrast with a vivid change in sonority. Within the quartet's more limited range of
volume and color, it must enlist other means to achieve rhetorical force and expressive accent: the dispersion of surface activity among rhythmically as well as

melodically independent parts contributes a vital source of intensity, especially in transition passages and development sections; and the device of withholding smaller note values for an extended span, only to unleash their energy full force at a crucial moment, serves to focus attention on progress toward major structural landmarks. The complementary effect of a well-timed shift from short to long note values may brake a seemingly unstoppable surface momentum; and the disruptive silence of a general pause can provide a powerful source of emphasis. Perhaps most impressive of all the quartet ensemble's special resources is the capacity for motivic development in which all four members participate.

As a virtually new genre in Haydn's time, the quartet was in a position to borrow and absorb from the surrounding musical environment. Its combination of textural plasticity and timbral neutrality—not to mention its emerging role as a medium for connoisseurs, whose appetite for musical wit and intrigue must be satisfied—enhanced its suitability for stylistic allusion and imitation. The symphony, for example, whose public façade would appear to be the antithesis of a quartet's drawing-room intimacy, served nonetheless as a model, sometimes with ironic intent. In addition to such obvious connections as the string-ensemble core, customary four-movement format, and affinity for the dialectic of sonata form, symphonic influence may be recognized in the occasional recourse to bold, texturally simple phrases in singing-allegro style,[8] the use of full-volume unisons, either for pronouncements or for consolidation and closure, and (specifically in Opp. 71/74 and 76/1) the device of an initial call to attention before the first movement's exposition proper gets under way.

More pervasive are the quartets' allusions to solo concerto and operatic aria, whose signature qualities of lyrical intensity, embellishment, and figural display Haydn had begun to explore in slow movements from the earliest quartets. From Op. 9 on, such elements flourish in first movements and to some degree in finales as well, most notably in connection with ritornello-like patterns of alternation between thematic statement and elaborate passagework.

Strict or ecclesiastical style, a recognized trait in chamber music by composers who catered to the conservative tastes of the imperial court, is less prevalent in Haydn, although by no means absent altogether. Such elements as canon, invertible counterpoint, imitative entries, suspension chains, cantus firmus–like melodies in long note values, fugal episodes, and full-scale fugues contribute as emblems of learned discourse, technical stringency, and lofty sentiment.

Balancing the quartets' absorption of elements from the realms of symphony, concerto, serious opera, and strict composition are their allusions to popular style, impressions of guileless spontaneity, and images of countryside music-making. This opposing facet comes to the fore in the unembellished, singsong melodies found among secondary-key areas of first movements, in principal as well as secondary or episodic material in rondo or rondo-like finales, or in dance movements, especially the trios. Often giving at least the impression of folk-music derivation, such melodies may invite us to hear reflections of the composer's own cultural background and his early musical experiences.[9]

Other relationships between Haydn's quartets and the traditions on which they draw may be sought in the realm of tonal usage and key association. As represented in table 2.1, Haydn's repertory of home keys embraces a total of fourteen possibilities, with key signatures that range from four sharps (E) to four flats (F minor). Within this spectrum, he gravitates toward a familiar core of major tonalities with few accidentals (well more than half the quartets are in major keys with no more than two sharps or flats) while demonstrating a certain bias toward the flat side. Notable in this regard is the absence of the sharp-laden keys A and E from all but one of the post–Op. 20 sets.

Can correlations be drawn between a quartet's key and its prevailing character or topical associations? This proves to be an elusive factor, in part because of such obvious variables as tempo, surface activity, and thematic contrast; but certain provisional observations may be made if, for example, we limit our scope to aspects of temperament or imagery in a first movement's opening thematic material.[10] Haydn's quartets in C major often display qualities of textural lightness and melodic simplicity at the outset (e.g., Opp. 33/3, 50/2, and 64/1) in ways that resonate with eighteenth-century associations of this key with purity and affective neutrality. Theorists' identification of G major with liveliness, cheer, and lyricism resound in several quartets in that key, notably Opp. 9/3, 33/5, 54/1, and 64/4. The pompous, militaristic connotations of D major would seem to make this key less appropriate for string quartets than for symphonies, among which it does indeed appear more often. But several theorists connect D major with gaiety instead of, or in addition to, martial qualities, and in so doing they suggest a resemblance between the key and its sharp-side neighbor, A, the latter key also linked to amorous passions. Here we can draw at least an oblique connection to Haydn's way with both keys in his quartets. Opening gestures of those in D as well as A are variously characterized by flashy or high-strung brilliance (as in Opp. 55/1 in A or 71/2 in D, following the slow introduction), open-air hunting- or gigue-style topics in $\frac{6}{8}$ time (Opp. 9/6 and 20/6 in A, Op. 17/6 in D), or else a more lyrical, pastoral quality (Opp. 64/5 and 76/5, for example, both in D).

Broad distinctions may be drawn between Haydn's approach to the keys just considered and the character of opening themes in his favored home keys on the flat side, E♭ and B♭. Here his usage tends to confirm theorists' descriptions of the latter tonality (e.g., tender, self-effacing) by providing the tonal setting for relatively intimate, reflective, or informal modes of expression. Opp. 55/3 (B♭) and 64/6 (E♭) both convey an impression of serenity at the start, and the opening of Op. 33/2 (E♭) is marked by tuneful innocence. The primary theme of Op. 76/4/i (the "Sunrise," in B♭) portrays a uniquely placid musical landscape; and Op. 50/1, also in B♭, has the most subdued beginning of all, leading off with two measures of quietly throbbing quarter notes in the cello.

TABLE 2.1 Distribution of home keys among the opus groups

Key	0	1	2	9	17	20	33	42	50	54/55	64	71/74	76	77	103
E♭ [10]	•	•		•	•	•	•		•		•	•	•		
B♭ [9]		•	•	•			•		•	•	•	•	•		
C [9]		•		•		•	•		•	•	•	•	•		
G [8]		•		•	•		•			•	•		•	•	
D [8]		•			•	•	•		•		•	•	•		
F [5]			•		•				•			•		•	
A [4]			•	•		•				•					
E [3]			•		•					•					
Dm [4]				•				•					•		•
Gm [2]						•						•			
Fm [2]						•				•					
Bm [2]							•				•				
Cm [1]					•										
F♯m [1]									•						

29

The key of E, encountered in Opp. 2/2, 17/1, and 54/3, represents Haydn's outer limit on the sharp side; and to at least some degree, we can detect a nervous intensity in the opening movements of these quartets that accords with contemporary descriptions of the key as "sharp," "fiery," "noisy," and "wild." The relatively small number of works in F (five, widely scattered through the repertory) cannot be easily explained, given the location of this key within the system's inner circle. Perhaps its neglect has to do with its apparent status as an in-between key, less suitable than D, say, for brilliant expression and also less closely linked with chamber style than B♭ or E♭.[11]

Haydn's home keys in minor, denizens of a sometimes severe, dark, or unstable realm, expand the available expressive range in several directions. Three minor keys on the flat side—D minor, C minor, and F minor—furnish the basis for opening themes that embody the gravity and melancholy traditionally associated with those keys. Haydn's G minor (Opp. 20/3 and 74/3) proves to be less serious and more highly energized at the outset (contemporary descriptions make note of this key's qualities of discontent, uneasiness, and agitation), whereas the openings of the two quartets in B minor (Opp. 33/1 and 64/2) both emphasize whimsy and ambivalence, the theorists' allusions to this key's gloom and artlessness notwithstanding. Finally, the lone quartet in F♯ minor, Op. 50/4, resists any easy characterization: certainly serious, with its forbidding unison in the opening measures, but also marked by a rhythmic life and motivic zeal that flies in the face of the melancholy attributed to this key by eighteenth-century writers.[12] (On the topic of minor tonality, additional mention might be made of Haydn's aversion to the key of A minor: he has no quartets, symphonies, keyboard sonatas, or keyboard trios in this key, which Ribock describes in Cramer's *Magazin der Musik*, 1783, as "the worst key of all, so sleepy, phlegmatic, that it should be perhaps the least used as a tonic.")

Elements of Wit, Irony, and Humor

The quartets' abundance of compositional techniques, traditional *topoi*, and key associations may be understood as part of a general celebration of musical diversity—embracing elements both exalted and commonplace, old and new, serious and comic—that informs much instrumental music of the time. The capacity to assimilate contrasting material within a coherent narrative stands as a hallmark of the age,[13] and the quartets may be admired for superbly realizing this tendency. But to speak only in terms of integration or accommodation is to oversimplify, for Haydn often seems more inclined to emphasize disparities and incongruities than to absorb them in any seamless aesthetic unity. A spirited orchestral tutti, involving a synchronized, collective effort, directed outward to a concert audience, may be mimicked by a string quartet, but scarcely without our noticing an ironic discrepancy between the image of a large-ensemble gesture and the intimacy of four solo strings. The first movement of Op. 76/1 begins with a stunning chordal announcement, underscored by double and triple stops in the upper parts. Yet any expectation of a full-voiced continuation evaporates immediately as Haydn reduces the sonority to an unaccompanied cello. This instrument's quizzical, baritone voice puts matters in a different light, mocking the bluster of the opening phrase, puncturing the inflated rhetoric, and introducing a more subtle brand of musical discourse.

Was it the stifling pretensions of the genre that made such a deflating stroke irresistible to Haydn? Whatever the reason in this particular instance, we can surmise from a broader perspective that he was often prompted by the quartet's natural intimacy and concentration to favor it for the cultivation of wit, irony, and humor. Encountered in all corners of the oeuvre, even among the earliest quartets, these overlapping areas of musical rhetoric share a common outlook by undermining our credulity and obliging us to take heed of the composer's artful, subversive presence. This aspect of Haydn's style involves both engagement and detachment on the part of listeners and performers. On the one hand, the music leads us into the trap of a deceptively predictable narrative; on the other hand, it removes us to a more objective vantage point from which to contemplate the habits and conventions on which our understanding normally depends.[14]

Haydn's wit, a virtually pervasive ingredient in the quartets, may be recognized in places where seemingly incompatible ingredients are brought into satisfying relationship, for example in Op. 55/1/iv, where the composer shakes an alla breve fugue subject from his sleeve just as a return to the rondo refrain is getting under way at measure 61. The refrain theme now dons the guise of a countersubject so that refrain and fugal episode become one. Irony describes situations marked by reversal, by outcomes that turn out to be the opposite of what was expected (for example, a transparent, pianissimo conclusion in place of a full-voiced peroration),[15] or by the use of elements for purposes utterly different from those for which they are normally intended: an opening gesture fashioned from materials best suited to a closing theme, or a passage of strict canonic imitation embedded in a rustic dance. Haydn's humor, a complex, many-sided element that seems to inhabit the very core of his musical personality,[16] often rises to the surface in moments of wit or irony whose unexpectedness or incongruity may infect listeners not only with amusement but even laughter. (That the composer himself was not immune is attested by a report of Muzio Clementi's, recorded by Charles Burney: "When he hears any of his own Pieces performed that are capricious he laughs like a fool.")[17] A concise example, from around the time of Clementi's anecdote, concerns Haydn's treatment of a recurrent motive in the scherzo of Op. 33/6. This three-note idea, announced by the first violin at the outset (bracketed in ex. 2.1a), quickly becomes a topic of dialogue and sequential repetition. Migrating from one instrument to another, it comes to dominate

almost every single measure; and in the approach to the end of the first reprise
(shown in ex. 2.1b), all three upper parts sound the motive in tandem just before forming a well-coordinated cadence. Naturally, we expect the ensemble to
recall this pattern at the end of the second part, and until practically the last moment (i.e., the middle of m. 25) the parallel is sustained, as shown in example
2.1c. But suddenly the viola, apparently unmindful of the approaching cadence,
or else determined to have another chance at the motive no matter what the consequences, presses on even as the others obey the decorum of a standard full close.
Given proper accentuation and physical gesture in performance, the effect can
be genuinely comical.[18]

There are elements of irony and fine-tuned artistry here as well: the viola's
"accidental" final statement of the motive happens to replicate the first violin's
opening notes, at pitch, so that the scherzo ends with a musical pun, closing just

EXAMPLE 2.1 Op. 33/6/iii

(a) mm. 1–2   (b) mm. 6–8

(c) mm. 24–26

Fine

as it had begun. Moreover, the viola's indiscretion serves to fill an otherwise vacant second beat, thus connecting either to the repeated strain or to the trio; and because the trio begins with a baritone-range cello solo, the viola's final notes play a mediating role, leading the music gracefully and thematically down toward the lower instrument's domain.

An especially potent strain of humor arises from Haydn's fondness for defeating expectations and thumbing his nose at commonplace formulas. Often, his comical disruptions are sharpened by expectations formed within the musical narrative. Most blatantly comical of all are the interruptive silences in Op. 33/2/iv (the "Joke"), climaxing with an unthinkable pause of four and a half measures whose odd placement—after a cadence that might have brought the work to a close, and before a disconnected reference to the refrain's opening measures—denies allegiance to any recognizable model for closure.[19]

More subtly blended with elements of wit or irony—and also drama—are Haydn's moments of context-related surprise, as in Op. 64/1/i (C major), where the recapitulation's retrieval of a forceful, repetitive closing figure (mm. 129–32, corresponding to that of mm. 55–58, near the end of the exposition) signals an imminent conclusion to the discourse. But Haydn annihilates expectations by undermining the harmony with the foreign tones A♭ and E♭ on the downbeat of measure 133. This destabilizing move suddenly opens up a field of play for unanticipated tonal and motivic possibilities, extending the recapitulation and enlivening it with fresh expressive content. In so doing, it holds a mirror to our customary dependence on structural models and the habitual, credulous attitudes on which those models seem to thrive.

3

Texture, Ensemble Technique, and Sonority

If the quartet's ability to shine as a consortium of solo voices is one of its most basic virtues, it is also one of the most complex. The prevalent stylistic norm of treble melody and accompaniment may at almost any point be temporarily challenged, destabilized, or overturned by usurping thematic action among other parts. The second violin may engage the first in argument or dialogue; the violins may expound in tandem, perhaps alternating with the viola and cello; the outer parts may oppose the inner; the cello may escape its duty as functional bass and temporarily control the principal line; or the instruments may all go their separate ways to create a texture of genuine polyphony.

The alternatives are truly legion, and Haydn is nothing if not resourceful in taking advantage of them. A quick pass through practically any of his quartets will yield a long tally of different textures, ensemble configurations, and patterns of thematic exchange among parts. But to list such possibilities would be only a raw first step. Given the genre's natural concentration on significant detail, every change in balance or relationship among parts invites analysis from the standpoint of musical rhetoric, structure, or compositional technique.

In varying degrees, writings that deal with Haydn's quartets and those of his contemporaries have addressed relevant matters of texture and ensemble technique, and there are major studies in which these topics are a central focus of attention. Levy's dissertation on the Parisian *quatuor concertant* examines the characteristics of that subgenre largely in terms of texture; Hickman's essay on the later-eighteenth-century Viennese quartet shows how divergent stylistic trends (including the Viennese *quatuor concertant* and the *quatuor brilliant*) are in part distinguished according to how thematic material is allocated among the parts; and Parker categorizes eighteenth-century quartets in terms of four kinds of discourse: the "lecture," in which the first violin predominates; the "polite conver-

34

sation," whereby thematic responsibility may pass more or less systematically from one part to another; the "debate" that arises when lower parts compete for attention without stepping out of their preordained roles as secondary or subsidiary voices; and the "conversation" that sets all four parts on a virtually equal footing.[1]

Other texture-related inquiries have focused more directly on the Haydn oeuvre. Schwindt-Gross's account of spatial, rhetorical, and dramatic phenomena in quartets of Haydn and Mozart spotlights their handling of the ensemble for complex strategies of motivic development. A dissertation by Moe traces patterns of change and development in Haydn's approach to texture from his earliest works in the genre through Op. 50; and Drabkin's book profiles a variety of salient textures, ensemble configurations, and idiomatic devices encountered throughout the opus groups.[2]

Drawing on the pertinent literature where appropriate, the account that follows surveys Haydn's use of textural possibilities and idiomatic sonorities for various structural and expressive goals. Our purpose is to affirm the importance of the topic and to provide a foundation for considering other aspects of style, design, and artistic significance in which the quartet's sound-resources prove decisive.

First Violin Predominance

Situations in which the first violin prevails as a main thematic voice make a natural point of departure. The contemporary preference for favoring the ensemble's top part has obvious practical purposes: given an amateur ensemble that includes members whose proficiency may be uncertain, it is wise for the composer to rely heavily on the presumed competence of a group leader. But there are structural and rhetorical considerations as well. A declarative, tonally grounded melody in the first violin denotes stability, assures maximum clarity of delivery, and lays the groundwork for later change and complication. In Haydn's quartets, this often entails clear distinctions at the outset between a sharply etched, rhythmically varied top line and a relatively neutral accompaniment among the lower parts, either sustained, arpeggiated, or broken into a patter of chordal repetition.

Although impressions of contrast between background and foreground may be blurred, and perhaps even temporarily erased, as a movement unfolds, there are also places where the first violin's predominance is accentuated by registral disparities between its voice and those of the lower parts. In an extreme case, from the slow movement of Op. 76/4 (m. 50), the first violin climbs nearly three octaves higher than the closely spaced harmony below before dropping precipitously to help define a structural landmark. Encountered in a slow-tempo soliloquy, a high-flying top part may suggest the commanding presence of an operatic singer or concerto soloist, and in opening Allegros and finales that indulge in soloistic display, soaring passages of figuration may promote headlong motion while focusing attention on the lead performer's virtuosity. These moments may be electrifying, but their resistance to a unified sonic picture can raise certain aesthetic questions. That listeners of the composer's own time may have harbored such questions is attested by a letter of 22 October 1783 from the Rev. Thomas Twining to the music historian Charles Burney. Twining writes of Haydn as follows: "His Quartetts spoil me for almost all other music of the kind. There are, in *them* too, some very fine, *serious* Cantabiles;—yet now & then in the midst of them, he takes a freak up to the top of the finger-board—& then, (to *my* ear, at least) the charm is dissolved—trick, caprice, & the difficulté vaincue, take place of expression & pathos.—It seems to me as if no Composer, or player cou'd be in earnest, in *altissimo:*—it is not the $\left\{\frac{\text{climb-at}}{\text{climate}}\right\}$ for it." In his reply of 10–12 November, Burney writes, "What you say of high Notes is as true as it is punnish & Comical."[3]

Overturned Authority, Thematic Diffusion, and Conversation

Contemporary misgivings notwithstanding, Haydn's freaks into a musical stratosphere can often be explained as rhetorical climaxes or well-placed moments of tension that call for quick resolution to a more stable disposition of parts and registers. But even without such daring exploits, the very presence of textures that spotlight the first violin may be heard, paradoxically, as a source of unrest—an imbalance that calls to be rectified by giving the lower voices more say in the musical discourse. At issue is a matter of expectation on the part of performers and listeners. In a symphony, say, or a soloistically conceived quartet, treble-dominated textures are customary. But for an idiom in which relationships among instruments are fluid and subject to change, the first violin's overbearing weight must at some point be relieved by shared thematic action among other parts. In a movement that embodies what Parker has described as a "polite conversation," the solution may involve a succession of solo phrases assigned to different ensemble members while the others oblige with suitable accompaniment;[4] but this is not typical of Haydn, for whom the appropriation of one instrument's theme by another is more likely to be charged with unpredictability, dramatic opposition, or textural complication. In a stirring example from the finale of Op. 76/6, the first violin's role is momentarily usurped by the gruff voice of the cello, whose entry at the start of the development section turns the entire discourse on its head. A previously airborne melody in major is now recast in minor at the base of the texture, whereas the accompanying chords, elevated in range and magni-

EXAMPLE 3.1 Op. 76/6/iv

(a) mm. 1–4

(b) mm. 67–70

fied by double and triple stops in the violins, take on a new, unsettling prominence (see ex. 3.1, which compares the opening phrase with the transformed recurrence in question).

More subtle brands of textural change and thematic migration typically arise
early in a movement, where an initial declaration draws other ensemble members into a musical dialogue. The opening of the D minor quartet, Op. 42, is an intriguing case, in part because of the textural complexity of the opening phrase itself
(see ex. 3.2). At the outset, full-voiced chords on alternate downbeats (mm. 1,
3, and 5) help secure the opening melodic arc to the movement's tonal and metrical foundation. The paired, rising inner parts balance the first violin's descending figure in measures 1 and 3, and the closer proximity of emphasized chords in
measures 5 and 6 (one on each downbeat) underlines the increasing melodic and
rhythmic intensity. Activity in the next to last measure of the phrase quickens
further, with chordal sonorities on each beat, while at the same time a measure
of equilibrium is gained as the second violin joins the first in melodic and rhythmic partnership.

The lower parts, vital but subservient voices so far, are doubtless more than
ready to take part thematically, and Haydn will duly oblige them in the phrases
that follow. First comes the cello's connecting upbeat, which fills the silence leading into measure 9; the viola then takes up the opening melodic figure, the second violin helps energize the upbeat to measure 10, and the configuration changes

EXAMPLE 3.2 Op. 42/i, mm. 1–12

Andante ed innocentemente

again in measures 11–12, where the harmony pivots to the relative major. As all this takes place, the continually changing sonority adds a rhythmic impetus of its own, helping to animate the transition and easing the change to a heightened level of surface rhythm in the phrase that follows. In the process, a fundamental ambivalence becomes manifest: changing ensemble relationships realize the medium's potential for participatory exchange—a palpable kind of string quartet equilibrium—even as they promote destabilization and goal-directed motion.

Haydn sometimes alters the principle witnessed above (first violin predominance, ultimately yielding to the lower parts' thematic participation) by assigning thematic leadership to another part at the outset. Given such an unstable premise, rebalancing the ensemble's hierarchy may prove to be a delicate matter. In the Op. 64/1 minuet, for example, the cello is likely to have our full attention at the very beginning; and yet the first violin has clearly reclaimed leadership by the end of the first strain (see ex. 3.3). In between, ensemble fluidity reaches a high level of finesse as elements of accompaniment and principal line intertwine, one shading almost imperceptibly into the other.[5]

As the phrase gets under way, the cello's gracefully arched line is joined from above by a pair of melodically stationary violins. But just as the cello lingers to

EXAMPLE 3.3 Op. 64/1/ii, mm. 1–8

reemphasize the dominant note G (m. 3), the previously immobile violins stir to action, partially upstaging the cello as they rise and fall in tandem and glide to an elegantly postponed cadence in the middle of measure 4. The consequent phrase both balances and intensifies: the viola enters to reinforce the violins in measure 5 but then joins the cello's ascent in measure 6; and the first violin responds by blossoming into a real melodic flourish in measure 7. The functions of melody and accompaniment are continuously in play, but their location is either indeterminate or subject to change; and in the seamless intimacy of their relationship we can catch a glimpse of Haydn's genius for string quartet technique at its best. The cello part unfolds as both principal line and foundation; the violins balance the roles of textural support and melodic thread; and the viola mediates between the ambivalent linear profiles above and below by switching allegiance in the course of the second phrase. Unsettled relationships help the music take flight by releasing the texture from the constraints of simple line and accompaniment and generating movement through the perpetually changing configurations of instrumental voices. Only in the last two measures do the parts line up in a familiar, fully scored arrangement of first violin melody and harmonizing support, although even here the viola claims melodic attention for an instant, recalling the cello's sixteenth notes from measure 2 while promoting acceleration to the cadence.

Silenced Voices

An obvious, ever-present threat to a string quartet's collaboration is the prospect of withdrawal by one or more of its members. A situation in which three instruments participate while an outer part remains silent may convey a restless, expectant quality, especially if this happens to be the start of a movement: the discourse has begun, but something essential is missing, and only the remaining part's entry will cure the unease.

Awareness of a missing voice is pointedly unsettling at the start of Op. 55/1/ii, where the first violin demurs, leaving a relatively fragile trio of lower voices to announce the principal theme. It is all the more reassuring, then, when the group's leader finally appears in measure 9 to head a fully assembled texture and take center stage as a soloist at last. Potentially more disturbing are moments when the cello drops out, removing the quartet's foundation and leaving the upper parts adrift. In the F♯ major Largo of Op. 76/5, marked "cantabile e mesto," the pervasive sadness deepens in the development section, whose modulations stray into alien territory. A V$_3^6$ chord in the distant key of G major, sounded in measure 49, then sustained by a fermata in measure 50, signifies a point of furthest remove. As the cello withdraws for the next four measures, the upper parts wander in tonal space, led by the viola, whose rare thematic prominence accentuates the general strangeness. Only with the reentry of the cello, confirming arrival in the more familiar terrain of F♯ minor, is a semblance of textural and harmonic stability restored.

Different in quality from Haydn's tensive, absent-voice situations are the unaccompanied duets, which have a tendency to establish their own fleeting sound-world of intimate partnership. In the opening of the slow movement in Op. 33/2, for example, the violins look on as the viola and cello, left to themselves, intone a mournful eight-measure theme. The trio of Op. 33/3/ii, by contrast, sparkles with the transparency of a staccato, middle- and upper-range duet of violins. An even more self-sufficient violin sonority informs the trio of Op. 9/4/ii, where continuous double stops in the first violin, joined by the second violin's single accompanying line, yields the relative fullness of three-part harmony.

Apart from cadenzas, solo lead-ins, or initial entries in points of imitation, single voices rarely stand alone in the quartets for more than a few beats. But there is one instance of a moderately extended solo at the very start: the first violin's famously ambivalent opening to Op. 64/2 (B minor), where the withholding of ensemble support immediately charges the atmosphere with wonderment and suspense. As shown in example 3.4, the first violin enters on the third degree of the scale and proceeds for nearly two measures to gyrate in a tonal no-man's-land between the realms of D major and B minor. The welcome arrival of the other instruments on the upbeat to measure 3 forms an unequivocal dominant seventh chord to pin down the work's tonal orientation at last.

Unified Ensemble Textures;
The Constraints of Learned Polyphony

How can we best describe the interaction witnessed in this example? Are the lower parts playing a prank on their leader by failing to lend harmonic and tex-

EXAMPLE 3.4 Op. 64/2/i, mm. 1–4

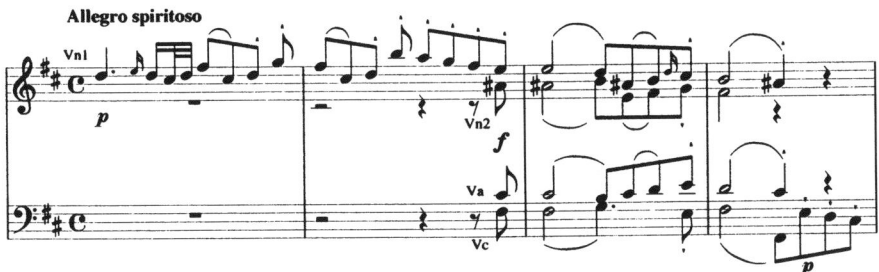

tural support to a problematical opening gesture? Or is the illusion of a per-
former-driven pantomime erased by the controlling hand of the composer,
whose string-pulling antics perplex everyone, performers and listeners alike?

Certainly there are many other situations in which impressions of free will
and conversational exchange are suspended by a larger, all-encompassing impulse that draws the instruments together as one. In some passages, all parts
blend in closely spaced, rhythmically uniform homophony, nullifying distinctions between principal line and accompaniment, and contradicting the more
normal give and take among individual lines. The resulting effect of a musical
parenthesis, suddenly planting us in a distant landscape, proves especially telling
when a tonal inflection accompanies the change in texture, and sustained tones
in all parts brake the surface-rhythmic momentum. (For a superb example, see
the finale of Op. 64/3, mm. 47–52, 103–10, and 174–81; this case is discussed in
chapter 14.)

A potentially more decisive unanimity arises from Haydn's four-part unisons.[6]
When heard at the start of a movement, unison texture can have a galvanizing
effect, commanding attention to a portentous announcement, as in the operati-
cally inspired Capriccio of Op. 20/2 or the opening movement of Op. 74/2, with
its fanfare-like call to order. Later in the course of a movement, the coalescing of
parts into a single line may designate a moment of consensus before the argument
turns in a new direction. In the finale of Op. 64/4, for example, we find a transition
theme that gains energy through incessant motivic repetitions (mm. 26–33), then
breaks into a run of continuous eighth notes in the first violin (second half of
m. 33) before sweeping the ensemble together in unison for a two-octave arpeggio (mm. 37–38)—a culminating gesture that clears the air and makes way for a
tuneful secondary theme (a comparable series of events spans mm. 115–25 in the
recapitulation). The ability of unison texture to signal resolution is realized on
numerous occasions, and it is featured memorably in the fugal finales of Op. 20/2

and 6, in which unison-charged perorations serve to overpower the centrifugal forces of polyphony.

Nowhere is the composer's hand a more dominating presence than in passages of rule-bound, equal-voice polyphony. In principle, learned counterpoint is a suitable discipline for the medium, given the premise of linear independence, not to mention the customary association with exacting technique and connoisseurship; and, as noted earlier, strict style was indeed a favored element in early quartets by several of Haydn's Viennese contemporaries. That Haydn himself was reluctant to highlight this topic extensively in his own earliest quartets may be partially explained as a matter of circumstance, notably the lack of a connection to the imperial court, where conservative styles were preferred. But he also may have been wary of imposing schematic designs on his music that would stifle more spontaneous exchange among the quartet's performers. In any event, his evidently cautious attitude persisted in subsequent quartets. Fugue and canon are most heavily concentrated in Opp. 20 and 76, yet even in these opus groups, learned style is by no means a dominant or pervasive quality.

Fleeting allusions to strict style occur throughout the repertory in the form of points of imitation in which a figure is taken up by each instrument in turn. Because of the innate formality of the device, combined with the textural discontinuity that it normally entails, a series of imitative entries serves well as a structural signpost: the start of a new phase of action and an opportunity to construct a four-voice texture afresh. The development section of Op. 2/1/i exemplifies such a scheme (see ex. 3.5a). This portion of the form gets under way by recalling the movement's opening chord and the first violin's continuation. The lower parts then pursue one another in imitation before the eventual reversion to a stable, melody-plus-accompaniment texture. The reuse of this same device in a much later movement (Op. 71/1/iv, quoted in ex. 3.5b) attests to its endurance. Here we find a similar pattern in reverse, as the development section begins with a subject in the cello before proceeding with imitative entries in successively higher parts.

Exerting tightest control on the relationship between parts are the sporadic instances of canon. On one occasion—the tumultuous "Witches' Minuet" of Op. 76/2—an entire rounded binary dance is suffused with strict canonic imitation, and the effect is rendered both strident and severe by the revival of a certain minuet texture first heard among the earliest quartets: violins in octaves, squared off against the lower parts, likewise moving in octaves.[7] Some passages of embedded canon are so brief and rudimentary as to go by almost unnoticed, except as extra complications within a context of rapid textural change. Others have a more arresting impact as they signal the change to a state of heightened technical stringency and rhetorical intensity. In the first-movement recapitulation of Op. 50/2, at a point where we might have expected a conventional first

EXAMPLE 3.5

(a) Op. 2/1/i, mm. 37–42

(b) Op. 71/1/iv, mm. 97–100

violin restatement of the primary theme (as in m. 21 of the exposition), the violins drop out and the lower parts proceed alone, locked in contrapuntal embrace to render the opening of the primary theme as a canon at the fifth (mm. 196–202). The violins are then made to respond, mirror-fashion, with their own primary theme–based canon in inversion, and the counterpoint becomes even more formidable as the lower parts reenter in canon at measures 207–8. Polyphonic momentum now persists for several measures before dissolving and making way for the return to a more predictable course of events.

Haydn's most ambitious examples of learned polyphony are the full-blown fugues that occur as final movements on three occasions in Op. 20 and once in Op. 50, and the later, embedded passages of fugal procedure found in several quartets from Opp. 54/55, 64, 71/74, and 76. Situated either in a middle portion of a movement or close to its end, each stands out as an event of highest importance. The elevation to a realm of serious polyphonic craft, flagged by the mandatory reduction of texture and concomitant announcement of a subject, temporarily transforms the discourse, as it channels the ensemble's energies into patterns of nearly equal linear engagement.

Special Colors and Idiomatic Techniques

If the ensemble configurations cited thus far can be said to benefit, as surely they do, from the instruments' timbral similarity—their ability to blend, or else to balance and complement one another interchangeably—then what can be said about places where Haydn oversteps his own constraints by indulging in special idiomatic devices or unusual coloristic effects? Peculiarities such as pizzicato, con sordino, bariolage, or robust multiple stopping have a natural tendency to call attention to themselves, inviting performers and listeners to enjoy the sheer novelty of a particular sound, or else pointing toward some topical association. By so doing, they disturb the relative neutrality and transparency on which quartet sonority more commonly relies.

Although such moments are rare on the whole, the earliest quartets display a concentration of choice examples. Their prominence here may be explained in part as a holdover from waning traditions of Baroque extravagance; but they also may be seen as reflections of a certain exploratory zeal, as if Haydn were intent on mapping out sonic territory for the new genre, with a particular eye for ways to compensate for its coloristic limitations. Yet even here he confines unusual sounds mainly to the dance-movement trios and interior slow movements. Outstanding cases include the second-movement trio of Op. 1/1, in which the fragile timbre of pizzicato violins alternates with bowed viola and cello, and the slow movement of Op. 1/6, whose haunting combination of con sordino first violin and plucked accompaniment wraps this technically simple movement in a state of reverie. (Could the composer of the spurious Op. 3/5 "Serenade" have had this movement in mind?)

Among later opus groups, the idea of enriching a quartet's character with evocative colors persists as a lurking possibility, and the rarity of such sounds heightens their impact when they do occur: comical glissandos in the Op. 33/2 trio; the nostalgic shimmer of pizzicato accompaniments in the slow movement of Op. 76/2; and the raucous, double-stopped sonorities that imitate bagpipes, most memorably in the first movement of Op. 76/3. Subtle but intriguing are the several instances of a *sopra una corda* technique in which an entire phrase is encompassed within the dark sound of the violin's lowest string, even though the line reaches well into the treble staff, as in Op. 20/6/i, measures 19–24.[8]

Bariolage, the device by which a single repeating pitch is played alternately on two adjacent strings,[9] stands out on one spectacular occasion—the finale of the quartet in D, Op. 50/6 (the "Frog")—as the center of attention. Here, the pungent sonority of fast, string-crossing As (played alternately on the open A string and the adjacent stopped D string) arises immediately as a thematic element to be explored and developed. The first violin's opening phrases present the idea in full array by engaging each of the possible string-pairs in turn (see ex. 3.6): A and D in measure 1; E and A in measure 5; and then, with the energy

EXAMPLE 3.6 Op. 50/6/iv, mm. 1–16 (violin 1 only)

of an emerging obsession, D and G in measures 9, 11, 13, and 15. Haydn concentrates the bariolage figure in the top part at the outset, but it proves contagious as the exposition proceeds, with all members of the ensemble succumbing to its bow-jostling spell. The second violin and viola pick it up before the end of the exposition; it eventually passes to the cello in the development section; and all four instruments give voice to its peculiar rasp and bow-arm gesticulations in the course of the recapitulation.

The strident ring of bariolage in Op. 50/6/iv sounds an instructive note on which to end this overview of Haydn's quartet-ensemble resources. The device itself is clearly peripheral to the composer's idiom, and the accent on this pungent effect doubtless qualifies the "Frog" as one of Haydn's most unusual-sounding quartet movements. Certainly it is one that cannot fail to make an indelible impression on first hearing.

In principle, such a case may pose a special challenge for performers, who face the task of absorbing a patently outsized coloristic device within a convincingly unified narrative. But this movement's sound effects, like other, inherently less striking sonorities, are no mere distractions. Far from cluttering the musical surface with aimless or unassimilated detail, they prove essential to the overall coherence of the design, working variously as agents of change, goal-directed motion, and structural delineation.

To begin with, the initial statements of the idea help shape the opening theme with particular clarity: first by underscoring the antecedent-consequent relationship of the opening phrase-pair (with the bariolage figure on the dominant, A, then its dominant, E), then by securing the latter part of the theme to the work's tonal center, D. The eventual migration of the figure to the second violin and viola toward the end of the exposition (mm. 74–75 and 77–78, respectively) helps round out the opening section. Its restoration to the first violin following the double bar highlights a major structural landmark; its long-awaited appearance in the cello, on the dominant note (mm. 135–36), signals the impending close to the development section; and the eventual four-way distribution of the

EXAMPLE 3.7 Op. 50/6/iv, mm. 240–43

figure (beginning with the viola in m. 203) enhances the summarizing character
of the form's last main portion. At the very end, eerie, simultaneous murmurings
of the idea in the three upper parts (mm. 240 and 242, shown in ex. 3.7) help
ground the tonal and thematic action by packing the instruments' bariolage
within a closely spaced tonic triad.

The interplay of musical form with sonority and ensemble technique often
proves subtler or more elaborate than that witnessed in the "Frog." Yet few cases
demonstrate with greater clarity the complementary processes by which a given
movement, seemingly designed with the intention to celebrate a peculiar color,
texture, or ensemble configuration, will draw on that very element as a principal
agent to drive the musical discourse and articulate its structure.

Part II: Formal Perimeters

4

Sonata Form

In Haydn's day, musical designs now recognized under the rubric of sonata form were an indispensable part of sonatas, trios, quartets, symphonies, and other multimovement genres. Their cultivation was linked to the growing importance of instrumental works as vehicles not only for refined technique but also for a degree of musical eloquence to rival that of compositions for church or theater.

Sonata form encompassed the large-scale symmetry of thematic statement (exposition) and recurrence (recapitulation), which together framed a development section that variously quoted, altered, and dissected previously heard themes in a context of general unrest. Tonally, the form emphasized a phenomenon of long-range tonal dissonance, evinced in the exposition's move to a secondary key, either dominant or relative major. Development section and recapitulation together were conceived as a response to the exposition's portrayal of duality or opposition, intensifying the tonal dissonance before resolving it through a tonally adjusted return of exposition material; and the two were most often cast as the second, extended part of a two-reprise design, typically supplied with the same scheme of double bars and repeat signs that had long been a fixture of binary dances and other relatively small-scale structures.[1] (A coda—a discrete, substantial appendage to the recapitulation proper—could take place either within or outside the customary second-part repeat.) The capacity of the form for musical intrigue and complexity, amply explored by Haydn, is in no small measure a consequence of the ambivalence by which it parses simultaneously in three parts (exposition, development, recapitulation) and two parts (exposition followed by its consequences in the combined action of the two latter sections).

Ingredients of a sonata exposition normally may be identified with specialized thematic functions and labeled accordingly: declarative statement in tonic (P), departure (T), arrival in the new key and the proposal of a new vantage point (S), then affirmation and closure (K). Applying this model to Haydn's string quartets requires caution, however. A given exposition may be too thoroughly infused with motivic process to permit the unambiguous labeling of functions; and even when the order of events is marked by thematic contrast or disjunction, the role of certain themes may prove ambiguous. The model nonetheless proves helpful for specifying normative procedures—many of which Haydn does indeed honor, whether in conventional or unexpected ways—as well as to measure and evaluate his various anomalies, alternatives, and digressions.

In view of the form's vast possibilities for thematic invention, elaboration, and structural intrigue, Haydn's inclination to favor it as a basis for both outer and interior movements is not surprising. Although its predominance was challenged by other designs for slow movements and finales (e.g., ternary, variation, rondo, and fugue), it was his standard choice for musically ambitious opening movements throughout the repertory. The rare exceptions are identified in table 4.1. One of the quartets in question, Op. 55/2, does in fact have a large-scale principal Allegro, but it comes second in the cycle rather than first. Haydn chose sonata forms for approximately two thirds of the quartets' finales, and in slow movements they occur about a third of the time. This last number grows to nearly half, however, if we count his so-called slow-movement forms in which the recapitulation follows the exposition immediately or after a grammatically simple transition.

Sonata Form in the String Quartets: Some Basic Considerations

The commanding presence of sonata forms in the quartets points to their central importance for Haydn's concept of the genre and its possibilities. Most important in this regard are the form's thematic and tonal complexities, which provided an ideal environment for strokes of surprise, thwarted expectation, overturned conventions, and the like. Also significant is the quartet's propensity for interaction among solo performers. In countless ways, the unfolding of a large-scale sonata form, with its polarities, fluctuating energies, and electrically charged borders between themes and sections, yielded opportunities for exploring varied relationships among parts and for generating, intensifying, and resolving the array of tensions to which Haydn's ensemble writing gives rise. An additional consideration has to do with Haydn's fondness (by no means restricted to quartets) for parody, intergeneric borrowing, and topical richness. Sonata forms, by accommodating disparate timbres, textures, themes, and rhythmic patterns, helped the quartet to mirror diverse customs, style topics, and expressive values while also (perhaps paradoxically) upholding the stature of the medium as a vehicle for pure compositional technique—the play of relationships within a more or less abstract musical narrative.

TABLE 4.1 First movements of Haydn's string quartets not in sonata form

Opus	Key	Tempo	Form
2/6	B♭	Adagio	Strophic variation
9/5	B♭	Poco adagio	Strophic variation
17/3	E♭	Andante grazioso	Strophic variation
55/2	Fm-F	Andante o più tosto allegretto	Alternating variation
76/5	D	Allegretto–Allegro	Nonstandard (*A B A' B'*)
76/6	E♭	Allegretto–Allegro	Strophic variation

As a result of their capacity for individualized design and expression, Haydn's sonata forms contribute to the unique profile of a given quartet, and the particular constellations of sonata form choices often apparent between quartets, or entire opus groups, helps clarify patterns of relationship and change throughout the oeuvre. At the same time, the composer's sonata form practices are grounded in various norms, tendencies, and consistent procedures that inform the repertory as a whole, and it is to these aspects that we now turn.

General Characteristics

Despite all variance from one work to the next, Haydn's sonata forms generally convey an impression of equilibrium, if not patent symmetry, between principal outer sections. Recapitulations often prove shorter, however, and in the movements that incorporate a coda or some other addendum, this last portion sometimes may be heard as a compensating factor. Development sections are typically substantial, most often consuming somewhere between and fifth and a third of the movement. Although these particular generalizations hold true throughout the oeuvre, certain distinctions are worth noting. Sonata forms in later works tend to be at least somewhat longer than such earlier counterparts as those of Opp. 9 and 17, although not to any uniform or consistent degree; and fast-tempo sonata forms in the very earliest quartets are generally short by comparison with those of the later sets, especially among first movements. Even if we were to reason that Op. 2/2/i, say, with 124 measures in $\frac{2}{4}$ time, seems comparable to Op. 9/4/i, which has seventy-five measures in common time, the comparison is misleading in light of the latter's far greater rhythmic density within the measure.

Additionally, the forms exhibit different properties according to their placement within the cycle. Opening movements, at least from Op. 9 on, tend to favor topical and expressive diversity, often allowing room for both solo theatrics and intimate dialogue; and even when there are close resemblances between themes, variety is assured by rhythmic contrasts and fluctuating levels of harmonic tension. More often than not, these characteristics go hand in hand with a relatively verbose, thematically varied development section. Finales, by contrast, often display a more streamlined approach to surface continuity—local, long-range, or both—sometimes at the expense of rhythmic diversity and harmonic detail. Their development sections tend to be proportionally shorter as a rule. Among the slow-tempo movements, showcasing the first violin's lyricism and decorative display sometimes entails minimal contrast in texture or rhythmic background within a section. Slow-movement development sections, like those of the finales, are for the most part proportionally more succinct than those of first movements.

Recognizing Haydn's general adherence to certain norms of design, character, and proportion is important for an appreciation of his aberrations, which tend to follow a logic of their own. Often it is not hard to find vital connections between an unusual large-scale design, as in Op. 9/6/i, for example, and the idiosyncrasies of its thematic material. Here, exactly halfway through the exposition (m. 26), an explosion of figuration in sixteenth notes—a level of surface activity withheld almost completely up to this point—coincides with arrival in the dominant key (1S in fig. 4.1). The impression of having shifted to a new plane of action is reinforced by the first violin's attainment of a fresh peak, e^3, and by the brilliance of a heightened tessitura. The salience of this event highlights the exposition's precisely balanced proportions and its attendant thematic duality: relatively homogeneous texture, emphasis on conjunct melodic motion, and a moderate rhythmic pace at the outset, as opposed to the secondary theme's rapid-fire, soloistic arpeggiation.

These features take on special significance as the movement continues, for both the accentuated contrast and the symmetry of proportion are destined to be realized on a higher order of magnitude. At measure 68, well into the development section and just beyond the midpoint of the movement, a cadence in the relative minor coincides with a recollection of the rhythmically animated secondary theme, as the first violin strikes the movement's highest pitch ($f\sharp^3$) on the downbeat, a step higher than the e^3 of measure 26. Marked by the same outburst of sixteenths heard at the middle of the exposition, this point stands out as a central pivot to the entire form, its moment of greatest intensity, and the apex of its melodic range (the high $f\sharp$ recurs in mm. 70 and 72). Solo figuration now persists, moving from the relative minor to the dominant (m. 74), then to the tonic in measures 79–82 (thereby prematurely recapitulating 1S material in the home key), and briefly to the subdominant before flowing without a break into the tonic-key retrieval of the primary theme at measure 86. The material that follows parallels the exposition in all essential respects but one: the fast-moving 1S, having been recalled in tonic already, is now exempted from further recurrence.

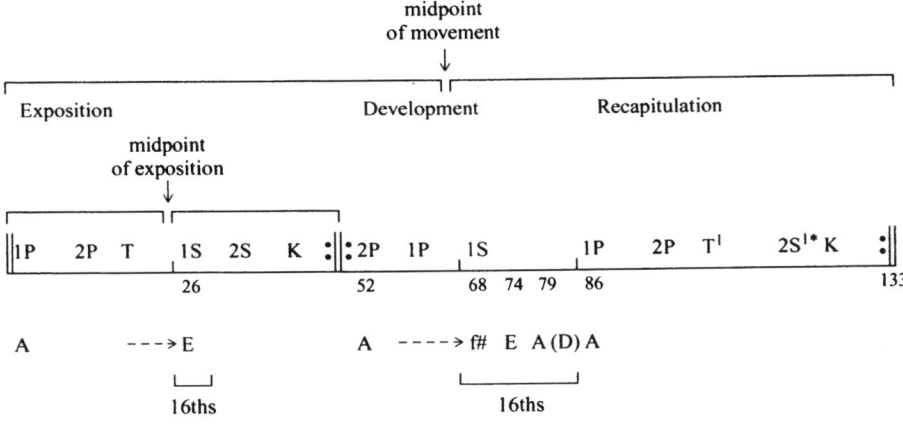

*The recurrence of 2S is preceded by a two-measure quote from 2P.

FIGURE 4.1 Op. 9/6/i

By concentrating on the fast-moving *1S* in the latter part of the development, then eliminating sustained sixteenth-note activity altogether from the main recapitulation, Haydn underscores the message of large-scale resolution: tonal restoration coincides with the return to a state of rhythmic equilibrium. But the plan also gives rise to a novel scheme of nested symmetry, as the exposition and the whole design both divide neatly in half. The movement thus embodies a palpable overall logic that partially overrides the customary model while at the same time confirming the principles of tonal polarity, contrast, and sectionalization on which that model rests. (The large-scale symmetry identified here is of course complicated, but not necessarily vitiated, by the binary repeats. At issue is the distinction to be drawn between the notated form, certainly capable of being appreciated by performers and listeners, and the actual temporal dimensions of the form as played.)[2]

The special design of Op. 9/6/i stands as a cautionary lesson: events in one part of a movement may be conditioned by those in another, if usually to a lesser degree than in this extraordinary instance. The form's sections are nonetheless worth examining in isolation, for just as a phrase may be taken out of context and examined as a structural entity, so the main parts of the quartets' sonata forms may be detached and explored provisionally as self-contained phenomena. Our principal concern in this endeavor is twofold: to identify elements and relationships that recur from one opus group to the next, thereby contributing to a larger picture of consistency as well as change in Haydn's approach to the genre, but also to make note of striking anomalies that may enhance the individuality of a movement by stretching, overriding, or transforming the composer's own customary procedures.

Expositions; The Medial Caesura

Haydn avails himself of several choices for getting a movement under way and then beginning the journey from tonic to a new key. Opening declarations, destined to figure prominently in the subsequent narrative, are often endowed with a clear and simple profile. However, they also may be marked by chromatic inflections or other destabilizing gestures that call for elaboration and eventual resolution; and if such elements of unrest are not present in an opening statement itself, they will likely emerge in the course of a varied or developed restatement, in a transitional phrase that emerges seamlessly from primary material, or in a newly introduced, contrasting theme.

The goal-directed motion to which the movement's initial destabilizing actions gives rise often leads to a provisional stopping point, not far from the middle of the exposition. This type of punctuation, identified by Darcy and Hepokoski as the "medial caesura," normally represents a point of release from the gravitational field of tonic and a platform for continuation in the new key.[3] Among the many sonata forms in the quartets that make use of the caesura, the event usually takes place within the middle third of the exposition, leaving room for one or more secondary themes—either substantially new or else derived from primary material—before the appearance of closing gestures to round out the section.

In movements of this type whose primary and secondary themes are not obviously related, the mid-exposition shift to a new key is typically accompanied not only by immediate change in rhythm, melody, and texture, but also by opposition or dichotomy with respect to the opening theme. Thematic contrast at this juncture is not Haydn's only alternative, however: instead, the mid-exposition break may lead to the recall of a principal idea in a new guise, as happens in roughly half the first movements and finales that honor the medial caesura, and in a few of the slow movements as well.

The idea of casting a previously heard theme in a fresh light is exemplified by the opening movement of Op. 64/6, where the caesura acts as a springboard for concentrated, polyphonically enriched development of the quartet's opening phrase, quoted in example 4.1a. In measure 24, the medial break is marked by rests in the lower parts as a rising chromatic line in the first violin connects from F, the dominant of the newly emerging key, to the new tonic, B♭, and the discourse resumes with the phrase shown in example 4.1b. Close resemblance to the opening theme is immediately apparent, and yet much is altered: the blended homophony of the opening phrase, whose image of serenity was enhanced by a

EXAMPLE 4.1 Op. 64/6/i

(a) mm. 1–4

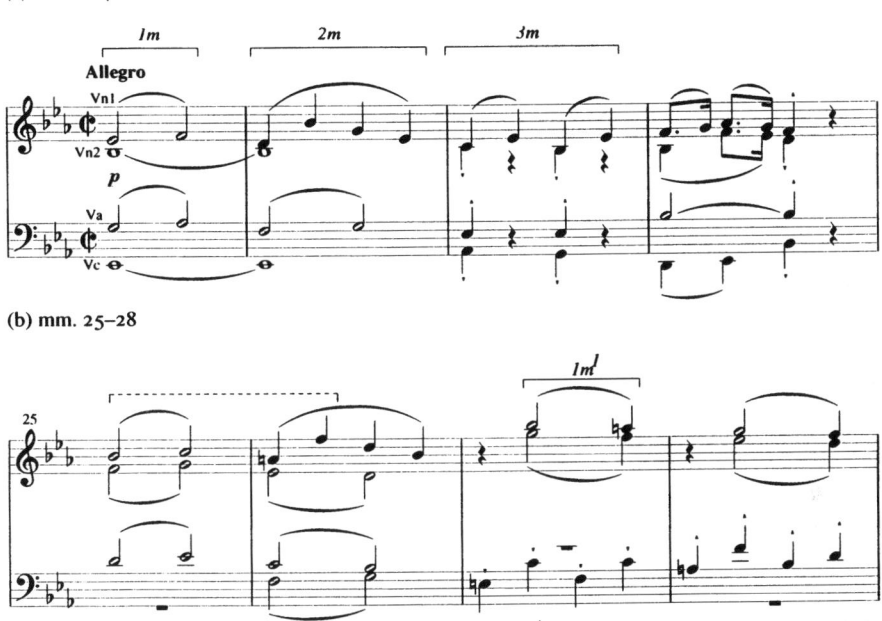

(b) mm. 25–28

stationary low E♭ in the first two measures, now yields to a more active texture. The cello holds back for one measure before entering with a fragment of canonic play with the first violin, marked by dotted brackets in the example, and the syntax becomes more complex as the violins elaborate a syncopated version of the opening two-note melodic gesture (1m) in inversion (mm. 27–28). Meanwhile, the cello's leaping staccato figure, passed to the viola in measure 28, furnishes beat-marking rhythmic support. Anything but a routine accompaniment, however, this proves to be a kind of developed conflation of the first violin's motives 2m and 3m from measures 2 and 3. The net result is a subtly complex transformation of the initial idea whose impetus will spearhead a rhythmically intensified drive to the end of the section.

The Continuous Exposition

By highlighting a structural pivot, the familiar device of the medial caesura gives palpable shape to a principle of tonal polarity, but it also entails a drawback: as a more or less centrally located stopping point, it impedes continuity at a point where Haydn often prefers unrelenting surface energy and motivic process. And in fact he often simply bypasses a mid-exposition break, thus allowing tonal unrest and rhythmic continuity to persist deep into the latter part of the section. When this occurs, we can say that the dynamic essence of a sonata exposition—the rhythmically energized propulsion from tonic to a new tonal center—has been privileged at the expense of balanced opposition or symmetry of proportions within the section.

Historians have attempted to describe Haydn's divergent approaches by distinguishing between "two-part" expositions (those with a medial caesura) and a "three-part" type (a class that embraces at least some of those that forgo the caesura in favor of extended transition).[4] But in light of the diverse procedures and the multiplicity of thematic events, cadences, and structural milestones that Haydn's expositions often entail, the more flexible term "continuous exposition" seems appropriate for cases in which open-ended elaboration persists through the middle portions of the section and confirmation of the new key is correspondingly postponed.[5]

The finale of Op. 33/1 in B minor, which Hepokoski and Darcy identify as a *locus classicus* for the continuous exposition, illustrates the method. An opening theme, progressing mainly in eighth notes and quarters, cadences on tonic in measure 12. The spark of sixteenth-note figuration ignites on the downbeat that follows, and this marks the start of a thirty-nine-measure trajectory, driven by a practically unstoppable show of virtuosity in the first violin, which will span the distance from tonic to the relative major (D). A decisive cadence, anticipated in measure 47, pins down the new key in measure 51, leaving a mere twelve measures of ensemble dialogue and closing formulas to dispel the charged atmosphere, achieve a more balanced relationship among the instruments, and draw the section to a close. The rapid-fire passagework lends velocity and surface glitter—a gratifying opportunity for brilliant execution—while supporting a span of tonal transition that encompasses more than three fifths of the exposition. Any possibility of structural symmetry is brushed aside in the process.

Most of the quartets' expositions follow either our first-described approach, with a medial caesura to separate primary and transition areas from secondary and closing material, or else a more process-oriented manner by which a phase of extended transition reaches into the latter part of the section to showcase figural display, motivic development, or interactive ensemble work. Others combine both tendencies by accommodating elements of balanced duality without permitting a letup in surface continuity. The first movement of Op. 55/1 in A, for example, begins with a wide-ranging, declamatory theme that happens to end, like that of Op. 33/1/iv, with a cadence in the twelfth measure. The extended transition that follows sounds restless and open-ended, with a continuous eighth-note impetus and a succession of chromatic inflections, although there is hardly any sense of departure from the orbit of tonic; and on the upbeat to measure 30,

EXAMPLE 4.2 Op. 55/1/i, mm. 29–32

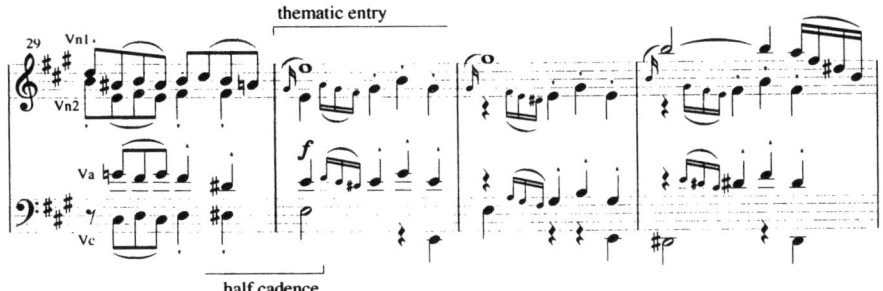

a rising chromatic line in the cello (C♯–D–D♯) seems to be steering toward an inflected half cadence on the dominant E (ex. 4.2). At this very point, close to the middle of the section, the first violin proclaims a variant of the movement's opening gesture, transposed from tonic to the dominant. The resulting elision, telescoping two measures into one, transforms what would have been a sacrifice of momentum into a new surge of energy, and the remainder of the section adopts the manner of a continuous exposition: the first violin unfurls a long span of triplet figuration, climbs to a peak of a^3, swoops to a low g♯, and eventually winds its way to a cadence at measure 48. The sixteen measures that remain allow for the relief of a lyrical violin duet prior to a series of punctuating moves that will close the exposition.

Still to be accounted for are some of Haydn's most intriguing strategies for parsing an exposition, those that make a game of the structural elements in play by setting up expectations of a conventional, stabilizing caesura, only to use the break as a platform for further unrest and development. In one artful instance, the first-movement exposition of Op. 71/3, Haydn embeds within the opening theme a forewarning of complications to come (see ex. 4.3a): the rapid acceleration from half note to sixteenths, which prefigures a longer-range tendency toward headlong action and resistance to temporal equilibrium. This trait manifests itself following a caesura at measure 43, whose accentuated V of V chords signal the end of a passage of tonal transition (see ex. 4.3b).

At this point, an unproblematical secondary theme might have been appropriate, but what we encounter instead is a polyphonically enriched transformation of the opening idea, whose unstable texture, harmony, and rhythmic impetus herald another span of transition. In its course, an infusion of sixteenth-note activity fuels the drive to a full cadence at measure 62, which is shown in example 4.3c. This structural landmark seems to stand as a sign of stability finally achieved, but such expectations are soon squelched by a new predicament: a throbbing dominant note sustains motion through the break; and as it persists,

EXAMPLE 4.3 Op. 71/3/i

(a) mm. 1–8 (violin 1 only)

(b) mm. 42–48

(c) mm. 61–67

(d) mm. 71–77

forming an undercurrent of harmonic tension, we hear what should be the eventual secondary theme—and so it is, in a sense, although there are odd contradictions at work. The absence of the cello from the theme's first five measures is a destabilizing agent in itself, as is the effect of a rhythmically misaligned canon between first violin and viola. Still more disturbing, however, is the fact that the principal line, derived once again from the main theme, has actually been restored to its original pitch level. The paradox is both subtle and profound: although we seem to have been propelled forward into the new key, melodically the exposition has shifted into reverse by recalling the opening theme's initial notes verbatim, just as they had appeared in measures 3–4 (see the brackets in ex. 4.3a and c). As if to make amends, this subversive thrust lasts only a few measures before the ensemble draws together once again for a full cadence in the dominant (m. 72). A stubborn force is still at work, however, and what follows turns out to be a rescored variant of the troublesome phrase quoted in example 4.3c, cheerfully adorned by a high-register, syncopated descant in the first violin (ex. 4.3d). Surface activity intensifies with a tumult of sixteenth notes beginning in the cello at measure 80, and it is only on the downbeat of measure 96, fourteen measures before the end of the exposition, that everyone joins forces once again for a cadence. By this time, any possibility of a relatively stable secondary theme area has been squandered, and the ensemble now forges ahead with a new idea that will lead through the double bar and repeat without any letup in surface momentum (see ex. 4.4, which shows the end of this movement's exposition and the start of its development section).

The Development Section

Apart from cases in which Haydn chooses not to call for a repeat of the exposition (Op. 76/5/iv and the slow movements of Opp. 1/3, 2/2, 20/5, 54/1, 71/2, 76/1, 4, and 5, and 77/1), crossing the threshold into the development section represents a thrust into new territory the second time around. The full stop and rest that most often marks this spot permits what follows to sound like a fresh start, a turning of the page to mark the onset of a new phase in the narrative. But sometimes there are complications, as when the development begins at the original pitch level with a literal or nearly literal recall of the primary theme for one measure or longer: a musical pun, in effect, by which the start of the new section seems momentarily indistinguishable from another return to the beginning of the movement (see Opp. 17/1/iv, 17/2/i, 20/1/iv, 20/5/iii, and 50/6/i).

In several first and last movements, forces of separation are mediated by the rhetorical device of immediate thematic connection, as in Op. 17/1/i, where the new section begins by passing the exposition's final closing idea to the cello, then treating it in dialogue between the two lower instruments. Continuity is thus assured, but there is a telling sense of reversal or change in temperament as well: harmonized first violin versus unaccompanied cello, major versus minor, and closed versus open (the melodic line had risen a half step to its resolution at the end of the preceding section; it now descends a half step to a leading tone, whose inherent tension, demanding a response, will set the development section in motion).

Haydn sometimes charges the very end of the exposition by destabilizing the harmony (most commonly by transforming the closing chord into a dominant seventh), by allowing surface activity to persist into the new section, or both. Such connective procedures may amount to nothing more than sustaining a melodic line while other parts momentarily rest to honor the sectional divide, but other times the ensemble's combined action helps erase any sense of a conventional punctuation. In Op. 71/3/i, the force of the first violin's cascading scale in measure 101 gives the impression of overshooting its goal (B♭, the local tonic) as the instruments join in unison to extend the line down to the low G (see ex. 4.4). They now rise together by degrees, introducing a salient repeated-note figure that will drive through the double bar and initiate the development section before stepping back to form an accompaniment to a new thematic entry in the first violin (m. 111).

If such resistance to closure may be heard as a refreshing alternative to the conventional full stop between exposition and development, there also exists the possibility of creating exaggerated discontinuity at this juncture, notably by jumping suddenly to a remote key as the new section gets under way. In Op. 54/3/i, all parts rest following a close on the dominant (B). The development then begins by stating the primary theme in a distant G major. Underlying the immediate impact of contrast in tonal color, however, are tangible elements of connection. To begin with, the change to G major had actually been anticipated several measures before the end of the exposition, where it was heard as a tonicized lowered submediant. Moreover, the status of B as a secure local tonic—and therefore its authority as a basis for registering tonal change—is undermined by significant chromatic inflections (C♮ and G♮) just before the double bar.

Taking the exposition's tonal dissonance as a point of departure, a development section is well positioned as an arena for locally engrossing moments of drama, suspense, or tantalizing humor, while at the same time generating expectations of ultimate resolution. But in addition to these forward-directed properties, the development affords a space for reflection and commentary: an opportunity to view the exposition in a fresh light, expand on its restricted tonal range, and engage in motivic process. The attendant freedom of syntax invites textural diversity and spirited ensemble play as themes variously undergo fragmentation, elaboration, and transformation. Principal lines and motivic figures typically migrate downward from the first violin, and conventional, treble-dominated sonority may

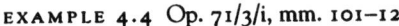

EXAMPLE 4.4 Op. 71/3/i, mm. 101–12

be further contested by contrapuntal technique or by other stratagems to give heightened importance to the ensemble's lower voices.

As a rule, tonal action in a development section complements that of the exposition simply by traversing other related keys. For major-key movements, this naturally entails a shift of emphasis to minor harmony, with allusions to keys based on the tonic scale's second, third, and sixth degrees standing in contrast to the exposition's tonic-dominant axis. In quartets as in Haydn's other instrumental genres, the last-mentioned of these minor keys, the submediant, enjoys favored status as a development-section goal.[6]

To specify Haydn's procedures more narrowly, the formula proposed by Leonard Ratner for the period as a whole proves useful: according to his model, a development section characteristically unfolds in two stages, the first leading to a so-called point of furthest remove, the second aimed toward the return to tonic.[7] Although many of the quartets' development sections conform more or less to this scheme, there are exceptions as well as much bending of the basic rule. In Op. 9/2/iv, for example, the development section comprises a single phase, essentially prolonging the dominant with no intermediate stopping point; and there are others that dwell with varying degrees of emphasis on two or more tonal regions in succession rather than highlighting a single principal goal. Momentary recollections of material in tonic (a possibility not excluded from Ratner's formula) are highlighted among several of the earlier quartets in a way that calls to mind a model described by H. C. Koch in his contemporary treatise on composition: begin with a statement on the dominant, step back momentarily to tonic, then proceed to another related key.[8]

Koch's allowance for an early, temporary return to tonic is especially worth noting in light of Haydn's occasional tendency, not only in very early works, to plant a conspicuous reference to the tonic key somewhere within the course of the development, as if to ponder the irony of its local presence in a part of the design where resisting the home key's gravitational pull might seem to be an important objective. In the first movement of Op. 17/1, temporary reversion to tonic materializes well into the latter part of the section, and because it coincides with a virtually exact quotation of the movement's opening measure, the event may be identified as a "false recapitulation": a preliminary, quickly abandoned return whose weight and timing might lead listeners to mistake it for the start of the recapitulation proper, or at least to recognize its similarity to that juncture in movements of similar construction and proportions.[9]

Notwithstanding the constant elements of Haydn's development sections, notably his enduring preference for the submediant as a tonal goal, there are changes in outlook over time. On the whole, later developments encompass a wider tonal spectrum than earlier ones (although there are in fact examples of relatively simple schemes in virtually every one of the later sets), and we can generalize by saying that the decisive move to a remote key—often explainable as a close relative of the tonic key's opposite mode (for example, the key of E♭ or A♭ for a movement in C major)—proves rare in development sections through Op. 42 but occurs on multiple occasions in all opus groups from Op. 50 on.

Aspects of Thematic and Rhetorical Profile

The vast majority of development sections in the quartets call on primary theme material as a point of departure. The order of events that follows is generally variable enough to ward off impressions of predictability, yet certain correspondences with the preceding exposition can sometimes be discerned.[10] (In fact, given the custom of beginning a development with a primary theme statement or derivative, even a single subsequent reference to later exposition material may suggest the possibility of significant relationship.) On a few occasions, the development in its entirety behaves almost as a species of parallel narrative, commentary, or dramatization with respect to the exposition. In Op. 33/5/i, the development mimics the exposition's thematic duality by beginning with the primary theme, then recalling the contrasting (but subtly related) secondary theme following a mid-measure rest close to the development's midpoint (m. 131, equivalent to m. 48, although without the fermata). The correspondence between sections, thus established, is enriched through Haydn's choice of key: by starting the development in tonic minor and eventually turning to the relative minor for the secondary theme, he creates something of a tonally darkened analog to the exposition's tonic-dominant polarity.

The development sections' penchant for fluid syntax and motivic fragmentation goes hand in hand with an accent on surface momentum, which in turn would seem to invite schemes of long-range, sweeping motion toward points of climactic intensity. That only a small number of the quartets' development sections unfold this way seems reasonable in light of the medium's natural affinity for intimacy, concentration, and detail. But on several occasions when Haydn does shape a development section more theatrically, we find him marshaling the ensemble's resources for brilliance and impact to splendid effect. In the finale of Op. 55/2, for example, the section begins on a note of urgency with nine measures of texturally unstable primary theme development nearly saturated with chromaticism (mm. 55–63). Surface activity then increases with a burst of sixteenth-note figuration that recalls a transitional passage from the exposition (mm. 34–40), and as the faster motion persists, the principal line rises above the staff, the cello descends, and a registral climax is attained on the downbeat of measure 70, marked by a four-and-a-half octave spread between highest and lowest pitches. The goal toward which all this action had been heading, a decisive cadence in the relative minor, is now deftly undercut, and the remaining six measures of the section will be absorbed in a rhythmically animated transition to the return at measure 78.

Altogether different from this case of unimpeded flow to a high point, yet also dependent on a driving rhythmic impulse, are those jarring moments where fast-paced activity comes momentarily to an abrupt halt: loud silences to tease, mark a change of course, or test the strength of a sustained argument by hindering forward motion. In one memorable instance, from the first movement of Op. 74/2 (F major), Haydn positions a full measure of dead silence as a central pivot in the form—measure 130, the exact midpoint of the movement—between a caesura on C major harmony (as V of F minor) and a startling continuation in C minor. A musical vacuum, the empty measure has the effect of swallowing up an anticipated arrival in the minor tonic as it clears the way for a new line of thought in an unanticipated key (ironically prepared, however, by the shared chord root between the two harmonies on either side of the break).

Conclusion of the Development Section

The question of how a development section ends takes us back to the theoretical model of a point of furthest remove, often the submediant, as a culmination of the development's centrifugal action. Although this is useful as a yardstick for Haydn's procedures, the potentially confusing "furthest remove" cannot always be equated with the most distant tonal center. Especially among quartets from

Op. 50 on, there are developments that lead to a remote key early in the section, as in the first movement of Op. 55/1/i (A major), where an initial span of transition veers from the dominant of E minor to the distant realm of C (m. 78), or even at the outset (for example, the first movement of Op. 54/3/i, with its immediate jump from the dominant, B, to the key of G).

In the two movements just cited, the appearance of a foreign key begins a modulatory process that eventually ends with a move to the submediant. The tonal path, in other words, has stretched from a distant region to a tonal orbit immediately adjacent to tonic, and from this point an imminent return to the home key is assured. Normally, a span of dominant preparation will intervene at this juncture, although there are several cases in which motion to the dominant of the relative minor actually marks the last event of the section before an unmediated return to tonic.[11] The first movement of Op. 54/3 (E major) is a striking example. Here, ongoing elaboration of the primary theme persists above a pedal point in the cello (G#, as V of C# minor) all the way from measure 98 to the very end of the development at measure 106.

In the vast majority of movements that do incorporate a preparatory dominant, this final piece of connective tissue seldom extends more than several measures. But even when the span is relatively long, it rarely entails dramatic or explosive gestures. Suppressed intensity better describes Haydn's typical procedure as motion either comes to a halt or else persists in the form of a thematic or accompanimental overlap, a wholesale elision at the join between sections, or the occasional, more delicate effect of a single, tenuous thread to reach across the divide and join with the start of the recapitulation. In an instance of this maneuver, from the finale of Op. 55/3, the returning primary theme is seamlessly embedded in the connecting solo line, so that it is only in retrospect that we can comprehend how the point of recapitulation has merged with the peak of the ascending scale on the upbeat to measure 66 (see ex. 4.5).

Recapitulation

As affirmed in writings by theorists of the time, including those of Koch, Francesco Galeazzi, and A. F. C. Kollmann, tonal resolution is the defining ingredient of what we understand as a sonata form's recapitulation.[12] But for present-day commentators, deriving their models from observed compositional practices as well as the classical theoretical accounts, large-scale thematic correspondences between outer sections prove no less germane than the question of tonal design,[13] and from this latter vantage point, the exposition and recapitulation may be perceived as more or less symmetrically balanced pillars of the form.

With respect to Haydn's practice, we can speak of a range of possibilities for proportion and thematic profile: on one end of the spectrum, the occasional oc-

EXAMPLE 4.5 Op. 55/3/iv, mm. 65–67

currence of a literal recapitulation whose duration and order of events closely matches that of the exposition; on the other, a final section so freely conceived as to challenge the very principles of thematic recapitulation and proportional equivalence. As a rule, recapitulations begin by restoring the home key simultaneously with a recurrence of the exposition's opening phrase. On rare occasions, this crucial thematic event precedes a delayed tonal return (as in Op. 33/3/i, mm. 108–10), or else the reinstatement of tonic coincides with something other than the primary theme. There are also a few cases in which the basic elements of thematic and tonal return come together on schedule, yet the moment is colored by harmonic ambivalence or uncertainty, as in the first movement of Op. 55/3 (B♭). The opening theme begins with a tonic note whose downbeat placement, long duration, and unison sonority help signify a stable point of departure (see ex. 4.6a). But the implications of this note are transformed at the start of the recapitulation (m. 129), where it now attaches to the end of a descending, dominant seventh arpeggio in the first violin (mm. 127–28; see ex. 4.6b). Embedded in this new context, the pitch sounds more like an appoggiatura than any definitive representation of tonic, especially as the motion from B♭ to A is now positioned to recall that of measure 127 (bracketed in ex. 4.6b), where the B♭ was heard as an accented dissonance. The lower parts reinforce this impression by entering on a dissonant chord, resolving to the dominant on beat 3, and withholding tonic harmony to the end of the next measure, midway through the phrase. The restoration of tonic therefore takes place not as a single, sharply focused event but as a gradual process.[14]

Apart from such rare aberrations, it is Haydn's practice to emphasize both tonal and thematic certainty at this juncture and thus to convey an apparent promise of stability and reconciliation. But what actually happens once the structural landmark has been reached is far from certain. Determining factors may in-

EXAMPLE 4.6 Op. 55/3/i

(a) mm. 1–4   (b) mm. 127–32

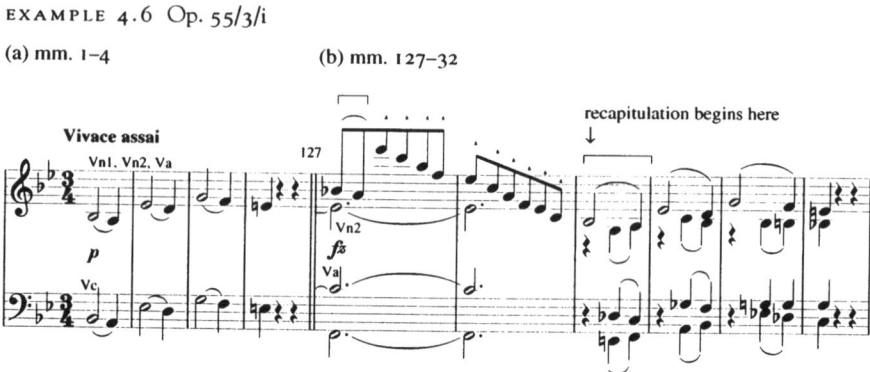

clude a particular recapitulation's obligation to trim material from the exposition that might otherwise seem redundant;[15] to respond to basic peculiarities of the preceding development section, thereby highlighting the interdependence of the form's principal sections; to promote undiminished attention to developmental process, novelty, and structural intrigue; or to achieve a rhetorical climax, perhaps realizing far-flung implications of a particular theme, enhancing the impression of long-range directional motion, or dramatizing the act of tonal reaffirmation.

Strategies that entail fresh development or special structural accent may stretch the size of the recapitulation considerably, as in Op. 64/1/i, where exposition and recapitulation contain sixty and seventy-seven measures, respectively, but such cases are not common. More typically, Haydn's preference accords with Koch's description of a plan in which "the most prominent phrases are now [i.e., in the recapitulation] compressed";[16] and there are some movements (Op. 9/4/i is an outstanding instance) in which abbreviation or compression shrinks the recapitulation to a fraction of the exposition's size.

Recurrence of Primary and Transition Material; The Secondary Development

Although it is common for Haydn to begin a recapitulation with the straight recurrence of an initial phrase, he seldom retrieves a primary theme unaltered in its entirety. Especially among the grammatically complex, fast-tempo first movements, the latter portion of an opening theme's recurrence tends to be varied, extended, rewritten, curtailed, or excised altogether. At issue is a basic difference in purpose between the form's outer sections: the need to establish a movement's tempo, character, and tonal focus invites repetition as a favored thematic process for the start of the exposition; in the altered context of a recapitulation, however, full recurrence may prove unnecessary, and the need to maintain momentum may be too urgent to permit the leisure of primary theme repetition. The question of superfluous recurrence is especially relevant to movements whose primary theme had been favored in the development section, as in Op. 9/4/i, where that section begins with an extended version of the opening phrase (*Pa*) in the subdominant (mm. 35–42), then proceeds to yet another varied statement of this idea in the dominant, beginning in measure 43. The recapitulation gets under way at measure 56, not by stating *Pa* yet again but by skipping ahead to a replica of the original restatement (*Pa¹*, corresponding to mm. 7–14). Redundancy and the risk of flagging momentum are thus avoided, but the choice of *Pa¹* at this juncture also lends a degree of structural continuity and large-scale integration, in that the relationship between the opening of the development (*Pa*) and the onset of the recapitulation (*Pa¹*) may be heard as a section-straddling expansion of the exposition's *Pa-a¹* logic in the original presentation of this material.

To follow the return of the opening theme with some version of the exposition's transition is an available option, assuming that the necessary tonal adjustments are made; but to the extent that this material was originally designed for modulation, it is now technically unnecessary, and it is thus likely to be abbreviated or altogether rewritten to form a fresh path into the latter part of the section. Exemplifying this approach, the recapitulation of Op. 50/6/i simplifies and telescopes a large swath of the exposition's transitional material (mm. 118–24, corresponding to mm. 16–33). That passage in the exposition had made a great show of pressing relentlessly toward the dominant, apparently well secured by measure 30, as a backdrop for the tonal shock of a heavily underscored ♭VI inflection shortly thereafter at measure 38. The recapitulation's much-abbreviated transition serves a simpler but no less urgent purpose in emphasizing a reestablished tonic while promoting a quickened pace of events as it aims for the analogous tonal deflection, consummated at measure 129 as a corresponding focus of intensity and color.

Different from movements that emphasize compression for the early portions of a recapitulation are those that indulge in a so-called secondary development,[17] digressing from the original order of events by interpolating a stretch of motivic elaboration, heightened ensemble activity, or tonal enrichment. Typically arising in the latter part of a primary theme's recurrence, the secondary development enlivens an otherwise predictable order of events as it resists the message of newly won stability. The first-movement recapitulation in Op. 33/5, for example, transforms the primary theme's restatement plus transition (mm. 25–48) into a span of textural novelty, energized motivic development, and tonal contrast (mm. 206–38). The exposition's opening twenty-four measures had come back intact (mm. 182–205); but now the viola and cello become metrically displaced, and the texture disintegrates into a rapid succession of three-note figures passed hocket-like between upper and lower parts. The ensemble's tonal bearings start to loosen as well, and the passage of motivic development that follows traverses G minor and E♭ (mm. 215–28) before steering back toward tonic for the return of the secondary theme in measure 239.

Recurrence of Secondary and Closing Material

According to Koch's prescription for the latter part of a recapitulation, "the second half of the first period [i.e., the exposition], or those melodic ideas of the first period which followed the V-phrase in the fifth [i.e., the caesura before continuation in the new key], is repeated in the main key and with this the allegro ends."[18] This rule obtains for many of the earlier quartets, and it proves viable to some extent among later works as well. Haydn often takes liberties with the standard formula, however, variously striving to keep the latter part of the form alive with unexpected turns of direction, or else bent on pursuing a long-range plan of elaboration and development. In the first movement of Op. 64/6, thematic activity in the recapitulation gives the impression of taking up where earlier segments of the form had left off. As shown in example 4.1, the secondary theme in the exposition had begun by subjecting the movement's opening idea to canonic imitation. The beginning of the development features a more extended canonic treatment; and in the recapitulation, a replica of the primary theme's opening phrase leads to yet another patch of strict imitation—the secondary development, in effect (mm. 102–7), whose contrapuntal impetus recalls that of the development section, but now with the pungent spice of grace notes on successive pitches in the leading and answering voices. Events that follow prolong the tendency toward cumulative change, intensification, and transformation. When the secondary theme comes back (m. 108), it is re-scored, telescoped by one measure to obliterate the canonic gesture, and enriched by new dissonant suspensions in the violins. The subsequent return of the closing theme (m. 118, corresponding to m. 36) turns out to be not a sign of impending conclusion but the introduction to another round of development: an interpolated recollection (mm. 123–34) of the principal idea whose hocket-style ensemble play brings the recapitulation to a climax of textural instability before resolving in a varied recurrence of the closing theme to rhyme with the end of the exposition.

Although the design just described may stretch the rule of transposed recurrence, it does come close to honoring a more liberal, twentieth-century version of Koch's dictum, the so-called sonata principle, by which material originally heard in a secondary key will be restored to tonic in such a way that "nothing is lost; everything that occurs will have its influence on the outcome and will have to be reckoned with before the piece is over."[19] There are situations, however, in which Haydn pointedly defies the sonata principle by deleting portions of secondary or closing material altogether, as in Op. 9/6/i, described earlier in connection with figure 4.1. The first appearance of the secondary theme (mm. 26–33) had marked the midpoint of the exposition; its recurrence, expanded to traverse several keys, coincides with the middle of the movement; and now, its form-defining duties having been discharged, it plays no role at all in the recapitulation.

The first movement of Op. 64/3 (B♭) presents a more blatant challenge to sonata form customs. The exposition features a particularly vivid contrast between a restless, motivically dense primary idea and a smoothly flowing secondary theme, which follows a medial caesura in measure 32. That this latter theme recurs in the heart of the development (m. 87, close to the midpoint of the movement) before disappearing for good, may suggest a plan similar to that seen in Op. 9/6/i, where a contrasting idea likewise served to designate both the middle of the exposition and central pivot to the form as a whole. But Op. 64/3/i seems more troublesome in two respects: first, the very salience of this movement's secondary theme as a well-formed, contrasting idea would seem to accentuate the tonal dissonance that a recapitulation is expected to resolve, normally by recalling that theme in tonic; second, the fact that the theme's development-section return is cast in the tonic minor means that the promise of a fully satisfying home-key return is never fulfilled. Is there some rationale behind the veiled, minor-mode recurrence of this material and its subsequent disappearance? As Hepokoski notes,[20] the exposition had already begun to darken the theme and compromise its structural weight by shifting from major to minor midway through its initial presentation (mm. 37–42). Its later recurrence in an unrelieved tonic minor, followed by an extension in which its melodic substance was fragmented, then dissolved altogether, may therefore be understood as the completion of a larger process: a strangely inflected narrative in which the secondary theme, tonally weakened at first by the turn to minor, is destined for extinction before the recapitulation ever gets under way.

Irregular Designs

Haydn occasionally challenges his own sonata form customs by circumventing any normally positioned boundary between the form's latter two sections. Easiest to explain are those cases in which the recapitulation appears to be foreshortened by some logically motivated omission of everything prior to the secondary theme, as in the finale of Op. 9/4, in which a close resemblance between the exposition's primary and secondary themes gives rise to a musical pun. The tonic key is reinstated at measure 73 with the semblance of a return to the movement's opening idea. However, this turns out not to be a version of the primary theme per se but its stand-in, the related secondary theme, first heard at measure 20. Restored to tonic, it serves to initiate an abbreviated recapitulation.

In several other instances of foreshortened recapitulation, a key ingredient is the persistence of developmental action well beyond the point where a return to tonic could reasonably have been expected. A prime example, the slow movement of Op. 20/3 (G major), begins its development by sounding the opening theme in the dominant, then tracing a modulatory route to the dominant of A minor (reached in mm. 64–65). The span encompassed so far is a bit short for a development section (its twenty-four measures barely exceed half the size of the exposition), and the meaning of the event that follows—a primary theme statement in C—therefore seems ambivalent: Could this be the start of a recapitulation that starts on the subdominant (rare for Haydn but not out of the question stylistically)? In fact, it prefaces a long, emotionally charged excursion, led by the high solo cello, whose lyrical voice persists from measure 70 to the downbeat of measure 84, where the arrival on a dominant plateau signals an imminent return to tonic. The movement now concludes not with a full recapitulation but with a replica of the exposition's latter part, restored to tonic (m. 89 corresponds to m. 19). (This scheme may be compared with that of the early Op. 2/4/i, represented in figure 8.1: uncanny resemblances between the two movements, despite rather extreme differences in tempo and character, include a comparably placed turn to the subdominant—following a cadence on the dominant of the supertonic—and the insertion of an additional span of development before a late return to tonic.)

There are other instances in which the development section, rather than overreaching normal limits, finds itself curtailed, at least temporarily, by an early return to tonic key and primary theme. This event may in turn yield to further excursion, as in Op. 1/2/i, so that elements of development and recapitulation intermingle, encroaching on one another's territory. Here the movement's opening phrase (*Pa*) returns at measure 56, after just eight measures of development over a dominant pedal, which seems too early for the start of a bona fide recapitulation, and a new phase of modulatory activity gets under way in measure 65. Only in measure 85 does the recurrence of exposition material in tonic resume with a tonally adjusted return of the exposition's second phrase, *Pa¹*. The resulting design, in which elements of elaboration and return alternate in the latter part of the form, has been aptly described as a species of disjunct recapitulation.[21]

Codas

In a large majority of the quartets' sonata-related forms, the end of the recapitulation corresponds to the end of the exposition, and with this the movement comes to a close. The correspondence may be only approximate, as when the exposition ends with destabilizing, transitional activity, and alteration is therefore necessary to bring about a satisfying conclusion. There are also numerous cases in which the point of decisive close at the end of the recapitulation is prolonged by several measures, sometimes through reiterations of a motivic figure, or else by a thematically neutral descent over a tonic pedal point.

More elaborate closing strategies may be found among sonata forms of the quartets' fast outer movements, which occasionally entail appendages that are structurally significant. The span in question may emerge seamlessly from the end of the recapitulation, and initially it may prove indistinguishable from a simple extension; but as it unfolds, it acquires identity as an event in its own right, defining its own field of action as a functionally discrete element in the design. Its nature varies considerably from one work to the next, although in a general sense it can be said to enrich the form with added motivic complication, harmonic emphasis, summarizing thematic recollection, or antic ensemble play, and thereby to end on a note of emphasized finality, mystery, comedy, or structural surprise in ways that, at least in retrospect, may have been anticipated by foregoing events. The term "coda," applied by Haydn and his contemporaries to specify various kinds of formal appendage, and subject to more narrow definition by later commentators,[22] serves as a convenient label for this phenomenon. Our use of the term in the discussion that follows will be deliberately restrictive in an attempt to capture palpable distinctions—but also pointed ambiguities—in Haydn's practice.

Easiest to specify, at least in certain outward respects, are those that fall outside the conventional double bar and repeat sign—presumably a reliable marker for the end of the recapitulation proper. In all, there are twelve movements that follow this scheme. Curiously, all but two occur in quartets before Op. 50 (see table 4.2).[23]

Although they differ in size, thematic content, compositional technique, and rhetorical significance, each has enough functional independence to be designated as a coda. Several ambitious ones constitute true perorations, developing important ideas as they form a resounding conclusion to the movement. Perhaps most memorable of all is the harmonically adventurous coda to Op. 20/5/i, which strays deep into remote tonal regions before swelling to forte, highlighting the restoration of tonic with scalar flourishes, then closing enigmatically with a pair of low-register chords sounded pianissimo. Others from among this list concentrate on the concise, valedictory recall of one or more themes, followed by either an energetic ringing down of the curtain (for example, Op. 17/4/iv) or a quiet retreat (as in Op. 9/5/iv). Still others play for humor, subtlety, or understatement, sometimes calling up fragmentary thematic recollections as a sign of wistful farewell.

By analogy with the codas listed in table 4.2, others may be recognized, not always unambiguously, in movements whose latter part is entirely enclosed by the conventional repeat, or else where a second-part repeat is absent. As a rule, such cases require a degree of parallelism between exposition and recapitulation, in order for us to have a clear idea of where the recapitulation per se leaves off and where the coda begins. In Op. 71/2/i, for example, a full recurrence of a tuneful closing idea (mm. 104–14) matches that theme's original appearance toward the end of the exposition (mm. 39–49). The remaining portion of the move-

TABLE 4.2 Sonata form movements in which the coda falls outside the repeat of the latter part

Opus	Key	Length
9/5/iv	B♭	19
17/1/iv	E♭	23
17/4/i	Cm	10
17/4/iv	Cm	18
17/6/iv	D	6*
20/5/i	Fm	23
33/3/i	C	17
33/4/i	B♭	4½*
33/6/i	D	16
42/iv	Dm	8*
71/3/i	E♭	28*
76/2/i	Dm	16

In all except those marked by an asterisk (*), connection from the end of the recapitulation to the start of the coda is accomplished by way of a second ending.

ment, measures 115–25, may therefore be appreciated as a coda: a span that embraces both a dense summary of thematic elements, including the specific recollection of an idea from the development section, and a bass line whose stepwise descent through the tonic scale (mm. 120–23) helps ground the movement's energies as the end approaches.

What motivates these codas? First of all, there are movements whose exalted rhetoric and seriousness of purpose call for something more emphatic than a simple equivalent of the exposition's closing theme: the first movements of Op. 20/5 (F minor) and 76/2 (D minor) stand out in this regard. In other cases, it appears that elements of fierce rhythmic or motivic intensity require the extra space of a coda to discharge tension and provide a suitably stable close. The opening movement of Op. 54/1, cast in a bright G major and charged with a near overabundance of energy from the start, gives the impression of an intense buildup of pressure in its recapitulation: Haydn telescopes the duration of the section by some twenty measures, and he crowds its surface with sixteenth-note figuration. Momentum now overflows from a varied recurrence of the original closing theme (mm. 107–13) to what may be described as an elaborate, thematically diverse coda whose salient events include the braking force of a phrase dominated by long note values (mm. 122–25) and a final burst of energy in which the exposition's opening and closing gestures are embraced in a single valedictory phrase (mm. 126–31).

The rationale for a coda is not always obvious, and in some cases it may be whimsical in intent. The finale of Op. 64/3, for example, presents a recapitulation that tracks the exposition closely enough to convince us that we can tell just where and how the movement is likely to end. All signals therefore seem clear as the exposition's closing phrases begin their timely recurrence (mm. 204–9, corresponding to mm. 67–72 in the exposition). But the second phrase, eliding with the end of the first at measure 209 (corresponding to mm. 72–79, with which the exposition had ended), goes off course: an elongated melodic arc defeats all expectations of immediate closure, although its registrally extended line—the f^3 of measures 214–15 is the highest note of the movement—does eventually lead to a decisive cadence at measure 225. And yet the action persists, this time with a recollection of the entire opening theme, no less, so that the movement's willful refusal to end begins to seem incurable. Along with this latest event comes a new promise, however: the latter part of the closing phrase (mm. 206–9) had actually made its first appearance as an ingredient of the primary theme (mm. 7–10). Will it return now, as part of the primary theme's surprise recall? If so, will it help restore order and bring about a satisfying conclusion after all? The closing formula does in fact reappear (mm. 232–35), but once again the movement declines to end: a succession of cadential figures, rests, and liquidating motivic fragments continues to tease for ten more measures before the long-delayed close finally transpires. Although comparable to other codas examined as a functionally discrete series of postrecapitulation events, this one seems inspired less by matters of necessity or rhetorical conviction than by an urge to engage us in a game inspired by the very topic of the coda as a musical entity.

Related Forms

Among the quartets' total of 107 fast, nondance movements whose design rests on a customary two-reprise foundation, just one, the diminutive finale of Op. 9/6, is too small to include within the domain of sonata form per se: its first reprise extends to a mere eight measures. In fewer than a dozen cases, the sonata model is compromised by a partial recapitulation, an intermingling of development and recapitulation functions, or by some other complication. Several of these exceptional movements have been cited.

Other two-reprise forms that stand outside the core sonata form repertory may be found among the slow movements. They include simple binary forms (Opp. 1/1/iii, 9/2/iii, 17/6/iii) with relatively concise first and second parts; rounded binary forms whose second part encompasses a tonally altered recurrence of first-reprise material (Opp. 1/2/iii, 54/2/ii); and several instances of what we have called "large binary" form: binary in profile yet cast on a larger scale, with differ-

TABLE 4.3 Instances of slow-movement form (sonata form without development)

Opus	Meter	Tempo	Key
9/3/iii	3/4	Largo	C (subdominant)
17/2/iii	¢	Adagio	B♭ (subdominant)
17/5/iii	3/4	Adagio	Gm (parallel minor)
33/3/iii	3/4	Adagio ma non troppo	F (subdominant)
33/5/ii	¢	Largo e cantabile	Gm (parallel minor)
33/6/ii	¢	Andante	Dm (parallel minor)
50/2/ii	¢	Adagio. Cantabile	F (subdominant)
50/5/ii	3/4	Poco adagio	B♭ (subdominant)
55/1/ii	2/4	Adagio. Cantabile	D (subdominant)

entiated themes and clearly marked cadences to punctuate the musical narrative within either part (Opp. 9/5/iii, 17/4/iii, 20/6/ii).[24]

Interior movements of another type, found on occasion in quartets from Op. 9 through Op. 54/55, follow a pattern often recognized simply as slow-movement form. The first part consists of a sonata-like exposition, not closed by a double bar and repeat sign, followed by a recapitulation[25] (see table 4.3; the fact that a transition may intervene can be a cause of ambiguity: to the extent that an elongated transition qualifies as a species of development, the distinction between sonata and slow-movement form is blurred). Designed to highlight a soloistic first violin, these forms call to mind contemporary operatic practices in which the setting of an aria text modulates to the dominant or relative major, then reverts to tonic as the text repeats;[26] and as with interior movements similarly inspired by aria- or concerto-like practices—for example, Op. 9/4/iii (sonata form) and Op. 17/6/iii (binary)—several in this group are adorned with cadenzas.

To ponder the quartets' many sonata- and sonata-related forms is to journey close to the heart of what these works represent as a facet of Haydn's artistic personality and a reflection of his compositional technique. Even the earliest quartets reveal a keen sense of the forms' capacity as vehicles for textural complexity, motivic process, and the realization of long-range structural implications. Haydn's spectrum of possibilities widened with his adoption of a thematically more complex, rhythmically more diversified idiom for his quartets of the late 1760s and early 70s (Opp. 9, 17, and 20). Subsequently, there was little evolution with respect to fundamentals. Rather, from this time on we find a perpetual demonstration of the form's resilience, its ability to accommodate novelty and experiment, and its elasticity in adapting to different parts of the cycle.

Basic to Haydn's strategy throughout the repertory is the reaffirmation of standard procedures on which listeners' understanding of a musical argument must be based. Exemplary or unproblematical sonata forms, with clearly defined structural hierarchies, unambiguous tonal paths, and transparent thematic designs, figure prominently in nearly every opus; and they serve as a foil for those that engage the listener in a game by thwarting expectations. Still others, encountered sporadically throughout the oeuvre, blatantly violate the composer's own models for large-scale design; but the environment of relative conformity in which they occur bestows meaning on them as acts of novelty or originality transferred from a more familiar place—as details within a conventional design—to aberrations affecting the design itself.

Of paramount importance in virtually all these forms is the composer's gift for articulating coherent relationships between the details of harmony, theme, and sonority, and the larger scheme from which they draw their expressive weight and rhetorical significance. Although an overview of the quartets' repertory of sonata forms can scarcely do justice to Haydn's ingenuity in this respect, it nevertheless serves as an illuminating backdrop for the more narrowly defined issues of form and movement type to be addressed in the chapters that follow, as well as for the more specific inquiry into individual opus groups that comprises the final part of our study.

5

The Dance Movement

The minuet, cultivated by earlier generations in private chamber music as well as in the ballroom, blossomed with fresh life in instrumental works by Haydn and his contemporaries. They embraced the stylized triple-meter dance as a standard movement type, and it became an absolute fixture of the Haydn quartet cycle. Always based on the tonic note of the home key, although not necessarily its mode (there are minor-key quartets with minuets in major), it guaranteed that at least one interior movement would reaffirm the tonal orientation of the cycle as a whole.

Ingredients of the familiar plan include the minuet proper, with binary repeats; a second minuet, or trio, also with binary repeats;[1] and the mandatory da capo recurrence of the minuet proper. Within a four-movement quartet, this minuet-trio complex comes either second or next to last, and in the early five-movement works it occupies both positions. Haydn's constancy in placing the dance-pair in every one of his quartets bespeaks a commitment to its inherent values. An emblem of aristocratic customs and manners, the minuet could bestow a degree of nobility and sophistication; and by virtue of its formulaic design, kinetic impulse, and tradition-bound constraints of rhythm, phrase, and melodic gesture, it complemented the expressive diversity, structural fluidity, and spontaneous rhetoric of adjoining slow and fast movements.

The dance movements were for Haydn more than a nod to tradition. Their all-too-predictable qualities furnished a basis for strokes of wit, novelty, and surprise, typically through rhythmic play, unexpected phrase lengths, motivic ingenuity, or unusual effects of dynamics, timbre, and texture.[2] Moreover, there are many instances, especially among quartets from Op. 33 on, in which a quickened tempo, streamlined rhythmic profile, or countrified tunefulness imbued the movements' character with a freer spirit. Indicative of a fresh perspective was Haydn's change of terminology for Op. 33, where the provocative label "scherzo"[3] replaced the otherwise standard "minuet" or "menuet." (The significance of Op. 33 as a landmark or turning point with respect to the dance movement should not be overemphasized: deviations from relatively conventional minuet practices did not begin with this opus; the Op. 33 scherzos are not uniformly adventurous; and Haydn did in fact abandon the term "scherzo" in favor of the older label for all his later quartets, despite the rebellious qualities they often display, including fast tempos, rhythmic disturbances, and odd phrase structures.)

The interplay of novel and old-fashioned elements—and the concomitant mixture of stately minuet characteristics with traits suggestive of rural dance steps—are recognized features of Haydn's approach to the dance movement in his quartets, symphonies, and other instrumental cycles. Exploring this phenomenon from various points of view, scholars have drawn comparisons with the adjacent repertory of Haydn's ballroom dances.[4] The pieces in question, variously labeled as minuets or German dances ("allemandes," "menuettini tedeschi," "tedeschi di ballo," "deutsche") survive in several collections from different times in the course of Haydn's career, as summarized in table 5.1.[5] They represent a direct encounter with social dance customs of the time, including both the refined steps of the minuet per se and the simpler, more energetic motions of popular or country dances;[6] and in this respect there are notable correspondences with Haydn's practices in the quartets.

Illustrating courtly manners, example 5.1 compares the first parts of two contemporaneous minuets: No. 4 from the early "Seitenstetten" ballroom collection and the fourth movement of the quartet Op. 1/3. Similarities include a principal line in which motion in half notes and quarters predominates, a sure sense of equilibrium or complementation in profile between first and second phrase, and a forthright, melodically active bass whose steady pace focuses attention on the beat as a primary metrical unit. The prevailing rhythmic and melodic composure, underscored by a felicitous balance of similar and contrasting measure-size

TABLE 5.1 Haydn's ballroom dances: Summary of principal surviving collections of dances scored for orchestra

Hob.	Title	Number	Date
IX:1	Minuetti ("Seitenstetten" minuets)	12	possibly by 1760
IX:5	Menuetti	6	1776
IX:7	Raccolta de menuetti ballabili	14	by 31 Jan 1784
IX:9	Six Allemandes; Menucttini tedeschi	6	by 15 Nov 1786
IX:11	Menuetti di ballo; Redout menuetti	12	1792
IX:12	Tedeschi di ballo; 12 Redout Deutsche	12	1792
IX:16	24 Menuetti	24	?ca. 1790–1800

EXAMPLE 5.1

(a) No. 4 from Hob. IX:1 ("Seitenstetten" minuets), mm. 1–8 (principal melody and bass)

(b) Op. 1/3/iv, mm. 1–8

units (in both phrases of the quartet movement, in the first phrase of the ball-room dance), typifies the elegance and noble simplicity with which the mid- to later-eighteenth-century minuet was identified, whether in the ballroom or the more private milieu of chamber-music performance.[7]

Example 5.2, by contrast, compares two dances in a less elevated style: No. 2 from the collection of twelve *Tedeschi di ballo* (or *12 Redout Deutsche*; 1792) and the third movement of the "Lark" quartet, Op. 64/5 (minuet). The opening phrases of both suggest a relatively heavy-footed step, with bass lines fastened to the tonic note, a vigorous, measure-level pulse, and simple melodic lines chiseled mainly from broken chords and scales. Heightened surface activity in either dance's third measure alleviates monotony, lends impetus toward the conclusion of the phrase, and helps convey the impression of a single unit of structure and motion. The second phrase in either piece builds on the increasing animation heard in the first, by falling through an extended flow of eighth notes in the ballroom dance while rising to a higher-register climax in the quartet. In both instances, streamlined action within the measure yields an impression of kinetic energy and directional motion spanning the entire eight-measure reprise.

Although elements of consistency over time may be traced in Haydn's cultivation of both high and low dance-movement styles, certain trends or patterns of change may be discerned, many aberrations and exceptional cases notwithstanding. To begin with, some of the shortest minuets and trios do indeed occur

EXAMPLE 5.2

(a) No. 2 from *Tedeschi di ballo*, mm. 1–8 (principal melody and bass)

(b) Op. 64/5/iii, mm. 1–8 (violin 1 and cello)

Menuet
Allegretto

among the earliest quartets; the minuets of later groups tend to grow progressively longer (this is less true of trios, whose dimensions are less subject to change over time); and one of the very last minuets, that of Op. 77/2, proves longest of all.

Somewhat more explicit tendencies can be seen with respect to the dance movements' tempo markings (see table 5.2): first of all the increasing occurrence of actual designations of tempo, not merely the generic label "minuet" or "menuet," through Op. 33 (one instance among the earliest quartets, three in Op. 9, four in Opp. 17 and 20, all six in Op. 33); second, a concomitant tendency in this portion of the repertory toward faster tempos (assuming that the allegretto and allegro markings represent an increase over some standard, tacitly understood tempo for the early, unmarked dance movements); and third, a trend toward faster tempos that encompasses the entire repertory, climaxing with the presto markings in Opp. 76, 77, and 103 (tempered in the last instance by the admonition "ma non troppo").[8]

Tempo correlates to some degree with distinctions between the different dance idioms: the traditional minuet, with its rhythmic diversity and stately pace, as opposed to the energetic *deutscher Tanz*. Relevant aspects of the more lowly style, occasionally found in earlier trios (more rarely in the minuet proper), and well established in several of the Op. 33 dance movements (scherzos as well as trios), include an accent on the measure rather than the beat as a temporal unit, the preference for uncomplicated, measure-outlining melodic figures, relatively slow harmonic rhythm, pedal points, and the grammatical plainness of alternat-

TABLE 5.2 Tempo markings for the dance movements

Op. No.:	0/1/2	9	17	20	33	42	50	54/55	64	71/74	76	77/103
Presto											1,6	77/1,2 103/ii[d]
Allegro					1[b],2 5		2			71/2 74/1	2,3 4,5	
Allegretto	2/4/iv	1[a],3 5	2[a],3 4,5	1[a],2 3,4	3,4 6		1[a],3 4,5 6	54/2,3 55/2	1[c],2 3,4 5,6	71/1 74/3		
No marking	0,1/1 1/2,1/3 1/4,1/6 2/1,2/2 2/4/ii 2/6	2,4 6	1,6	5,6		ii		54/1 55/1,3		71/3 74/2		

Tempos indicated here correspond to those represented in *JHW* 12/1–3, 5–6 (for Opp. 0, 1, 2, 9, 17, 20, 33, 64, 71/74, 76, 77, and 103) and the Doblinger series, ed. Landon and Reginald Barrett-Ayres (for Opp. 42, 50, and 54/55).

[a][Un] poco allegretto

[b]Allegro di molto

[c]Allegretto ma non troppo

[d]ma non troppo presto

ing tonic and dominant harmony. Although the more exalted manner is never completely supplanted, later dance movements almost never recapture its spirit to the extent witnessed among the earliest minuets. In this respect, the repertory as a whole may be seen to reflect a recognized, larger development by which aristocratic customs lose ground to a more inclusive aesthetic.[9]

Example 5.3 highlights the general trend toward a measure- rather than beat-oriented rhythmic impulse by comparing the openings of four dance movements from different phases of Haydn's oeuvre. (The particular choice of examples must not be interpreted as an attempt to overstate the case for evolutionary change: it should be kept in mind that early dance movements sometimes exhibit rustic qualities more commonly found in later opus groups, and later examples occasionally incline toward a stately, beat-oriented pace.) The first minuet quoted (Op. 9/4/ii, shown in ex. 5.3a) displays several traditional minuet-style traits, notwithstanding the disturbance of a downbeat rest in measure 3, which work to emphasize the quarter note as a salient unit of activity: a melodically active bass, a variety of note values in the principal melody, including a beat-outlining group of sixteenth notes, and relatively fast harmonic rhythm (six changes of harmony in four measures). Example 5.3b, from the Op. 20/5 minuet, embodies a different kind of movement, with plainer surface-rhythmic and melodic activity in its outer parts and a slower rate of change in harmony. Each downbeat marks the start of a new pattern; at the same time, similarly weighted quarter notes help sustain a beat-level pulse. Progressing to example 5.3c, which quotes from Op. 50/3/iii, we find a minuet whose opening phrase clearly highlights the measure as a rhythmic entity. Especially in measures 1 and 2, downbeat energy is first discharged and then reabsorbed in anticipation of the downbeat that follows, so that action within the measure is subordinated to a measure-level impulse. Finally, in example 5.3d, from the beginning of Op. 76/1/iii, beat- and measure-level activity is simplified to such a degree that the entire measure seems to go by as a single pulse within a higher-level metrical frame; and the fact that the treble line's initial pitches in each measure traverse an archetypal four-note macroline G–A–C–B (scale degrees 1–2–4–3) enhances the impression of a large-scale unit of motion.

A complicating element, one that to some extent runs counter to other trends toward rural simplicity and down-to-earth accessibility, involves the expanded boundaries of harmonic relationship sometimes found among later dance movements. Examples include the minuets of Op. 50/3 (in E♭, with a move to G♭ in the second reprise), Op. 55/2 (in F, shifting briefly to E♭), Op. 74/1 (in C, with a second reprise that jumps immediately to A♭), and Op. 103/ii (in D minor, with an accent on chromaticism and prolonged harmonic tension). The more isolated phenomenon of remote relationship between minuet and trio occurs on just four occasions: Op. 74/1 (in C, with a trio in A major); Opp. 74/2 and 77/2 (both in

EXAMPLE 5.3   Beat- versus measure-level activity
(violin 1 and cello)

(a) Op. 9/4/ii, mm. 1–4

(b) Op. 20/5/ii, mm. 1–4

(c) Op. 50/3/iii, mm. 1–4

(d) Op. 76/1/iii, mm. 1–4

F, each with a trio in Db); and Op. 77/1 in G, whose trio is likewise cast in the lowered submediant (Eb).

The opposite phenomenon—restriction to utterly minimal tonal action—occurs more commonly among earlier dance movements but is by no means limited to them. Relatively extreme cases include Op. 20/6, whose minuet and trio both unfold in a pure A major with no more than two pitches foreign to the tonic scale (E♯ and D♯ in the trio, mm. 24 and 26, respectively), and the two-reprise forms in addition to the Op. 20/6 minuet that have no accidentals at all: the minuets of Opp. 1/3/ii and 2/2/iv and the trios of Opp. 1/6/ii and 64/4.

The Minuet Proper

Dance movements in the quartets typically begin by presenting either a principal melodic line with harmonizing accompaniment or else (especially in earlier quartets) the polarized texture of treble and bass moving in counterpoint. Although having all ensemble members engaged from the start is normal and natural to the genre, there are more than two dozen instances of a more tentative, interrogative, or ambivalent opening in which one or more parts are withheld: thus the minuet of Op. 50/5 leads with an unaccompanied first violin solo, that of Op. 55/2 presents an extended duet of first violin and viola, and that of Op. 64/1 begins with a solo cello accompanied by a pair of violins. Often the instruments group and regroup in pairs as a minuet unfolds—a trait scarcely restricted to this movement type but nonetheless one of its distinctive features—almost as if to suggest a ballroom's pairing of dance partners. Ensemble partnerships are especially conspicuous in certain of the earliest quartets where a fourth-movement minuet follows a slow movement that had favored the first violin exclusively; and in both Op. 2/1 and 4 we can recognize a three-phase progression, beginning with a soloistic Adagio, proceeding to a courtly minuet with instruments sounding in pairs, and moving from there to a less formal style of dance in the trio: a virtual musical itinerary leading from opera house, to ballroom, to village square.

Within the first reprise, the minuets' pitch range is seldom more than moderately wide, the harmony is predominantly consonant and diatonic, and tonal action entails either beginning and ending in tonic or (more commonly) progressing to the dominant or relative major key. Most often, this first segment spans eight, ten, or twelve measures, with four-measure phrases, sometimes elongated by two-measure extensions, being the norm. These technical constraints, which describe a sizable majority of the minuets, perhaps may be heard as a metaphor for the circumscribed space in which the dancers perform their steps. Minuets that stretch or break the prevailing norms are by no means rare, and examples may be found in all opus groups. They include those whose first reprise is marked by an ascent to a high register (Op. 20/2), unusual phraseology (Opp. 0/ii, 54/1), abnormal length (as in Op. 77/2, with a first reprise that extends to twenty-four measures), metrical dissonance (Op. 20/4), or extremely fast tempo (Op. 77/1). Such challenges to Haydn's own conventions may signal entry into a realm of stylistic transformation where minuet-like traits prove conspicuous by their very absence.

The Second Reprise

Conceived as the response to a normally concise first part, the second reprise unfolds through such processes as motivic development, rhythmic and melodic alteration or contrast, and harmonic excursion, sometimes incorporating an emphasized
apex of pitch, dynamics, or harmonic intensity before a return to stability. Simplest in overall structure, although sometimes procedurally complex, are those
that complement the first reprise to create a straight binary form, as in Op. 2/4/iv,
whose first part comprises a pair of vividly contrasted, four-measure phrases: loud
versus soft, staccato versus legato, middle register versus low. The second reprise
both elaborates and reconciles the juxtaposed contrasts, offering two identical
two-measure units that incorporate elements from both phrases of the first part,
then progressing to a climactic passage that attains a peak of f^3 (m. 14) before recalling the staccato quarter notes of measure 3 (m. 15) as it begins the descent to
a cadence in the same register with which the movement began. Minuets whose
second part similarly complements or intensifies the first comprise scarcely more
than a handful, scattered among quartets through Op. 20. In every instance but
one (Op. 9/2), the first part ends either in the dominant key or on a dominant
chord; and in all but two cases, the second part exceeds the first by four or more
measures (see table 5.3).

In contrast to these simple binary structures, the vast majority of Haydn's
quartet minuets may be described as rounded binary forms whose second reprise
begins with a span of development or contrast (which can simply be labeled B)
before a substantial return of first-reprise material (A), which may be literal, tonally
adjusted, or otherwise altered, and that may be followed by a supplementary ap-

TABLE 5.3 Simple binary-form minuets

Opus	1st repr.	2d repr.	Comments on the design of the 2d reprise
1/2/ii	12	18	Altered recurrence of mm. 1–4; then new material follows
2/4/iv	8	12	1st-reprise motives elaborated; final phrase recalls 1st-reprise material
9/2/ii	10	10	Corresponds closely to 1st reprise
9/4/ii	20	28	Extends and elaborates 1st-reprise material, largely retaining its order
17/3/ii	16	16	Corresponds approximately to 1st reprise; appendage recalls 1st phrase
20/4/iii	8	12	Elaborates opening material; latter part corresponds closely to 1st reprise
20/6/iii	8	12	Motivic development and new material; replica of opening phrase at end functions as an appendage

TABLE 5.4 Rounded binary minuets with literal, or nearly literal, recurrence of first-reprise material (‖ A :‖:B A :‖)

Opus	‖ A	:‖: B	A [+appendage]:‖	Comments on appendages
1/1/ii	10	14	10	
1/4/ii	8	14	8	
0/ii	7	14	7	
1/6/iv	9	14	9	
2/2/iv	12	18	12	
9/3/ii	12	6	12	
9/5/ii	8	12	8	
20/1/ii	8	16	8 + 12	Elaborates and summarizes A and B material
33/2/ii	10	14	10	
33/3/ii	10	14	10	
33/4/ii	8	8	8	
33/5/iii	10	22	10	
33/6/iii	8	10	8	
50/2/iii	8	16	8[a] + 18	Develops and recalls A, rises to a climax
50/3/iii	12	24	15[a] + 6	Recalls A material
50/6/iii	8	16	8	
54/1/iii	10	14	11[a] + 9	Recalls and intensifies A material
54/2/iii	8	16	8 + 14	Echoes A material, rises to a climax
54/3/iii	8	22	8	
64/3/iii	14	18	17 + 9	Extends, recalls, and develops A and B material[b]
64/4/ii	8	16	8	
71/2/iii	10	9	9	

[a]Ends with a deceptive, extended, or otherwise incomplete cadence.

[b]Additional complications are illustrated in figure 5.3.

pendage. The simplest rounded binary designs are those, listed in table 5.4, in which the first reprise begins and ends in tonic, and its material comes back literally, or nearly so, in the latter part of the second reprise. The form is thus anchored to a pair of structural pillars whose tonal stability frames volatile activity in between. Examples of this type occur in nearly all opus groups, with a particular concentration in Op. 33. All are in major, and in most instances the central area of the form involves modulation, or at least allusion, to the dominant. (Several traverse other related keys, and one, Op. 2/2/iv, has no modulation at all.)

The quartets' other rounded binary minuets prove more complex than most of those listed here, because they involve alteration or expansion of first-reprise material rather than simple recurrence. More often than not, they incorporate a substantial appendage prior to the close (as in the six exceptional cases noted in table 5.4). The result is a kind of form in which the latter part of the second reprise may exceed its obligatory function of recurrence (literal or tonally altered) by offering fresh intrigue or heightened rhetorical emphasis.

The repertory of these forms is substantial, comprising almost fifty minuets, and their formal diversity covers an impressive range of possibilities. Most straightforward are those in which first-reprise material returns largely intact apart from simple tonal adjustments and appendages. More complex situations include several (mostly early) minuets whose point of return is colored by imitative entries, canon, or by changes in harmonic orientation and melodic profile. Other cases, both early and late, involve variation or extension of returning first-reprise material.

Certain connotations of the minuet—notably its formality, stylized demeanor, and impressions of physical presence and motion—naturally suggest the appropriateness of a full-bodied cadence to mark the end of the dance and bring all action to a stop, and yet there are those that end by dropping to a quiet dynamic level in the manner of a quizzical afterthought. In Op. 64/6/iii, for example, an evidently premature closing phrase (mm. 29–32) drives to a reassuringly decisive cadence on the downbeat of measure 32 (see ex. 5.4). To all intents and purposes, this would seem to mark the end of the minuet. But this is not what happens. Instead, a quietly mocking, metrically out-of-kilter addendum in measures 33–36 transpires as an impudent, parenthetical comment on the preceding action.

Trios

Bracketed by the minuets' statement and recurrence, and thus positioned to serve as an interlude or digression from the main line of thought, the trio tends to be relatively compact, and in fact there are no more than twenty quartets, distributed among earlier as well as later opus groups, with trios either equal in size to their respective minuets or longer. The trios often impress us with a certain pithy, sometimes almost static quality, the result of dwelling on a single figure, motive, rhythmic impetus, or timbre. To cite a striking example, every measure in the

EXAMPLE 5.4   Op. 64/6/iii, mm. 29–36

Op. 71/2 trio contains the same, hauntingly persistent figure, although its disposition among the ensemble members changes repeatedly, especially in the second reprise: dotted half notes in one or more parts as the backdrop for a pattern consisting of a rest on beat 1 followed by dissonant attack on beat two which is slurred to an upward or downward resolution on beat 3.

For the vast majority of trios, the tonal center is the same as for the minuet, with the opposite mode being chosen in nearly half these cases. Several others, mostly early, are cast in closely related keys: dominant, subdominant, relative minor, or submediant. As noted earlier, four quartets from the 1790s venture to a more distant key for the trio: major submediant in Op. 74/1, lowered submediant in Opp. 74/2, 77/1, and 77/2.

With respect to overall structure, Haydn avails himself of approximately the same options for trios as for minuets, although in accordance with the trios' tendency toward greater concision and uniformity, he has more trios than minuets in simple two-part binary form (listed in table 5.5), fewer trios with supplementary appendages, and more instances in which the return in a rounded binary form is shorter than the first reprise. Among this last-mentioned group is a type not found in any of the minuets: one in which the first and second reprise are of equal length (eight measures each), and the return consists solely of a replica or variant of the opening four-measure phrase.[10] A distinctive touch in a number of the rounded binary trios involves the return of the principal melodic line in a different register or instrumental sonority, as in Op. 71/3, where the trio's opening melodic descent in the cello, initially unaccompanied, undergoes a thorough

TABLE 5.5 Trios in simple binary form

Opus	1st reprise	2d reprise
1/1/ii	14	14
1/6/ii	8	12
2/6/iv	8	8
9/2/ii	8	14
9/4/ii	8	8
17/1/ii	10	22*
33/1/ii	14	12
33/4/ii	9	10
42/ii	8	8
54/2/iii	10	16
55/3/iii	8	12

*The long second reprise is a special case but nonetheless belongs in the binary category with respect to tonal and thematic content.

transformation in character as it returns in the latter part of the second reprise. Here it sounds not in the cello but three octaves higher in the first violin, reinforced by the second violin from below, and further harmonized by a rising line in the viola. Coloristic nuance thus takes precedence over the more common rhetoric of straight recurrence at this crucial moment in the form. (Although specially featured among the trios, the device does occur in several minuets as well.) Finally there are trios, yet to be discussed, in which the second reprise is incomplete—cut short to make way for a transition back to the minuet, and therefore not subject to repetition.

Relationship between Minuet and Trio: Some Representative Instances

In what respects do the dance movement's two elements form a complementary, dialectic, or mutually reinforcing pair? There are instances in which the trio simply sustains the minuet's key and temperament while proposing a new theme to be elaborated. More often, elements of contrast between minuet and trio—a switch to the opposite mode, or the appearance of a new texture, sonority, or rhythmic impetus—suggest an opposing argument or altered perspective: perhaps a descent from noble deportment to the rustic simplicity of a Ländler,[11] a switch from relatively serious discourse to comedy, or a moment of relief or introspection following a minuet's frenetic energy, as in Op. 77/2, in which the richly blended, lower-range legato of the trio materializes as an oasis, an inviting retreat from the minuet's metrical discord and overwrought development. Reduced or simplified texture—as if delivering an aside or adopting a more intimate tone—is a customary attribute of trios, and there are many that feature either a smaller ensemble (e.g., two violins only in Op. 9/4; first violin, viola, and cello in Op. 20/6), lightened or fragmented texture, or else a solo escapade by one ensemble member (usually the first violin) that limits the others to the status of background accompaniment.

A different kind of approach prevails in quartets where the protected space of the trio provides a forum for technical difficulty, timbral novelty, rhythmic peculiarity, or some other more or less extreme idiosyncrasy not easily accommodated elsewhere in the cycle. We find such an approach in the gyrating canonic figures of the Op. 33/6 trio, the violin duet in Op. 33/3, and the rhythmic *imbroglio* of Op. 9/3, where individual lines assert independence from each other in a welter of ties and forzato accents.

Contrast between the dance movement's two portions is mitigated on several occasions in which the latter sustains, elaborates, or transforms material from the former. Samples include Op. 64/1, in which the beginning of the trio materializes as a variant of the minuet's initial rising, triadic figure, recast now in

EXAMPLE 5.5 Op. 20/2/iii, mm. 53–60

minor as a topic for reflective dialogue among the upper three instruments, and Op. 20/2, quoted in example 5.5, where the first violin's graceful descent resumes in the trio as a melodically prominent line in the cello. In several respects, this minuet and its trio may be heard as opposites (most obviously in mode, major vs. minor), and yet the effect of an ongoing melodic process, passed at this moment from highest to lowest instrument on a shared middle C, counters disparity with a palpable unifying thread.[12]

Run-On Connections

There are situations in which a harmonically unstable transition replaces the trio's customary full close in the local tonic key.[13] This transforms the minuet-trio juxtaposition into something akin to a rondo's transition from episode to refrain, or perhaps the open-ended connection between second and third parts of a ternary form. In four of the ten cases in question, the transition is complicated by a deceptive or ambivalent harmonic path: rather than moving directly to the minuet's dominant as a springboard for the return, the connecting passage steers toward some other dominant instead—V of vi (Opp. 17/2, 74/1), V$^6_5$ of ii (Op. 20/1), or V of iv (Op. 20/3). Dance movements with open-ended trios divide into two groups procedurally as well as chronologically: each of the earlier examples involves a curtailed or interrupted second reprise (shown in table 5.6a), whereas the later ones all incorporate a complete or virtually complete trio before adding a transition as a relatively separate event (table 5.6b).

Just as Haydn challenged the separation of trio and minuet, he chose on two occasions (Opp. 20/2 and 54/2) to leave the preceding slow movement open-ended and harmonically unresolved, thereby linking it to the minuet-trio complex and thus counteracting the latter's traditional isolation from other components of the cycle—its somewhat marginal stature, in other words, as a topically old-fashioned movement, rhythmically inclined toward the mechanical and not infrequently marked for stylistic eccentricity or parody.

TABLE 5.6 Dance movements with open-ended trios

	Minuet	Trio	Comments
(a) Second reprise interrupted (hence no repeat of this incomplete portion)			
Op. 9/1/ii	C	Cm	8 mm. of dominant preparation after a cadence in Gm.
Op. 17/2/ii	F	Dm	6 mm. of V in D minor, with a final A tied to the opening A of the minuet.
Op. 17/5/ii	G	Gm	4 mm. of dominant preparation, with allusions to the upbeat figure of the minuet.
Op. 20/1/ii	E♭	A♭	2d reprise modulates to Fm and culminates on V $^6_5$ in that key.
Op. 20/2/iii	C	Cm	10 mm. of dominant preparation.
Op. 20/3/ii	Gm	E♭	2d reprise modulates to Cm and ends by prolonging a dominant pedal in that key.
(b) Second reprise completed, repeated, then followed by a transition			
Op. 74/1/iii	C	A	Full close in A; then a 16-m. transition leading to V of Am.
Op. 74/2/iii	F	D♭	Full close in D♭; then an 11-m. transition to a thrice-repeated cadence on V of F minor.
Op. 77/1/iii*	G	E♭	Avoided close in E♭; then a 12-m. transition leading to the dominant of G.
Op. 77/2/ii	F	D♭	Full close in D♭; then a 9-m. transition, labeled "Coda," ending on V in F.

*First and second reprise written out rather than indicated by repeat signs.

Questions of Proportion

Although Haydn inclines toward dance forms whose second reprise is somewhat longer than the first, there are times when he seems intent on defying any sense of normality in this regard, and examples of radically lopsided proportions are to be found in most opus groups from Op. 20 on. As listed in table 5.7, thirteen two-reprise dance forms (eleven minuets, two trios) have a second part that reaches more than four times the length of the first. (This chosen cutoff point is basically arbitrary; the forms it isolates are not significantly different from others whose second reprise is also quite long, although somewhat less so.)

By dwarfing its first part—the statement of a principal argument, in effect—an exceptionally long second reprise strains the idea of simple complementation within a two-part form. The motivation for such an imbalance may be explained in terms of rhetorical amplification (expanding on first-reprise material with unusual verbosity), willful violation of normal boundaries and proportions (by virtue of extended phases of repetition, elaboration, or contrast), or perhaps the virtual transformation into something more elevated or complex than a conventional

TABLE 5.7 Minuets and trios with greatly
extended second parts (measure counts are
adjusted to exclude written-out or varied repeats)

Minuets	1st reprise	2d reprise	Total length
Op. 20/1/ii	8	36	44
Op. 20/3/ii	10	42	52
Op. 50/2/iii	8	42	50
Op. 50/5/iii	8	33	41
Op. 54/2/iii	8	38	46
Op. 64/1/ii	8	36	44
Op. 64/5/iii	8	34	42
Op. 74/2/iii	8	33	41
Op. 76/4/iii	8	42	50
Op. 77/1/iii	12	58	70
Op. 103/ii	8	38	46
Trios			
Op. 76/3/iii	8	36	44
Op. 76/4/iii	8	38	46

dance form. In the Op. 64/1 minuet (represented in fig. 5.1), the second reprise
begins with an eight-measure phrase that modulates to the dominant. After four
measures of transition, the anticipated recurrence of first-reprise material begins,
although with drastically altered scoring (the cello's initial solo now sounds in
octaves by the violins). Subjected to internal expansion and augmentation,
what had been an opening four-measure idea now stretches to twelve measures
(mm. 21–32), likewise ending in a deceptive cadence, and the twelve measures
that follow offer a balancing response while continuing to pursue the topic of development and expansion.

Structurally more intriguing is the A minor trio of Op. 76/3. As shown in
figure 5.2, the long second reprise begins with twelve measures of elaboration
(4 + 8), and this span culminates on a dominant chord, sustained by a fermata
in measure 76. A normal, rounded binary design would result if we were simply
to delete the following sixteen measures (bracketed in the diagram) and proceed
directly to the final phrase-pair, whose eight measures constitute a tonally altered recapitulation of the first reprise. The bracketed measures, thematically related to the rest of the trio but set apart by a change in mode from minor to
major, actually comprise a perfectly symmetrical, self-contained binary structure

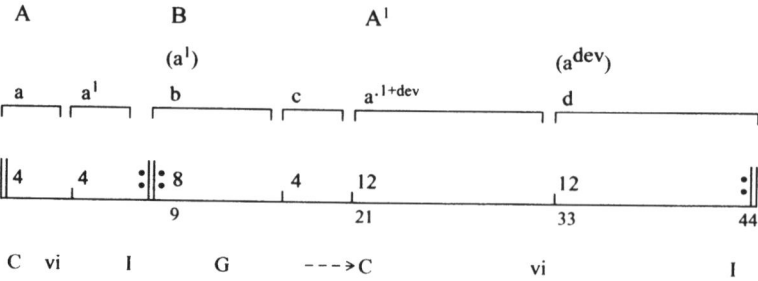

FIGURE 5.1 Op. 64/1/ii, minuet

without repeats, wedged in the middle of the second part. Gracing the trio with an island of tranquility and modal contrast, this inspired moment of relief from the surrounding gloom lends depth and complexity to an otherwise transparent design.[14]

One of the most puzzling cases of unbalanced proportions, the Op. 64/3 minuet, appears to question the form's basic alignments of theme, key, and structural articulation. As represented in figure 5.3, the first part highlights the disparity between contrasting topics: a yodeling melody (phrases *a* and *b*) and a horn-call idea that sprouts from the end of *b* and superimposes a virtual duple meter on the end of the section (labeled *c* in the diagram; ex. 5.6 quotes *a* and the end of *b*, mm. 11–12, plus the horn figure, mm. 13–14). The second reprise behaves in a manner comparable to other rounded binary minuets with extended second parts: a modulation to the dominant, a transitional passage leading back to tonic, an elaborated return, and a closing appendage.

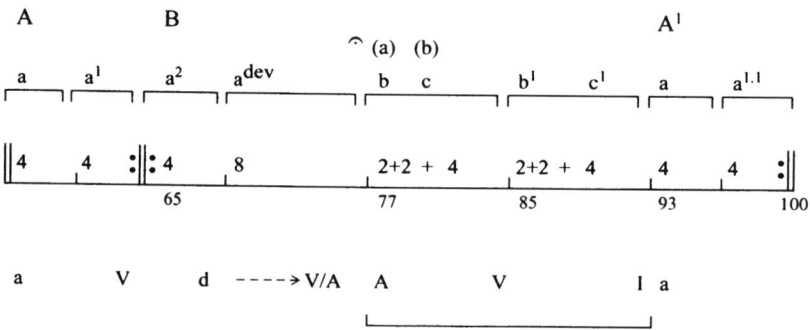

FIGURE 5.2 Op. 76/3/iii, trio (The bracket beneath the main diagram marks an embedded binary form within the second reprise.)

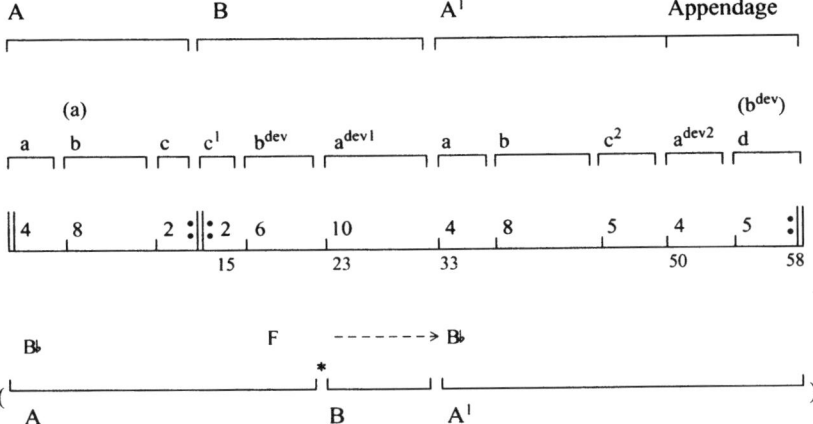

FIGURE 5.3 Op. 64/3/iii (Hypothetical divisions marked by brackets below the main diagram represent the rounded binary design that would result by a shift of the double bar and repeat signs from measure 14 to measure 22.)

But another interpretation suggests itself. Suppose we were to remove the double bar and repeat signs from measure 14 (not unthinkable, as the violins' horn-fifths scarcely represent a convincing point of sectional division), and relocate them to measure 22, where all parts come together for a full cadence in the dominant? The redrawn second reprise would now encompass a ten-measure span of development, mostly prolonging the dominant (mm. 23–32), followed by a varied, slightly extended recurrence, in tonic, of measures 1–22 (our hypothetically extended first reprise). The logic unmasked by this relocated divide (marked by an asterisk in the diagram) would appear to be unassailable. By contrast, Haydn's actual placement of the double bar in measure 14 seems oddly out of kilter: by intersecting the horn-fifths theme c (which continues in the lower

EXAMPLE 5.6 Op. 64/3/iii

(a) mm. 1–4   (b) mm. 11–14

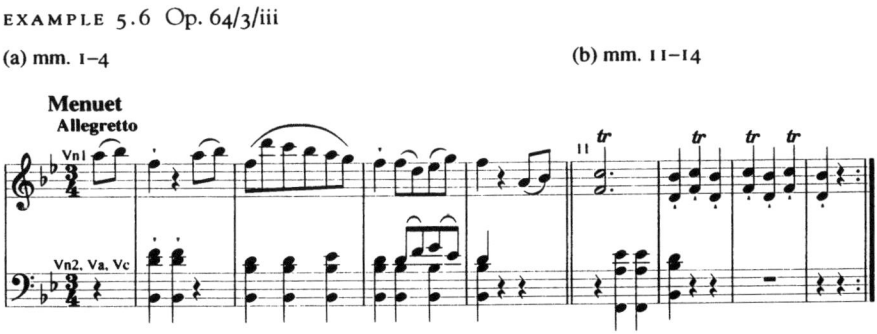

instruments in mm. 15–16), it fails to coincide with a satisfying cadence and obliges the second reprise to begin, still in tonic, with an awkward resumption of a metrically dissonant figure. In sum, several kinds of structural tension suffuse the design and enhance the impact of its eccentric character: an inconclusive opening section prefaces a complex, multifaceted second reprise; the close in the dominant at measure 22 proves heavier and more tightly coordinated than the punctuation between principal sections; and the elongated span of recurrence, nearly twice as long as the first reprise, must not only repair the fissure that had divided the horn call into two separate events but also rationalize it as a metrically dissonant parenthesis between relatively stable, metrically conformant phrases.[15]

Digressions from Customary Dance-Movement Style

Deviations from Haydn's norms for sonority, harmonic succession, melodic profile, and rhythmic organization occur sporadically throughout the repertory. No single opus group consistently undermines the impression of general adherence to dance-movement protocol, and there are few instances in which the transgressions affect more than one or two aspects of style or design. It often happens that a patently capricious minuet or trio actually reinforces certain dance-movement conventions even while violating others. Such compensating factors not only reaffirm Haydn's allegiance to the form's attributes and values but also help guarantee the impact of novelties and digressions when they do occur. The first violin's climb to an exceedingly high register at the end of the Op. 42/ii minuet (mm. 27–28) comes as an exhilarating surprise, but the rounded binary form it punctuates is otherwise normal; and the melodic gesture by which the high notes are attained—an extended rising scale—proves intimately related to the scalar figures that had occupied every one of the minuet's preceding phrases. Likewise, the extreme contrast of sonority embraced by Op. 33/3/ii—a richly blended, low-register scherzo proper engaging all four parts continuously, followed by a brittle, middle- to upper-register duet for violins in the trio—is balanced by the adherence to conventional practices with respect to harmony, rhythm, phrasing, and large-scale form.

The impact of a genuine harmonic shock is rare among the dance movements (although to be sure, the number of odd or individualistic harmonic details is legion), and it is worth noting that several of the most striking cases arise not as unique, unexplained disturbances but as part of a larger, cyclic phenomenon. To cite one instance, the minuet of Op. 50/4 (F♯ major) plunges suddenly and noisily into the key of the flat submediant, D major, shortly after the start of the second reprise. However stunning at the moment of its occurrence, the tonal surprise is both enriched and mitigated by recognition of its relationship to an earlier shift to D major at the start of the first-movement development section—likewise heavily emphasized, although less tonally disruptive as the subdominant of the preceding relative major, A.

More commonly encountered are the rhythmic disturbances by which Haydn delights in contradicting the very essence of minuet gesture and motion. Means at his disposal include the fermata and general pause as well as ties across the bar line; second- or third-beat accents; conflicting accents among different parts; and the implied change of meter that arises from repetitive rhythmic and melodic figures that occupy two beats instead of three. Although such complications occur repeatedly in nearly every opus group, the total number represents a minority of the total repertory, and the cases of emphasized or prolonged disturbance rarely involve both minuet and trio. Instead, they often serve as elements of contrast between the two, the syncopations or metrical dissonances of one set off in relief against the more conformant rhythms of the other. In a memorable example from the Op. 54/1 trio, the metrical flow broadens from $\frac{3}{4}$ to an implied $\frac{3}{2}$ in an almost Brahmsian roll at the start of the second reprise (mm. 53–56). The systematic compression of melodic and surface-rhythmic action now shifts the metrical focus to an implied $\frac{2}{4}$ (mm. 57–58) before the temporarily suppressed triple meter finally reemerges in measure 59.

By maintaining a place for the traditional minuet-trio complex in their quartets and other instrumental cycles, Haydn and his contemporaries affirmed their appreciation of its familiar, repetitive qualities, and perhaps for some of its special connotations as well. A link with the past, it signified the vitality of inherited musical traditions. It also reinforced a key aspect of the elusive dialogue between the composer and those who would enjoy his wordless creations as performers or listeners—namely, the comprehension of an instrumental work as one instance of an enduring model. However deeply a Haydn string quartet may impress us by its wit and novelty, its many fixed elements—none more closely prescribed than the conventions of the dance movement—oblige us to understand it at least partially as the realization of a preordained pattern or roster of standard ingredients.

As the preceding overview indicates, Haydn took advantage of the form's prospects for musical experiment and adventure while at the same time taking pains to honor its resistance to change. Paradoxically, the dance movements represent both a thread of continuity stretching across the entire oeuvre, and a persistent, convention-flouting play with stylistic norms, customary musical designs, and listeners' expectations. Viewed from this perspective, they constitute a showcase for some of the most basic mechanisms that inform Haydn's approach to the quartet.

6

Variation

Variation form in the quartets may be viewed as one aspect of a much larger realm of variation procedure, an element of Haydn's compositional technique whose influence is felt across the entire range of forms and movement types among works in this genre.[1] Encompassing melodic decoration, altered repetition, rescoring, polyphonic enrichment, and the like, variation technique proves congenial to the quartet medium in important ways. The instruments' combination of timbral balance and technical agility accommodates strategies for thematic redistribution and migration, and the environment of intimate discourse among individuals makes an ideal forum for elaboration, commentary, and reflection. The rhetorical emphasis conveyed by varied repetition can help compensate for the quartet's limited capacity to accentuate or persuade through massed sonority, vivid timbral contrast, or volume. Variation can enhance the intimacy of our dialogue with the composer of a quartet by inviting us to contemplate relationships between the altered version of an idea and its unadorned progenitor; but it can also sharpen our responses as performers and listeners by spotlighting factors of execution. Notated embellishments that mimic improvisation can suggest artless spontaneity as interest shifts from the unfolding of a structure to the decoration of musical events already heard. In the process, we may experience the illusion of liberation—or at least momentary relief—from the composer's controlling presence.

Haydn's practice of altering the recurrence of musical ideas—whether motives, phrases, or larger segments—is part of a pervasive inclination toward surface continuity and elaborative process, and it claims an important place among his techniques for musical design and expression. In a sonata form, for example, fashioning primary and secondary themes so that the latter arises as a variant of the former helps amplify the importance of a principal idea while at the same time informing an exposition's tonal opposition with an ingredient of unity and coherence. Correspondingly, the alteration of a theme when it comes back in a recapitulation can lend an element of freshness and vitality to offset impressions of sameness or familiarity.

Of more direct impact is the immediate varied repetition of an idea, which typically calls attention to itself as a local phenomenon; but it also may have larger consequences, as in the first-movement exposition of Op. 17/1, in which the varied repetition of a phrase lends weight to the process of confirming a secondary key. As quoted in example 6.1, measures 25–26 help to energize the advance toward an anticipated close in the dominant by presenting a barrage of sixteenth notes, and the heightened activity propels the first violin's line toward a melodic peak, a³. Goal-directed motion now resumes, but after two measures Haydn elides the expected cadence (m. 31) with an animated variant of the phrase begun in measure 25, accelerating the rhythm from straight sixteenth notes to triplets while preserving the original melodic outline, increasing momentum by continuing the triplet impulse through the rising scale, and maximizing the effect of surface-rhythmic contrast as the line once again reaches the high a³ (m. 33). The varied repetition gives the first violin an extra opportunity for solo display—decoration as an end in itself—but it also lends force to the exposition's tonal trajectory, and by redoubling the suspense of an awaited moment of tonal confirmation, it enhances the weight of the full cadence that finally brings the section to an end.

In contrast to the melody-outlining diminutions seen in example 6.1, there are instances of variation in which the original melody persists as a constant element, or cantus firmus, while secondary or accompanimental material changes. At the start of Op. 20/5/iii, the first violin states an unadorned, siciliana-style theme, accompanied by chords in the lower parts. The restatement that follows (mm. 9–16) recalls the opening melody intact for four measures, but the fabric is enriched by fresh activity and altered relationships among the parts: the principal melody migrates from first violin to second; and the former, now liberated from thematic responsibility, proceeds to spin a thread of decorative commentary on its own. Leaving the melody untouched helps sustain an atmosphere of serenity, whereas the overlay of figuration adds color and sets the stage for further elaborations as the movement unfolds.

Different from either melodic outline or cantus firmus procedure is the practice of allowing only the original bass line and harmony, or perhaps the harmony alone, to persist while ensemble members indulge in freely conceived material. An instance of this technique may be seen in the Op. 71/3 minuet, following a cadence in tonic partway through the second reprise (m. 25). Here a nine-measure phrase (mm. 26–34) unfolds, derived from the movement's opening melodic gesture. The tension of its restless, oscillating harmony eventually resolves with the drive toward a cadence, quoted in example 6.2a. This action proves insufficient to bring matters to an end, however, and the argument continues with a variant of the phrase. The violins initiate a dialogue in which elements of the original

EXAMPLE 6.1　Op. 17/1/i, mm. 25–43 (violin 1 only)

idea are at first embedded; but in the closing measures of the phrase, shown in example 6.2b, the first violin takes the liberty of ascending to a climactic c^3, and the second violin moves more freely as well, yet the harmony remains the same as in the preceding phrase.

The three techniques we have described—melodic outline, cantus firmus, and constant bass (or constant harmony), to adopt the categories proposed by Sisman—provide a handy if not thoroughly inclusive framework for considering Haydn's use of variation as an ingredient of a theme or as the principal motivation for an entire section or movement. The latter phenomenon, variation form, elevates the technique as a musical value on its own terms, permitting performers and listeners the luxury of fullest concentration on details of relationship between model and variant.

Haydn's variation-based designs may be grouped into four distinct categories, as represented in table 6.1:[2] (1) *varied reprise*—structures in which the repeat of the first part is not marked by a double bar and repeat sign but is written out with

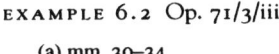

EXAMPLE 6.2 Op. 71/3/iii

(a) mm. 30–34

(b) mm. 39–43

added embellishments and rhetorical gestures; (2) *ternary*—A B A¹ forms in which the third section is an embellished version of the first; (3) *strophic*—movements consisting principally of a series of two or more variations on a binary or rounded binary theme; and (4) *alternating*—forms related in principle to strophic variation but enriched by the interpolation of two or more segments in the opposite mode.[3] As for the column labeled "other" in the table, neither of the two movements listed can be described as a variation form pure and simple, although both are sufficiently dependent on variation-related procedure to merit inclusion in the table. Omitted altogether from the table are two hybrid forms that incorporate variation technique (Opp. 71/2/iv and 76/4/iv) and also the rondo finale of Op. 33/4, whose refrains are varied.

Varied Reprise

Beginning with Op. 9 and extending through Op. 33, Haydn cultivated a certain type of vocally inspired, soloistic Adagio designed to showcase decoration in a

TABLE 6.1 Variation movements in the Haydn quartets
(The five columns are arranged to highlight the chronological distribution of different variation types.)

Strophic	Varied reprise	Alternating	Ternary[a]	Other
2/6/i				
9/5/i	9/2/iii			
	9/4/iii			
17/3/i	17/4/iii			
20/4/ii	20/6/ii			
33/5/iv	33/3/iii	33/6/iv		
50/1/ii		50/4/ii		
50/3/ii				
	(54/2/ii)[c]		54/3/ii	
55/3/ii		55/2/i		
64/1/iii			64/3/ii	
64/2/ii			64/4/iii	
			64/5/ii	
			64/6/ii[d]	
		71/3/ii	71/1/ii[d]	
74/2/ii			74/3/ii	
76/3/ii			76/2/ii	76/5/i
76/6/i[b]				76/6/ii
77/2/iii				
			(103/i)[d]	

[a]Excluded from this list are two finales (Opp. 54/2/iv and 64/5/iv) that may be construed as ternary, but that bear little significant resemblance to the core repertory of interior, slow-tempo forms in this category.

[b]Strophic variations, followed by a (partially) fugal summation in which a final variation is embedded.

[c]Technically an instance of varied reprise, though it differs in style and concept from others in this category: hymn-style melody persists in lower instruments as a cantus firmus, while the first violin has free elaboration.

[d]Included here since they are slow-movement ternary forms like the others, but variation in the recurrence of the *A* section is underplayed in Opp. 64/6/ii and 71/1/ii, and virtually absent from Op. 103/i.

varied first part. (See table 6.2, where basic elements of the movements in question are summarized and compared; as noted in table 6.1, one later instance, Op. 54/2/ii, qualifies technically as a species of varied-reprise form, although it differs from the other movements listed in basic matters of theme, formal premise, and texture.)

How did the notion of a varied reprise come about, and what was its special appeal? For insight into contemporary musical practices by which these move-

TABLE 6.2 Slow movements with varied first reprise

Opus	Key	Meter	Tempo	Form
9/2/iii	Cm	$c-\frac{3}{4}$	Adagio–Cantabile	Intro., binary (irreg.) with abbreviated 2d reprise and cadenza
9/4/iii	B♭	¢	Adagio. Cantabile	Sonata form with short development (10 mm.) and cadenza
17/4/iii	E♭	$\frac{3}{4}$	Adagio. Cantabile	Large binary with cadenza
20/6/ii	E	¢	Adagio	Large binary
33/3/iii	F	$\frac{3}{4}$	Adagio ma non troppo	Slow-movement form with transition to recap (6 mm.)
(54/2/ii	Cm	$\frac{3}{4}$	Adagio	Rounded binary; mm. 1–8 repeated with free elaboration in vn1)

ments may have been inspired, it is helpful to consider C. P. E. Bach's reflections on extemporized variation in his *Versuch über die wahre Art das Clavier zu spielen* (*Essay on the True Art of Playing Keyboard Instruments*), part 1, 1753, as well as certain remarks in the preface to his 1760 *Sechs Sonaten für Clavier mit veränderten Reprisen* (Six Keyboard Sonatas with Varied Reprises). In the treatise, Bach cautions that "many things . . . cannot be readily varied" and declares that "all variations must relate to the piece's affect, and they must always be at least as good as, if not better than, the original. . . . Constant attention must be given to preceding and succeeding parts; there must be a vision of the whole piece."[4] Noting in his preface to the sonata edition that varied repetition is expected of every performer, he argues as follows: "But supposing the performer has the wherewithal to vary a piece appropriately: is he disposed to do so at all times? Will unfamiliar pieces not give rise to new difficulties in regard to [variation]?" Bach addresses the dilemma by supplying varied repeats that release performers from the task of "either inventing their own, or having others write them out and learning them from memory with great effort."[5]

Haydn's varied repeats in the movements included in table 6.2 resemble those of Bach's sonatas by mimicking the spontaneity of improvised embellishment. In so doing, they turn what would otherwise have been a prerogative of the performer into a vehicle for the composer's own rumination on the musical discourse at hand.

Generally speaking, the five primary examples of this device follow a similar course of action in their first parts: a tonally stable theme (preceded in Op. 9/2/iii by an operatic-style introduction, mm. 1–8), subsequent expansion in range and expressive scope, and eventually a decisive close in the secondary key. Melodic delivery falls mainly in the hands of the first violin, whose trills, turns, leaps, and salient melodic peaks signify a solo presence even in this first phase of the form. But then comes the varied reprise: diminutions enliven the melody, fracturing some of the pitches that had previously been sustained, and streams of figuration in small note values engulf passages originally marked by rhythmic variety. The resulting gain in momentum accentuates the impact of melodic goals and structural punctuations. Soloistic intensity tends to slacken, at least temporarily, as the varied reprise comes to an end, and in three instances (Opp. 9/2/iii, 20/6/ii, and 33/3/iii) Haydn's telescoping, inflecting, or eliding of the divide between sections helps compensate by quickening the turn to a new, less solo-dominated phase of action. The impression of having pressed the varied-reprise technique almost to exhaustion is especially pronounced in Op. 9/2/iii: the abbreviated second part barely lasts long enough to accommodate a hasty return to tonic, preparation for an improvised cadenza, and a final closing formula. Op. 17/4/iii differs from this plan by fully honoring the break between sections and then proceeding to a substantial-size second part; but the first violin nonetheless earns relief from sustained solo effort by temporarily passing responsibility to the cello, whose sixteenth-note figurations predominate for a full nine measures (mm. 71–79).

In addition to the core repertory of varied-reprise slow movements, Haydn sometimes altered his binary repeats within one or more segments of a composite form—a local phenomenon, not necessarily soloistic in character. Instances of this device, listed in table 6.3, occur with some frequency among ternary, strophic, or alternating variation forms, including the early strophic variations of Op. 2/6/i, whose time of composition likely predates any contact with Bach's *Versuch* or with his sonata edition cited earlier.[6] Additionally, there are several dance movements and rondos in which altered repeats add decoration, textural variety, contrapuntal intrigue, or extra rhythmic life.

Ternary Variations

Although Haydn abandoned the idea of an ornate, varied-reprise Adagio after exploring this type in Opp. 9, 17, 20, and 33, he did retain something of its spirit and technique among later slow movements cast in ternary form—a plan in which a contrasting middle section (B) unfolds between presentation and recurrence of an A section that comprises a two-reprise entity in itself. Table 6.4 lists the interior movements in question. All begin and end in major, all feature marked harmonic contrast in their middle sections, and six (Opp. 54/3/ii, 74/3/ii, and the four ternary movements of Op. 64) have middle sections with parallel-minor key signatures.

To what extent does Haydn apply soloistic variation procedures to these movements? In Op. 103/i, recurrence is virtually literal; in Op. 71/1/ii, a peculiar array of disjunct grace notes colors the A theme's recurrence; and in Op. 64/6/ii, there are changes in the distribution of lines among the parts, but new decorative embellishment is mainly confined to two measures in the first violin (mm. 56–57).

TABLE 6.3 Other instances of notated repeats* involving variation procedures

Opus	Key	Meter	Tempo	Location of varied reprise
1. Strophic variation movements				
2/6/i	B♭	$\frac{2}{4}$	Adagio	Variation 4, 1st and 2d reprise
9/5/i	B♭	$\frac{2}{4}$	Poco adagio	Variation 4, 1st and 2d reprise
33/5/iv	G	$\frac{6}{8}$	Allegretto–Presto	Variation 3, 1st and 2d reprise
50/3/ii	B♭	$\frac{2}{4}$	Andante più tosto allegretto	Variations 2, 3, 1st reprise
64/1/iii	F	$\frac{2}{4}$	Allegretto scherzando	Variation 2, 1st reprise
64/2/ii	B	$\frac{3}{4}$	Adagio ma non troppo	Theme, 1st and 2d reprise
74/2/ii	B♭	$\frac{2}{4}$	Andante grazioso	Variation 3, 1st reprise
2. Alternating variation movements				
33/6/iv	D	$\frac{2}{4}$	Allegretto	Both variations of major theme: both parts
50/4/ii	A	$\frac{2}{4}$	Andante	1st variation of major theme: 1st reprise
55/2/i	Fm-F	$\frac{2}{4}$	Andante o più tosto allegretto	1st variation of minor theme: 1st reprise
				1st variation of major theme: 1st reprise
				2d variation of major theme: both reprises
3. Ternary slow movements				
64/3/ii	E♭	$\frac{2}{4}$	Adagio	*A*: 1st and 2d reprise; *B*: 1st reprise
64/4/iii	C	$\frac{2}{4}$	Adagio. Cantabile e sostenuto	*A*: 1st and 2d reprise
64/6/ii	B♭	$\frac{3}{4}$	Andante	*A*: 1st reprise; *A'*: 1st reprise
76/2/ii	D	$\frac{6}{8}$	Andante o più tosto allegretto	*A'*: 1st reprise

4. Other movements: rondo (Opp. 33/4/iv, 54/1/iv), minuet (Opp. 50/1/iii, 55/2/iii, 77/1/iii), nonstandard (Op. 76/5/i)

Opus	Key	Meter	Tempo	Location of varied reprise
33/4/iv	B♭	$\frac{2}{4}$	Presto	1st and 2d recurrence of refrain, 1st reprise (mm. 77–84, 155–62)
54/1/iv	G	$\frac{2}{4}$	Vivace	1st full recurrence of refrain, 1st reprise, mm. 102–9
50/1/iii	B♭	$\frac{3}{4}$	Poco allegretto	minuet: 1st reprise varied
55/2/iii	F	$\frac{3}{4}$	Allegretto	minuet: 1st reprise varied
77/1/iii	G	$\frac{3}{4}$	Presto	minuet: 1st reprise varied
76/5/i	D	$\frac{6}{8}$	Allegretto–Allegro	mm. 1–8 varied in mm. 9–16 (deceptive cadence in m. 16)

*Certain instances have been excluded from the table because the repeats are nearly literal. Two involve initial structural changes (Op. 54/2/iv: first binary form; Op. 76/4/iii: trio, 1st reprise); three have structural alterations at the end: deceptive cadence or truncation (Op. 54/2/iv: fast-tempo binary form; Op. 64/6/ii: *A*, 2d reprise; Op. 76/4/iv, *B*, 2d reprise); one has various minor changes (Op. 77/1/iii: trio, both reprises).

TABLE 6.4 Interior slow movements in ternary form

Opus	Key	Meter	Tempo	Form of *A* section
54/3/ii	A	3/4	Largo. Cantabile	Rounded binary
64/3/ii	E♭	2/4	Adagio	Binary
64/4/iii	C	2/4	Adagio. Cantabile e sostenuto	Rounded binary
64/5/ii	A	3/4	Adagio. Cantabile	Rounded binary
64/6/ii	B♭	3/4	Andante	Binary
71/1/ii	F	6/8	Adagio	Rounded binary
74/3/ii	E	¢	Largo assai	Rounded binary
76/2/ii	D	6/8	Andante o più tosto allegretto	Rounded binary
103/i	B♭	2/4	Andante grazioso	Rounded binary

Most of the other ternary movements have third sections whose greater wealth of embellishments, diminutions, and amplified points of contrast recall the earlier Adagios' varied repeats; and in several cases, Haydn adds an extra layer of complexity by inserting varied-reprise technique within one or more parts of the form, thereby incorporating elements from the earlier Adagios in two respects: the immediate, altered repeat of one or more subsections as well as the higher-level plan of decorating a recurring principal section.

Haydn's ternary movements obviously differ from the earlier varied-reprise forms in their accent on variation procedure in the last section, a circumstance that entails a different perspective: here the middle portion of the form, perhaps not unlike that of a da capo aria, represents a counterforce to be weighed against an initial proposition. The final section is thus charged with reaffirming order and reestablishing tonal equilibrium, and the added element of variation—enriching, amplifying, and persuading—invites an eloquent response to the *B* section's contrasts.

Op. 54/3/ii vividly illustrates this play of forces. An idyllic mood prevails throughout the first part (mm. 1–24), but this quality is shattered by the *B* section (mm. 25–38), whose throbbing sixteenth notes underlie spans of solo figuration in thirty-second notes and even sixty-fourths. A semblance of stability is eventually regained in the A^1 section, but not without a new element of agitation that transforms recurring material into a showcase of solo display, complete with rising and falling lines in sixty-fourth notes as well as turns and other embellishing figures. The heightened activity suggests nothing less than a mingling of the *A* and *B* sections' disparate elements, the middle portion's disturbance enduring as an implacable undercurrent while the final section runs its course.

Of the ternary designs with embedded altered repeats in one or more sections, Op. 64/6/ii may be singled out for the subtlety with which the device en-

riches the movement's final portion (the A^1). Here a nearly straightforward recurrence of the opening eight-measure strain flows seamlessly into a variant in
which the principal melody passes continuously from one voice or register to
another: violin 2 (mm. 55–56), violin 1 (mm. 57–58), cello (mm. 59–60), violin 1 (mm. 61–62; see ex. 6.3, which compares the statement and recurrence in
question: mm. 47–54 vs. 55–62). Overlapping the last of these thematic migrations, a derivative of the cello's arpeggiation of measure 52 materializes high in
the first violin (m. 60); and as this thrust continues into measure 61, it merges
with recollections of the first violin's own line from measure 53 as it aims toward a
cadence in measure 62 (now an octave higher than in the corresponding m. 54).
By virtue of the melodies' shifting locations and the plasticity of their changing
profiles, performers and listeners are drawn into an engrossing web of intertwined
relationships between the original idea and its varied repeat.

The phenomenon of ternary variations calls to mind two additional cases,
neither of which actually belongs to our family of interior slow-tempo movements
of this type. The first of the two, Op. 71/2/ii, is a sonata form, but the soloistic
manner of its exposition resembles that of the earlier Adagios with varied reprise,
and its recapitulation highlights diminutions and other decorative touches that
invite comparison with a ternary variation's third section. Altogether different
in character, although nonetheless related in principle, is the opening movement of Op. 76/5, whose scheme of opening section (A), contrast (B), and embellished recurrence (A^1), all marked allegretto, leads to an allegro whose elaboration of material from the preceding A and B sections carries the movement to
a brilliant conclusion.

Strophic Variation

More numerous than either varied-reprise or ternary forms, Haydn's strophic
variations span virtually the entire oeuvre, with at least one example in each
opus group. Nearly all begin with a two-reprise form (Op. 76/3/ii is the exception) followed by a succession of variants, each of which normally retains the
underlying shape and harmonic content of the theme itself. Duple meter and flat
key signatures are preferred choices in all phases of the repertory, and with one
exception (Op. 50/1/ii, which proves less conventional in several respects), each
of the two-part themes has a first reprise of eight measures. (Table 6.5 provides a
summary overview. Variations that diverge significantly from the form or harmonic basis of the theme are mentioned in annotations that accompany the table;
also flagged are two cases, Opp. 50/3/ii and 77/2/iii, in which the strophic design
is complicated by developmental episodes.)

Harmonic simplicity tends to go hand in hand with the strophic variations'
accent on rhythmic life and decorative melodic play, but not always. Exceptions

EXAMPLE 6.3 Op. 64/6/ii, mm. 47–62. Statement and varied repeat compared

TABLE 6.5 Strophic variation movements

Opus	Key	Meter	Tempo	Form (B = binary; RB = rounded binary)
2/6/i	B♭	$\frac{2}{4}$	Adagio	B: 4 variations (varied reprises in Var. 4)
9/5/i	B♭	$\frac{2}{4}$	Poco adagio	RB: 4 variations (varied reprises in Var. 4)
17/3/i	E♭	$\frac{2}{4}$	Andante grazioso	B: 4 variations
20/4/ii	Dm	$\frac{2}{4}$	Un poco adagio e affettuoso	B: 3 variations, reprise of theme, and coda
33/5/iv	G	$\frac{6}{8}$	Allegretto–Presto	B: 3 variations and coda (varied reprises in Var. 3)
50/1/ii[a]	E♭	$\frac{6}{8}$	Adagio	B: 3 variations and coda (Var. 2 in minor)
50/3/ii[b]	B♭	$\frac{2}{4}$	Andante più tosto allegretto	RB: 3 variations, added segment between Vars. 2 & 3 (Var. 1 in minor; varied 1st reprise in Vars. 2 & 3)
55/3/ii[c]	E♭	$\frac{2}{4}$	Adagio ma non troppo	RB: 2 variations and coda
64/1/iii	F	$\frac{2}{4}$	Allegretto scherzando	RB: 2 variations (varied 1st reprise in Var. 2)
64/2/ii	B	$\frac{3}{4}$	Adagio ma non troppo	B: 3 variations and coda (reprises of theme varied)
74/2/ii[d]	B♭	$\frac{2}{4}$	Andante grazioso	RB: 3 variations and coda (Var. 2 in minor; varied 1st reprise in Var. 3)
76/3/ii	G	¢	Poco adagio. Cantabile	4 variations on a theme in *a a b c c* form
76/6/i	E♭	$\frac{2}{4}$	Allegretto–Allegro	RB: 3 variations and a (partially) fugal summation
77/2/iii[e]	D	$\frac{2}{4}$	Andante	RB: 3 variations; added segments between theme & var. 1, and between vars. 1 and 2

[a]Var. 2 digresses from both the harmony and the phrase structure of the theme.

[b]Var. 1 digresses from the harmony as well as the melodic profile of the theme; the added segment (8 + 6) has a repeated first part that modulates to the dominant (unlike the theme), and its abbreviated 2d part is open-ended.

[c]Var. 2 is developmental, digressing from the form of the theme; the end of the 2d reprise is truncated.

[d]Var. 2 differs substantially from the theme in design, harmony, and melodic profile.

[e]Var. 1 is curtailed; var. 2 is extended; the end of var. 3 is altered and merged with a brief extension.

to the rule of limited harmonic color and tonal range include the chromatic extravagance of the Op. 20/4/ii coda, the several major-key strophic variations (for example, Op. 50/1/ii) that incorporate a harmonically enriched variation in minor, and the slow movement of Op. 64/1, where a move to the parallel minor (F minor) and its relative major (A♭) are featured within the theme itself.

A certain "walking" style[7] figures prominently among the strophic variations' themes, with a metrically regular stride that accommodates sharply outlined melodic profiles while avoiding the rhythmic density and expressive accents more commonly encountered in varied-reprise and ternary movements. And whereas variation procedures in those other two types often highlight the original theme's points of contrast, the strophic forms incline more toward uniformity or homogeneous continuation within a given variation.[8]

Haydn draws from the full range of variation technique in his strophic forms, although there are certain differences of emphasis between one phase of the oeuvre and the next. It is mostly among earlier works that he uses constant bass or constant harmony procedure. (That he may have regarded such a simple premise as too old-fashioned or thematically loose-jointed for extensive use among later works is easy to imagine.) Correspondingly, his later fondness for cantus firmus technique seems understandable in light of the limitless opportunities it offered for contrapuntal invention, coloristic accompaniment, and ensemble interaction. Melodic outline technique, which in Haydn's usage typically involves delicate balances of melodic freedom and constraint, could be said to mediate between those other two possibilities as a source of expressive nuance as well as decorative extravagance.

Different techniques often occur within a single strophic variation movement, and on occasion they combine or intermingle in ingenious ways. In Op. 76/6/i, for example, Haydn draws on cantus firmus and melodic outline procedures to explore the idiosyncrasies of an ungainly, antic theme (quoted in ex. 6.4) whose peculiar traits include a series of short-breathed, two-measure units stubbornly separated by rests (mm. 1–12, 17–22), spans of jarring dotted rhythms (mm. 13–15, 28–32, 34–35), and a succession of disconcerting hiccups (mm. 23–27) before the final phrase of the second reprise.

As the variations unfold, the theme as cantus firmus is joined by other voices whose counterpoint either magnifies the eccentricities or else compensates for hindered momentum. In the second reprise of the first variation, for example, an unaccompanied duet (mm. 45–52) places the halting melody in the second violin while the first lends continuity by spinning out a continuous thread of sixteenth-note figuration below. In the opening phrase of variation 3, Haydn elaborates on the stop-and-go jerkiness of the theme by having the viola and cello chime in a measure late with a comparably disjointed series of two-measure particles (mm. 110–13). Then a welcome torrent of sixteenth notes at the start of that variation's second reprise (mm. 117–23) transports us to a realm of (apparently) freewheeling embellishment, but here, as in the previously cited figural work from variation 1 (mm. 45–52), there is also an abundance of control. The sixteenth-note figures of measures 45–52 faithfully trace the profile of the lowest sounding part from measures 9–16 (see ex. 6.5a and b, where the corresponding passages are sampled), and in measures 117–24 the principal melody itself is animated by the craft of melodic outline variation as it combines impressions of untrammeled rhythmic flow with calculated melodic constraint (ex. 6.5c; see the circled pitches in the examples, which represent points of connection with the theme's unembellished gestures of mm. 9–12).

EXAMPLE 6.4 Op. 76/6/i, mm. 1–36 (violin 1 only)

Haydn's strophic formats typically favor events and processes of the moment, and as the variations present themselves, comparison with the theme in its original form is generally of paramount interest. To varying degrees, however, attention may also be directed to larger unifying forces. On a basic level, the principle of periodic return, continually retracing the theme's temporal framework, imposes a kind of large-scale rhythm whose cohesive force is enhanced in the four earliest strophic variation movements (those of Opp. 2/6, 9/5, 17/3, and 20/4) by having the original melody return virtually intact after a series of diminution-rich variations—a signal that the variation process has come full circle, perhaps, or has exhausted itself and is ready to conclude. In both Opp. 2/6/i and 9/5/i, the returning theme is treated to a varied first and second reprise. This valedictory adornment elevates the theme's stature while at the same time accelerating the structural rhythm (or rather setting up a new rhythm of alternation between unadorned statement and varied repeat) as the movement nears its end.

A degree of cohesion can also be sensed in variation movements that trace a long-range thematic trajectory by having the theme migrate among the instruments from one variation to the next. In Op. 76/3/ii, for example, the path of the

EXAMPLE 6.5 Op. 76/6/i

(a) mm. 9–12

(b) mm. 45–48

(c) mm. 117–24 (violin 1 only)

Emperor's Hymn through the ensemble may be heard as an inverted arch extending from the theme through the final (i.e., fourth) variation: violin 1, violin 2, cello, viola, violin 1. An all-encompassing directional force arises in strophic movements that feature patterns of progressive surface diminution, sometimes intensified by quickened rates of change in other elements along the way. In Op. 9/5/i, for instance, the original theme moves mainly in quarter notes and eighths; the first variation introduces sixteenth-note diminutions; the pace quickens in variation 2 with streams of triplet sixteenths and moments of rapidly changing relationship among parts; and in variation 3, rhythmic acceleration culminates with figuration in thirty-second notes.

Still other manifestations of large-scale profile are felt in strophic movements that incorporate a variation in tonic minor (Opp. 50/1, 50/3, and 74/2).

The change of mode suggests removal to a shadowy, unsettled space from which the return to major emerges as a kind of renewal—a resumption of the main line of thought—and thus a decisive turn in the projection of the movement's design. In Op. 50/3, the form is later complicated by an open-ended segment (beginning at m. 81) whose special thematic intrigue—the altered, transposed recurrence in measures 89–92 of a melodic thread from the latter part of the variation in minor (mm. 41–42)—marks this as a crucial juncture in the form. A related case of complex strophic design, the third movement of Op. 77/2, features two interruptions of the strophic sequence (mm. 23–39, 59–73), almost in the manner of a rondo form's episodes, the second one involving a turn to the opposite mode.[9]

As indicated in table 6.5, several of the strophic forms incorporate the rhetorical weight of a bona fide coda. That of Op. 20/4, the first of these cases, turns out to be among the most emphatic in its implications for large-scale cohesion. The stratagem of building to a climax is embedded within the theme itself, whose gradually approached melodic apex (d^3, mm. 16–17, underscored in m. 16 by the urgency of an augmented sixth chord) comes just before its final cadence in measure 18. The coda, beginning in measure 89, interrupts the theme's summarizing return at this very point, using the climactic note as a springboard for a cadenza-like series of culminating events whose heightened intensity has the effect of projecting the shape of the theme (i.e., its property of building to a climax) onto the scale of the entire movement.[10]

Alternating Variations

The category of so-called alternating variations encompasses a small but distinguished group whose members are dispersed among several middle and later opus groups (see table 6.6). Although related to strophic variations in technique and process, each embodies an added dimension of systematic contrast: the insertion of two-reprise segments in the opposite mode between theme and first variation, and then at least once more before the end of the movement. The opposite-mode idea, variously designed to counter, complement, or transform the movement's initial theme, proposes a contrasting argument whose impact helps motivate the subsequent course of events. In keeping with the potential depth and expressive range of such a scheme, alternating variation served Haydn as a vehicle not only for interior slow movements but also for a finale (Op. 33/6 in D) and a formidable first movement (Op. 55/2 in F minor).

Comparably ambitious in matters of variation technique, contrast, and polar opposition, the alternating variations follow a plan in which there are basically two separate tracks—the opposing-mode themes and their respective variations— with elements such as texture, register, melodic gesture, and surface rhythm working to underscore the difference in harmonic color between major and minor.

TABLE 6.6 Alternating variation movements

Opus	Key	Meter	Tempo	Form	Comments
33/6/iv	D	$\frac{2}{4}$	Allegretto	M-m-M-m-M	Subtle relationships between M and m; varied reprises in the major-key variations
50/4/ii	A	$\frac{2}{4}$	Andante	M-m-M-m-M	Subtle relationships between M and m; varied 1st reprise in 1st major-key variation
55/2/i	Fm-F	$\frac{2}{4}$	Andante o più tosto allegretto	m-M-m-M-m-M	m and M related; varied 1st reprise in 1st minor & 1st major variations; varied reprises in 2d major variation
71/3/ii	B♭	$\frac{2}{4}$	Andante con moto	M-m-M-M-m-M-coda	M and m related; 2d m differs from first

The movements vary in the degree of unifying relationship between their two themes. Whereas both share virtually the same opening melodic figure in Op. 55/2/i before going separate ways, resemblances are more obscure in Op. 50/4/ii: here the minor theme holds a dark mirror to the graceful opening gesture—the first violin's embellished upward skip and stepwise descent to tonic—with its menacing plunge to the cello's low C and subsequent prolonged ascent to tonic (mm. 20–25).

A more elaborate play of reflecting surfaces informs Op. 33/6/iv, where aspects of duality and contrast are mediated by a logic of reversal and hidden resemblance. The opening gesture of the major theme, a downward leap in the first violin, is opposed by a wide upward jump in the cello at the start of its minor counterpart; and the interval series in the minor theme's second measure, which the cello approaches by step from above (diminished fourth, minor second, major third) unfolds as a varied permutation of that heard in the second measure of the original theme, duly approached by step from below (minor second, minor third, perfect fourth).

Op. 71/3/ii stands out as the most intricate of the group thematically as it mixes aspects of similarity and contrast between alternating themes, and between the two minor-mode sections as well. The first minor portion, longer than the principal major theme and substantially different in harmonic structure, follows an independent course melodically as well, although the opening theme's gestures are clearly recalled in both its first and second reprise. The second minor segment, postponed until the completion of two major-key sections—a literal return of the first theme and a melodic outline variation—embodies elements of both the initial major theme and the earlier minor portion; but it is not closely tied to either, and it takes a fresh harmonic route in the first reprise, modulating to the relative major rather than the dominant.

There is actually an exquisite irony in this move, given the peculiar tonal schemes of both the original theme and the initial minor segment: the normal pattern for a binary form in major with a modulating first reprise is of course to go to the dominant, thereby privileging major harmony; and for a binary form in minor, the corresponding norm is to modulate to the mediant key (i.e., the relative major), thereby brightening the harmonic color in the course of the first reprise. Perversely, Haydn does the opposite in the opening segments of this movement: the major theme (quoted in ex. 6.6a) modulates to the mediant, D minor, effectively darkening the tone, whereas the first minor segment goes to the minor dominant, privileging minor. The second minor segment's garden-variety move to the mediant can therefore be heard as the emergence of an unexpected connection with the opening theme's odd modulation to its mediant.

But there is more to it than this, for the fresh endorsement of conventional practice that the modulation represents resonates with the major theme's resolution of its own tonal peculiarity in avoiding a standard movement to the dominant. Following the second minor segment (mm. 73–88), we encounter an incomplete version of the major theme's first reprise (mm. 89–96, repeated in mm. 97–104 and followed by a four-measure extension), which at last is harmonically transformed to end in the dominant. The disembodied sparkle of staccato sixteenths that characterizes this passage conveys a sense of growing distance from the movement's established play of contrasts; but at the same time, the revised tonal path (i.e., the straightforward modulation to the dominant) signifies a new, corrective proximity to recognized conventions.

What happens now may be described as a coda, beginning in measure 109, whose thematic recollections and developments prove both familiar and novel, reassuring yet also unexpected. First, a replica of the principal theme's opening phrase (mm. 109–12, quoted in ex. 6.6b) promises a return to stability, and while the following measures' echoes in the viola (mm. 113–14) and cello (mm. 115–16) signify persisting unrest, this action is overlapped by a powerful token of resolution: an elongated, transformed version of the first part's closing gesture (mm. 116–18, corresponding to mm. 7–8) in which the original harmony and melodic line are redirected to end squarely on tonic.

More transparent structurally, the opening movement of the "Razor" quartet, Op. 55/2 in F minor, is the only member of the alternating variations group to begin in minor, so that the scheme of modal change unfolds in reverse. Two comparably sized themes (twenty-six and twenty-four measures, respectively) are each treated to two full variations in alternation. Along the way, divergent approaches to cantus firmus and melodic outline underscore differences in character between the two opposing segments. Whereas the initial minor variation has

EXAMPLE 6.6 Op. 71/3/ii

(a) mm. 1–8 (violin 1 only)

(b) mm. 109–18

the first violin tear through the theme's melodic profile in angular triplet figures (especially in the second reprise, mm. 67–84), the first major variation makes amends with conjunct, rhythmically consonant diminutions and straightforward arpeggiations (mm. 93–116). In a comparably stark juxtaposition of contrasts, the second minor variation locks the first violin and viola in octaves (mm. 117–22, 125–27, 133–41) against growling passagework in the bass line, whereas a portion of the second major variation awards the melody itself to a lyrical, high-tenor cello (mm. 151–74), adorned by a halo of first violin figuration. The two themes are sufficiently close melodically, at least in their opening gestures, to imply that the second is a transformation whose more affirmative spirit will prevail in the end. The impression of major transcending minor, enhanced by the peculiar timbral brightness of the final variation, is confirmed by a major-mode appendix (mm. 191–202), in which allusions to the rising broken-chord figures that the two themes had shared provide a satisfying, thematically integral close to the movement as a whole.

∾

The technically circumscribed realm of variation forms, however limited in matters of thematic diversity, development, and hierarchic complexity, offered invaluable opportunities for Haydn to exercise his penchant for soloistic embellishment and rhetorical amplification as well as ensemble interplay, and in this capacity they lent an element of continuity in his approach to the genre. Movements based on variation models presented performers and listeners with familiar ingredients to be contemplated against the background of related examples from other opus groups and other repertories. But Haydn also arranged for some of the variation forms to change over the course of his career. Op. 20/4/ii raised strophic variation form to a new level of drama and expressive force, positioning it as a minor-mode interior movement and locating its rhetorical climax within an extended, theatrical coda. The varied-reprise Adagio furnished a showcase for operatic display; and although that form was discarded after Op. 33, its soloistic manner was later reclaimed in a different guise with the ternary variations. Meanwhile the alternating variations, beginning with the finale of Op. 33/6, gave rise to new possibilities for expressive contrast, thematic relationship, and harmonic color; and certain strophic forms, otherwise the most predictable of variation types, were enriched by episodic insertions as well as other kinds of reshaping. Finally, in several movements from Op. 76, Haydn exceeded customary variation-form boundaries altogether by inventing unusual designs marked by polyphonic technique and structural complexity.

Collectively, the quartets' variation movements stand out as a momentous accomplishment, affirming the enduring validity of traditional mechanisms while at the same time reveling in their elasticity and susceptibility to change. By placing variation forms in different positions within the cycle, Haydn demonstrated their adaptability to various functional requirements and confirmed their efficacy as a complement to the artifice, narrative depth, and formality of other movement types. Their decorative, coloristic properties were thereby shown to be consistent with the highest aspirations of the genre.

7

Other Forms: Fugue, Rondo, and Miscellaneous Nonstandard Designs

Categories of form surveyed in the preceding three chapters—sonata and related two-reprise designs in fast and slow movements, the minuet-trio complex, and the principal types of variation form—account for nearly nine tenths
of the repertory. Among quartets before Op. 20, the sole exceptions are a small
group of fast-tempo, ternary da capo movements found in Opp. 1 and 2. Thereafter, most occasions on which Haydn stepped outside his own normal boundaries involved alternative approaches to the finale: fugue in Opp. 20 and 50;
rondo, beginning with Op. 33; and a miscellany of irregular or hybrid designs in
later quartets, variously involving aspects of sonata, rondo, variation, and con-
certo-related procedure. To these may be added a scattered assortment of aberrations, comprising several slow movements and one finale that defy categorization altogether in terms of recognized models.

Earliest and structurally least complicated are the da capo forms, all marked
presto, situated as middle movements in Opp. 1/3 and 2/6 (the two early five-
movement cycles that had begun with slow movements) and as finales in Op. 1/3
and 4. Each of these symmetrical, three-part structures sandwiches a contrasting
middle part between an initial closed form and its literal recurrence—a plan that
succeeds in highlighting contrast (tonal, textural, rhythmic, and melodic) in a
movement of substantial size without transcending the simple realm of two-reprise
conventions on which most of the principal and middle portions of these forms
are based.

Fugal Finales

Next chronologically are the three fugues of Op. 20,[1] Haydn's first departure from
his practice up to this point of concluding with a relatively lightweight sonata

form, some other two-reprise design, or a da capo scheme. The decision to side-line those choices in favor of learned polyphony may be linked to the generally high ambitions that mark this opus, as well as to a special concern for cyclic unity and coherence. A well-turned fugue, aspiring to sublime complexity and persuasive rhetoric, is ideally suited to the role of culmination: a natural apex of technical stringency, linear density, and ensemble energy, and hence a long-range goal toward which the action of previous movements had been striving. Cyclic unity and integration were ideas within Haydn's purview, especially at this point in his career, and his Op. 20 fugues may be heard as manifestations of the tendency.

Learned style, with fugue as its capstone, was an available ingredient for Viennese composers of Haydn's day, and Haydn himself had practiced fugal technique in his baryton trios of the previous decade; his Symphonies Nos. 3 (by 1762) and 40 (1763) have fugal finales;[2] and there are instances in his previous quartets of canonic imitation (in the trio of Op. 17/1/ii and in Op. 17/4/i, for example) as well as points of free imitation with parts entering one by one. From this perspective, the full-scale fugues in Op. 20 may be seen not as stylistic aberrations but as manifestations of a viable, current technique.

Certainly the Op. 20 fugues stand out as superlative examples of their kind, enjoying the medium's capacity for rhythmic precision and melodic agility while demonstrating fugal ideals of linear independence, unity, and continuity. It is easy to imagine that these examples of exalted craftsmanship were welcomed and appreciated by chamber-music connoisseurs. The idiom was one with which they would have been familiar; the quartet, with its arrangement of solo parts to match soprano, alto, tenor, and bass voice ranges, made a suitable foundation for fugal discourse; and in the absence of any explicit formal prototype, the finales embodied fresh solutions to problems of large-scale design. Moreover, to the extent that they were actually heard as climactic events within their respective cycles, they invited contemplation of large-scale coherence as an issue of structural and aesthetic importance.

Haydn attached a label to each of the fugues to specify the number of subjects it encompassed: two in Op. 20/5, three in Op. 20/6, four in Op. 20/2. The distinguishing tags notwithstanding, all three may be described technically as double fugues: each begins with a principal subject accompanied by a countersubject that figures prominently, if not consistently, in subsequent statements. The additional specified countersubjects in Op. 20/6 and 2 play lesser roles, but they nonetheless contribute to the prodigious rhythmic and melodic diversity—and the considerable polyphonic complexity—that characterize both these movements.[3]

Other resemblances confirm impressions of family relationship. The fugues' principal subjects all start on the fifth scale degree, and each has a tonal answer that begins on the tonic note and moves to the dominant. In each case, the initial exposition embraces five entries: two pairs of subject-answer units, giving each ensemble member a chance to state the principal subject, plus an additional entry

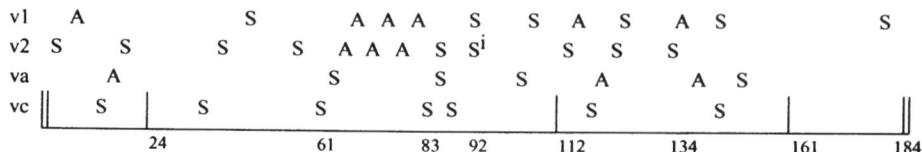

(a) Op. 20/5/iv

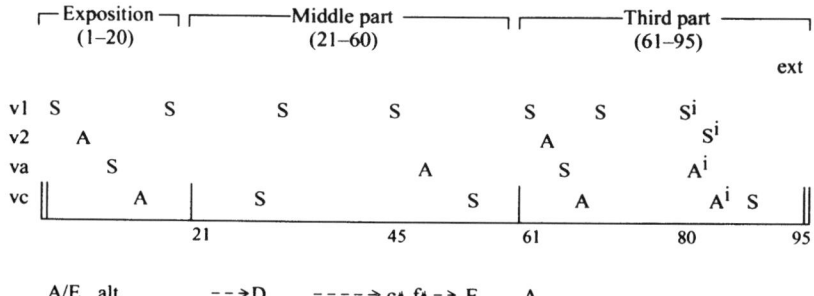

(b) Op. 20/6/iv

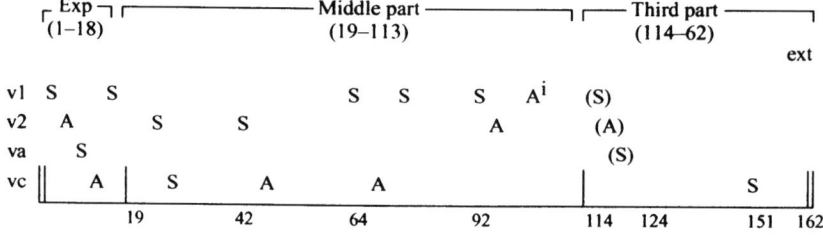

(c) Op. 20/2/iv

(S = principal subject, A = tonal answer, the superscript "i" denotes inversion. Not all entries identified in the diagrams are complete, although all are substantial representatives of either subject or answer.)

FIGURE 7.1 The three fugal finales of Op. 20: Nos. 5, 6, and 2

in tonic, restored to the voice by which it was stated at the outset (see fig. 7.1). The next phase comprises an extended middle section in which the tonal focus changes repeatedly in the course of episodic passages and further statements of the subject and countersubjects. A final portion dwells on tonic; and, to counter the harmonic stability that now predominates, activity increases in other elements, variously including surface rhythm, textural density, and notated or implied dynamics. A concentration of special devices late in the movement (such as stretto, pedal point, inversion, and canon) helps build to a rhetorical high point and resounding conclusion, especially in Op. 20/5 and 6.

Curiously, all three fugues are inscribed at their head with the marking *sempre sotto voce*, perhaps cautioning performers to honor the learned atmosphere with a measure of emotional distance and a rarefied, uniform balance among parts. But the pent-up energy thus entailed would seem to call for eventual release, especially given the imperative of cyclic culmination; and Haydn does in fact signal the ultimate change to a fuller volume—with the help of explicit dynamic markings in Op. 20/5 and 2, and by implication in Op. 20/6, where vigorous unisons and double-stopped chords in the closing measures clearly demand at least a forte rendition.

A closer view of the fugues reveals points of individuality and stylistic differentiation. In the F minor fugue, an alla breve time signature and archetypal subject in long note values stand out as markers for the *stile antico*, and elements suggestive of strict style are cultivated throughout: a preference for conjunct melodic lines, apart from the featured leaps of its "pathotype" theme,[4] relatively long note values, and copious display of learned techniques, including canon, inversion, and stretto at successively shorter time intervals. Distinctly more modern in character and technique, the A major fugue has a subject that mixes a variety of shorter note values and is further enlivened by short rests, wide leaps, and sequential repetition, all of which provide the basis for episodes based on subject material, sometimes involving the stretto-like effect of entries in close imitation (for example, mm. 25–26 and 35–37). The most complex of the three stylistically is the C major fugue of Op. 20/2, whose dancing subject in $\frac{6}{8}$ time, enriched by a chromatic passing tone, joins a multiplicity of countersubjects as a basis for continuously changing relationships among parts, variously involving inversion, chromatically inflected sequence, canon, and dialogue.

For the finale of Op. 50/4 in F♯ minor, a special case in several respects, learned style provides a means to crown a serious, disturbing quartet in a difficult minor key.[5] As in Op. 20, the very presence of fugue signifies cyclic culmination, a quality enhanced here by the device of a principal subject that summarizes and reassembles motivic elements from previous movements.[6] At the same time, however, cohesion is tempered by stylistic disparities within the fugue itself—most notably its lightly tripping gait in a fast $\frac{6}{8}$ time, a quality that belies the sobriety of learned style and the dark connotations of the subject's "pathotype" profile,[7]

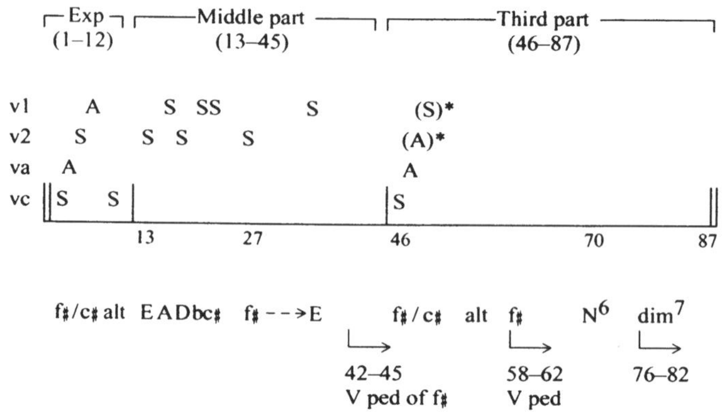

┌─Exp─┐ ┌──────Middle part ──────┐ ┌──────────Third part ──────────┐
(1–12)   (13–45)   (46–87)

v1   A   S SS   S   (S)*
v2   S   S S   S   (A)*
va   A   A
vc   ‖S   S │   │S   ‖
          13   27   46   70   87

f♯/c♯ alt E A D bc♯   f♯ - ->E   f♯ / c♯   alt f♯   N⁶   dim⁷
                                        └─→   └─→   └─→
                                        42–45   58–62   76–82
                                        V ped of f♯   V ped

_____

*First measure only.

FIGURE 7.2 Op. 50/4/iv

although to some extent the contradictions may resonate with the rhetorical and affective complexity of the work as a whole.

Despite all similarities to the fugues of Op. 20, and despite the special intensity of its climax—which features a richly scored outburst of Neapolitan harmony (m. 70), simultaneously with a climb to the movement's highest pitch, g^3—the Op. 50/4 fugue marks a retreat from the technical ambitions of Op. 20. Shorter than the earlier fugues, and designed to permit fewer entries of the principal subject, it makes proud display of fugal technique at the outset but then relaxes the commitment to equal-voice polyphony as the movement progresses (see fig. 7.2). The subject as an intact thematic unit is abandoned relatively early. In a decisive move placed just after the midpoint (m. 45), a pregnant silence prepares the way for a pattern of stretto entries (mm. 46–49), which eloquently confirms the restoration of tonic while revisiting the initial order of entering parts (lowest to highest). Polyphonic activity continues for a dozen measures more, the last four over a pedal point; but now the coalescing of all parts in unison (mm. 62–64) signifies the near-surrender to rhythmically synchronized, vertically oriented textures.

Paradoxically, the last movement of Op. 50/4 may be regarded both as an affirmation of learned polyphony and a belated acknowledgment of its limitations. The Op. 20 fugues were exemplary by comparison, brilliantly displaying the quartet's potential for motivic concentration, linear continuity, four-part interaction, and rhetorical persuasion within a contrapuntal discipline. And even if polyphony was occasionally relieved by passages of relatively homogeneous rhythm and galant-style figuration, such digressions were subordinate. In Op. 50/4, Haydn makes more prominent use of textures that involve repetitive surface patterns and a melody-plus-accompaniment alignment of parts, especially in connection with structural landmarks and moments of expressive impact, so that the movement vacillates between opposing styles, and the tensions between them furnish an expressive compositional resource.

Was the ambivalence of such a design, mixing strict and free technique, a viable alternative for future developments? Whatever the merits of learned polyphony as the starting point of a musical narrative, the realm of free style claimed obvious advantages, offering room for the music to rest, breathe, and enjoy the play of diverse sonorities to which the quartet was so well adapted. It is scarcely surprising that in subsequent quartets that straddle the two domains, the hierarchic relationship between them is overturned: free style—with its familiar symmetries and patterns of repetition, recurrence, and contrast—conclusively subsumes strict composition, whose elevated rhetoric and exacting technique relinquish their place as a movement's controlling impetus without being discarded altogether as a source of enrichment within a larger design.

Rondo Forms

For the quartets of Op. 33, generally lighter and more accessible than those of Op. 20 and evidently targeted for a less exclusive market, the quest for an alternative type of finale led in a new direction—namely, to the currently fashionable rondo, whose characteristic virtues of tunefulness, rhythmic life, and sharply defined sectional contrasts underlined its attractiveness as an uplifting conclusion to a multimovement cycle. In keeping with what we can presume to be Haydn's eye toward popular appeal, this form must have seemed an irresistible choice.[8]

The plan adopted for Op. 33's three rondos features a recurrent, cheerful refrain in binary or rounded binary form; two episodes, offering opportunities for contrast as well as motivic development; and a coda at the end. Apart from their comparable size and formal arrangement, resemblances among them include the choice of a fast duple meter, either $\frac{2}{4}$ or $\frac{6}{8}$; the similar preference for short motives that lend themselves to repetition as well as variation, permutation, and migration among the parts; and (in Op. 33/2 and 3) a sense of accumulating momentum that enhances the suspense of the forms' transition passages and helps motivate the special punch lines that adorn the endings. Such family resemblances notwithstanding, each of these finales has a distinctive character, and each displays a somewhat different approach to realizing a rondo's possibilities. In No. 3, an utterly simple, repetitive melodic premise gives rise to a masterpiece of thematic unity, motivic concentration, and diversity of ensemble technique. Almost every melodic gesture stems from the initial two-note figure, which continually undergoes repetition, inversion, and other operations in which all instruments take part.

No. 2 (the "Joke"), justifiably famous for the comical disjunctions of its closing measures, is also rich in playful manipulation of the form's rhythms of contrast and recurrence. To begin with, the second reprise of the rounded binary refrain

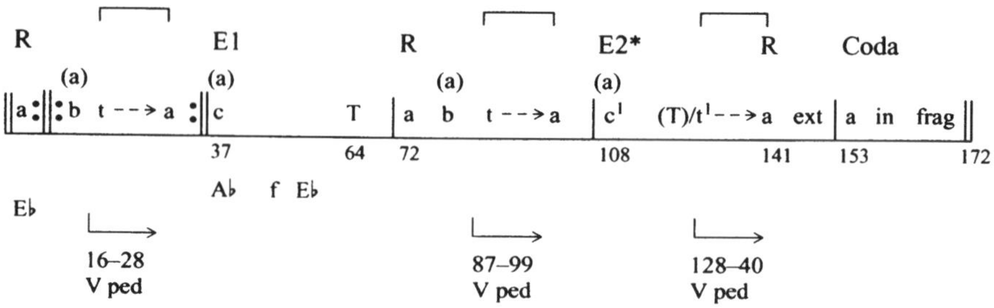

```
       ┌───┐                 ┌───┐          ┌───┐
  R    │   │    E1      R    │   │   E2*    │   │   R      Coda
       (a)        (a)             (a)           (a)
  ‖a:‖│:b  t --→ a :‖ c      T │ a  b  t --→ a │ c¹ │ (T)/t¹--→a ext │ a  in  frag ‖
                    37          64  72              108         141    153      172
  Eb
                   Ab  f  Eb
  └──→                          └──→              └──→
  16–28                         87–99             128–40
  V ped                         V ped             V ped
```

*The opening four measures of E2 vary those of E1.

FIGURE 7.3 Op. 33/2/iv

has sufficient breadth to encompass thematic development, a brief inflection to the dominant, and a transition (t in fig. 7.3) to the return, so that the refrain as a whole traverses on a small scale the form's larger, periodic dispositions of statement, departure, transition, and recurrence. This in itself is not unusual; what is distinctive is the way Haydn bestows exaggerated emphasis on the second-reprise transition, positioning it as a tense moment of inhalation before the awaited recurrence of first-reprise material and actually lending it more upbeat energy than the subsequent, larger-scale connection (T) from the end of the first episode to the refrain.

But why? A reason for this oddity emerges as the form continues to unfold (see fig. 7.3): when the end of the second episode (E2) segues as expected into a transition that will lead to the refrain's third appearance at measure 141, what we hear is not a replica of the preceding transition to the refrain (i.e., mm. 64–71) but something that sounds more like a variant of the long upbeat passage embedded within the refrain's second reprise (mm. 16–28, 87–99). It leads not to a full statement of the refrain but to the recurrence of a single eight-measure phrase-pair, and the formal ellipsis that results gives rise to a tight and unexpected unity: the transition in question (mm. 128–40), related, as we have noted, to the transition that unfolds within the second reprise of the refrain, now comes into its own by assuming a higher-level function, joining the second episode to a partial statement of the refrain, and thus mediating between smaller and larger dimensions of structure as the rondo heads toward its celebrated conclusion. Paradoxically, the full stop in measure 148 sounds both satisfying (it presents a solid, decisive punctuation) and incomplete (we have been cheated out of a large portion of the refrain): a suitably unstable environment for the perplexing adagio of measures 149–52 and the bizarre coda that follows.

The finale of Op. 33/4 (represented in fig. 7.4) differs from either of the other two rondos by calling for a full close rather than an open-ended transition between episode and refrain. (The passage marked T in the sketch is indeed transitional, yet it is neither fluid nor charged with anticipation. Preceded by a full close and capped by nearly a full measure's rest, it acts as a developmental inter-

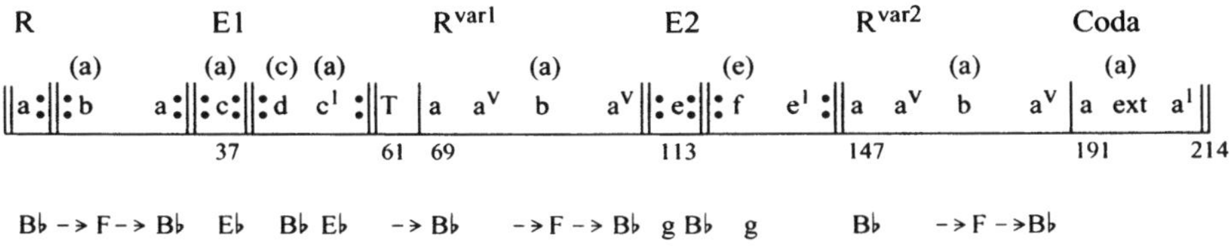

R	E1	R^{var1}	E2	R^{var2}	Coda

(a)	(a) (c) (a)		(a)	(e)	(a)	(a)
‖a:‖:b	a:‖:c:‖:d c¹ :‖	T ∣ a a^V b	a^V ‖:e:‖:f e¹ :‖	a a^V b	a^V ∣ a ext a¹ ‖	

37	61 69	113	147	191 214

Bb -> F-> Bb Eb Bb Eb   -> Bb   -> F - > Bb g Bb g   Bb   -> F ->Bb

FIGURE 7.4 Op. 33/4/iv

lude that puts distance between the first episode and the returning refrain as it negotiates the tonal shift from subdominant to tonic.) The emphasis on separation resembles the usual segmentation of variation forms, and in fact there are variation techniques in play: the second appearance of the refrain quickens the pace with sixteenth-note diminutions, and its final occurrence transforms some of the theme's repeated notes and broken-chord figures into wide-leaping gesticulations. The adornment of second and third refrains with diminutions and leaps points up the rondo's susceptibility to variation as an antidote to the monotony of unaltered recurrence—an issue of particular relevance to the quartet, with its predilection for detail and the corresponding tendency to avoid pure repetition.

The scarcity of relatively simple rondo forms subsequent to Op. 33 reflects Haydn's growing tendency to charge his last movements with elements of unpredictability, rhetorical impact, and structural novelty. Only two later finales, those of Opp. 54/1 and 64/6, resemble the Op. 33 rondos closely enough to be labeled unproblematically as examples of the type. Like the last movements of Op. 33/3 and 4, both are whirlwind finales in $\frac{2}{4}$ time, and both have rounded binary refrains that (as in Op. 33/2) focus attention on a second-reprise transition whose suspenseful qualities prepare the return to first-reprise material (see the sketch of Op. 54/1/iv in fig. 7.5, where the transition in question is marked *t*). Also similar to both Op. 33/2 and 3 is the suspense of transitional gestures between episode and refrain (those of Op. 54/1/iv are marked *T* in the sketch). However, neither of these later rondos retains a comparably simple plan of alternation between refrain and episode. In Op. 54/1/iv, for example, the form's first two segments—initial refrain and first episode—conform to basic rondo expectations; but the second refrain is strangely destabilized by a digression to the mediant, B minor, at the start of its second reprise, followed by a close in the dominant of that key, F♯ minor. In effect, Haydn has joined a statement of the refrain's first part to a segment that would seem appropriate as the first reprise of a minor-key episode; he thus collapses both functions—refrain and episode—within a single formal unit (labeled R + E₂). After a brief transition, a fully intact refrain (with varied first reprise) restores order temporarily. But starting with measure 132 (*E₃*), the movement's course veers once again toward the unpredictable: a low-register musical afterthought, quietly commenting on the preceding phrase, a further span of developmental transition, and a recall of *a¹* that flows directly

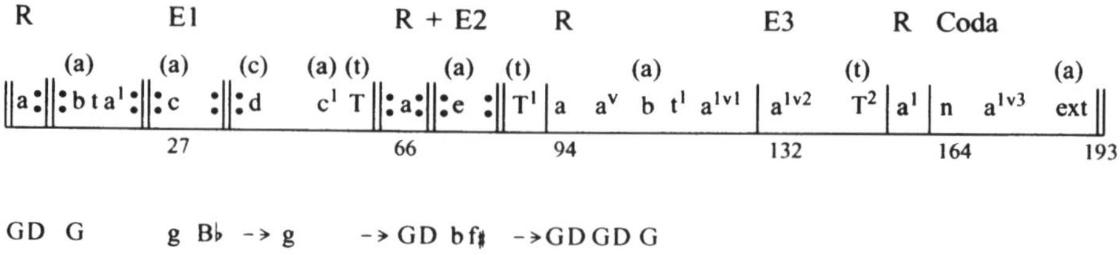

R   E1   R + E2   R   E3   R   Coda

(a)   (a)   (c)   (a) (t)   (a)   (t)   (a)   (t)   (a)

‖a:‖:b t a¹:‖:c   :‖:d   c¹ T ‖:a:‖:e :‖T¹│a   aᵛ b t¹ aˡᵛ¹ │ aˡᵛ²   T² a¹ │ n   aˡᵛ³ │ ext‖

       27   66   94   132   164   193

GD G   g B♭ -> g   -> GD bf♯   ->GD GD G

FIGURE 7.5 Op. 54/1/iv

into a brilliant coda, complete with scale- and arpeggio figures, final references to the refrain, loud unison punctuations, and a quizzical, high-register ending, sounded pianissimo.

Rondo-Variation Hybrids

In two finales from subsequent opus groups (Opp. 71/2/iv and 76/4/iv), the combination of rondo and variation yields unconventional results quite unlike the relatively transparent, varied-refrain scheme witnessed in Op. 33/4/iv. The first of these two hybrids begins with a rounded binary refrain (mm. 1–20), proceeds to a developmental episode that opens in the parallel minor, and then continues with a varied recurrence of the refrain. The order of events so far suggests a rondo or perhaps a ternary variation form. But instead of confirming either model, the movement proposes another variant of the refrain, having accelerated from allegretto to allegro, before winding up with an exuberant coda. Contributing to the impression of a rondo-related form, despite these structural peculiarities, are the suspenseful transitions that preface major landmarks in the form: the initial return of the refrain at measure 47; the change of tempo and second return at measure 75; and finally, with still more dramatic emphasis, the start of the coda at measure 95.

Haydn recalls key features of this finale in the last movement of Op. 76/4. Resemblances include a rounded binary refrain (enhanced in this instance by the distinctly rondo-like gesture of an elongated transition to the a^1 portion of the ‖ a : ‖ : b a^1 : ‖ design), the parallel-minor episode, and the long anacrusis (mm. 69–74) to the return. As in Op. 71/2/iv, the refrain is now varied, and once again an onrush of new activity lies in wait. As the tempo rises to più allegro (m. 110), the ensemble races through thematic particles as it presses toward a climax: the change at measure 128 to a still faster tempo, più presto, and another variant of the refrain, now fragmented and abbreviated, before the onset of a coda at measure 150. As in Op. 71/2/iv, neither rondo nor ternary variation adequately describes the movement's profile, although most of its ingredients are accounted for if we regard it as a hybrid comprising elements of both.

Sonata-Rondo Forms

Likewise recognizable as hybrids or mixtures are the last movements of Opp. 74/2 and 76/2. In this related pair of duple-meter finales, Haydn plants rondo trademarks within the structural outlines of a sonata form. Both movements begin in the manner of a rondo with a rhythmically impulsive, two-reprise theme; but instead of continuing with a rondo-type episode, they both proceed in the manner of a customary sonata narrative, with a modulatory transition, confirmation of the new tonal center with a secondary theme, and a closing idea to round out the exposition (but not the binary double bar and repeat signs that might otherwise be expected at this juncture).

The subsequent course of events in both cases is informed by rondo as well as sonata-like elements, the latter predominating: a sonata-style development section, a rondo-like anacrusis and return to the refrain, and a recapitulation of transition, secondary, and closing material. (Op. 76/2/iv features the additional complication of an eventual transformation from minor to major at m. 180.)

Irregular Forms Involving Fugal Procedure

If Haydn's return to fugue in the Op. 50/4 finale signified a refusal to abandon strict style as an alternative, even as he loosened some of its burdensome constraints, then a move witnessed in Op. 54/55 may be regarded as a next logical step: the insertion of a fugal passage within a movement controlled on the whole by some other structural principle. The two cases in question, the finale to Op. 55/1 and the fast second movement of Op. 55/2, both capitalize on the ability of fugue to command attention, elevate the prevailing tone, and complicate the musical narrative while at the same time strengthening its coherence and sharpening its profile.

The underlying model for Op. 55/1/iv is that of a rondo. After a full-size rounded binary refrain and an episode that migrates to the dominant, a telltale anacrusis and dominant pedal point lead us to anticipate an impending return. For an instant, the reappearance of the opening thematic figure, in tonic, fulfills expectations; but reassuring signs vanish instantly with the surprise appearance of a fugue subject in long note values and the remolding of the refrain theme into a fast-moving countersubject. As a genuine fugal exposition now gets under way, the viola's repeated-note entry, in effect a second countersubject, underlines the impression of a connection to the opening of the movement by appropriating the refrain's quarter-note impetus while the first violin proceeds in eighth notes (see ex. 7.1, which compares the opening theme, mm. 1–4, with the announcement of the strict-style subject in mm. 61–64). Inscribed in this fugal enterprise is

EXAMPLE 7.1 Op. 55/1/iv

(a) mm. 1–4 (violin 1 only)

(b) mm. 61–64

a musical pun with at least two distinct facets: first, the sober intrusion of a subject (virtually identical in rhythm, and partially similar in melodic profile, to the opening five-note pathotype figure of Op. 20/5/iv) in a way that transforms the rondo theme by adopting it as a countersubject; second, the ambivalence of the movement's time signature, initially understood as a species of modern, fast common time, designated by the signature ¢. With the entry of the subject, the connotations of the signature are temporarily transformed, as if by magic, from modern common time to the old learned-style alla breve.[9]

The contrapuntal escapade lasts for about forty measures, a bit more than a fourth of the movement, before dissolving to make way for a final recurrence of the refrain. In effect, Haydn invokes attributes of fugue—an alla breve subject in whole and half notes, the elevated rhetoric of a fugal exposition, and the relentless momentum of rhythmically independent polyphony—to enrich the texture of an otherwise normal rondo and create an ingeniously streamlined design by collapsing two structural elements, refrain and second episode, into a single event.

For Op. 55/2 in F minor, Haydn reverses the standard order of first and second movement types, and a meaningful connection might thus be made between two destabilizing elements in question: the change in cyclic profile on the one hand, the intrusion of fugal polyphony on the other. The movement as a whole exudes a dark intensity reminiscent of the two earlier minor-key quartets in which fugue had played a part, Op. 20/5 in F minor and Op. 50/4 in F♯ minor. From this perspective, it would appear that Haydn has deliberately chosen two radically opposing environments to showcase this opus group's two excursions into the realm of learned style: a bright, sharp-key rondo finale and a somber, F minor principal Allegro in sonata form.

The exposition of Op. 55/2/ii bestows special importance on the movement's primary theme by highlighting its distinctive opening gesture—a pair of long note values, the second a fifth higher than the first—at the outset and at the start of both the transition (T) and secondary theme (S). That it also should dominate the development section seems almost inevitable; and, after two statements, in the submediant (D♭) and major mediant (A), respectively, it takes on the exalted status of a fugue subject, to be treated to a succession of eight entries that will lead through several keys. The first violin's eventual entry (m. 125) proves to be the last, reaffirming the tonic key in the same register in which the movement had begun, and thus serving as a covert point of recapitulation, embedded within the final stretch of the fugue-like process before polyphonic energies are dispersed over a dominant pedal point. After a change of signature to F major at measure 145, the movement concludes with a straightforward return of secondary and closing themes in tonic major. Much as the fugal display in Op. 55/1/iv embraced both refrain and episode, that of Op. 55/2/ii straddles and partially conflates two normally discrete functions, development and recapitulation, by weaving a recapitulatory statement of the primary theme within the surrounding fugal discourse.

Among the fugal exploits of subsequent opus groups, first to be cited is the finale of Op. 71/3, which merges fugue and rondo in a manner reminiscent of Op. 55/1/iv. The logic is similar, but there are added complications: this time, the polyphonic adventure begins right after the end of the initial refrain (m. 31), with a subject arising directly from the rhythm and melodic profile of the refrain theme itself. Eventually, an extended passage of liquidation and transition (mm. 52–68) returns us to the opening theme, and thus it appears that refrain and fugal episode will be distinguished as separate entities rather than intertwined as in Op. 55/1/iv. But a major change is in store: at measure 73 (an approximate midpoint of the form), the fugal impetus revives. A semblance of the original subject and countersubject now interrupts what had promised to be the start of a genuine refrain, and a new span of polyphonically enriched development unfolds. Finally, beginning in measure 88, the refrain recurs fully intact—a welcome, stabilizing pillar in the latter part of the form—prior to the whirlwind coda that follows a fermata in measure 124. Here the irrepressible topic of polyphony comes to the fore once again, with a series of imitative entries based on the principal theme and a final torrent of sixteenth-note figuration derived from the first episode and the countersubject introduced at measure 31.

The role of fugue proves less complicated in the ternary (A B A¹) finale of Op. 64/5, whose perpetual-motion, rounded binary A leads without a break into the B section, as the first violin's incessant sixteenth notes pass almost imperceptibly from first violin to second and the harmony darkens from major to minor. Simultaneously, the spotlight shifts to a new melodic idea, a fugue subject declaimed in eighth notes and syncopated quarters, which now subsumes the sixteenth-note patter as a countersubject. (Here a comparison may be drawn with the fugal escapade in Op. 55/1/iv, whose principal subject likewise arises as a new element while a derivative of the opening theme sounds in counterpoint.) After five entries, encompassing the tonic minor and several related keys, a developmental episode builds to the movement's melodic peak, g^3, prior to a long span of preparation for the A section's varied return. The energy generated by all this polyphonic action gives the impression of outweighing the subsequent A^1, so that the substantial coda that follows (mm. 103–28) proves to be a satisfying way to brake the accumulated momentum, balance the B section's intensity, and bring the movement to a close.

The potentially riveting effect of fugue, entailing the shift to an elevated plane of action and the driving energy of polyphonic development, was a resource that Haydn continued to explore in the quartets of Op. 76, but from a different perspective: on three occasions here, he posits fugal technique not as a technically brilliant centerpiece embedded within a more or less familiar design but as a source of affirmation or rhetorical climax in the latter part of a movement characterized by structural, tonal, or thematic peculiarity. Op. 76/5/i implicates fugue in a design that seems both logically coherent and deliberately ambiguous. In basic terms, the movement could be described as a moderately paced $A \, B \, A^1$ form in which an embellished but abbreviated A^1 is capped by an allegro appendage in which brilliance and complexity (including a span of polyphony based on a subject derived from the principal theme of A) help drive the movement to a stunning conclusion. But other elements in play call for a more nuanced description. To begin with, the subject, along with its accompanying countersubject, had actually been introduced in the B section. Moreover, the fugal texture dissolves well before the end of the movement in a series of flourishes recalled directly from the latter part of B. In effect, the B section and closing portion are so intimately related that the latter may almost be heard as an elaboration of the former, accelerated in tempo, recast in tonic major, intensified by fugal technique, and tonally stabilized to form a brilliant conclusion. From this vantage point, the movement may be seen as dividing into two main parts ($A \, B \mid A^1 \, B^1$) with the principal modulatory action taking place in B. That neither way of classifying the form proves thoroughly satisfactory need not be seen as a fault of the music or its analysis: ambivalence seems essential to the movement's character, a palpable source of the restlessness conveyed by this unconventional design.

In Op. 76/6/i, Haydn introduces fugue as a means of discharging accumulated tension in a strophic variation form whose cantus firmus treatment of a strangely halting, repetitive theme had given rise to an ever-increasing feeling of pent-up energy. The subject, derived from the theme's first reprise, coincides with the shift in tempo from allegretto to allegro (m. 145); and the sense of release, of being propelled into a new orbit, is underlined by the new rhythmic life of a relatively fast-moving countersubject. After four entries and several measures of

elaboration, we encounter what seems at first to be merely a new entry of the subject in the first violin, now in C minor (m. 179). But there is more to it than this:
as the line unfolds, pivoting harmonically to E♭ and discarding the fugue subject's
trail of sixteenth notes, distinct recollections of the theme itself come into
focus—an impression confirmed by the cello, beginning on the upbeat to measure 185, whose line (through m. 186) recalls that of the theme at the close of
the first reprise (E♭–A♭–A♮–B♭, corresponding to the first violin in mm. 7–8). The
experience of a structural *double entendre* continues in the seven measures that
follow (mm. 187–93): this phrase may be heard as a crowning rhetorical flourish,
with recollections of the subject above an embellished pedal point; but it also
turns out to be an abbreviated reconstitution of the theme's first reprise (cunningly inflected in m. 192), an octave higher than the original pitch level; and
the second reprise that follows, starting in measure 194, actually recapitulates that
of the third variation.[10] Elements of fugal climax, variation, and recapitulation
are thus drawn together, and the movement closes with a brilliant addendum to
the theme's final cadence.

Curiously, the last of Haydn's quartet movements to display fugal technique
lies in closest proximity to the one just considered: the second movement of
Op. 76/6, designated "Fantasia." Given that term's association with a tradition of
improvisation, Haydn's choice to affix it here helps justify—or at least give warning of—the movement's extraordinary liberties in matters of form and tonal organization. The key itself is unusual: a distant B major, which may be understood
as an enharmonic equivalent of C♭, logically related to the quartet's home key as
its lowered submediant. Stranger still is the fact that the entire first half of the
piece (through m. 59) bears no key signature—actually a reasonable anomaly in
light of the wrenching tonal shifts that accompany the principal theme's varied
repetitions in this part of the movement, and that would cause portions of the
music to bristle with accidentals even if a key signature had been in place. When
the signature of B major does finally appear at measure 60, this marks a crucial
turn of events—a long-awaited point of tonal stabilization and, after a solid four-
measure phrase in the restored home key, the start of an elaborate fugal excursion on a subject derived from the theme's opening two measures. Fugal texture
dissolves by measure 88, and the eventual reinstatement of the first violin as an
uncontested lead voice (m. 95) marks the start of an extended peroration to ground
the movement's far-flung energies and negotiate a quiet conclusion.

Other Nonstandard Designs

Haydn's evocative label for the Op. 76 movement just described recalls a similar
inspiration from an earlier phase of his career: the slow movement of Op. 20/2,
designated "Capriccio"—another case of a colorful term whose suggestion of improvisatory freedom resonates with the digression from standard procedure.[11] In

this earlier instance, the underlying topic is a parody of operatic practices, beginning with a portentous C minor unison, then proceeding with passages reminiscent of arioso, recitative, and lyrical aria. As the action proceeds from one theatrical moment to the next, we may enjoy the experience of a dream-like escape from the constraints of a self-contained instrumental form. And yet a logical tonal design, well coordinated with principal thematic events, helps bestow order as it frames the drama: the stage is set in tonic; an extended modulatory path to G minor (mm. 8–25) connects a pair of arioso-like phrases for solo cello; a bifocal cadence at measure 33 (V of C minor to I in E♭) marks the boundary between the movement's two main sections; and a transition following the aria portion steals wistful glances back to the aria theme (mm. 52–54; 55–57) before steering toward the dominant of C minor in preparation for an open-ended connection to the dance movement.

In several other unusual movements, the course of events at any given time follows a grammatically normal path, yet the form as a whole resists conformity to a structural stereotype. Perhaps the least complicated example of this type is the E♭ Largo of Op. 33/4, whose overall outline bears resemblance to that of a slow-movement form. What complicates matters is the instability of the secondary material, which is tonally enriched and open-ended in both exposition and recapitulation. The exposition slips from the major dominant to its parallel minor, then touches on that key's relative major, D♭, before negotiating a three-measure transition to the recapitulation (mm. 23–25). As the recapitulation proceeds, the transposed replica of these events leads to E♭ minor and eventually to G♭, three measures before an additional return to the primary theme in tonic (m. 53) restores tonal stability for good.

More intriguing in relation to formal convention is the slow movement of Op. 42, in which a centrally placed close in the dominant (m. 28) divides the movement into two principal parts. In fact, Haydn had originally placed double bars and repeat signs here and at measure 52, five measures from the end,[12] in the manner of a binary form (‖ A B B^{1} : ‖ :C A : ‖ Ext). But there are elements that resist a simple binary interpretation, notably the self-enclosed nature of A, which ends in a full stop, and the peculiar shape of B B^{1}, which taken out of context would appear to comprise the first part (plus varied repeat) of a two-reprise form in its own right. When the discrete segments are viewed in this light, the result is a distinctly symmetrical design in which A and its recurrence stand as tonally stable pillars to frame two unstable portions (B and C) that flank the central pivot.

The slow movement of Op. 33/2 likewise makes ample allusion to formal conventions without lapsing into any standard arrangement of parts (see fig. 7.6).[13] The first section, which begins with a twice-stated eight-measure sentence (P), resembles a sonata exposition, complete with transition (T) and secondary theme (S). But the sonata model is soon contradicted by an immediate reversion to the principal theme in tonic, following the end of S in measure 31. A slow-movement

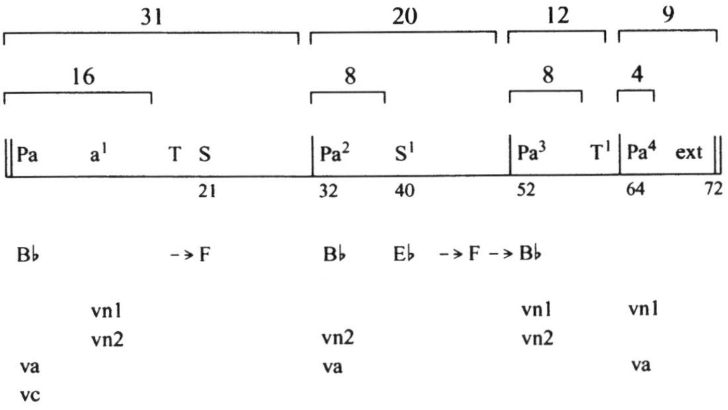

```
        31                    20           12        9
┌──────────────────┐  ┌────────────┐  ┌──────┐  ┌──────┐
        16                    8             8        4
┌──────────┐          ┌──────┐       ┌──────┐  ┌──┐
‖Pa    a¹    T   S │Pa²    S¹ │Pa³    T¹│Pa⁴   ext‖
                21      32    40        52        64       72

B♭              -> F   B♭     E♭   -> F -> B♭

         vn1                          vn1      vn1
         vn2           vn2            vn2
    va                 va                       va
    vc
```

FIGURE 7.6 Op. 33/2/iii

form without development? Possibly, although the recurrence of the secondary theme in the subdominant at measure 40 is disturbing, as is the series of events that follows: two additional recurrences of *Pa* (the second abbreviated), with a return to *T* intervening. Crucial to this movement's haunting effect is the persistence of its principal idea, presented always as a duet whose participants change from one occurrence to the next, as indicated beneath the diagram. The relatively agitated transition and secondary material repeatedly set this tranquil thought in relief as the movement unwinds, and a semblance of sonata logic is inscribed in the recurrence (in reverse order) of *S* and *T*. The different guises in which the opening theme appears belong to the rhetoric of variation, and the multiple recurrences after contrast suggest rondo elements as well. Most telling of all is the scheme of progressively shorter time intervals between statements of *P* (delineating four sections lasting thirty-one, twenty, twelve, and nine measures, respectively) and the concomitant shrinking of the theme itself: sixteen measures in the opening section, eight measures in each of the middle portions, and four at the close—a palpable acceleration in structural rhythm whose underlying directional thrust helps validate the peculiar liberties of the form.

Concerto-Related Forms

A final category of exceptional movements encompasses those whose designs betray the influence of the solo concerto, with its characteristic play of contrast between solo and ritornello. Starting with the earliest quartets and extending through the repertory are movements that highlight the first violin as soloist; and among later works are some that engage various instruments in stretches of concertante-style figural display. The course of events in such a movement is sometimes marked

by a veritable scheme of alternation between texturally consolidated, thematically salient phrases and intervening passages of relatively florid, rhythmically
continuous figuration. Inevitably, differences in volume and timbre prove subtler
than those of a concerto movement with orchestral support; yet the ritornello-
like effect is often unmistakable, and there are a number of movements whose
overall shape, however abnormal or ambiguous when heard solely in terms of a
sonata form model, proves readily explainable when viewed as an amalgamation
of ritornello and sonata principles.

Especially notable in this respect are the slow movements of three quartets
from the 1780s, Op. 33/5, Op. 50/2, and Op. 55/1, each of which comprises two
principal parts, exposition and recapitulation, with an intervening transition whose
function proves analogous to that of a central ritornello. In two of these movements, the concerto-like manner is underscored by notated cadenzas (mm. 41–50
in Op. 33/5; mm. 28–33 and 61–67 in Op. 55/1), and all three share the structural peculiarity of beginning with an eight-measure statement that closes with
a cadence in tonic. In each case, this opening idea may be heard as a ritornello,
because it serves to introduce the movement's principal theme in preparation for
the more pointedly soloistic discourse that follows (i.e., the first solo proper, culminating with a trill and cadence in the secondary key). In the two later instances,
Opp. 50/2/ii and 55/1/ii, Haydn reinforces the analogy with an opening ritornello
by withholding the first violin from thematic participation at the outset—a tactic
that permits it to enter as a fresh solo voice after the cadence, an octave higher
than the second violin's introductory statement. (In Op. 55/1/ii, the first violin
is silent altogether for the first eight measures.)

~

Given the structural ingenuity, expressive depth, and general vitality of the
quartets' fugues, rondos, and other exceptional schemes, it may seem odd that
Haydn chose not to draw on their possibilities more often. His indulgence in formal hybrids and other nonstandard designs was especially cautious, almost systematically so, as if having tried something new, he was sooner or later moved to
return—but often just once—to reexamine, validate, or amplify: there are two
sonata-rondo hybrids with refrain-like opening themes (Opp. 74/2/iv and 76/2/iv),
two rondo-type last movements with fugal episodes (Opp. 55/1/iv and 71/3/iv),
two post–Op. 33 finales that incorporate a change of tempo while combining elements of rondo and variation (Opp. 71/2/iv and 76/4/iv), and two unusual first
movements that culminate with a display of fugal technique (Opp. 76/5/i and
76/6/i). Even the Op. 20/2 Capriccio and the Op. 76/6 Fantasia make a pair,
given the extraordinary liberties subsumed by their similarly suggestive titles.

The potential attractiveness of such schemes notwithstanding, Haydn may
have felt he had good reason to use them sparingly. Much of the delight of his

more customary forms, after all, comes from his gift for inviting us to participate knowingly in the unfolding narrative while stretching the stylistic norms on which that narrative is based. As we join in the game, a particular transformation or aberrant detail can be recognized as a challenge to assumptions founded on our prior musical experiences. From this perspective, we can imagine some reluctance on Haydn's part to test the patience of his admirers with baffling structures and the attendant impression of their inventor's overbearing presence. The promise of intimate communication, permitting performers and listeners to concentrate on intricate details without being excessively mystified by the larger design, was a touchstone of Haydn's idiom. The rare occurrences of unusual forms help define and illuminate the space in which the more reassuring dialogues take place. By specifying certain perimeters of his oeuvre, their presence sharpens our understanding of his genius for reconciling convention and novelty in the works that lie within.

Part III: The Opus Groups

8

The Earliest Quartets
(ca. 1755–60 [?ca. 1757–59])

Op. 0; Op. 1 Nos. 1, 2, 3, 4, and 6;
Op. 2 Nos. 1, 2, 4, and 6

We can be thankful to Griesinger's volume of *Biographische Notizen* for a portrayal of the setting in which Haydn's first quartet came about: the gatherings at Baron Fürnberg's castle, the members of the ensemble that performed, including the composer himself, and the fond reception by which "Haydn took courage to work further in this form."[1]

Griesinger sheds no useful light, however, on the matter of when the event in question took place. His odd comment that Haydn was eighteen years old at the time (which would take us back to ca. 1750, the beginning of his adult life, before he would have had a chance to build a reputation or attract a patron's notice) cannot be accurate. Given what is known of Haydn's association with Fürnberg, the available record of his other activities during the years in question, and various additional pieces of evidence, a probable date would be circa 1755–57.[2] The musical craftsmanship on display also points to a later date. Technically polished and stylistically consistent, but at the same time resourcefully varied in texture, sonority, and thematic invention, all ten quartets bespeak a well-honed knowledge of contemporary musical customs and an ability to make wise compositional choices. In short, they reveal Haydn not as a beginner but as an accomplished artist with a distinctive voice of his own.

Could any of the quartets have originated later than the decade of the 1750s? In the absence of evidence to the contrary, datings beyond 1760 are possible, although speculation along these lines must take into account not only the quartets' stylistic resemblances to one another (suggesting a relatively narrow time frame between first and last), but also the composer's changing circumstances, most notably his entry into Prince Esterházy's service in 1761. His employer's requests for music in other genres, along with the new burden of administrative responsibilities, likely would have left him little time or motivation to continue writing string quartets.

The earliest datings, derived from contemporary manuscripts or catalogues, provide upper limits to the time of composition but are in fact all too late to shed much light on the matter: 1762 for Opp. 1/1, 2, 3, and 6, and 2/4 and 6; 1763 for Opp. 1/4, 2/1, and 0; and 1765 for Op. 2/2.[3] (Regarding the opus number designations, there is no indication that Haydn himself intended to number the earliest quartets or to distribute them in specific sets; and their collective appearance in Paris and Amsterdam prints, from which the traditional numbering derives, was a development for which he was not directly responsible. In references to early catalogue entries and manuscripts, our use of the standard numbers is purely a matter of convenience.)

No autograph manuscripts are known to survive for any of the earliest quartets. However, listings in the composer's *Entwurf-Katalog* attest to the authenticity of all but one (Op. 1/6 is not listed); and all but Opp. 0 and 2/4 are represented by sources of good pedigree (i.e., manuscript copies that can be linked directly with Haydn himself and his circle), two of which appear to include corrections in the composer's hand.[4] Numerous other manuscript copies of these works survive, and their geographic distribution, along with the additional evidence of listings in contemporary thematic catalogues, attest to the early works' appeal among widening circles of amateurs in the 1760s. It is possible that Haydn himself may have actively promoted their dissemination, once he had the resources to hire professional copyists and market his works, although there is little in the way of proof for this.[5]

In any event, circulation of the quartets through manuscript copies was eventually joined by the printed editions that extended their reach and enhanced their composer's reputation. As summarized in table 8.1, the process began with prints issued by the Parisian publishers La Chevardière and Huberty in 1764. Before long all ten quartets were represented, but not without a degree of confusion as to the genre or authorship of certain works included in the published sets: the prints issued by La Chevardière and Hummel comprised six compositions each, in accordance with prevailing custom; but as indicated in our table, only one collection (item 3, Hummel's Op. 1) consists purely of Haydn quartets. Others mix quartets with works belonging properly to other categories, some not even by Haydn.

The first batch of quartets to appear comprised the four included in La Chevardière's 1764 print (item 1), where they stand beside a pair of flute quartets by Carl Joseph Toeschi, here erroneously attributed to Haydn. La Chevardière's later reissuing of the authentic Haydn works (item 6), now supplied with the opus number 4, sheds the Toeschi pieces and replaces them with an additional authentic quartet (which became known as Op. 1/6) and a symphony (now designated as No. 107), scored here for strings alone.

In 1765, J. J. Hummel of Amsterdam offered a collection (item 3) that included the four quartets found in La Chevardière's original 1764 print, plus Op. 1/6

TABLE 8.1 Haydn's early quartets published in Paris and Amsterdam, 1764–68. Dates are given as in *JHW*, 12/1, *Kritischer Bericht*,* except for item 6. In column 3, standard opus numbers are listed sequentially and not in order of appearance in the collection.

Publisher	Date	Haydn quartets	Other works
1) La Chevardière	1764[a]	Op. 1/1–4	2 flute quartets by Toeschi[b]
2) Huberty (titled *Simphonia a più strumenti obligati*)	1764[c]	Op. 0	none
3) Hummel, Op. 1	1765[d]	Op. 0, 1/1–4, 6	none
4) La Chevardière, Op. 3	1766[e]	Op. 2/1, 2, 4	3 sextets for 2 horns and strings, 2 by Haydn (Hob. II:21, 22; see 5 below), one spurious (Hob. II:F5)
5) Hummel, Op. 2	?1766[f]	Op. 2/1, 2, 4, 6	Op. 2/3 and 5 (= Hob. II:21, 22, without the horn parts; see 4 above)
6) La Chevardière, Op. 4	1768[g]	Op. 1/1–4, 6	Op. 1/5 (= Symphony No. 107, here scored for strings alone)

[a]Advertised on 30 January.

[b]See Hoboken, *Werkverzeichnis*, 1:361.

[c]Based on the dating of a Huberty catalogue.

[d]Advertised on 13 April.

[e]Advertised in March.

[f]Announced as forthcoming on 8 September 1766 (Johansson, *Hummel*, 1:80).

[g]Advertised in April (Johansson, *French Music Publishers' Catalogues*, 74).

*For further information on the early publication history of the quartets (including relevant bibliographical references), see Feder, *Kritischer Bericht*, 25–30.

and another quartet, not represented in either of the French publisher's compilations but previously published by Huberty in Paris under the anomalous title *Simphonia a più strumenti obligati* (item 2); Hummel assigned this group the opus number 1. A year later, in 1766, La Chevardière published three of the remaining quartets not included in previous collections, along with three sextets for strings and horns (item 4); and Hummel's closely related publication, which may have come out in the same year, dropped one of the sextets in favor of the one remaining true quartet (item 5). With this last effort, all ten quartets were represented in published form, and when Ignaz Pleyel undertook an authoritative *Collection complette des quatuors d'Haydn* at the start of the nineteenth century, the models he chose for the two groups to be designated as Op. 1 and Op. 2 went back, respectively, to La Chevardière's Op. 4 (item 6) and Hummel's second collection (item 5). Unfortunately, this decision meant that the quartet we recognize as Op. 0 was excised from the canon, and it gave rise to two misapprehensions: first, that there were two discrete groups of quartets in question (rather than a

more arbitrary allocation of individual works); second, that the two groups together comprised twelve true quartets (Op. 1/5 is a symphony, as we have noted,
and Op. 2/3 and 5 originated as sextets). As for Op. o, this piece was destined to
remain obscure until the early twentieth century, when its authenticity was
freshly acknowledged and its odd opus number assigned to indicate its affiliation
with the nine other quartets represented in the traditional Opp. 1 and 2.

Is there any significant correlation between the traditional opus numbers
and the order in which the quartets may actually have been composed? As the
early publication projects did not begin until 1764 (probably several years, in
other words, after the last of the quartets had been written), there seems no reason to suppose that the works accumulated for publication by La Chevardière,
Huberty, and Hummel in 1764–65 (collectively representing Opp. o, 1/1–4, and
1/6) necessarily originated before those published subsequently (for example, La
Chevardière's Op. 3, representing Op. 2/1, 2, and 4). Nevertheless, certain evidence may suggest a somewhat earlier date of composition for those published in
1764–65. In Haydn's *Entwurf-Katalog*, begun in 1765, the quartets recognized as
Op. 1/3, 4, 2, o, and 1 came first. Listed in this order on page 3, each was originally designated by the term cassatio. Op. 2/4 follows Op. 1/1 on the same page
but is called a divertimento, and Op. 2/6, listed on page 4, also bears the label divertimento. Finally, on page 5 come the only ones actually entered in Haydn's
hand, Op. 2/1 and 2, and both are given as divertimenti (the others are in the
hand of Haydn's copyist Joseph Elssler).[6]

Whatever this distribution of listings means with respect to relative dates of
composition, there might be some significance in the way the generic titles are
assigned (cassatio vs. divertimento), even though these labels are unspecific and
virtually interchangeable in mid-eighteenth-century usage. According to an account by a contemporary,[7] Haydn himself appears to have used the word cassatio for the earliest of these works; and if this is true, he must at some later point
have changed his mind about their proper designation: not only are the two
quartets he himself entered labeled divertimento, but Elssler's original labels on
page 3 were later altered by Haydn (from cassatio to divertimento).

Stylistic Overview of the Quartets as a Group

How can we best characterize the early quartets, and to what extent do they cohere as a group? Each displays a variety of topics, textures, and compositional
techniques, which likely reflect the composer's everyday musical experiences while
contributing to his cultivation of a personal idiom. Their ensemble technique
spans a range of possibilities, with elements of simple melody and accompaniment sometimes appearing side by side with allusions to the disciplines of canon,
two-voice counterpoint, and imitative polyphony. Within a given quartet, high-

spirited movements with tempo markings of allegro or presto stand in contrast to the courtly manners and whimsy of the moderate-tempo dance movements, and the soloistic idiom typical of the Adagios provides opportunities for melodic decoration as well as expressive intensity.

According to the predominant large-scale design, an elaborate slow movement stands as a proud centerpiece to the cycle; flanking it on either side are a pair of minuet-trio complexes, each in itself rendered symmetrically as a three-part da capo form, while extroverted, quick-tempo movements begin and end the cycle (see table 8.2, in which the quartets' movement sequences are displayed). Two variants of the model, seen in Opp. 1/3 and 2/6, disturb the large-scale equilibrium by switching the slow movement to the beginning and placing a fast A B A da capo form in the vacated middle position. There were to be no sequels to the first of these alternative plans, that of Op. 1/3, which begins with a slow-tempo sonata form; but the exceptional procedure for Op. 2/6, leading off with a set of variations, was one to which Haydn would return on several later occasions.

As can be seen in table 8.2, proportions among the different movement types tend to be approximately similar from one quartet to the next. In several that do have relatively long fast movements or Adagios, greater length is matched by greater internal complexity, as in Op. 2/2 and 4, both of which do indeed appear to come relatively late in the works' chronological sequence. Such distinctions notwithstanding, the quartets betray a general impression of consistency in form and procedure, and many generalizations to be made about a given work apply equally well to the others.

The Fast-Tempo Movements

Two in each work, variously assigned to first, middle, or last position, the quartets' fast movements abound in beat-marking rhythmic patterns and melodic materials that derive mostly from triadic, scalar, repeated-note, or neighbor-note gestures. Simple meters prevail ($\frac{2}{4}$ and $\frac{3}{8}$), although Haydn does choose the greater metrical complexity of $\frac{6}{8}$ for three first movements (Op. 1/1 and 6; Op. 2/4).

The full-fledged sonata forms with which most of the quartets begin and end include polished models of structural cohesion as well as thematic contrast and diversity. The first violin naturally bears chief melodic responsibility, and yet the other instruments participate thematically in dialogues and partnerships that reinforce the logic of an unfolding design. The first movement of Op. 1/4 illustrates both the thematic resourcefulness of these forms and the liveliness of their textures. As shown in example 8.1, the primary theme alone displays a wealth of interactions. The initial resonance of double stops in the first violin, supported by chord roots in the cello, echoes in the inner parts' slurred afterbeats (mm. 1–4). A competitive exchange of triple-stopped chords between the violins intensifies

TABLE 8.2 Summary statistics for Opp. 0, 1, and 2; SF = sonata form, M/T = minuet/trio, special titles in brackets (For measure counts that accompany the designated forms, "r" denotes the presence of one or more written-out repeats.)

Op.No.	Hob.No.	Movement				
		i	ii	iii	iv	v
0	II:6	E♭ $\frac{2}{4}$ Presto SF 92	E♭/Cm $\frac{3}{4}$ M/T 28/32	B♭ ¢ Adagio SF 76	E♭ $\frac{3}{4}$ M/T 32/30	E♭ $\frac{2}{4}$ Presto SF 74
1/1	III:1	B♭ $\frac{6}{8}$ Presto SF 62	B♭/E♭ $\frac{3}{4}$ M/T* 34/28	E♭ e Adagio Binary 42	B♭ $\frac{3}{4}$ M/T 26/16	B♭ $\frac{2}{4}$ Presto SF 68
1/2	III:2	E♭ $\frac{3}{8}$ Allegro molto SF (irreg.) 128	E♭/B♭ $\frac{3}{4}$ M/T 28/30	B♭ e Adagio Rounded binary 26	E♭/Cm $\frac{3}{4}$ M/T 26/30	E♭ $\frac{2}{4}$ Presto SF 78
1/3	III:3	D $\frac{3}{4}$ Adagio SF 88	D/G $\frac{3}{4}$ M/T 20/24	D/Dm $\frac{2}{4}$ Presto ABA Da capo [Scherzo] 24/31	D/Dm $\frac{3}{4}$ M/T 28/24	D/Bm $\frac{3}{8}$ Presto ABA Da capo 50/48
1/4	III:4	G $\frac{3}{8}$ Presto SF 158	G/Gm $\frac{3}{4}$ M/T 30/28	C e Adagio ma non tanto SF 42	G/Gm $\frac{3}{4}$ M/T 26/32	G/Em $\frac{2}{4}$ Presto ABA Da capo 71/28
1/6	III:6	C $\frac{6}{8}$ Presto assai SF 64	C/F $\frac{3}{4}$ M/T 36/20	G $\frac{2}{4}$ Adagio SF (irreg.) 62	C/Cm $\frac{3}{4}$ M/T 32/40	C $\frac{2}{4}$ Allegro SF 76
2/1	III:7	A $\frac{2}{4}$ Allegro SF 110	A/Am $\frac{3}{4}$ M/T 24/28	D $\frac{2}{4}$ Adagio SF 72	A $\frac{3}{4}$ M/T 26/16	A $\frac{2}{4}$ Allegro molto SF 79
2/2	III:8	E $\frac{2}{4}$ Allegro molto SF 124	E/Em $\frac{3}{4}$ M/T 24/30	A e Adagio SF 42	E/Em $\frac{3}{4}$ M/T 32/30	E $\frac{2}{4}$ Presto SF 123
2/4	III:10	F $\frac{6}{8}$ Presto SF (irreg.) 86	F/B♭ $\frac{3}{4}$ M/T 36/28	Fm $\frac{3}{4}$ Adagio SF 92	F/B♭ $\frac{3}{4}$ Allegretto M/T 20/22	F $\frac{2}{4}$ Allegro SF 76
2/6	III:12	B♭ $\frac{3}{4}$ Adagio Strophic var. 120(r)	B♭/E♭ $\frac{3}{4}$ M/T 35/24	E♭/A♭ $\frac{2}{4}$ Presto ABA Da capo [Scherzo] 42/16	B♭/B♭m $\frac{3}{4}$ M/T 28/16	B♭ $\frac{3}{8}$ Presto SF 75

*The designation for trio is "Minuet secondo."

EXAMPLE 8.1 Op. 1/4/i, mm. 1–12

the discourse (mm. 5–8); the lower parts then withdraw in order to spotlight a rhythmically accelerated solo flourish (mm. 9–10), and finally all parts join to form a cadence (mm. 11–12).

A different kind of ensemble play animates the open-ended counterstatement that follows: after a replica of the opening four measures (13–16), the instruments gather on the downbeat of measure 17 for a loud tonic chord, intensified by triple stops in the inner parts, and this surge of energy and volume signals the start of a new phase of action. Spirited into the orbit of the dominant, the first violin and viola take off in dialogue (mm. 18–25), exchanging an arpeggiated sixteenth-note figure, which they pass to the second violin (mm. 26–32) for yet another timbral contrast before the first violin jumps back into the fray, sounding high above the others prior to the descent to a full cadence in the new key at measure 40. At this juncture, the complexion changes again as the ensemble pulls back to pianissimo. The lower parts mimic the violins' impertinent, paired eighth-note asides (mm. 42–44), and the air of conspiracy then deepens as an inflected sixth scale degree hints at a turn to the minor. After a moment of breathless suspense, crowned by a fermata in measure 48, a new sonority breaks the spell: a rising four-part unison (m. 49, repeated in m. 53), an emblem of consolidation as the exposition nears its conclusion.

The development section pursues the theme of rapidly changing ensemble relationship by interspersing recollections of previous dialogues and points of contrast with strident unison interjections (mm. 59–100). And the recapitulation, having begun with an almost literal recurrence of the movement's opening phrases, confronts us with a major sonority-related surprise at measure 117: a loud subdominant chord, so fully scored that it engages no fewer than ten of the upper instruments' twelve strings. This is a stroke of rhetorical exaggeration, as well as a fitting culmination to the pattern of ever more dense, multistring chords: double stops at the outset; alternating triple stops in the second phrase; fuller-voiced sonority at measure 17 with triple stops in the two inner parts; then finally this magnified equivalent of that earlier chord, comparably positioned as a springboard for the transition theme's dialoguing figuration.

Can distinctions be drawn between the fast opening movements and the character of their corresponding finales? The latter tend to focus on a narrower range of thematic contrast, and their accent on surface momentum readily suggests a headlong rush to the finish. Key differences in quality and function are inscribed to some extent in the outer movements' opening ideas, generally more expansive in first movements, more compact in finales. Op. o, exemplifying this trait, begins with an unaccompanied announcement by the first violin: a signal that the quartet's narrative is about to begin. The second violin joins two measures later, to be followed by the two lower instruments in turn, each taking the same introductory bow. It is not until the middle of measure 10 that all parts sound together, and not until measure 15 that we have a sense of the ensemble's full engagement in a rhythmically and melodically continuous discourse. The finale, by contrast, brings all four parts into play at the outset, presents a scurrying thematic idea in sixteenth notes as early as measure 2 (pointedly different from the first movement's initial quarter- and eighth-note pace), and launches into a steady stream of sixteenths as early as measure 10.

Whether fashioned to begin the cycle or draw it to a close, the sonata form movements mostly resemble one another with respect to overall structure, with expositions separated from the remainder of the movement by standard binary repeats, generally sizable development sections, and recapitulations whose order of events proves usually at least roughly comparable, and in some cases nearly identical, to that of the opening section. Several of the first movements do surprise, however, by digressing from the normal procedure and substituting an alternative logic.

This is clearly the case in Op. 2/4/i (F major), whose exposition is followed by an initial stretch of development, fourteen measures long, that ends with a jolt (m. 48). A half cadence in the supertonic at this point, emphasized by a round of chordal impacts, is dramatized by a general pause in measure 49—an early example of Haydn's using this device to accentuate a moment of suspense or structural punctuation (see fig. 8.1). Could what follows be the start of the recapitulation? The preceding span of development seems brief relative to the length of the exposition (thirty-four measures), and the V of ii chord on which motion has come to a stop tells us that expectations of a return to tonic are premature. The pause is too emphatic to be heard as a mere breathing space, however; in fact, the course of events that follows sends mixed signals, recalling the opening of the

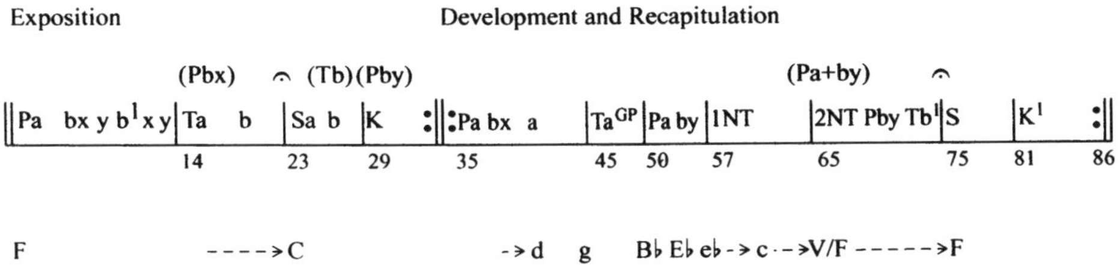

Exposition   Development and Recapitulation

(Pbx)	⌢ (Tb)(Pby)							(Pa+by)	⌢		
‖Pa bx y b¹x y	Ta b	Sa b	K :‖	‖:Pa bx a	Ta^GP	Pa by	1NT	2NT Pby Tb¹	S	K¹	:‖
14	23	29	35		45	50	57	65	75	81	86

F ----→C →d g Bb Eb eb-→c--→V/F -----→F

FIGURE 8.1 Op. 2/4/i

exposition while at the same time pointedly evading tonic: first by shifting to the subdominant, Bb (securing a bifocal connection to the preceding half cadence— V of G minor to Bb), then passing through several other keys before settling on a half cadence in F (m. 64). At this point, we can hear allusions to primary theme material, tethered to a dominant pedal, but not until the return of the secondary theme at measure 75 is the home key reaffirmed. Basic sonata form elements are accounted for, but the dynamic intersection of key and theme is such that reentry into the orbit of tonic is postponed to the last twenty-three measures— not much more than a quarter of the movement's total length.[8]

How can we best interpret such formal idiosyncrasies, which seem potentially baffling when viewed next to the more predictable opening movements? Although the design just examined may be a stylistic aberration when measured against the norms of late-eighteenth-century sonata form, it might not necessarily have seemed so to Haydn's mid-century contemporaries; and the composer himself, far from attempting to perplex or astonish, may instead have been exploring ways to individualize the logic of a first-movement form by complicating (and perhaps thereby validating) an inherently straightforward principle of close correspondence between outer sections.

The Dance Movements

Given the substantial size of the minuets and trios, and the fact that there are two of them in each work, they bear obvious weight as an ingredient of the cycle. Stylistically, their range extends from courtly elegance to impressions of rough-hewn comedy, and their various binary and rounded binary schemes allow for much variety of structural detail in the relationship between first and second parts. The minuet proper normally relies on the first violin to project relatively long, gracefully arched phrases. Melodic delivery is often enhanced by having the second violin move in tandem with the first, either in thirds, sixths, or octaves, and the viola frequently doubles the cello's beat-marking bass; yet there is also room for the textural complexity of changing alliances among parts and snippets of imitative polyphony.

In several instances (usually involving the second of a quartet's two min-uets), Haydn showcases the stark sonority of two-part counterpoint with upper and lower parts both paired in octaves. The minuet of Op. 1/3/iv is one of two in which this texture is sustained throughout: an elegantly sculptured melody in the violins, predominantly conjunct and rhythmically varied, is set off against a viola/cello line whose dogged succession of leaping and stepwise quarter notes, moving variously in parallel or contrary motion to the violins, occasionally drops out for a beat or two to let them shine through unaccompanied. Such octave-based sonorities evidently did not go unnoticed by Haydn's contemporaries. A critic writing in the Hamburg *Unterhaltungen* in 1766 states that "whether [Haydn's] minuets in octaves are for everyone, I will leave undecided. They are good for entertainment; but one is thereby easily given to imagine that one is hearing beggars, father and son, singing in octaves."[9] Later that same year, an essay in the *Wiener Diarium* titled "Von dem wienerischen Geschmack in der Musik" (Con-cerning the Viennese Taste in Music), thought to have been written by Carl Dit-ters,[10] countered with a favorable view of Haydn's octave-doubling technique and declared it to be the composer's own invention.[11]

The trios, abounding in character, novelty, and topical variety, are a natural locus for contrast against the backdrop of the minuet proper, and the impression of crossing into a different realm of sonority and atmosphere is often pronounced. In Op. 1/6/iv, for example, the minuet had been dominated throughout by stri-dent octave doubling and two-part counterpoint. Its end comes with a feeling of relief and expectation of change, and the start of the trio does not disappoint: the cello temporarily drops out, and a solo first violin breaks the silence in the guise of a country fiddler, marking the opening downbeats with embellished quarter notes, while the inner parts sustain motion with lilting staccato after-beats. A more intense character informs several trios (notably in Opp. 0/ii and 2/2/ii) in which the darkening of tonal color from major to minor gives rise to an adventure in chromaticism; and in Op. 2/1/ii, the change to minor furnishes a backdrop for novel, exotic sonority as each instrument unfurls its own layer of sound and rhythmic impulse: pizzicato downbeats in the cello; virtually nonstop leaping quarter notes in the viola, likewise sounded pizzicato; a barrage of broken-chord figures in the second violin; and the first violin itself, poised above the rest of the ensemble as a soloist, bounding through rhythmically differentiated arpeg-giations before driving to a cadence.

The Adagios

Haydn fashions most of the quartets' slow movements as expressive solo vehicles for first violin. As such, they stand equally aloof from the mechanical energy of the fast movements, the formality of the minuets, and the coloristic impetus of the trios. The predominant two-reprise format provides the basis for an exalted style of melodic delivery, with sharply outlined declarations, wide leaps—sometimes extremely wide—within phrases, a propensity for trills, appoggiaturas, and other decorations, a tendency to climb high above the accompanying parts, and in one case, Op. 2/2/iii, a pair of bona fide cadenzas (mm. 15 and 39).

The movements differ from one another in their degree of embellishment and rhythmic detail, in the density and rhythmic impetus of their accompaniments, and in the extent of interaction between soloist and second violin. Whereas Op. 1/6/iii displays a wistfully amorous, richly decorated melody, veiled in a con sordino haze and weightlessly supported by a pizzicato accompaniment, the central movement of Op. o is more austere melodically; and in the slow opening movement of Op. 1/3, the second violin joins the first in an elegant duet whose interwoven lines and rhythmically undifferentiated bass resemble the manner of a Baroque trio sonata.[12]

Motivic Process

Haydn's gift for motivic elaboration—building a phrase from a melodic or rhythmic kernel, fashioning subsequent phrases as variants or derivatives, and thus bestowing cohesion on a developing, goal-directed narrative—proves already well developed among these works, especially in fast-tempo movements such as Op. 1/3/iii that take advantage of the medium's capacity for thematic banter between parts (see ex. 8.2). The initial idea, an arpeggiated figure followed by an appoggiatura (mm. 1–2), invites a balancing response in the second violin, the appoggiatura now resolving in the opposite direction. Measure 5 inverts the staccato arpeggiation to coincide with the shift of tonal focus to the dominant (mm. 5–6), and the strain closes by intensifying the leaping motion, then dispensing with the appoggiatura altogether (mm. 7–8).

The second part begins by proposing an altered replica of the opening exchange: first the melodic compass narrows as the harmony veers to E minor (mm. 9–12), then widens to form still another pair of variants with the promise of imminent return to tonic (mm. 13–16). Meanwhile, the pattern of change in the appoggiatura's direction—descending in measure 2, then rising in measure 4—is mapped onto a larger, eight-measure span (mm. 9–16) and reversed: rising in measures 10 and 12, falling in measures 14 and 16. The next four measures masquerade as an oasis of contrast, a momentary withdrawal of surface energy before a drive to the close, yet there is a palpable connection with measures 1–4: the violins exchange variants of the appoggiatura idea in augmentation, while arpeggiating motion persists in the lower voices. Finally (mm. 21–24), the violins join in a variant that welds the dialogue of measures 5–8 into a streamlined phrase that propels the music to a decisive conclusion.

EXAMPLE 8.2 Op. 1/3/iii, mm. 1–24 (violins only)

Development of an initial idea may give rise to actual thematic contrast while at the same time contributing to a larger impression of unity. In the finale of Op. 1/1, the dotted rhythm plus triplet (marked *1m*) lends energy and thematic identity to an opening six-measure phrase, quoted in example 8.3a. In the transition that follows, the inner parts' recollection of *1m* secures a tight connection to the principal idea, but now *1m* is paired in dialogue with a new figure in sixteenth notes (ex. 8.3b). Once the new key has been secured, measures 18–21 deliver a degree of thematic contrast while drawing a connection to the opening triplet idea and its previous developments (see ex. 8.3c): the inner parts' variant of *1m* begins the phrase, while the first violin's response (*2m*) reverses the direction of the triplet and shifts from the end of the measure to the beginning. The measures that follow take still another step in the process of variation and transformation: first a reiteration of *1m* (m. 22, as in m. 18), then a series of telescoped reiterations of *2m* that lead down through the octave to a cadence on the downbeat of measure 26 (see ex. 8.3d). At this point, an extension furnishes another particle of relationship, recalling the sixteenth-note arpeggiation first sounded in measure 8 and stretching the phrase begun in measure 22 to six measures, so that it balances the length of the opening idea.

Aspects of Harmony, Rhythm, and Phrasing

That some of the designs cited above offer little in the way of harmonic intrigue need not be regarded as a drawback: there is more than enough motivic work and textural diversity to occupy our attention, so that a simple harmonic backdrop

EXAMPLE 8.3 Op. 1/1/v

(a) mm. 1–6 (violin 1 only)

(b) mm. 7–12 (violins and viola)

(c) mm. 18–21 (violins and viola)

(d) mm. 23–27 (violin 1 only)

may be appreciated as a desirable constraint. And yet the harmony is by no means always bland. Even in movements with minimal tonal action, there are instances of suspense or rhetorical impact where this element plays a key role, as in the first-movement development section of Op. 1/1 in B♭, where the foreign tones D♭ and G♭ sound a note of gravity as they steer the harmony momentarily to B♭ minor on the threshold of the recapitulation.

Apart from such an occasional change of mode, the earliest quartets seldom venture further afield than keys with one accidental more or less than tonic, although distant areas are sometimes touched on in passing. Haydn's preference for a conservative tonal idiom, tailored for structural coherence but occasionally embellished with color and novelty, is matched by a related approach to matters of rhythm and phrasing. On the whole, these works tend toward metrical conformity and surface continuity, with few disruptive syncopations, moderate to fast rate of chord change, and much reliance on regular phrase rhythm in the presentation of harmonically stable themes. Strategically placed fermatas (as in Op. 2/1/iii, just before the recapitulation) lend an occasional element of temporal elasticity and rhetorical accent, and in the trio of Op. 2/4/iv, we find an early but brilliant instance of a phrase whose metrical implications disagree with the bar line. What happens is that a rhythmically halting but metrically congruent figure in the first reprise, bracketed in example 8.4a, is recalled at the beginning of the second part in a curiously telescoped form. The second-beat rest has been excised so that a two-beat pattern results, as shown in example 8.4b (mm. 29–34). In this compressed version, the pattern contradicts the triple meter so thoroughly that if performers heed the implied accents of melody, harmony, and surface rhythm and ignore the bar lines, the phrase will suggest momentary removal to an altogether different dance step, that of the duple meter bourrée. To represent the aural phenomenon of a virtual change in meter, example 8.4b includes a re-barring of the passage.

Phrase structures in the earliest quartets, although seldom predictable to the point of mechanical sameness—and always informed by a variety of small-scale melodic shapes, processes, and changeable relationships between harmony and metrical accent[13]—are often ordered to sustain a regular two- or four-measure phrase rhythm over the course of a theme or section. In Op. 1/4/i, quoted earlier in example 8.1, four detached, one-measure units of rhythm and sonority form a coherent four-measure phrase. The next segment, comprising an identical pair of open-ended, two-measure ideas, flows into yet a third kind of melodic construction, a continuous melodic arc that spans four measures to close on the downbeat of measure 12. Along the way, a certain dynamic balance arises between accelerating surface rhythm and the progressively expanding melodic units (one, two, then four measures): a subtle yet significant source of cohesion in the midst of diversity in melody, texture, surface rhythm, and ensemble play.

A more intricate phraseology marks the last movement of Op. 2/4, in which a scheme of altered phrase lengths serves to highlight key differences in function between the form's outer sections. The movement begins with a quizzical mixture of equilibrium on the one hand (a pair of equal-sized phrases, the first cadencing on tonic, the second on the dominant) and unrest on the other. The phrases in question are each five measures long (3 + 2; see ex. 8.5a), and the tension that naturally accompanies their lopsided phrase rhythm, underscored by the disturbance of syncopation, lends propulsion toward an eventual cadence in the dominant by the end of the following phrase (mm. 11–18). In the recapitulation, Haydn reshapes his material in ways that help neutralize the exposition's destabilizing forces in the interest of resolution and closure. To begin with, the

EXAMPLE 8.4 Op. 2/4/iv

(a) mm. 21–24 (violin 1 only)

(b) mm. 29–34 (violin 1 and cello), rebarred below to show the implied meter

energy-packed transition phrase cited above (mm. 11–18) is almost entirely deleted, but not quite: a patch of that theme's main idea, comprising pairs of six-teenth notes in downward sequence, comes back as part of an ingeniously altered version of the recurring primary theme. The opening five-measure statement returns intact (mm. 49–53): however, the latter part of the responding phrase (mm. 54–60, quoted in ex. 8.5b) absorbs the sixteenth-note idea as it expands to a full four measures—a stabilizing element in itself. Additionally, its end is altered to rhyme with the antecedent phrase in the descent to a cadence in tonic—a reversal in harmonic direction with respect to the end of the original consequent phrase (m. 10), and thus a sure sign of restored tonal stability.

Questions of Cyclic Character and Cohesion

From among the ten early quartets, we can designate at least five (Opp. 0; 1/1, 2, and 6; 2/1) as members of a central, normative group, with first movements and finales in sonata form, and third-movement Adagios cast either in the dominant or subdominant key. Two others come close to membership in this group: Op. 2/2, whose unusually large-sized outer movements set it somewhat apart from the others, and Op. 2/4, whose main digressions from the norm are the structural pecu-

EXAMPLE 8.5 Op. 2/4/v (violin 1 only)

(a) mm. 1–10

(b) mm. 49–60

liarities of its opening movement and the unique choice of tonic minor for the Adagio.

Each of the remaining quartets diverges from the model in more striking and significant ways, and each merits notice not only for its structural aberrations but also for the issues it raises regarding cyclic design. Op. 1/3, with an engrossing slow movement at the start and fast-tempo da capo forms for both middle movement and finale, least resembles the others in format. Its various middle sections (i.e., the dance-movement trios and the B sections of the fast movements) are marked by tonal diversity: G for the second-movement trio, D minor in both third and fourth movements, and B minor in the finale. From another perspective, the work proves uniquely consistent tonally in that it clings to the home key of D major as principal tonic for all five movements. The opening Adagio is of particular interest, not only for the fact of the slow movement's promotion to first place, but for the resulting concentration of formal complexity and expressive weight at the head of the cycle.

Op. 2/6, although obviously comparable to Op. 1/3 in its nonstandard tempo sequence, embodies a special cyclic feature of its own with respect to large-scale harmonic design: the keys for the middle sections of its interior movements trace a progressive descent into the flat side of the tonal spectrum. The second-movement trio is in E♭ (three flats), the subdominant of the home key of B♭; the middle movement, with E♭ now as a point of departure, reaches down a fifth to A♭ (four flats)

for its B section; and the fourth movement dips even further, to five flats, by veer-
ing to the tonic minor for its trio.

Is this flat-side journey a significant cyclic phenomenon, and can it be heard?
When the second-movement trio begins, shifting the focus from tonic to subdominant (foreshadowed by the V^7 of IV harmonies near the end of the minuet
but otherwise a fresh sonority at this point), the effect of a shaded, quiet space is
enhanced by the first violin's initial retreat to a long-sustained, middle-register
bb^1 (mm. 36–41) and by the subsequent descent to bb (m. 45, the lowest principal melody note of the movement). The impression of withdrawal, relative to the
immediate surroundings, is still more pronounced in the middle section of the
third-movement Scherzo (mm. 43–58): here, the accompanying parts' repeated
notes, afterbeats, and sustained tones are pointedly subdued by comparison with
the A section's thematic energy and diversity. Meanwhile, the motivically
repetitive first violin part reaches no higher than eb^2, a whole octave lower than
the pitch ceiling of the A section. The opening of the fourth-movement trio
(mm. 29–32) conveys a sense of turning inward, to a state of calm reflection, not
only by its low register, sustained tones, and utter melodic simplicity, but by the
underlying stasis of a reiterated tonic pedal point in the viola and cello.

With the start of the presto finale comes a fresh torrent of sixteenth notes
that all but buries the foregoing images of peace and seclusion. But then, as if
casting a backward glance at those quiet moments before dashing to the end, the
start of the second reprise reduces the dynamic level, darkens the harmony from
major to minor, and slows the pace by sustaining a single pitch (f^2) in the first
violin above a murmur of slurred eighth notes in the second violin, viola, and
cello (mm. 34–37).

Perhaps the most telling signs of cyclic strategy are those witnessed in the G
major quartet, Op. 1/4, a piece whose basic structure proves unusual only in substituting an A B A da capo scheme for the normal sonata form finale. What merits attention here is not so much formal oddity as the preoccupation with a certain rhetorical device: an emphasis on multiple-stopped chordal exclamations
whose salient recurrences promote cyclic cohesion and intermovement resonance.
The quartet's home key of G major is a good one for this idiomatic effect, given
the congenial match between its principal harmonies and the instruments' open
strings (particularly the violins' G and D, and the viola's C and G). We have encountered richly scored chords that incorporate those sounds at important junctures in the first movement (mm. 17 and 117), and we will meet them again as
the work proceeds. In the second-movement trio, for example, triple-stopped
chords in the first violin are a principal thematic event, declaimed repeatedly as
if in protest to the threatening G minor unisons of the lower strings (ex. 8.6a).
Bright, triple- and quadruple-stopped G major chords announce the opening phrase
of the finale's A section (ex. 8.6b) and the B section's second reprise (ex. 8.6c,
which shows the attack on this chord following the second violin's connecting

EXAMPLE 8.6 Op. 1/4

(a) ii, mm. 31–34

(b) v, mm. 1–4

(c) v, mm. 79–81

(d) iii, m. 22

sixteenth notes in m. 79). Such richly scored accents are not common among the quartets. Their forceful imprint in this work stands out as a characteristic sound; and each is so conspicuous, so seemingly out of place in its local context as to call attention to others heard elsewhere in the cycle. Most significant in this respect are the quadruple-stopped chords that the violins proclaim like a pair of exclamation points at the very heart of the middle slow movement. This old-fashioned-sounding solo for first violin, with Baroque-like echo figures in the second violin played con sordino, seems an unlikely environment for the *Sturm und Drang* of heavy, declamatory accents. However, midway through the form, where a move into the key of G minor is confirmed as the bass line comes to a halt on this temporary tonic (m. 22), the first violin responds on beat 2 with an astonishing sonority, a quadruple-stopped G minor chord, to be followed immediately by an odd but perfectly logical stroke, given the movement's premise—a con sordino, quadruple-stopped echo in the second violin (ex. 8.6d). What could this pair of events signify if not a cyclic milestone, a large-scale structural pivot, or a centrally placed, modally inverted reminder of the work's tonal center and its recurrent, unifying sonority? (In an aftershock to the oversized chordal impacts in m. 22, the violins play a corresponding pair of triple stops to accentuate a cadence in F, the movement's subdominant, in m. 25. Locally a pivotal event in its own right, this is the last full cadence before the recapitulation; and perhaps significantly, it coincides with the movement's golden section.)

Stepping back to judge the significance of the earliest quartets, it may be helpful to speak of two opposing yet complementary tendencies. A degree of conformity and predictability in matters of cyclic design, formal outline, and stylistic convention within the different movement types is readily apparent; and from this vantage point, Haydn appears to be establishing stylistic perimeters and defining the basic terms of a new genre. But countering this tendency is an unmistakable bent for novelty and invention, manifested in any number of ways and destined to stand out against the backdrop of otherwise normal surroundings. In effect, predictable features and idiosyncrasies complement one another in an idiomatic chamber style that balances rhetorical clarity with engrossing detail.

That performers and listeners of Haydn's day took notice of these works is apparent in the quartets' dispersal through published editions and manuscripts in the 1760s and well beyond; and their transmission in arrangements for other instruments (e.g., lute, keyboard four hands, keyboard and strings, violin, and cello), as well as for voice and keyboard, further attests to their enduring popularity. The early quartets and their composer were forces to be reckoned with, as is evident from the words of praise as well as censure found in contemporary critical, historical, and anecdotal writings. Differing assessments of an early Haydn trademark—the two-part counterpoint in octaves found in several of the minuets—were noted earlier in our discussion. One of the writings in question, the 1766 *Wiener Diarium* essay, defends Haydn as "the darling of our nation" and describes his "cassatios, quartets and trios" in terms of "a pure and clean water, over which a southerly wind occasionally ripples, and sometimes rises to waves without, however, losing its bed and course."[14] Looking back from a somewhat later time, Gerber's *Historisch-biographisches Lexikon der Tonkünstler* of 1790 refers to the general sensation caused by the quartets as they became known around 1760;[15] and Reichardt, in his *Vertraute Briefe*, fondly recalls the singular aesthetic pleasure of his early acquaintance with one of them.[16]

Although comparison with later accomplishments may be inevitable (as it was, in fact, among Haydn's own contemporaries),[17] these works merit recognition as genuine musical inspirations. Given their command of contemporary forms and styles, plus their well-placed moments of wit and surprise, they rank among Haydn's most important early achievements in instrumental music. Together they represent a milestone in the development of Haydn's craft and musical outlook, and a starting point for his cultivation of the string quartet as an independent genre. They may lack the syntactic richness that informs the later opus groups, yet they can claim something unique and special of their own as reflections of a restless and inventive musical personality, equally intent on celebrating and challenging mid-century customs of musical style and design.

9

Op. 9 (ca. 1768–70)
and Op. 17 (1771)

The quartets of Opp. 9 and 17 merit honor as a landmark in the repertory, for with these works Haydn regained a foothold on a medium that had been paramount to his early achievement as a composer, but that he seemed to have abandoned under the pressure of other commitments. As if resuming an interrupted endeavor, the new works recall many of the earlier quartets' stylistic hallmarks; but they also embody a reassessment of possibilities and an exploration of new directions.

The decision to survey both groups in a single chapter should be understood not as a quest for economy in presentation but as the response to compelling forces in the music itself. Either set can stand on its own, to be sure; and yet the two are bound by a web of correspondences so dense that it seems only reasonable to understand them as two facets of a single inspiration, the latter working to amplify, question, or otherwise complement the implications of the former.

It was noted in chapter 1 that Boccherini's first published set of string quartets had appeared in 1767, and that Haydn's employer and his first violinist Tomasini may have heard these works during a sojourn in Paris in the fall of that year. Whether or not this circumstance was a factor in stimulating Haydn's re-engagement with the genre, it would have been not long after the travelers' return that Haydn set about to write his own first, bona fide quartet opus: a group presumably conceived as a set from the start.

What can be determined about the works' time of origin? For the Op. 9 quartets, nothing so concrete as a dated autograph exists, and the surviving authentic copies for two works of this set, Nos. 1 and 4, cannot be placed within a time frame any narrower than the years 1769–73.[1] More helpful is the fact that all six were registered by the Leipzig publisher Breitkopf in the 1771 supplement to his thematic catalogue of manuscripts for sale.[2] That year is thus secure as an upper limit, but a still earlier date is likely in view of the fact that the Op. 17 quartets

are known to have been completed in 1771. Additional clues may be gleaned
from the entries for Op. 9 in Haydn's *Entwurf-Katalog*: it seems clear from their
placement that they were recorded no earlier than 1768, and Webster has argued
cogently that they may in fact have been entered somewhat later, possibly as late
as 1770.[3] For the quartets of Op. 17 we are on firmer ground: an autograph manuscript containing all six works (variously titled "divertimento a quatro" or "divertimento") survives with the date of 1771.[4]

Like their predecessors, the new quartets circulated in the form of manuscript copies before finding their way (much more quickly now than before) into
the hands of foreign music publishers: prints for the two sets began to appear
with Hummel's editions, Op. 9 in 1771 or 1772 (as Op. 7), and Op. 17 in 1772
(as Op. 9). Among the various early prints, several are notable for the precedents
they established: for Op. 9, the edition by Anton Huberty in Paris, advertised on
30 March 1772, provided the first instance of both the traditional opus number
(i.e., Op. 9) and the sequence of works within the set that later became standard
through Pleyel's *Collection complette*; for Op. 17, the traditional sequence first
appeared in Hummel's Amsterdam edition, in press as of 18 May 1772, and the
now-standard opus number was first assigned in Sieber's Parisian edition, advertised on 10 May 1773.[5]

The order in which the quartets were numbered and presented did indeed
vary from one early edition to the next, and the numbers that eventually became
standard have no claim to authority. Yet for both sets there are grounds for determining what could be described as an authentic sequence. For Op. 17, we
have the autograph manuscript, in which the order is 2, 1, 4, 6, 3, 5 with respect
to the traditional numbering, and this series is confirmed by the order of entries,
all notated in Haydn's hand, in the *Entwurf-Katalog*. Because the catalogue entries for Op. 9 are likewise in Haydn's hand, even though there are no surviving
autographs it seems reasonable to draw the analogy with Op. 17 and regard the
Entwurf-Katalog sequence—4, 1, 3, 2, 5, 6—as authentic.

Given that the works in question appear to have been intended as components of six-item series rather than as completely autonomous pieces, the matter
of numbering would seem to be worth contemplating. But what actual significance do the orderings have? Whether or not they have anything to do with
order of composition is unknowable; and their implications for performance would
seem to be limited, although perhaps not altogether negligible. Performers and
their listeners who ventured to consume an entire opus at a sitting might be able
to appreciate a certain long-range play of contrasts or even the intimation of an
overarching musical narrative. A complete reading of Op. 9 according to the authentic order would thus start off on a note of theatrical intensity with the D
minor quartet (No. 4) and end cheerfully with a far less taxing work in A major
(No. 6). No similarly obvious progression in mood, character, or tonality would
obtain for Op. 17, however: the first quartet in this series (No. 2 in F) makes a

bright splash but is otherwise not particularly well suited for the role of a starting point, while the musical complexities and technical challenges of the last
(No. 5 in G) would probably lead even stalwart connoisseurs to the brink of exhaustion. More important than the quartets' order, perhaps, is the pervasive evidence of a calculated balance of consistency and diversity from which impressions of a distinctive opus character may be discerned.

Initial Generalizations on Style and Design

Changes in fashion and compositional technique that had accrued since the
time of the earliest quartets are duly reflected in Haydn's instrumental works
from the early to mid-1760s; and among the new quartets it is not surprising to
find corresponding differences in style with respect to the pre-Esterházy works.
Especially in their sonata form first movements, the quartets of Opp. 9 and 17
display far greater diversity of surface rhythm and theme as well as a generally
more ambitious approach to form and motivic development. Points of connection to the early quartets are nonetheless apparent, especially among the interior
movements and finales, and are perhaps quite deliberate in light of those previous works' enduring popularity. Keeping up with contemporary trends was obviously an important aim; but if Haydn was motivated to explore, extend his reach,
and respond to changing tastes, he also had reason not to abandon certain traits
that had helped sustain the success of his earlier accomplishments.

As witnessed in table 9.1, the most decisive change in overall design is the
abandonment of a five-movement format. Haydn now chooses to eliminate the
second of the two dance movements, and the center of gravity shifts accordingly:
the interior Adagio, no longer favored as a quartet's centerpiece, yields in importance to a relatively long, technically exacting first movement, cast as a sonata
form in all but two cases. The exceptions, Opp. 9/5/i and 17/3/i, are strophic
variations, similar in style to the first movement of Op. 2/6.

Essential to the character of the refashioned cycle is the heightened importance given to the first violin at the outset, both as a commanding thematic presence and a vehicle for brilliant execution. It is as if the soloistic manner, previously concentrated in an interior slow movement, is now permitted to spread to
other parts of the cycle, especially the more elaborate, grammatically complex
first movements in common time, whose broad underlying motion, affirmed by the
tempo designation moderato, accommodates a new wealth of foreground detail.
The first movements' proportions are by and large more expansive, and development sections in particular have grown in relative size and rhetorical importance.

The dance movements of Opp. 9 and 17, similar in many respects to those
of the earliest quartets, may be viewed as tangible points of connection with the
earlier endeavors. Several of the minuets are scarcely distinguishable from their

TABLE 9.1 Summary statistics for Opp. 9 and 17

Op.No.	Hob.No.	Movement			
		i	ii	iii	iv
9/1	III:19	C e Moderato SF 72	C/Cm $\frac{3}{4}$ Un poco allegretto M/T 34/28	F $\frac{6}{8}$ Adagio SF 67	C $\frac{2}{4}$ Presto SF 156
9/2	III:20	E♭ e Moderato SF 109	E♭ $\frac{3}{4}$ M/T 20/22	Cm e-$\frac{3}{4}$ Adagio–Cantabile Binary (irreg.) 61(r)	E♭ e Allegro di molto SF 57
9/3	III:21	G e Moderato SF 81	G $\frac{3}{4}$ Allegretto M/T 30/21	C $\frac{3}{4}$ Largo Slow-mvt. 73	G $\frac{2}{4}$ Presto SF 138
9/4	III:22	Dm e Moderato SF 75	Dm/D $\frac{3}{4}$ M/T 48/16	B♭ e Adagio. Cantabile SF 76(r)	Dm $\frac{6}{8}$ Presto SF (irreg.) 93
9/5	III:23	B♭ $\frac{2}{4}$ Poco adagio Strophic var. 124(r)	B♭ $\frac{3}{4}$ Allegretto M/T 28/16	E♭ $\frac{3}{4}$ Largo. Cantabile Large binary 71	B♭ $\frac{2}{4}$ Presto SF 218
9/6	III:24	A $\frac{6}{8}$ Presto SF 133	A/Am $\frac{3}{4}$ M/T 34/34	E e Adagio SF 57	A $\frac{2}{4}$ Presto Rounded binary 53
17/1	III:25	E e Moderato SF 110	E/Em $\frac{3}{4}$ M/T 50/32	Em $\frac{6}{8}$ Adagio SF 75	E $\frac{2}{4}$ Presto SF 237
17/2	III:26	F e Moderato SF 100	F/Dm $\frac{3}{4}$ Poco allegretto M/T 34/28	B♭ e Adagio Slow-mvt. 90	F $\frac{2}{4}$ Allegro di molto SF 169
17/3	III:27	E♭ $\frac{2}{4}$ Andante grazioso Strophic var. 99	E♭ $\frac{3}{4}$ Allegretto M/T 36/28	A♭ $\frac{3}{4}$ Adagio SF 85	E♭ e Allegro di molto SF 69
17/4	III:28	Cm e Moderato SF 130	C/Cm $\frac{3}{4}$ Allegretto M/T 40/40	E♭ $\frac{3}{4}$ Adagio. Cantabile Large binary 107(r)	Cm ¢ Allegro SF 136
17/5	III:29	G e Moderato SF 89	G/Gm $\frac{3}{4}$ Allegretto M/T 32/24	Gm $\frac{3}{4}$ Adagio Slow-mvt. 80	G $\frac{2}{4}$ Presto SF 135
17/6	III:30	D $\frac{6}{8}$ Presto SF 200	D $\frac{3}{4}$ M/T 22/20	G e Largo Binary 43	D $\frac{2}{4}$ Allegro SF 147

predecessors in melodic style and rhythmic impetus, and only a few significantly exceed their predecessors in size. There are nonetheless some important novelties, most notably the intrigue of open-ended trios in Opp. 9/1 and 17/2 and 5, and the metrically dissonant escapades of Opp. 9/3 and 17/5 (anticipated, to be sure, by the Op. 2/4/iv trio), as well as other signs of change in approach—for example, fewer passages in which the viola and cello proceed in unison or octaves, and less indulgence in textures that pair upper and lower parts in two-part counterpoint. Two special sounds—con sordino and pizzicato—disappear altogether as part of a general retreat from the colorful sonorities, chromatic inflections, and theatrical contrasts that had distinguished some of the most memorable early trios.

Resemblances to the earliest quartets are unmistakable among the new interior Largos and Adagios, where the emphasis continues to fall on soloistic delivery by the first violin. Following Haydn's own precedents, several of the new slow movements begin with introductory or ritornello-like phrases in the manner of a concerto; and that quintessential marker of concerto style, the cadenza, is now a recurrent feature, especially in Op. 9. Different from any of the earlier Adagios is the adoption of varied-reprise forms, which provide a basis for lavish spontaneous-sounding decoration.

Among the finales of Opp. 9 and 17, points of connection with the early quartets include the persistence of a very fast $\frac{2}{4}$ meter (on eight occasions), an accent on restless momentum, and a fondness for rapid-fire eighth notes among the accompanying voices. These enduring preferences are easy to understand in light of the new format, by which a dense, detail-laden slow movement comes directly before. A feeling of relief now attaches to the abrupt shift in tempo and mood, which breaks the slow movement's spell, clears the air, and makes way for a high-energy finish to the cycle. Syntactically less complex than the sonata form opening movements, the new finales play a distinctive role within the cycle. Their streamlined, often repetitive melodies and sweeping transitions help convey an impression of finality, an ultimate untangling of disparate strands in the musical discourse. Proportions are generally enlarged by comparison with the earliest finales, and the longest, that of Op. 17/1, stretches to more than three times the size of the shortest finale among the earlier works, Op. 1/1/v. But there is one striking exception, the breathless finale of Op. 9/6, whose singular compactness, velocity, and emphasis on exuberant closing formulas all contribute to the image of a musical punctuation mark for the cycle, and perhaps for the opus as a whole.[6] Within its fifty-three-measure span, the first reprise consumes a mere eight measures, and a large portion of the second reprise consists of closure-affirming addenda to the main design.[7]

Headlong momentum, typical for the new finales as it was for their predecessors, gives rise to strokes of surprise, suspense, or sudden change in color and surface activity. In the last movement of Op. 17/4, for example, the pulsating eighth notes that underlie the secondary theme come to a dead stop on the downbeat of measure 32 (m. 100 in the recapitulation). Something must be done to compensate or regroup, and so the first violin now begins to sparkle with a new sonority—a series of string-crossing flourishes, sounded in alternation with stubborn chords in the lower parts—as if struggling impatiently to restart the action (see ex. 9.1a, which quotes from the exposition). The effort extends for a full four measures before progress resumes toward a brilliant high point and ultimate descent to the close. Haydn may have modeled this passage on a no less cunning precedent of his own, from the finale of Op. 2/2, quoted in example 9.1b, in which ruptured surface activity likewise gives rise to a call for renewed action by the ensemble leader, underscored in this earlier instance by the telescoping effect of progressively shorter time intervals between string-crossing exclamations.

Aspects of Rhythm and Meter;
The Moderato Compound $\frac{4}{4}$

Basic to the style of the new quartets is their adoption of certain metrical conventions. No fewer than half of the interior slow movements, for example, explore the expressive and decorative possibilities of a stately $\frac{3}{4}$ time. Haydn had chosen triple meter for the opening Adagio of Op. 1/3 and the middle movement of Op. 2/4; but slow triple time is otherwise absent from the earlier quartets (perhaps with good reason, because $\frac{3}{4}$ is already richly represented in those five-movement works by their pairs of minuet-trio complexes). More significant than the endorsement of a slow $\frac{3}{4}$ itself is the attendant rhythmic diversity, as in the Largo of Op. 9/5, where sustained sonorities at the beginning are disturbed by a flurry of thirty-second notes as early as the end of measure 2 in a gesture that anticipates the wealth of small-note figuration—engaging sixteenth-, triplet sixteenth-, and thirty-second-note activity—that informs the subsequent course of events.

EXAMPLE 9.1

(a) Op. 17/4/iv, mm. 33–36 (violins only)

(b) Op. 2/2/v, mm. 37–43 (violin 1 only)

Likewise bursting with rhythmic detail are the new common-time opening movements, which display a metrical type that writers of the time describe as the compound $\frac{4}{4}$: the notated measure essentially combines two measures of $\frac{2}{4}$ time, a practice that readily leads to situations of ambiguity—and perhaps near-equality— of metrical accent between first and third beats.[8] Frequently encountered in other eighteenth-century vocal and instrumental repertories, it was only now to be used by Haydn for first movements of his quartets, where it supersedes his earlier preference for $\frac{2}{4}$, $\frac{3}{8}$, and $\frac{6}{8}$. Typically, the quarter note defines a basic pulse, while a nearly pervasive motion in eighth notes sustains momentum. Sixteenth notes are common in principal lines and accompaniments, and there are some extended stretches of triplet sixteenths in addition to decorative figures involving thirty-second notes (the latter occurring more often in Op. 9 than in Op. 17).

The layered metrical continuum thus described invites thematic diversity as well as contrasting activity among simultaneously sounding parts, and it promotes the excitement of rhythmic acceleration in anticipation of a structural goal or rhetorical climax. But in addition to the sweep of a long melodic trajectory, this brand of common time also lends itself to the quintessential intricacy and concentration of chamber style; and because of the ambivalence of the compound measure as a metrical unit (depending on the context in question, the accentual force of beat 1 may scarcely differ from that of beat 3), it invites phraseological intrigue. Themes may unfold not only in a mixture of two- and four-beat units (the latter aligned variously with the beginning or the middle of the measure) but also in occasional six-beat units that straddle the notated bar lines. Haydn makes splendid use of these possibilities in the first movement of Op. 9/1, starting off with a pair of three-measure phrases, the second a variant of the first (see ex. 9.2). The three measures that follow (mm. 7–9) push forward and destabilize by forming a pair of one-and-a-half-measure units; and whereas metrical stability is partially reclaimed as the theme continues, the unit-halving impetus— and the attendant impression of acceleration—persists, notably in the change from one-measure ideas in descending sequence (mm. 11–12) to a pair of highly energized half-measure figures in measure 13. This pattern intensifies the approach to an inflected half cadence in measure 14, sharpens the directional thrust of the theme in its entirety, and lends an additional touch of unity by recalling a similar pattern of unit-halving acceleration within the theme's very opening measures (indicated by brackets in the example).

In a more extreme case of rhythmic play, from the first movement of Op. 17/5, Haydn reaches beyond the ambivalence of half-measure displacement to a perilous loosening of the metrical fabric. Toward the end of a long development, the texture thins to an open-ended melodic stream in the first violin, unaccompanied except for sporadic chordal accents in the lower parts (mm. 59–68). The violin's meandering line implies no strong or regular grouping of beats, and the punctuating chords mostly do not coincide with notated downbeats. Instead,

EXAMPLE 9.2 Op. 9/1/i, mm. 1–14 (violin 1 only)

their unpredictably placed impacts temporarily obliterate any sense of a measure-level continuum. Metrically adrift at a precarious moment of retransition, we find our attention drawn with peculiar intensity to the first violin's improvisatory-like connecting thread.

A further possibility to which the first movements' common time gives rise is the sudden, momentary cancellation of foreground detail, which depending on context may work to create dramatic surprise, rhetorical emphasis, or comical interruption. In one example, from Op. 17/2, the customary buildup of energy and momentum has led to a melodic peak (m. 27 in the exposition, m. 88 in the recapitulation), and the culminating trill over dominant harmony that follows promises imminent resolution and stability. But the cadence is avoided, harmonic progress stalls, and after two and a half aimlessly repetitive measures, surface motion practically expires. The ensemble drops back to a quiet dynamic level, and all parts join in a moment of contemplation, a mystifying temporal parenthesis (mm. 32–33; 94–95) that momentarily banishes eighth- and sixteenth-note activity just before a final run to the close.

Expanded Harmonic Resources

Concomitant with the new rhythmic diversity in Opp. 9 and 17 is an expanded harmonic range, and here comparison with the earlier works is likewise revealing. Haydn had previously chosen to reserve the slow interior movements for intricate solo work, and he had sequestered a good deal of harmonic richness in several of the dance-movement trios. Now, just as he allows elaborate figuration to color all movements in the cycle, harmonic complication becomes more pervasive as well. In a particularly impressive instance, the first movement of Op. 17/6 (D major), harmonic intrigue begins with an extended transition theme that bends from major to minor as it unfolds. A prolonged arrival on the dominant of the new tonal center (A) certifies that a structural dividing point has been attained (mm. 40–43), but the harmony is still lodged in minor: a modal threshold has yet to be crossed before the music can proceed in a securely established, major dominant. This is eventually accomplished by the appearance of a primary theme derivative in the major dominant at measure 57, but meanwhile the minor dominant persists as the local tonal foundation: the cello drops by a major third from its perch on V of A minor to C (m. 45), in the manner of a bifocal cadence—a coherent but nonetheless surprising move, and an entire phrase now unfolds on this remote but logically approached plateau (mm. 45–50). This elaborated tonal path, duplicated within the orbit of the home key in the recapitulation, elevates the parallel minor and its relative major to positions of central importance as it extends the tonal reach of the movement's outer sections.

Deflections from major to minor lead still farther afield amid the lushly romantic strains of the Op. 17/3 Adagio, where the oddity of venturing into alien terrain is underscored by the fact that the movement's key already lies far to the flat side of the tonal spectrum—the relatively rare Ab major. The opening theme, a warbling duet for violins, leads to a half cadence in measure 12. The next several measures mark time on the dominant, as if in a trance, before slipping into minor (m. 19) and then ranging progressively deeper into flat territory: Gb (the mediant of Eb minor), Gb minor, and finally to that distant key's submediant chord, Ebb, before eventually gliding back to a restored major dominant. (A corresponding passage in the second reprise traces a path through Ab minor and its submediant, Fb, before the ultimate return to Ab.)

Motivic Development;
Intermovement Motivic Relationships

The cohesive force of motivic process, already well developed among the earliest quartets, now reaches new degrees of refinement, especially in the rhythmically dense environments of the opening movements in compound $\frac{4}{4}$ time. That of Op. 9/1, cited in connection with example 9.2, represents a veritable playground of motivic elaboration, as seen in example 9.3, where melodic processes in the primary theme's opening three measures are pinpointed. The opening gesture, consisting of a pair of upward-leaping sixteenths followed by a sustained note, generates at least five—possibly six—tangible derivations just within the opening phrase. Each signifies resemblance to, while at the same time tracing a pattern of progressive removal from, the initial idea: (1) a narrowed leap prior to beat 3 in measure 1, with the sustained note now positioned as an appoggiatura; (2) a widened leap on the upbeat to measure 2; (3) the leap now further widened to a seventh just ahead of beat 3 in that measure; (4) an inverted leap on the upbeat to measure 3, followed by a shortened appoggiatura; (5) a rhythmically altered leap from the end of beat 1 to beat 2 in measure 3, followed again by a shortened appoggiatura. Finally, we can perhaps identify a more remote variant that completes this series of progressive transformations as it leads to the end of the phrase in the middle of measure 3: at the end of beat 2, the vertical distance between upbeat notes has shrunk to a downward whole step (G–F), but the dotted rhythm links this upbeat figure recognizably to that of (5), and the appoggiatura, now further compressed rhythmically, initiates a stepwise descent whose boundaries recall the initial motive's leap of a fourth.

Evidence of an extended range of motivic control is subtle yet persuasive, not merely informing thematic process within movements but crossing the boundaries between them, and perhaps even lending a measure of cohesion to an entire cycle. In the F major quartet, Op. 17/2, the melodic succession F–E stands out at the head of the first-movement primary theme, and later derivatives of this germinal two-note idea acquire sufficient emphasis to be recognized as a unifying thread[9] (occurrences include i, m. 100; ii, mm. 1–5 and 33–36; and iv, mm. 1–4 and 118–30).

An even more palpable sense of intermovement connection can be felt in Op. 9/4 (D minor), largely through the recurrent, close proximity of two tense, unstable pitches, C♯ and B♭, together with the more stable D and A to which they attach. Ingredients of this composite idea first materialize in measure 2 (quoted in ex. 9.4a), and their developments cast a long shadow as the work progresses.

EXAMPLE 9.3 Op. 9/1/i, mm. 1–3 (violin 1 only)

EXAMPLE 9.4 Op. 9/4

(a) i, mm. 1–3

(b) i, mm. 73–75 (second ending; violin 1 only)   (c) ii, mm. 1–4 (violin 1 only)

(d) ii, mm. 46–48   (e) ii, mm. 49–51

(f) iv, mm. 1–4

As shown in example 9.4b, a restless permutation of the four-note complex (labeled *m*) highlights a melodically salient diminished seventh B♭–C♯ as it concludes the first violin's angular descent at the end of the first movement; and as early as the upbeat to the minuet's second measure (ex. 9.4c), the intensity of that moment is rejoined as the four notes of *m* unfold in retrograde (*m¹*). Both the B♭–A and C♯–D successions make summarizing recurrences at the end of the minuet proper (ex. 9.4d), and the idea evolves further in the D major trio (mm. 49–50, quoted in ex. 9.4e), as its elements divide into neighbor-note figures in the first violin (A–B–A) and second (D–C♯–D). This last configuration anticipates the four notes' subsequent appearances, restored to minor, as part of the inner- and outer-voice duets heard at the outset of the finale (ex. 9.4f).

Aspects of Relationship between the Two Opus Groups

How close are the correspondences between Opp. 9 and 17? The two sets share enough common ground stylistically to be viewed as a natural pair, but a host of more explicit connections may be identified as well, as if Haydn viewed the latter set not merely as a sequel, but as an opportunity to rethink, elaborate, and expand on the previous venture from several perspectives, including aspects of form and style in individual movements, matters of cyclic profile, and the design of the set as a whole. We can see at the outset that each opening movement in Op. 9 belongs to a distinctive stylistic category, especially in its initial statement, and that each may readily be matched with a counterpart in Op. 17: "singing allegro," Opp. 9/3 and 17/2, with bold opening phrases supported by pulsating chordal accompaniment; turbulent or eccentric minor, Opp. 9/4 and 17/4; pastoral or gigue-like, Opp. 9/6 and 17/6, both marked presto in ⁶⁄₈ time; "walking"-style theme and variations, Opp. 9/5 and 17/3; decorative galant, Opp. 9/1 and 17/5, with ingratiating themes and an abundance of diminutions; and thematically austere/concerto-like, Opp. 9/2 and 17/1, characterized by relatively mechanical, chord- and scale-outlining themes and an accent on soloistic figuration.

From a broader perspective, either opus reveals a set of three major-key cycles— Op. 9/1, 2, and 3; Op. 17/1, 2, and 5—that display an array of stylistic norms: a moderate-tempo opening movement in common time, a structurally uncomplicated slow movement designed as a solo vehicle for the first violin, and a substantial-size finale that gains momentum (especially in Op. 17/1 and 5) from spans of repeated-note accompaniment. Seemingly to compensate for a general drift toward conformity, only two of the dance movements in this category, those of Opp. 9/2 and 17/1, are unproblematic technically: Opp. 9/1, 17/2, and 17/5 are complicated by open-ended connections from trio to minuet; and both Opp. 9/3 and 17/5 are spiced with metrical dissonance. Furthermore, none of the three Op. 17 works may be described as altogether normal in tonal usage: No. 2 incorporates the relatively rare choice of a trio in the relative minor, whereas both Nos. 1 and 5 are single-tonic compositions—the first of their type among the quartets, and a precedent for a small but significant number of later instances. Among the slow movements in question, two explicit pairs may be identified: those of Opp. 9/1 and 17/1, both cast in ⁶⁄₈ time with traits of the siciliana, including dotted rhythms on the downbeat and a persistent long-short-long-short accompaniment pattern that serves as the backdrop for a first violin soliloquy; and the minor-key Adagios of Opp. 9/2 and 17/5, which make prominent allusions to the operatic stage—the former through its contrast between portentous introduction and lyrical aria, the latter by displaying passages of instrumental recitative.

By comparison with the six works considered so far, the three remaining quartets of either set are characterized by pronounced individuality. As shown in table 9.2, however, each has a more or less explicit counterpart in the neighboring set.

Additional observations are in order. The slow movements of the two minor-key quartets (Opp. 9/4 and 17/4), in related major keys, stand out in particularly sharp contrast to the minor-key discourse of their respective outer movements, and the accent on contrapuntal technique in their finales lends an air of seriousness that to some extent transcends Haydn's own predilection for lighthearted closing movements. Opp. 9/6 and 17/6, obviously related by their choice of a dance-like $\frac{6}{8}$ meter at the outset, have peculiarly similar slow movements as well: the primary thematic ideas of both involve a long-sustained tonic note in the melody, figuration in parallel thirds and sixths in the inner parts, and beat-marking repeated notes in the cello (see ex. 9.5, which compares their opening measures). In both cases, the characteristic pairing of inner voices persists throughout much of the movement.

Interwoven among the many correspondences between Opp. 9 and 17 are signs of a more developed idiom in quartets of the later set. On average, individual movements are longer. Some, like Op. 17/6/i, with its embrace of intermediate key areas within both exposition and recapitulation, are significantly more complex grammatically. Elements of contrast within and between themes are sometimes more pronounced, and points of climactic intensity often exceed those of the previous opus. Such differences may suggest a more practiced hand or a greater degree of technical assurance. But might Haydn also have had in mind

TABLE 9.2 Representative shared characteristics in each of three pairs of quartets

Op. 9/4 in D minor; Op. 17/4 in C minor

  i: shortened and altered recapitulation
iii: varied-reprise form, marked adagio, with the modifier cantabile
iv: opening theme that begins in two-part counterpoint

Op. 9/5 in B♭; Op. 17/3 in E♭

  i: two-reprise theme, 20 measures long, followed by four variations (Op. 9/5 closes with a brief appendage)
ii: minuet and trio both in tonic major
iii: $\frac{3}{4}$ meter; extraordinary textural density
iv: soloistic first violin writing emphasized

Op. 9/6 in A major; Op. 17/6 in D major

  i: gigue-like, in $\frac{6}{8}$ time, marked presto
iii: closely related in theme and accompaniment; characterized by dense texture

EXAMPLE 9.5

(a) Op. 9/6/iii, mm. 1–2

(b) Op. 17/6/iii, mm. 1–2

the growing competency of his performers and listeners? Having mastered the difficulties of the first set, were they perhaps ready for something more challenging?

Other thoughts come to mind, for if Haydn's Op. 9 quartets suggest a critique of his own earlier works in the medium—adopting, amplifying, and further developing some of their elements (soloistic Adagios, fast $\frac{2}{4}$ finales), while abandoning others (the five-movement format and the relatively short, high-speed opening movements)—might Op. 17 be understood as a critique of Op. 9, variously challenging, destabilizing, or indulging in ironic commentary, while at the same time building on its precedents?

To start with the D minor quartet, Op. 9/4, whose opening Moderato is perhaps more distant from the sound-world of the earliest quartets than any other movement in the new opus: this work enjoys special stature as Haydn's first quartet in minor, and he has evidently used the occasion to peer deeply, especially in the first movement, into a terrain of *Sturm und Drang* theatrics, rife with syncopations, chromatic inflections, dynamic shocks, explosive melodic thrusts, dissonant chords sustained by fermatas, gasping pauses, and unsettling pianissimos. Signs of unrest are evident at the outset, where a throbbing octave- and repeated-note bass underlies the relatively hollow sonority of an opening call from which the second violin mysteriously withdraws after a single eighth note. A replica of the opening bass motion returns to accompany the surging intensity of measures 15–16, where note values in the principal line extend from whole to thirty-second. The impetus of the octave-spanning thrust up to bb^2 carries over into the overwrought passagework that follows (mm. 17–22), and the first violin's triple-stopped chords that straddle the bar line between measures 22 and 23 sound like a desperate attempt to stabilize the headlong activity. Surface energy is suppressed for only a few measures, however, and intensity soon reaches new heights in the closing theme (beginning in m. 27), whose waves of triplet sixteenths variously engage all four members of the ensemble.

What are the implications of this piece for its successor, the first movement of Op. 17/4 in C minor? Is there room for development along similar lines? A semblance of minor-key foreboding does persist in the mystery and portent of the later quartet's opening gesture, its several points of drastic contrast in surface rhythm, its jarring passages of beat-by-beat alternation between loud and soft dynamics, and its descent to a conspiratorial, low-register pianissimo at the end. (Here, for the first time among the quartets' first movements, the closing phrase stands outside the recapitulation proper as a species of coda.) On balance, the later opening movement evinces a dryer, more distanced manner than its D minor predecessor. A less insistent rhythmic energy makes for a more austere, even-tempered delivery; and new elements of wit, irony, and thwarted expectation emerge to replace—or perhaps act as commentary on—the earlier movement's overdrawn gestures and mannerisms.

There is in fact evidence of a reversal in emphasis: whereas a relatively secure tonal foundation in Op. 9/4 provided a basis for stormy dynamics, rhythm, and texture, Op. 17/4 lessens those latter distractions in favor of an ongoing game of tonal uncertainty and ambivalence. The works' shared initial gesture—a rising third in half notes—is no longer a token of tragic expression. The interval has been changed from minor to major, and its accompaniment has been stripped away to pose a tonal riddle: the two unaccompanied half notes E♭–G represent members of a triad, but which one? By the time the line reaches up to C on the downbeat of measure 2, the meaning of those notes as third and fifth of a tonic triad proves unequivocal in retrospect (ex. 9.6a). But then a restatement in measures 9–10 veers from the path by sounding B♭, a step lower than the C of measure 2 (ex. 9.6b). The move is doubly ironic: the first violin's line now fulfills the initial implications of a simple triadic continuation (E♭–G–B♭) even as it points toward a new key, the emerging relative major; but the new tonal orientation thus implied is itself simultaneously undermined by the second violin's accompanying D♭, which turns the harmony into V⁷ of A♭. Later, when the opening call returns to articulate the boundary between exposition and development, the process of tonal deception and reinterpretation continues as the crucial third note (now A♭) comes one step lower than the last time (ex. 9.6c), so that the interval E♭–G now turns out to represent the lower tones of a dominant chord (E♭–G–B♭) in that previously foreshadowed key of A♭ major. The development section sustains the impression of a veritable tonal guessing game by configuring statements of the two-note figure and its continuation alternately as

EXAMPLE 9.6 Op. 17/4/i

(a) mm. 1–3   (b) mm. 9–10

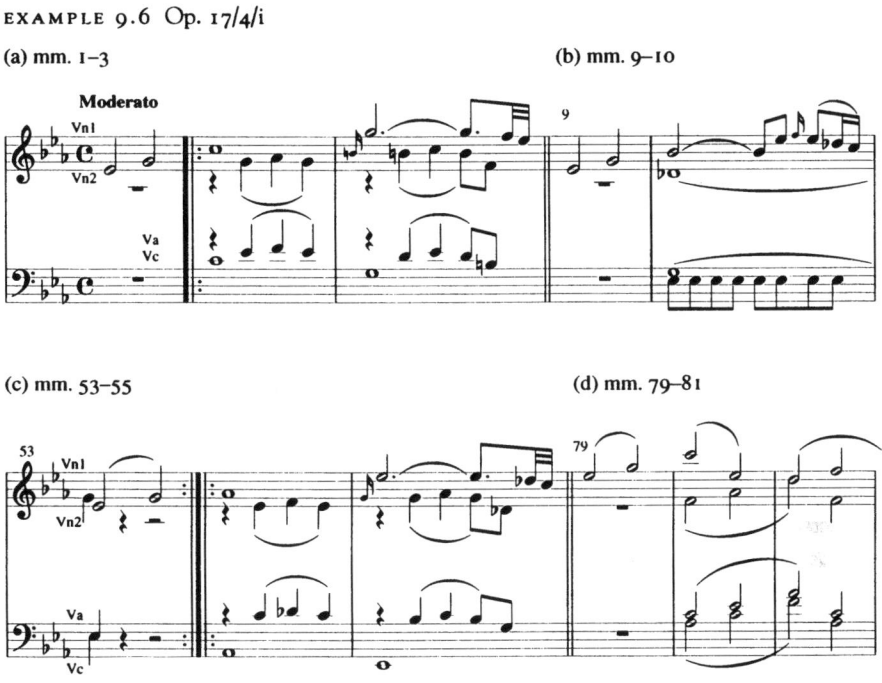

(c) mm. 53–55   (d) mm. 79–81

an arpeggiated chord in root position (Ab–C–Eb in mm. 60–61) and first inversion (Bb–Db–Gb in mm. 62–63).

Late in the section, the return of the two unaccompanied notes Eb and G (though now sounding an octave higher than in measure 1) suggests that we may possibly have arrived at the start of a recapitulation (m. 79; see ex. 9.6d). Yet even though the first violin now climbs to the high C as expected, the entering lower parts confirm our suspicion that all was not quite right by harmonizing with something other than the anticipated C minor (namely, a first-inversion F minor chord). The span of disembodied canonic imitation that now unfolds (mm. 80–85) works to sustain an aura of tonal ambivalence and indirection, impressions enhanced by the uncanny uniformity of half-note rhythm in all parts. When the canonic passage finishes, the return once again to the Eb–G figure (m. 86), now restored to the original octave, suggests that the recapitulation is finally about to begin in earnest (notwithstanding the Eb harmony on this measure's downbeat). But once again Haydn treats us to a stroke of irony and deception: the third note of the theme is not the expected C but Bb, as in measure 10. This has the effect of turning the action of recapitulation on its head by recalling elements of the restatement before the opening statement itself, which will not be heard until measure 92.

Among the dance movements of Opp. 9 and 17, rhythmic disturbances may be heard collectively as a challenge to the (for the most part) greater metrical conformity of the earlier minuets and trios. But distinctions become apparent when we compare the later sets' dance movements with one another. The metrical *imbroglio* in the trio of Op. 9/3/ii, for example, is framed on either side by a reassuringly normal minuet, and the trio itself begins on a peculiarly tentative note, with two violins in quiet counterpoint, but with no agreement on where the accents should fall or just how the melody and rhythm should line up with the meter. The metrically coordinated entry of the lower parts on the upbeat to measure 35 promises greater stability, and the phrase ends with all metrical dissonance resolved. The second reprise rejoins the topic of metrical conflict, with ties and second-beat accents in the first violin, before bringing all parts into alignment as in the end of the first reprise.

By contrast, this movement's rhythmically dissonant counterpart, the minuet of Op. 17/5, not only entertains a more disruptive brand of metrical play but gives it a position of great prominence within the minuet proper. Trouble begins early in the second reprise, where the lower parts imitate the violins' anapestic rhythm a beat too early (compare ex. 9.7a and b). Conflict intensifies two phrases further on, where the rhythmic figure (bracketed in the examples) spawns a variant, just two beats long, and the second violin chases the first after a single beat (ex. 9.7c). Here, any trace of normal $\frac{3}{4}$ time disappears as every successive quarter note through the middle of measure 18 competes for attention as a downbeat. The disturbance is then amplified in measures 25–26: the full ensemble now engages in canonic imitation, the paired lower parts imitating the paired violins at the time interval of a single beat.

Further differences between Opp. 9 and 17 can be sensed in Haydn's approach to the idea of the open-ended trio, which in both groups involves impressions of a musical puzzle or impasse as the expected completion of the trio's second reprise is averted. In Op. 9/1 (C major) the trio's second part had begun normally enough with a rising sequence of phrases, first on E♭, then F minor, then G minor. But after a cadence in this last key (m. 54), the harmony inexplicably freezes: the cello proceeds to reiterate the note G no fewer than twenty-four times, marking each downbeat with a descent to the lower octave—a pointed anticipation of the oom-pah-pah bass heard at the start of the minuet proper—while the violins cycle aimlessly through a variant of the trio's own opening melodic figure. Going nowhere, the ensemble gives up, in effect, after seven hopelessly repetitive measures, and proceeds directly back to the minuet (thereby resolving the tension of a persisting dominant of C) without having brought the trio to a full close.

Revisiting this idea in the dance movement of Op. 17/5 (G major), whose trio is in the parallel minor, Haydn likewise conveys the idea that the latter part of the trio has lost its way in a series of motivic repetitions (mm. 45–52). But

EXAMPLE 9.7 Op. 17/5/ii

(a) mm. 1–2   (b) mm. 9–10   (c) mm. 17–18

these are now configured more ominously as a melodic sequence that begins innocently on g^1 (mm. 45–46) before seeming to spin out of control in a succession of rising fourths: f^1 (mm. 47–48), bb^1 (49–50), then eb^2 (51–52). Where can the pattern go from here? As if in desperation, a loud, four-fold exclamation on a V_5^6 chord of G (mm. 53–54) puts an abrupt end to the upward cycling as it heralds a brief motivic anticipation of the minuet's return.

In the other open-ended trio, that of Op. 17/2/ii, Haydn tinges the device with irony and eccentricity by ending stubbornly on the dominant of the trio's own tonic (D minor) rather than turning to that of the minuet proper (F). As in Op. 9/1, motivic repetitions based on the trio's main idea act to stretch out the immobilizing harmony, and it is only in retrospect that we can appreciate the logic of the return: the sustained A in the first violin joins seamlessly with that same A on which the melody of the minuet begins, and the underlying harmony (V of vi from the standpoint of the minuet's overriding tonic) resolves directly to the minuet's return in the manner of a bifocal cadence. In this instance, the trio's independence is further sacrificed (and the cohesion of the movement as a whole correspondingly enhanced) by the ingenious rhetoric of thematic overlap: the principal idea of the trio springs directly from the closing figure of the minuet, so that the trio is bound to the minuet on both ends.

The persistence of first violin–dominated slow movements in Opp. 9 and 17 naturally affirms Haydn's enduring penchant for showcasing the ensemble's group leader as a star performer. But there are also signs of a tendency to undermine his own inclination in this regard (perhaps no less in Op. 9 than in Op. 17) with strokes of irony and antic parody. The Largo of Op. 9/3, for example, begins with an exalted ritornello, as if furnishing the backdrop for a forthcoming solo entry. But the anticipated aria never materializes. What happens instead amounts to an abandonment of the operatic stage for a more secluded, mystified space of shimmering instrumental color and metrically disoriented arpeggiation. The broken-chord figures in question, shared by the violins, roll by in mechanically repetitive triplet sixteenths, yet the descending arpeggiation has four notes, not three, always beginning on the second note of the measure, so that melody and meter are perpetually out of phase. The oddity of this arrangement is enhanced by a scheme of alternation between quasi ritornello and metrically dissonant figuration, and by the insertion of improvised cadenzas (mm. 34, 69), as if to underscore the paradox of simultaneously embracing and denying the customary formulas and gestures of an operatic-style solo.

Operatic allusions are a more vivid presence in the G minor Adagio of Op. 17/5, which moves from a ritornello at the start (mm. 1–10) to a full-blown imitation of obbligato recitative. In the course of this mock-tragic monologue for first violin, sighs and repeated-note pleas are punctuated by expressive pauses, amplified by repeated-chord figures in the lower instruments, and interrupted by quasi-orchestral unison admonitions. The melodious legato theme that follows (now in the relative major) bespeaks consolation as it completes the picture of an operatic scena embedded within the movement's overarching two-part design. This can sound deeply moving if performed with conviction; and yet the device can also be read as a tongue-in-cheek parody of the composer's own conventions, and an intriguing case of Haydnesque detachment by which performers and listeners are invited to appreciate the play of unforeseen relationship and stylistic transformation.

Haydn's favored slow-movement alternative to the operatic aria model for highlighting the first violin, the technique of varied reprise, is convincingly realized on two occasions among the interior slow movements of Op. 9 (Nos. 2 and 4). But in the slow movement of Op. 17/4, Haydn takes the decorative abundance of a varied reprise to comical extremes. As shown in example 9.8, which compares the second phrase of the first part (mm. 5–10) with its varied recurrence (mm. 38–43), the altered version overcrowds the original line with adornments at virtually every turn.

Among the finales of Opp. 9 and 17, signs pointing to a developing view of the genre's character and technical possibilities prove no less telling than for other portions of the cycle. Particularly intriguing in this regard are several finales (most notably those of Opp. 9/3 and 5; 17/1, 5, and 6) that finesse the opportunity for culminating energy, volume, or rhetorical weight, and instead pull back as the end draws near, allowing climactic forces to dissolve in a "negative culmination" that turns customary closing strategies upside down.[10]

The irony of the design is enhanced in Op. 9/3 by the way the end revisits the movement's whimsical opening call, sounded by the violins alone as if catching the lower parts unaware. In the exposition, what had started as a full-volume rush to the end of the section tapers off prematurely several measures before the double bar. To fill the ensuing silence, the violins quietly take up the opening idea, now in the dominant key, then pass it to the viola and cello, whose echo-like iteration serves to punctuate the section. This amounts to a structural pun: since the development section begins with a statement of the fully harmonized

EXAMPLE 9.8 Op. 17/4/iii (violin 1 only)

(a) mm. 5–10

(b) mm. 38–43

theme first heard at measure 5, the recall of the preliminary gesture acts not only as an afterthought to close the exposition but as an upbeat to the development section, comparable to that heard at the outset of the movement. This much seems logical as a bridge to the new section, but it also gives rise to a comical redundancy if the exposition repeat is taken, for the closing measures to the exposition will now constitute an upbeat to the upbeat. The end of the recapitulation finds matters in a particularly delicate state, for here the parallel recall of the opening upbeat figures, restored to tonic, naturally supplants any customarily full sonority in the approach to the close, and the burden of conclusion to the movement and to the cycle will now fall on the simple pianissimo cadence by which they are followed (mm. 137–38).

For the finales of Op. 17/1, 5, and 6, Haydn builds on the idea of negative culmination, with endings that convey a reluctance to bring matters to a close, even as the thematic substance of the movement slips away and dissolves into nothingness. In Op. 17/1, such a scenario unfolds as part of a witty play of theme allocation, tonal relationship, and structural proportion. A transition theme (1T, mm. 13–22) starts out on a promising note, elaborating the primary theme's opening melodic figure sequentially and animating the musical surface with a continuous flow of eighth notes. But rather than proceeding toward the orbit of the dominant as expected, the theme veers disturbingly in the opposite direction, to the subdominant. A second transition theme (2T, mm. 23–34) compounds the problem by confirming the wayward tonal move for a full six measures before eventually redirecting its energies toward the dominant. Both themes figure prominently in the course of the development section (1T in mm. 97–126, 2T in mm. 127–37), and in both instances the recurrence begins on the same pitch level as in the exposition. Haydn's omission of these themes from the recapitulation therefore seems justified: their return has been taken care of, albeit prematurely. Sectional proportions are compromised, however, because the recapitulation turns out to be substantially shorter than either exposition or development. More seriously, the tonal oddity of that early move to the subdominant remains unresolved, and this circumstance forms the basis for a trenchant afterthought: an appendage to the form that offers a nearly literal recall of $1T$ (mm. 216–25), followed by the beginning of $2T$ (mm. 226–29, analogous to mm. 23–26). This last-minute retrieval of salient material from the exposition promotes finality and proportional balance, but the movement is still off center tonally, lodged in the same subdominant region toward which those themes had originally been directed. Haydn now resolves the dilemma in the simplest possible way by shifting from the subdominant to the home key for a tonally resolved allusion to $2T$ as the movement draws quietly to a close.

~

Infrequently performed and overshadowed by later opus groups that enjoy the lion's share of critical attention, the quartets of Opp. 9 and 17 must nevertheless play a crucial part in any coherent survey, for there is a sense in which both groups, taken together, constitute a foundation for Haydn's subsequent endeavors in the medium: the distribution of diverse movement types and models for form and topic within an opus group, the choice of a standard four-movement cycle, and the establishment of certain consistencies and points of contrast within the cycle. These include aspects of textural and motivic complexity in a technically demanding first movement, the persistence of the slow movement as a vehicle for solo violin, the concentration of stylistic eccentricity and novelty—as well as reaffirmation of tradition—in the dance movement, and the preference for an extroverted, whimsical finale in which relatively uniform surface energy promotes large-scale resolution but also serves as a backdrop for rhetorical impact or surprise.

The many resemblances between Opp. 9 and 17 underscore the impression of a systematic exploration of available conventions and styles, and they demonstrate Haydn's concern for questions of design on the largest scale: the four-movement cycle as a whole and its place within an opus group of six quartets. Correspondences between the two sets furnish a basis for appreciating their differences. The latter group expands on forms, styles, and gestures explored in the former, and it also parodies them through strokes of Haydnesque wit and irony. In effect, Op. 17 affirms the validity of the Op. 9 models while at the same time interrogating them. In this respect, Op. 17 clearly sets a course for the future. As will be seen in the next chapter, Haydn would lose little time in further stretching, questioning, and digressing from his own newly established models for form and procedure.

10

Op. 20 (1772)

No musically informed contemporary of Haydn's could have failed to be impressed by the appearance of Op. 20 so closely on the heels of Opp. 9 and 17, and yet so different in character and technique. Certainly there are points of connection with the preceding quartets: lively interaction among ensemble members, continuous elaboration of pithy motives, and perpetually changing textures are all telltale signs of the same musical personality at work. There are extended passages—and indeed several entire movements—that betray the close proximity of these works to those just completed. But even as they point to an uninterrupted flow of inspiration, a persistence of whatever stimulus it was that led Haydn to turn his attention to the genre at this point in his career, the new quartets break fresh ground in matters of cyclic profile and opus design, and they far exceed their immediate predecessors in musical wit, technical sophistication, expressive range, and formal variety.

What could have motivated Haydn to digress so sharply from previous technical and stylistic constraints? One clue concerns the negative assessment of his music that a North German critic had voiced in 1771, just before Op. 20's time of origin. The writer scorns the "emptiness, the strange mixture of comic and serious, of the trifling and the moving" that he attributes to Haydn, along with several lesser (although by no means unknown) composers: Carl Joseph Toeschi, Christian Cannabich, Anton Filtz, Gaetano Pugnani, and Carlo Antonio Campioni. Referring to their trios, but also their quartets, the author goes on to deplore their "great ignorance of counterpoint."[1] That such criticism rankled seems apparent from certain comments that Haydn made in his autobiographical sketch of several years later (1776): "In the chamber-musical style I have been fortunate enough to please almost all nations except the Berliners," who are "incapable of performing some of my works, and are too conceited to take the trouble to understand them properly."[2] Could the quartets of Op. 20, with such manifest difficulties as their exacting fugal technique, be understood as a musical answer to the Berliners and other detractors? If so, theirs was a complicated response: although a high level of craftsmanship and invention is unmistakable throughout the set—nothing in these works could reasonably be described as empty or ignorant contrapuntally—the contradictory elements of comic and serious are, if anything, more blatant and intricately intertwined here than in many of Haydn's previous instrumental compositions.

That Haydn himself regarded these quartets as a special achievement may be sensed in the diverse, florid manner of the Latin inscriptions he appended to them in the autograph manuscripts.[3] Like the less wordy formulas that typically adorn his manuscripts, they represent offerings of praise, acknowledging divine guidance. Whereas the plain "Laus Deo" appears just once (No. 5), others are more verbose, like the "Laus Deo et Beatissimae Virgini Mariae" in No. 6, or more emphatic, as in the "Gloria in Excelsis Deo" of No. 4. Collectively, they resonate with the works' overall impression of variations on a theme, each realizing Haydn's freshly expanded conception of the genre in its own particular way.

What can be said about the order of quartets within the set? Whereas the authentic sequence for Op. 17 is clear, because Haydn notated those quartets in a single manuscript, each quartet of this group was prepared as a separate, unnumbered entity. (Each bears the date 1772 and the designation "divertimento a quattro.") The order in which they appear in the Entwurf-Katalog, (5, 6, 2, 3, 4, 1)[4] would seem to be authentic by analogy with Op. 17, whose entries in the catalogue match the order in the manuscript. An additional consideration is the fact that different shades of ink and different papers may be discerned among the manuscripts: primarily light brown ink and one type of paper for Nos. 5, 6, and 2, medium to dark brown ink and mainly another paper type for the remainder.[5] Significantly, the quartets comprising the first, lighter-ink group all happen to be the ones that incorporate the fugal finales. Moreover, the order in which the Entwurf-Katalog lists them corresponds to their fugues' designated number of subjects in ascending order: two subjects in the fugue for No. 5, three for that of No. 6, and four for the fugue of quartet No. 2.[6]

Despite the patent logic of the catalogue listing, which gives pride of place to the quartets with fugues and arranges them systematically, any such scheme was ignored by the publishers who took the initiative of distributing the quartets in printed editions. The earliest of these appears to be that of the Parisian publisher La Chevardière (advertised on 4 November 1774), who gave them their designation as Op. 20 and placed them, with no obvious rationale, in the order 1, 5, 2, 6, 3, 4. The traditional sequence, which became standard with Pleyel's Collection complette, is traceable to two other early editions: that of Hummel's Op. 16, advertised on 10 November 1779, and Blundell's London edition (also designated Op. 16), datable to 1778–80 by means of the publisher's address on the title page.[7] (It was the title page of Hummel's edition, adorned at the top by a sunburst-framed visage, presumably a representation of Apollo, that inspired the familiar nickname of this set as the "Sun" quartets.) That the question of the quartets' ordering remained unsettled, possibly even in Haydn's mind, is shown by a much later, supposedly authorized edition by Artaria. Here the quartets were presented in two parts, both as Op. 32, and ordered 1, 6, 5 and 4, 2, 3. The two parts were advertised respectively on 3 May 1800 and 8 April 1801 in the *Wiener Zeitung*, with the claim that the edition represented corrections made in Haydn's own hand and under his supervision.[8]

Points of Connection with Opp. 9 and 17

Strands of continuity are apparent in the way Haydn took pains to preserve elements of his previous quartets' cyclic designs, even as he exercised new alternatives (see table 10.1). The reaffirmation of an existing formula is most fully expressed in the E♭ quartet, Op. 20/1, whose overall profile seems not unlike that of Op. 9/1, for example, with its similar sequence of tempos and movement types.

Op. 20/6 in A may be cited for its intimate connections to both Opp. 9/6 and 17/6, at least in its opening and slow movements. All three cycles in question are in sharp keys (D or A), and the fast $\frac{6}{8}$ time with which they all begin stands in contrast to their pensive slow-movement soliloquies (situated in second place rather than third in Op. 20/6). The first movement of Op. 20/6 specifically recalls that of Op. 17/6 in highlighting the shift from major to minor in the course of both exposition and recapitulation; and impressions of a special bond between the two A major works, Opp. 9/6 and 20/6, are reinforced by a thematic correspondence in the outer sections of their first movements: in both cases, comparably situated full cadences (mm. 41 and 123 in Op. 9/6/i, mm. 55 and 154 in Op. 20/6/i) serve to usher in a tuneful phrase whose relative simplicity helps ground the preceding action as the close of the section draws near (see ex. 10.1a and b).

In a particularly intriguing case of interopus correspondence, Haydn revisits the metrical uncertainty of a passage from the development section of Op. 17/5/i by building a more complex span of metrical disorientation into the outer sections of Op. 20/3/i. Late in the exposition, a repetitive three-beat figure in the first violin suggests a momentary change from duple to triple meter (mm. 71–75), to be followed by a four-beat variant (mm. 75–77). But the accompanying chords in measures 73, 75, and 77 confuse the issue by reinforcing the pattern's third (or fourth) beat instead of the perceived downbeat (ex. 10.2a). A corresponding, more extended passage in the recapitulation begins much like the first, adding to

TABLE 10.1 Summary statistics for Op. 20

Op.No.	Hob.No.	Movement			
		i	ii	iii	iv
20/1	III:31	E♭ e Allegro moderato SF 106	E♭/A♭ 3/4 Un poco allegretto M/T 44/22	A♭ 3/8 Affettuoso e sostenuto SF 96	E♭ 2/4 Presto SF 160
20/2	III:32	C e Moderato SF 106	Cm e Adagio Nonstandard [Capriccio] 63	C/Cm 3/4 Allegretto M/T 56/30	C 6/8 Allegro Fugue [Fuga a 4to soggetti] 162
20/3	III:33	Gm 2/4 Allegro con spirto SF 270	Gm/E♭ 3/4 Allegretto M/T 52/36	G 3/4 Poco adagio SF (irreg.) 113	Gm e Allegro di molto SF 104
20/4	III:34	D 3/4 Allegro di molto SF 298	Dm 2/4 Un poco adagio e affettuoso Strophic var. 122	D 3/4 Allegretto M/T [Menuet alla zingarese] 20/16	D e Presto e scherzando SF 126
20/5	III:35	Fm e Moderato SF 159	Fm/F 3/4 M/T 53/46	F 6/8 Adagio SF 85	Fm ¢
20/6	III:36	A 6/8 Allegro di molto e scherzando SF 164	E ¢ Adagio Large binary 79(r)	A 3/4 M/T 20/22	A e Allegro Fugue [Fuga con 3 soggetti] 95

EXAMPLE 10.1 (violin 1 only)

(a) Op. 9/6/i, mm. 42–45

(b) Op. 20/6/i, mm. 55–59

a superimposed triple meter the same unsettling discrepancy in accentuation between melodic pattern and accompanying chords (mm. 218–25; the chords are marked by asterisks in fig. 10.1). Matters then become more complicated, and in fact almost Stravinsky-like, as the first violin deviates from the established figure—shortening it by a beat (mm. 225–26), then extending the scalar descent by two beats (mm. 226–28). And yet at the same time (beginning in m. 226) a degree of metrical clarity emerges as the chordal accents coincide with the melodic line's apparent downbeat (see ex. 10.2b). As shown in the example, the passage ends by trimming the figure to an initial upbeat plus upward leap (mm. 232–33), augmenting the leap's note values (m. 233) and reducing the distance between perceived downbeats. Reinstatement of the notated meter thus coincides with the liquidation of the recurrent metrically dissonant idea.

Other instances in which Haydn builds on the preceding quartets' novelties involve tonal derailment and digression, as in the chromatic maze of the Op. 20/5 first-movement coda, whose sheer audacity recalls that of the adventurous Op. 17/3 Adagio. Here, in one of Haydn's most inscrutable harmonic passages of all, the tonal detour transpires quietly, engulfed in a deceptive state of rhythmic and melodic calm (mm. 136–45). But its impact is unmistakable: by threatening to undermine tonal stability at the last moment, the precarious move to a far-fetched key (B♭♭ minor) lends rhetorical emphasis to the full-volume retrieval of tonic (m. 148) and to the summarizing thematic gestures with which the movement ends.

Equally important precedents for Op. 20 are found in the dance-movement trios of Opp. 9/1, 17/2, and 17/5, in which Haydn circumvents the standard practice of a full close at the end of the second reprise. He now recalls the integrated-trio scheme on three occasions (Nos. 1, 2, and 3), although only that of No. 2 involves a straightforward dominant lead-in to the recurrence of the minuet. In the Op. 20/1 trio, integrative intentions are signaled by an anticipation of the minuet (mm. 62–66) that prevents the trio's second reprise from coming to a full

EXAMPLE 10.2 Op. 20/3/i

(a) mm. 70–77

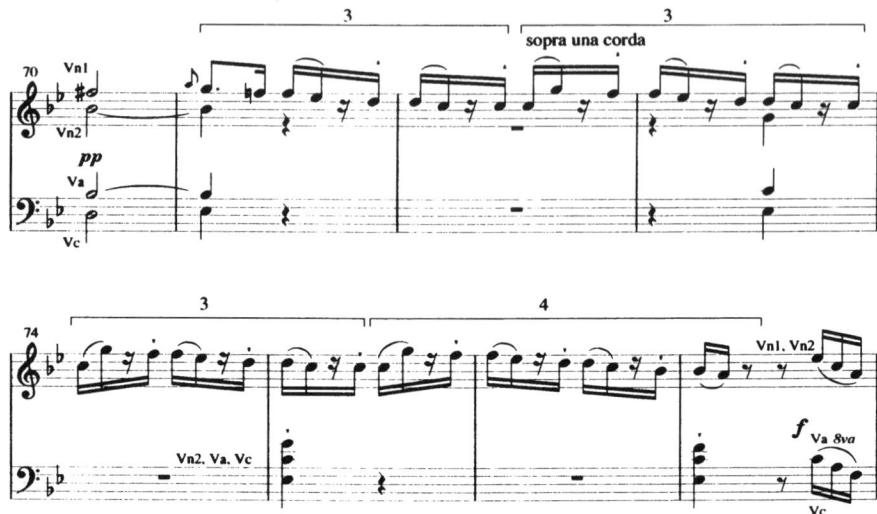

(b) mm. 224–33

close. The foreshadowing gesture turns neither on the home-key dominant nor on V of vi, however, but on V_3^6 of ii (i.e., F minor, the relative minor of the trio): a false connection at the point where a seamless junction was to have been expected. The trio of Op. 20/3 is comparably peculiar, with an abbreviated second reprise that comes to rest on V of iv with respect to the home key (i.e., C minor, the relative minor of the trio, just as in Op. 20/1). One other dance movement

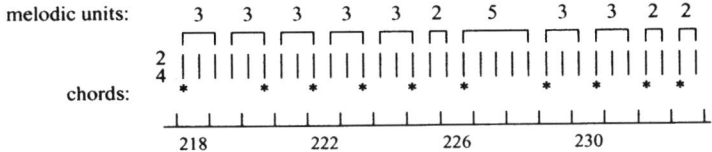

FIGURE 10.1 Op. 20/3/i, mm. 218–33

merits mention in this context, that of Op. 20/5, in which minuet and trio are joined at the other end: a second ending at the close of the minuet proper elides with the start of the trio, so that the two connect without a break.

New Ingredients

If some aspects of the Op. 20 quartets follow paths similar to those traced among the preceding works, we can also recognize a complementary urge to break new ground and redefine the boundaries of the genre. With regard to texture and ensemble technique, there is less reliance on the first violin as a primary thematic voice and a new diversity of ensemble textures in which thematic responsibility passes freely among all four performers. The inclination toward equality is most famously realized in the three fugal finales, but there are also manifestations of an emerging Haydn specialty: conversational textures with instrumental roles so intertwined that they defy categorization as separate strands of theme and accompaniment. No less demanding than traditional polyphony, this kind of ensemble work requires special concentration on the part of listeners, and from the players it exacts heightened attention to nuances of articulation, phrasing, and ensemble balance.

Novel departures from the first violin's predominance inform the opening themes in Op. 20/1 and 2, which taken together traverse a veritable catalogue of ways to distribute line and accompaniment among members of the group. Ironically, the process in both instances parodies a distinctly old-fashioned textural premise, that of the Baroque trio sonata. Op. 20/1/i begins by pairing first violin and viola above a staid bass line in the cello. The second violin remains silent until the downbeat of measure 7, and at this point the lower parts unexpectedly switch roles: the cello elects to sing in tandem with the second violin while the viola provides a bass. Op. 20/2/i likewise begins with a trio of instruments, but conventional relationships are more radically altered at the outset: astonishingly, a melodious, tenor-range cello stands out as the highest sounding part, joined below by the second violin, while the viola acts as the bass. Meanwhile, the first violinist looks on (perhaps genuinely bemused, at least on first encounter with the work), biding time until the start of the second phrase on the upbeat to measure 7.

The cello's liberation from standard bass-line duty, as in the opening of Op. 20/2, is a key ingredient in certain passages that either resist separation into principal line and accompaniment, or that elevate the cello to the status of a soloist. Both tendencies are deftly combined in the second variation of Op. 20/4/ii, where the instrument's lumbering yet expressive, wide-ranging presence commands attention at the start of the first reprise (mm. 37–40). The cello persists as leading voice through the start of the consequent phrase that follows (mm. 41–42, as shown in ex. 10.3). But then the center of attention begins to shift, and even though the cello continues to provide color and rhythmic impetus, the first violin advances to the foreground (m. 43). As the outer voices negotiate their changing relationship, we cannot necessarily pinpoint the cello's surrender as principal line. For an elusive moment, as that instrument's melodic thrust begins to dissolve in broken-chord figuration, thematic line and accompaniment blend seamlessly into one another.

The cello's heightened importance in sonata form contexts is exemplified in Op. 20/3/i, where its resonant voice takes the lead early in the recapitulation (m. 174), thus challenging customary ensemble relationships and breathing fresh life into the musical narrative. This passage foreshadows the cello's high profile in the quartet's third movement, which stands out as one of Haydn's most romantically expressive Adagios. The instrument conveys yearning and pathos toward the end of the exposition as it climbs to a sustained d^2 (mm. 35–37), overreaching both inner voices and overlapping the first violin's figuration. But Haydn saves its moment of greatest eloquence for the second part. Beginning in measure 70, the movement's golden section, the principal theme passes to the cello, whose long, plaintive phrase is supported by the first violin's figuration above, the second violin's broken-chord patterns in its own register, and the viola's throbbing bass below.

Expanded Diversity among Movement Types

Basic to Op. 20's overall profile is the new multiplicity of choices for tempo, meter, character, and tonal procedure. Among first movements, the consistency that had prevailed in Opp. 9 and 17 (each had incorporated four moderato opening movements in common time, one $\frac{6}{8}$ Presto, and one slow variation movement) is abandoned in favor of a greater variety of types. Only two of the six bear simply the tempo marking moderato, whereas each of the others is a differently modified allegro. Along with the customary common time and previously established $\frac{6}{8}$, there are examples of $\frac{2}{4}$ and $\frac{3}{4}$, and several instances of unusual section length or proportion, notably an exceptionally long development section in No. 4, a much shortened recapitulation in No. 2, and an extended coda in No. 5.

Among slow movements, the range of alternatives embraces four different form types, four different tempo markings (although five are in fact some type of

EXAMPLE 10.3 Op. 20/4/ii, mm. 41–44

adagio), and six different meters, so that all the time signatures to be found any-where among Haydn's quartets are represented: $\frac{3}{8}$, $\frac{2}{4}$, $\frac{3}{4}$, $\frac{6}{8}$, $\mathbf{c}$, and $\mathbf{\phi}$. In matters of texture and temperament, the slow movements span an especially wide spectrum, including the meditative, homogeneous blend of No. 1; an operatic Adagio in No. 2 (titled "Capriccio") that juxtaposes lyrical solos with ominous unison decla-mations; an embellished soliloquy for first violin in No. 6; and a multiplicity of textures in the variations of No. 4, which give all ensemble members a chance to enjoy the limelight, if only momentarily in the case of the inner parts.

The dance movements contribute to the general theme of diversity, not-withstanding the customary limitations of meter, form, and style that define this movement type. Only two are content to stay in tonic major for the trio, whereas each of the others proposes a different relationship: subdominant (No. 1), paral-lel minor (No. 2), submediant (No. 3), and parallel major (No. 5); and as noted earlier, tonal variety is further enriched by the device of an indirect dominant preparation to the return in two of the three movements with open-ended trios (V_3^6 of ii in No. 1; V of iv in No. 3). Moreover, the minuets and trios alike en-compass an impressive range of topical allusion, character, and rhythmic com-plexity, with examples of innocence and simplicity (No. 6, both minuet and trio), courtly manners (No. 5, minuet), country dance (No. 3, trio), and rhyth-mic *imbroglio* (No. 4, minuet).

Diversity of movement character and design has the natural consequence of accentuating the uniqueness of each quartet. But there is an additional compli-cation: a complementary network of similarities among analogous movements in different quartets, each varying the treatment of a common problem or idiosyn-crasy. There are three fugal finales, all distinct from one another in terms of meter, number of subjects, particular usage of fugal procedures, and overall design; two first movements (those of Nos. 1 and 2) have opening themes that invoke the manner of a trio sonata in different ways but with similar effect; and three dance movements have run-on trios, each negotiating a different species of harmonic connection to the recurring minuet.

Aspects of Cyclic Design; Cyclic Integration

Surveying the quartets' different movement types in view of their individuality as well as the relationships that connect them sheds light on the methodical nature of Haydn's procedures, the scope of his ambition, and the ways in which he either builds on his own precedents or surmounts their limitations. But what about the individual quartets to which these movements belong? To what extent do we find either the persistence of familiar practices or the development of a new apparatus for the design of a four-movement cycle? The clearest outer sign of a fresh outlook is Haydn's decision to reverse his customary order of interior movements (dance movement second, slow movement third) for three of the new works, Nos. 2, 4, and 6. More richly scented with musical significance is the fact that two of the Op. 20 quartets are cast in minor. This seems significant in itself (no other set has more than one), but what attracts particular notice is the profound difference in temperament and expression between them, well exemplified by their respective opening movements: volatile, capricious, and spontaneous in No. 3, not unlike the instrumental idiom of C. P. E. Bach, as opposed to even-tempered and serious in No. 5, more in the manner of Gluck's tragic theater style.[9]

Intersecting the minor-quartet phenomenon is this opus group's accent on single-tonic designs that explore different patterns of alternation between major and minor modes. Whereas No. 5 (F minor) frames a placid F major trio within a stern F minor minuet before proceeding to a slow movement in major, No. 2 (C major) reverses both the interior movement sequence and the corresponding modal relationships, offering a minor Adagio in second place and a minor trio for the third-movement dance complex. No. 4 (D major) reserves minor tonality for the slow movement only.

All six works, with the partial exception of No. 1 (cited earlier for its resemblances in overall design to works from Opp. 9 and 17), show signs of balancing the traditional emphasis on intermovement contrast with a measure of long-range cohesion. This latter tendency is scarcely new—we have seen examples among the earliest quartets—but it does take on fresh urgency in Op. 20, and it may be seen as part of a general concern for cyclic integration in Haydn's instrumental works from around this time.[10]

Impressions of cyclic cohesion are especially pronounced among the quartets that incorporate fugal finales (Nos. 5, 6, and 2). Given their polyphonic intensity and rhetorical heft, the fugues tend to outweigh their respective quartets' interior movements and even rival the opening movements in importance; and the dynamic profile of a given fugue, with its build to a high point before the close, is thus replicated on a larger scale by the cycle as a whole, whose learned-style finale embodies the quartet's greatest degree of ensemble engagement, surface continuity, and technical sophistication.

Op. 20/5 in F Minor

The F minor quartet, distinguished by the exalted manner in its outer movements, and endowed with the inherent constancy of a single-tonic design, strikes a serious tone at the outset by the combination of minor tonality, beat-marking rhythmic impulse, and continuity of texture, register, and line. The two middle movements sustain these qualities in different ways. The minuet proper evinces a reserved, courtly manner with the help of an even-tempered quarter-note pace, self-assured (although scarcely simple or conventional) melodic delivery, and clarity of relationship among parts; and the elision that links the end of the minuet to the start of the trio ensures seamless continuity between the two dances. The Adagio presents another facet of elevated style, invoking the realm of serious opera with a lyrical siciliana. The first violin mostly dominates the scene as an expressive soloist, alternating plain thematic delivery with passages of coloratura; and chordal accompaniments, often favoring a persistent, long-short-long-short rhythmic pattern, lend background support.

The closing fugue transcends the middle movements' worldly images of courtly dance and theater with its alla breve signature, archetypal subject in long note values, and learned contrapuntal idiom. Certain long-range harmonic implications are now realized as the fugue subject passes through the key of Gb (mm. 61–64), thereby securing a connection with allusions to Gb and Gb minor in the first-movement coda.[11] The fugue's integrative importance is further underscored by an analogy that becomes apparent between the profile of the first movement, capped by the impact of a harmonically and thematically elaborate coda, and that of the work as a whole, crowned by the intensity of a polyphonic tour de force.

Op. 20/6 in A

Op. 20/6 resembles the F minor quartet in that both works culminate in the eventual shift from free, mostly treble-dominated textures to the rigor of fugal procedure. But it is also quite different, occupying the opposite end of the set's tonal spectrum (i.e., A major, with three sharps), evoking a generally lighter, more carefree manner in its first movement, and tempering the finale's strict style with greater rhythmic and melodic agreement between parts. As we have seen, there are family resemblances between this work and the two sharp-key quartets from the preceding sets, whose first movements likewise dance in $\frac{6}{8}$ time (Opp. 9/6 in A and 17/6 in D). In Op. 20/6, the persistence of an open-air, pastoral quality is affirmed by an unmistakable thematic correspondence between the beginnings of the first movement and the minuet (ex. 10.4a and b).

Indications that this work might continue on its idyllic path to the end, as did its sharp-key relatives in Opp. 9 and 17, are reinforced by the implications of another thematic connection, the one noted earlier between the first movements of the two A major quartets (i.e., Opp. 9/6 and 20/6; see ex. 10.1). In light of this resemblance in spirit between the two quartets' opening movements, might we reasonably anticipate some similarity between their respective finales? As noted in the previous chapter, the last movement of that earlier work stands as one of the lightest, most inconsequential finales in the repertory: a duple-meter presto whose first reprise consists of a single, nonmodulating pair of four-measure phrases. Viewed in this light, the advent of a full-scale closing fugue must be regarded as a momentous change in direction. However, in light of the movement's sprightly subject, its fast-paced motivic interplay among voices, and its embrace of a countersubject (first heard in the top part, mm. 6–7) that seems as closely allied with free style as with strict, this finale may be heard as a meeting ground of divergent idioms and a demonstration, perhaps, of their reconciliation.

Op. 20/2 in C

The last of the three cycles with fugal finales makes an especially persuasive case for long-range coherence. Like the F minor quartet, this is a single-tonic work that invokes the opposite mode to accomplish change in mood and color for both the slow movement and the dance-movement trio. Tonal sameness enhances cyclic cohesion, but in this instance it also promotes run-on connection between movements: there is no full close between the slow second movement (in C minor), which ends on a dominant chord, and the start of the minuet (C major); and the C minor trio is likewise open-ended, using that same dominant harmony (identically scored) as a connector to the return of the minuet. Consequently, the only interior full stop is the close of the minuet proper, before and after the trio.

As if to promote an overall sense of natural, effortless continuity, the boundary between slow movement and minuet is softened by the latter's opening gesture, gentle and hesitant, which prolongs a tonic chord across the bar line in all three upper parts, so that the characteristic motions of the dance emerge only gradually from the preceding movement's dissolution. A clear break separates minuet and trio; but the latter's open-ended second part, which tapers off in a succession of dominant chords, adds to the theme of integration not only by joining

EXAMPLE 10.4 Op. 20/6

(a) i, mm. 1–2   (b) iii, mm. 1–4

seamlessly to the repeat of the minuet, but by recalling the suspenseful aura of the similarly voiced dominant chords heard at the Adagio's midpoint and close.

With regard to the border between first and second movements: although marked by a full stop, it is nonetheless compromised in significant ways. First of all, the first movement's abridged recapitulation causes a destabilizing imbalance of proportions and a corresponding sense of acceleration in the large-scale structural rhythm (each principal section is shorter than the last). Added to this is a late inflection to minor (mm. 95–101, analogous to mm. 36–42 in the exposition), which leaves a mere five measures for a hasty reinstatement of major before the close. Combined with a quiet dynamic level, this tonal darkening so near the end helps temper the impact of closure as it anticipates the minor mode of the movement that follows.

From a still broader perspective, we can attribute integrative significance to the very opening of the work, where aspects of theme and texture signify a foretaste of the last movement's turn to fugal procedure. As noted in our discussion of textural elements, Haydn fashions the opening phrases in the manner of a trio sonata—in itself an emblem of an older, contrapuntal tradition—and in so doing mimics a fugal exposition's tonal play: presentation of a subject in tonic (mm. 1–6); a switch in scoring and register to herald a restatement, analogous to a fugal answer, on the dominant; and still a third (curtailed) entry, restored to tonic, which further extends the analogy with fugal procedure before the business of tonal transition gets under way.

As for the fugue itself, the choice of $\frac{6}{8}$ meter and a gigue-like character leaven the fugal discipline with an element of galant-style play; and as the movement unfolds, passages of ensemble dialogue, featuring rhythmically synchronized motion in parallel thirds and sixths, contribute to the sense of a stylistic amalgam. Disparities between the fugue and the preceding movements are thus softened, and the fugue's plausibility as a crowning, summarizing event is correspondingly enhanced.

Op. 20/3 in G Minor

Integrative forces in the G minor quartet, although not always so obvious as some of those witnessed earlier, are nonetheless unmistakably at work, some of them powerfully connected to the quartet's chief idiosyncrasies. To cite one instance: at a point roughly two thirds through the first-movement exposition (m. 64), an abrupt halt on F, the dominant of the relative major, is followed on the next downbeat by an utter non sequitur—a fortissimo fanfare, poised on a first-inversion Bb triad, with no compelling relationship to the immediately preceding or following material. At best, the chord acts as an assertion of the relative major where none was called for, and an overly portentous introduction to the skittish measures of violin solo that follow. Moreover, the fanfare's implication of some imminent, fully endorsed relative major will never be realized: the exposition skirts any decisive closing gesture by dissolving in a state of harmonically unstable transition. The oddity of this juncture takes on new significance in the recapitulation: the analogous fanfare recurs in measures 212–13, but the harmony is now transformed to a diminished seventh chord—an electrically charged inflection of the home key's dominant—to announce the extended violin solo with sharply focused intensity and thereby clarify the thread of the argument instead of intruding as an element of distraction.

Stepping back to view the quartet as a whole, can we attribute larger significance to the first movement's peculiarities? Notwithstanding the recapitulation's efforts to extract elements of coherence from volatile, disparate materials, it would be hard to imagine this movement as a finale. It leaves too palpable a sense of unresolved issues, and this is a point to which the final measures call special attention—first by giving voice to residual tensions in a stunning, fortissimo outburst, and then by suppressing them in an understated final cadence, marked piano. But if the first movement leaves certain matters unresolved, we can still recognize a complementary relationship between its outer sections—exaggerated unrest in the exposition, a more rationally ordered discourse in the recapitulation—and this in turn may be heard as the model for a larger-scale relationship between the outer movements of the cycle.

Specifically, the finale pointedly resembles the first movement in matters of texture, dynamics, rhythmic action, and thematic content. Similarities include a contrapuntally conceived primary theme whose leading voice, leaping up to an initial downbeat, triggers an immediate stepwise response; a prominent stepwise descent from Bb to F# (heard as a secondary line in the cello at the start of the first movement, then promoted to the status of a principal idea at the beginning of the finale); a special abundance of thematically salient neighbor-note gestures; and a frequently occurring oscillation figure involving groups of four sixteenth notes.

Countering the outer movements' resemblances are some equally prominent differences in syntax. Relative to the first movement's interruptions and fractured narrative, the finale proposes the reassurance of greater local continuity, goal-directed movement, and logically articulated punctuations between phrases and themes. Moreover, although the first movement and finale come to a similar kind of close, with recollections of an opening theme amid images of retreat, the finale embodies a special sense of resolution by its luminous, last-minute switch from minor to major—a sure sign of reconciliation achieved and peace restored at last.

Meanwhile, the end of the last movement embodies another summarizing trait by weaving together gestures that highlight the leading tone (F♯), on the one hand, and the lowered seventh scale degree (F♮), on the other. This juxtaposition of contrary forces resonates with elements of the first movement, most notably the close proximity of C♯ and C♮ in the opening principal line; but at the same time it evokes memories of one of the work's oddest, most daring moments: the undisguised clash between F♯ and F♮, a diminished octave above, in the opening phrase of the minuet (see ex. 10.5). What could Haydn have had in mind here, apart from the shock of willfully violating a rule of counterpoint at the apex of the movement's opening phrase? Locally, we can appreciate this event as part of a musical pun: the melodic profile of the second phrase is almost the same as the first, but this time Haydn redirects the harmony toward a full cadence in the dominant. In the process, the offending false relation is banished altogether.

A larger role for the incongruous relationship of F♯ and F♮ comes into view when we turn to the dance movement's main structural divides, namely, the end of the minuet proper and the interrupted, transitional close of the trio, both marked by a halo of tantalizing ambiguity. At the end of the minuet, occurrences of the cello's neighbor-note F♯ coincide with the first violin's descent from F♮ (mm. 47, 49, and 51). For the duration of this repetitive closing idea (mm. 47–52), the combined effect of three elements—a recurrent lowered seventh in the first

EXAMPLE 10.5 Op. 20/3/ii, mm. 1–10

violin, a prevalent B♮ in the second violin (mm. 48, 50, and 52), and a species of embellished pedal point on G below—is to give the harmony the feel of a prolonged dominant (i.e., G as V of C minor) rather than a G tonic.

Impressions of tonal ambivalence are underscored when we compare this passage with the end of the trio, where several of the same forces hold sway; but now the balance weighs still more heavily in favor of a dominant function, as if we were somehow headed toward a resolution to C minor rather than the G minor of the minuet's return: both the B♮ and the F♮ are now embedded in a principal descending line, the F♯ is reduced to a recurrent lower neighbor in eighth notes (further minimizing any significance it might have as a leading tone), and the first violin continually arpeggiates a C minor triad. A common preoccupation with the juxtaposition of F♯ and F♮ highlights the connection of these passages to the minuet's opening phrase, with its inclusion of both pitches in a simultaneous, dissonant event. The diminished-octave clash may thus be heard in retrospect to have spawned an element of unity between the dance movement's two parts, even as it works to undermine their tonal stability; and it is this very tonal uncertainty that will be rectified by the close of the finale, whose own play with F♯, F♮, and B♮ promotes cyclic integration not merely by recalling an earlier movement's peculiarities but by embracing them in a satisfying conclusion (ex. 10.6).

Op 20/4 in D

The D major quartet is marked by relatively extreme disparities in character between movements, so that its single-tonic format may be heard as a compensation for intermovement contrast: at least there is an enduring key center to which all movements can relate. Yet another cyclic phenomenon may be appreciated as well, a scheme of progressive descent from serenity and composure at the outset to raucous play in the latter part of the cycle, where a spirit of abandon tests the strength of standard movement forms and the norms of cyclic organization.

Signs of disruption are actually apparent within the opening movement, notwithstanding the mood of rare tranquility in which it begins. The stately pace of relatively long note values in $\frac{3}{4}$ time almost suggests a courtly minuet topic that has been displaced from its normal, interior location. But a more impatient motion in triplet eighths challenges the initial pace as early as measure 31. The faster surface action takes hold for longer spans from measure 43 on, sustaining the sense of a contest between opposing forces—dance-like grace versus impetuous display—as a prominent feature of the movement in all principal sections.

An impression of overstepped limits proves more explicit in the second movement, where the strophic variation format eventually loosens to accommodate an impassioned coda whose unruly series of contrasting events, including a

EXAMPLE 10.6 Op. 20/3/iv, mm. 99–104

long descending sequence, a unison fortissimo climax, and a succession of dissonant, forzato accents, threatens to overshadow the variations themselves.[12]

However willful its rhetoric, nothing in this second-movement coda prepares
us for the wild escapade that follows: a travesty of the traditional dance, which
Haydn titles "Menuet alla Zingarese." Here, in place of courtly manners, the
upper and lower parts enact a barbaric struggle as syncopated accents conflict not
only with the bar line but also with one another.

The finale upholds the general tendency of Op. 20 to make the cycle's last
portion count, in one way or another, as a crucially important element in the design. But rather than elevating the discourse through learned style, say, as did the
three fugal finales, this movement follows a path more in keeping with the daring qualities heard in previous parts of the cycle: the opening movement's unsettling triplets, the second movement's dramatized, improvisatory coda, and the
exotic minuet. Descending still further from any pretensions of high style, the
Op. 20/4 finale indulges in comical exclamations, pauses, and sometimes baf-
flingly sudden changes of topic or direction of thought.

The first violin sets an impudent tone by racing through a matched pair of
skittish, two-measure ideas (mm. 1–4) and a whimsical flourish (mm. 5–6) before joining the rest of the group in a profoundly different gesture: a forbidding

unison in minor (mm. 7–8), colored by a strange and difficult interval, the diminished fourth. This startling event grounds the initial melodic flight with a note of gravity and portent. But no sooner has the point been made than the first violin breaks off on its own, momentarily demolishing all trace of seriousness as it mocks the ominous interval in chattering sixteenth notes. Then just as quickly and arbitrarily, the full ensemble reconstitutes itself, resumes the stern, momentum-braking announcement, and then concludes the idea on a unison half cadence in measure 11 (ex. 10.7).

As if heedless of the rebuke, the first violin takes up the narrative thread once again, recalling the opening measures and then directing the principal line toward the new key. But a turn to the dominant minor (m. 22) soon leads to a mid-exposition crisis—a temporary impasse, with gaping silences, stuttering dotted rhythms, and a stubbornly repeated motive whose traversal of a diminished fourth (G♯ to C in mm. 28–30) may be heard as another mocking commentary on the earlier, all-too-serious unison pronouncement. Surface activity picks up once again in measure 33, and as the end of the exposition draws near, the movement's comic impulse resurfaces in the second violin's repeated off-beat eighth notes (mm. 43–46), each adorned with the irreverent spark of a grace note from below:[13] a colorfully exotic effect, like the similar device heard in the finale of Mozart's Violin Concerto in A, K. 219. Given that there is virtually no letup of energy in the rapid-fire, repetitive fragments that close the exposition, we might expect a similarly energized conclusion to the movement as a whole. But the end of the recapitulation backs off instead, descending in the second ending, yielding to and coming to rest on the same low-register tonic chord that had rung down the curtain on the first movement.

Early in this chapter we noted the proximity of Op. 20 to a certain negative critique of Haydn's craft, and among the musical excerpts we have examined, there are some whose ambition and ingenuity could easily be cited as evidence that Haydn was bent on proving himself to real or imagined critics. But along with samples of exemplary artistry and technique, there are other passages whose audacity points to an attitude of disdain for conventional proprieties and the narrow-minded judges who would uphold them. How else to explain such a case as the latter part of the Op. 20/3/i development section, beginning with measure 141, where an astonishing scheme of false starts, interruption, resumption, and disintegration (partially quoted in ex. 10.8) seems to anticipate the modernist languages of Bartók or Stravinsky? In measure 141, a main thematic idea is recalled from the opening of the movement. But after gaining momentum through sequential repetition (mm. 143–44), the figure is abruptly silenced, cut off midstream as an unrelated (but thematically important) figure, different in texture, dynamics, and register, fills the void—only to be thwarted just as suddenly after two measures. The descending-sequence figure, having been summarily interrupted, strives to regain the upper hand but is blocked again. In the measures

EXAMPLE 10.7 Op. 20/4/iv, mm. 7–11

that follow, the contest of mutually confounding thematic particles continues, although now in a telescoped or chopped-off version, as the two elements alternate, disintegrate, then finally make way for the formation of a new trajectory (at m. 154) that will lead to the recapitulation in measure 165. The mystifying interruptions and juxtapositions fly in the face of conventional discourse. This seems basic to their purpose; and yet it could be said that the passage follows a perverse logic nonetheless, wrapping up the development section with a summarizing encounter of thematic ingredients: one, marked x in the quoted excerpt, accomplishes a prolonged stepwise descent whereas the other, marked y, prefigures the return to the movement's home key by its downward motion to the tonic note G.

As for Haydn's flouting of convention in the Op. 20/4 minuet, where heavily accented hemiolic patterns—layered, displaced, and distributed among different parts—give rise to utter metrical confusion, here we can likewise appreciate a certain rationale behind the audacious façade. Reckless, headlong motion early in the phrase, where every beat vies to express the accentual thrust of a downbeat, serves to motivate the tonal change from tonic to dominant. Then, as the confusion dissipates, a quickened surface rhythm helps maintain momentum as the end of the reprise draws near. Yet even here, a trace of hemiolic ambivalence

EXAMPLE 10.8 Op. 20/3/i, mm. 141–53 (first violin only)

persists (mm. 6–7), especially in the bass line, as surface duration, melody, and dynamic accent fall into alignment with the meter (the second reprise revisits this order of events and actually extends the span of metrical dissonance by four measures).[14]

On occasion, Haydn takes an opposite (but no less impudent) tack by constructing an image of deliberate pedantry, as in the thoroughbass numbers affixed to a passage in the slow movement of Op. 20/5 (mm. 53–55), along with a curious Latin inscription for the first violin (see ex. 10.9). The passage in question features a meandering, figural line of thirty-second notes, supported by chordal accompaniment in the lower parts. Conveying a spirit of improvisational freedom, the solo line does not always agree with the harmony of the accompanying chords: from measure 54 through the middle of measure 55, it is only after the chord sounds that the first violin catches up, so to speak, to acknowledge the underlying harmony by touching on one or more of its pitches. Lest there be any question about the technique in operation here, Haydn takes pains not only to label it—"per figuram retardationis"—but also to identify the underlying chords with their appropriate thoroughbass symbols.[15]

Mock-pedantry can likewise be sensed in Haydn's systematic labeling of his three closing fugues, collectively an emblem of high style and learned technique. Rather ostentatiously, he designates the finales of Nos. 5, 6, and 2 as fugues with two, three, and four subjects, respectively; and in the first of the series, the alla breve fugue in F minor, he marks the appearance of learned devices with appropriate verbal signposts: "al rovescio" in measure 92, "in canone" at measure 145 (the "al rovescio" label is also found in the finales of No. 6, mm. 80 and 83, and No. 2, m. 102).

But to pursue the question of the fugues a bit further: whatever inspired Haydn to undertake such designs for three of the Op. 20 quartets, surely their purpose was not merely to prove a point to critics; and yet if there was a higher purpose to their inclusion, then the question naturally arises as to his satisfaction with the result and his subsequent decision to abandon fugue as the principal basis for a quartet movement (except for one later occasion, the finale of Op. 50/4). Within the domain of a fugue's subject-based linear continuity, there was little place for the narrative conventions, customary landmarks, or proportional schemes that normally govern a sonata form, rondo, or minuet, and hence no corresponding basis for the kind of expectation-thwarting intrigue so basic to Haydn's style. Yet fugues did offer immense possibilities for motivic development and harmonic excursion; and through their association with compositional rigor, they could help, at this juncture in Haydn's career, to certify the attainment of a new level of sophistication.

On balance, it would seem reasonable to regard Op. 20 as a connoisseur's showcase for some of the medium's most advanced, most widely ranging possi-

EXAMPLE 10.9   Op. 20/5/iii, mm. 53–56

bilities up to this time. Gerber acknowledged as much in his 1790 *Lexikon*, identifying these works with Haydn's attainment of "full greatness as a quartet composer."[16] For other composers, the Op. 20 quartets were a source of keen interest and a model worth studying and emulating. The Andante con moto of Mozart's String Quartet in E♭, K. 428, appears to derive directly from the Affettuoso e sostenuto of Op. 20/1. Beethoven copied this quartet in his own hand, and the influence of its slow movement (whether directly or through Mozart's example) can be sensed in quartet movements of his that embrace similarly homogeneous textures, most notably Op. 59/3/ii. Also noteworthy is the fact that Johannes Brahms once owned the autograph manuscripts for the entire set, and in fact took pains to make corrections based on the autograph in his pocket score edition.[17]

The apparent significance of Op. 20 for Haydn's own later directions may be described as both varied and diffuse. There was no immediate sequel—he did not return to the genre until after the start of the next decade—and none of the subsequent opus groups closely resembles this set in outlook or design, with the partial exception of Op. 50, in which ingredients such as a fugal finale (Op. 50/4), the preoccupation with intermovement thematic relationship, and the tendency to juxtapose disparate or seemingly incompatible ideas may all be cited as points of resemblance.

Several of Op. 20's precedents were to prove decisive: the revised sequence by which the slow movement was placed second, the minuet-trio third, became nearly standard from Op. 50 on; and each full set of quartets beginning with Op. 50 follows the example of Op. 20 in casting at least one interior slow movement as a strophic variation form. The general tendency to endow the finale with special weight—if not culminative significance—is traceable to this opus as well. Techniques for distributing thematic interest among all the instruments, displayed prominently in Op. 20, may be seen as models for Haydn's subsequent approaches to ensemble play, and the new role of the cello as a soloistic or theme-carrying voice—in different registers and various formal contexts—is likewise a feature of this set to which later quartets will turn, although seldom with as much zeal as in these early examples.

Perhaps most important of all as a precedent for Haydn's later endeavors is the new accent on innovation itself. As Haydn proceeds, underlying consistencies in design and technique will persist; but from Op. 20 on, he will position the quartet as a forum for novelty—and at least occasionally, as an opportunity to reinvent some of the basic assumptions on which his concept of the genre rested.

Op. 33 (1781) and
Op. 42 ([?1784–] 1785)

It was in early December 1781 that Haydn wrote to an illustrious contemporary from Zurich, the theologian and physiognomist J. C. Lavater, in connection with his newly completed set of quartets.[1] Recognizing that there are many music connoisseurs and patrons in Zurich and Winterthur, and eager to sell copies of the quartets by subscription, he asks Lavater's help in making known their availability. His letter begins on a note of flattery but then quickly turns to the matter at hand: "As one reads, hears, and relates, I myself am not inept, in that my name . . . is known to great acclaim in every country." A statement of simple truth, this last phrase stands as a reminder of the circumstances under which the works were conceived and the high expectations that must have attended their appearance.

The quartets are composed, Haydn famously writes, in "*a new, quite special way, for I haven't composed any for 10 years.*" In so declaring to Lavater and to other potential buyers, Haydn was exaggerating slightly (the Op. 20 quartets are dated 1772), but the remark is well taken nonetheless—an apology for neglecting the genre and ceding leadership to others, and also a rationale for the change in approach to be expected by performers and listeners. Under these conditions, could they have been written in anything other than a "new, quite special way"?

By undertaking to enlist subscribers, Haydn was assuming the role of an entrepreneur, exercising his new rights (as specified in the redrawn contract of 1779 with Prince Esterházy) to distribute his music as he wished. In the case of the quartets, it appears he had a twofold scheme in mind: to have them published, but to offer them beforehand to a select group of connoisseurs in the form of manuscript copies. Participating patrons would thus be able to enjoy the privilege of owning, performing, and discussing the quartets—brand-new inventions by a much talked-about composer—before they became available to the public at large. (In addition to the communication cited, two other letters survive, out of a probable total of some sixteen,[2] in which Haydn offers manuscript copies of the quartets by subscription.)

As for the other part of the plan, selling the new works to his publisher for distribution as prints, Haydn's letter to Artaria of 18 October mentions "6 new quartets which will be ready in 3 weeks," and an enclosure to the letter clarifies that four of the planned set of six are complete.[3] Publication was thus imminent; and the fact that the extant letters to subscribers are dated 3 December implies that the set was finished by that time. Meanwhile, it was important to satisfy those subscribers as promised with their prepublication copies. Timing was critical, in other words, and Haydn was understandably vexed when all did not go as planned. Before the end of the month (29 December), Artaria seemingly jumped the gun by announcing in the *Wiener Zeitung* that the set was being engraved and would be available in four weeks. This prompted an irate response from Haydn, who wrote several days later (4 January) to complain that the integrity of his offer had been compromised by the premature announcement. His next letter to Artaria, dated 20 January, was more conciliatory, acknowledging a misunderstanding, or at least a lack of sufficient caution, on both sides. In the end, Artaria delayed publication for several months, and the edition evidently did not appear until April 1782 (advertised on 17 April). But in the meantime Haydn had apparently also sold the set to Hummel, and in a letter to Artaria of July 1782 he tries to extricate himself from an awkward situation by casting blame on Artaria's "over-hasty announcement," which had obliged him to offer his quartets "all over the place."[4]

Judging from the correspondence cited here, it seems safe to place the date of completion for the quartets in late autumn 1781, sometime between the message of 18 October to Artaria and the letters of 3 December to Lavater and others. No autograph manuscript exists for these works,[5] but one of the copies, an incomplete set at the library of the Benedictine Monastery at Melk, is thought to represent one of the sets that Haydn sold to subscribers.[6] The copy in question, in which just four of the six works are extant, was prepared by an Esterházy scribe whose hand also can be recognized in a fragment believed to come from another subscription copy. The fragment was evidently cut from a title page to the cello part, whose first page of actual music can be seen on the reverse. The title, in Haydn's hand, reads "Sei quartetti. di me giuseppe Haydn ppria. Prego umilmente d'osservare il piano, e forte" (Six quartets. by me Joseph Haydn in my own hand. I humbly ask you to observe the piano and forte [dynamic markings]).

The four separate manuscripts comprising the incomplete Melk source bear numberings that correspond to the sequence in Artaria's edition—5, 2, 1, 3, 6, 4 with respect to the familiar, traditional numbering. Artaria's ordering, further confirmed by the fragment, which shows the first quartet in this copy to have been No. 5, may thus be regarded as an authentic order.[7] The familiar number sequence, made standard by Pleyel's *Collection complette*, follows that of an early edition published by Sieber in Paris, advertised on 16 January 1783.[8]

The nickname "Russian" with which Op. 33 has long been identified evidently originated with the dedication of the quartets to the Grand Duke of Russia, later Czar Paul, in Artaria's reprint of the set (not the original edition). The choice of dedicatee is likely to have been inspired by an occasion in late December 1781, when a quartet of Haydn's, presumed to be one from the new set, was featured in a private concert given by the grand duchess during the couple's sojourn in Vienna.[9] (Two other nicknames are associated with the set: "Gli scherzi," which comes from the fact that the dance movements are labeled "Scherzo," and the "Maiden" quartets, which—as with Op. 20—derives from the title page design of Hummel's edition.)

Initial Notes on Style

Haydn may easily be forgiven for boasting of a "new, quite special way." Obviously, he deemed it important to describe the quartets in terms that would spark curiosity and enhance their attractiveness; and if they did not exactly offer a sweeping departure from his previous works, they nonetheless represented a significant recasting of the genre with regard to character, tone, and technical aspiration. Certain differences between the new works and their predecessors doubtless reflect changes in fashion: the Op. 20 quartets' figural detail and contrapuntal artifice may have appealed to connoisseurs in the early 1770s, whereas the more easygoing manner of Op. 33 would seem more in keeping with a current fondness for natural sentiment, melodic simplicity, and structural transparency. Tendencies in this direction can be found in Haydn's other instrumental music of the time. Among his symphonies from the mid-1770s to 1781, for example, a prevailing "artistic stance of entertainment"[10] suggests a general shift of focus in compositional ambition and aesthetics as well as an acknowledgment of contemporary popular taste. Haydn's experience as director of the Eszterháza opera theater also may be cited as a likely source for some of the new quartets' distinctive traits, notably their rhythmic fluency and bantering ensemble play.

Germane to the question of an altered approach in Op. 33 is the matter of Haydn's revised contract, which gave him the right to sell his own compositions: evidently less concerned now with such local constraints as a patron's requests, a particular performer's technique, or the idiosyncratic tastes of those within his immediate circle, he now faced the prospect of writing explicitly for subscription and publication. The circles in which his music was purchased, performed, and admired were destined to expand, and we can readily imagine his wanting to please new customers for whom comic opera, street songs, or popular dances might have more appeal than the learned discourse of Op. 20.

Inseparable from Haydn's presumed concerns for salability and popular appeal are the pervasive signs of an altered artistic outlook and a new depth of insight into the nature of the genre and its possibilities. Outstanding in this respect, if not altogether new with this opus, is the concentration on motivic process and the accompanying preference for textures that distribute thematic interest among all members of the ensemble. In addition, there are new approaches to opus design, cyclic profile, and movement type, all to be explored in the discussion that follows; but it is important to note at the outset that the more novel elements are often found side by side with practices that recall Haydn's earlier quartets.

Overview of the Opus; Characteristic Aspects of Form and Movement Type

Turning to table 11.1, we find a new term for the dance movements (scherzo) and a fashionably new form (rondo), as well as signs of a tendency to relinquish some of the formal diversity and technical ambition of Op. 20. The tonal spectrum has been narrowed (the range of home keys extends from two sharps to three flats), and tonal action within movements is correspondingly less adventurous, with fewer occasions for emphasized remote relationship and nothing so radical as the Op. 20/5/i coda, with its excursion to a region of harmonies with double flats. As Haydn now returns to the practice of including a single quartet in a minor key, the number of movements in minor shrinks to six, counting dance-movement trios (in Op. 20 there were nine, and even Op. 17 had as many as eight); and in view of the recognized affinities between minor tonality and troubled or impassioned expression, the altered balance may be seen as part of a general inclination toward a lighter, more easygoing manner.

As for the design of the individual quartet cycle, Haydn casts as many as half the quartets (Nos. 2, 3, and 4) in a single mold, one that he perhaps felt would prove specially attractive in its distribution of contrasts in tempo, meter, and character: a thematically varied sonata form at the outset, marked allegro moderato in each case; a fast or moderately fast dance movement in second place; a contemplative, slow-tempo third movement in $\frac{3}{4}$ time; and a grammatically simple, high-speed rondo. Against this backdrop, Op. 33/5 and 6 stand out as exceptional, No. 5 beginning with a long, very fast movement in $\frac{2}{4}$, comparable to that of Op. 20/3, whereas the first movement of No. 6 resembles those of Opp. 9/6, 17/6, and 20/6 in its lively $\frac{6}{8}$ meter and pastoral character. However different from each other, the two works are also significantly related. Both are single-tonic cycles, and each locates a soloistic, minor-key slow movement in second place, so that the impact of juxtaposed opposites (fast vs. slow, major vs. minor,

TABLE 11.1 Summary statistics for Opp. 33 and 42

Op.No.	Hob.No.	Movement			
		i	ii	iii	iv
33/1	III:37	B♭ c Allegro moderato SF 91	Bm/B♭ $\frac{3}{4}$ Allegro di molto S/T [Scherzo] 36/26	D $\frac{6}{8}$ Andante SF 92	B♭ $\frac{2}{4}$ Presto SF 194
33/2	III:38	E♭ c Allegro moderato SF 90	E♭ $\frac{3}{4}$ Allegro S/T [Scherzo] 34/34	B♭ $\frac{3}{4}$ Largo e sostenuto Nonstandard 72	E♭ $\frac{6}{8}$ Presto Rondo 172
33/3	III:39	C ¢ Allegro moderato SF 167	C $\frac{3}{4}$ Allegretto S/T [Scherzo] 34/16	F $\frac{3}{4}$ Adagio ma non troppo Slow-mvt. 91(r)	C $\frac{2}{4}$ Presto Rondo [Rondo] 170
33/4	III:40	B♭ c Allegro moderato SF 89	B♭/B♭m $\frac{3}{4}$ Allegretto S/T [Scherzo] 24/19	E♭ $\frac{3}{4}$ Largo Nonstandard 63	B♭ $\frac{2}{4}$ Presto Rondo 214(r)
33/5	III:41	G $\frac{2}{4}$ Vivace assai SF 305	Gm ¢ Largo e cantabile Slow-mvt. 53	G $\frac{3}{4}$ Allegro S/T [Scherzo] 42/20	G $\frac{6}{8}$ Allegretto–Presto Strophic var. 106(r)
33/6	III:42	D $\frac{6}{8}$ Vivace assai SF (irreg.) 164	Dm ¢ Andante Slow-mvt. 50	D $\frac{3}{4}$ Allegretto S/T [Scherzo] 26/24	D $\frac{2}{4}$ Allegretto Alternating var. 114(r)
42	III:43	Dm $\frac{2}{4}$ Andante ed innocentemente SF 105	D/Dm $\frac{3}{4}$ M/T 28/16	B♭ ¢ Adagio e cantabile Nonstandard 57	Dm $\frac{2}{4}$ Presto SF (irreg.) 103

*Trio not specified in Op. 33.

etc.) registers early in the work. Moreover, both have last movements that explore new approaches to variation form. Previously a slow-tempo, highly embellished affair suitable either for the beginning of a quartet or an interior position (as in Op. 20/4/ii), variation now becomes the basis for a finale, with a quickened tempo, a corresponding release from decorative detail, and an emphasis on predictability, tonal stability, and momentum. Op. 33/1 in B minor, obviously unique by virtue of its minor key, resembles Nos. 2, 3, and 4 in its order of interior movements as well as its allegiance to the custom of a moderately fast opening movement. Unlike any of the others, it poses the challenge of a finale in sonata form.

A clear sign that Haydn has embarked on another course with Op. 33 is his decision to abandon fugue and its associations—learned, transcendent, resistant to whims of fashion—in favor of an equivalent emphasis on the rondo, designed for popular appeal and positioned to end the cycle in a spirit of carefree exuberance.

All three of the rondos conform to the same basic formula, with three occurrences of a two-reprise refrain (the third occurrence is abbreviated in Op. 33/2), a pair of episodes interspersed, and a coda. The lightweight, tuneful refrains of Op. 33/2/iv (a gigue-like country dance) and No. 3/iv (evidently derived from a traditional Croatian melody)[11] are treated to nearly literal recurrence, whereas that of Op. 33/4/iv is subjected to variation, and in this respect it occupies a middle ground between two discrete form types represented among other finales in the set: strophic variation versus five-part rondo. (Correspondingly, the alternating variation scheme of Op. 33/6 may be described as a mixture of rondo-like recurrence and variation.) Perhaps as an antidote to formal simplicity and repetitiveness, all three rondos feature comical end games, leading us through a series of false starts, pauses, fragmentary thematic utterances, or other signs of disintegration to spotlight the inevitability of closure while at the same time preventing its coming about in any decisive, predictable way.

If the finales' wit and popular appeal underscore the distance between Opp. 33 and 20, then the new quartets' slow movements may be heard on the contrary as a site of connection with Haydn's established practices. Op. 33/3/iii, for example, revisits the varied-reprise idea previously encountered in Opp. 9/2, 9/4, 17/4, and 20/6 as a showcase for soloistic decoration. Specially featured in this instance is a transitional phrase that partially loosens the notated triple meter by superimposing patterns in an implied $\frac{2}{4}$. First heard in measures 14–18, treated to flowing embellishment in measures 43–47, then subjected to further decoration in the second part (mm. 75–79), the rhythmically unsettled passages allow the first violin a glimmer of freedom from prevailing metrical constraints.

The practice of reserving the slow movement as a vehicle for expressive solo display is further sustained in Op. 33/5, whose Largo e cantabile begins in a concerto-like manner with a ritornello: a solidly scored, initial statement, punctuated by a full cadence, that will introduce a more expansive, open-ended span suggestive of a concerto movement's first solo (one that in this instance begins to modulate after a single measure of tonic stability). The analogy seems apt in spite of the fact that the first violin is present from the start. Its role in the opening measures is straightforwardly thematic, and the ritornello-like impression is confirmed by the gruff closing figure that separates it from the narrative that follows. Recurrences of this figure will highlight the persistence of concerto-like procedure at two landmarks later in the form: the transition from the end of the second solo (m. 38) to a notated cadenza (which begins in m. 41) and the immediately ensuing close of the movement (mm. 51–53).

The Scherzos

Nothing in the outward appearance of these quartets captures the spirit of novelty and liberation so well as the new label "Scherzo" for each of the dance movements (curiously, the trios are not titled). But does the music itself live up to the raciness of the name? In some respects, these movements remain tied to conventional practices. The scherzo proper is invariably designed as a rounded binary form of small to moderate size, with a span of modulatory or tonally unstable activity early in the second reprise. The trios, although structurally diverse, all adhere to customary two-reprise formats. There are no tonal surprises: the trios simply sustain the tonic key or else change to the opposite mode, and there are no instances of run-on connection as seen on occasion in previous opus groups (Opp. 9/1; 17/2 and 5; 20/1, 2, and 3).

With regard to mood, character, and pace, the dance movements present anything but a unified picture, and at least one, the scherzo proper of Op. 33/4, actually comes close to the dignified manner of a courtly minuet. Others digress from traditional decorum with an accelerated speed and heightened rhythmic propulsion. For the first time, all dance movements in a set have actual tempo markings; and also for the first time (in Nos. 1, 2, and 5) the specified speed is faster than allegretto. In Nos. 1 and 5, the combination of slow harmonic rhythm, long melodic trajectories, and repetitive rhythmic figures implies a pace in which the measure eclipses the beat as primary metrical impulse.

The dance movements' promise of playful adventure is most fully realized in the scherzo of Op. 33/5, where gyrating arpeggiations in the principal line (mm. 1–3) keep performers alert and listeners off balance by superimposing a surrogate duple impulse on a fast-charging repeated-note background (see ex. 11.1). Only with the lunge to a dissonant accent on the downbeat of measure 4, marked forzato, do all parts join in confirming the notated downbeat. An initial four-measure unit has thus been achieved, internal complications notwithstanding, so that we can expect a comparable-size unit to follow and thereby uphold a conventional, periodic norm of four-measure phrase rhythm. This anticipated out-

EXAMPLE 11.1   Op. 33/5/iii, mm. 1–10 (violin 1 only)

come seems close to fulfillment in the three, metrically stabilized measures that follow (mm. 5–7), and we have every reason to expect a cadence in measure 8 to balance the metrical and harmonic accent of measure 4. But what Haydn offers instead is a loud silence—a vacuum to absorb the previous measures' energy, derail the phrase rhythm, and annihilate expectations. When the displaced cadence does materialize following the vacant measure, it comes quietly (the marking is piano) as an ironic afterthought in place of the full-volume close we had been led to anticipate. This order of events recurs almost verbatim at the end of the second reprise, but the impact of thwarted expectation is now intensified as the final cadence is rendered still more quietly (i.e., pianissimo).

The format of principal dance plus trio naturally invites contrast. Op. 33 is no exception in this regard, and several of the trios stand out for their elements of novelty and surprise. In Op. 33/2, for example, a whimsical blend of high and low styles in the scherzo serves as a platform for the trio's sound-picture of a tipsy village fiddler, totally engrossed in his song, who sways to the lilt of a rustic accompaniment as his left hand slides with abandon over the fingerboard.

A comparably stunning pair of images inspires the dance movement to Op. 33/3. A subdued, darkly colored scherzo, marked sotto voce, confines all four instruments to their lowest registers as it blends their voices in close harmony. Then comes the trio, with a drastic change of register, timbre, and theme to dispel the somber tone. The lower parts drop out altogether, the first violin jumps to the bright A and E strings, altogether unused in the scherzo, and the violins proceed to sing like a pair of birds.

Special Points of Connection with Op. 20

The serene Op. 33/3 scherzo, maximally differentiated from the violin duet with which it is paired, merits attention from a different perspective as a case of resemblance to the preceding opus. The stately triple-meter pulse, homogeneous texture, and lower-register timbres are all unmistakable reminders of the opening movement of Op. 20/4. And at one point in the scherzo (mm. 15–18), the similarity actually embraces melodic gesture and surface rhythm, not merely the more general aspects of mood and sonority (see ex. 11.2).

EXAMPLE 11.2

(a) Op. 20/4/i, mm. 19–24

(b) Op. 33/3/ii, mm. 15–18

This pair of excerpts may be read as one of several signs that Op. 20 was more than a distant memory as Haydn undertook the Op. 33 quartets. These were the products of a new decade and were tailored to different tastes, but such factors scarcely preclude the possibility of recaptured, reanimated trains of thought, or the adaptation of previously developed ideas to the requirements of a new project. There are places in Op. 33 that in fact suggest a deliberate effort to revive or transform material from the earlier opus, notwithstanding the lapse in time between them. To begin with, the first movement of Op. 33/6 bears a certain family resemblance to those of Opp. 9/6, 17/6, and 20/6: each has a key signature of two or three sharps and a fast compound duple meter (Op. 33/6/i will turn out to be Haydn's last of this type), and it may or may not be purely coincidence that Opp. 20/6/i and 33/6/i have exactly the same measure count (164). A different kind of relationship to Op. 20 may be seen in the Op. 33/5 finale, which suggests a synthesis and transformation of two slow-movement types encountered in Op. 20—the siciliana of No. 5, with its signature dotted-rhythm patterns, and the strophic variations of No. 4. In devising a movement that appropriates key elements of both, Haydn changes the location to the end of the cycle and quickens the pace: first to allegretto, then eventually to presto for a whirlwind conclusion that, for good measure, recalls the concern for cyclic cohesion witnessed in Op. 20 by retrieving the stepwise dominant-to-tonic figure with which the first movement had both opened and closed.

More carefully concealed resemblances may be traced between the outwardly dissimilar opening movements of Opp. 20/3 and 33/5. The two complement one another modally (the former is in G minor, the latter in G major); each stands out as the sole opening movement of its set in $\frac{2}{4}$ time (noteworthy in light of the rarity of opening movements in duple meter from Op. 9 on); both are long, 270 and 305 measures, respectively; and both have exceptionally fast tempo markings (allegro con spirto, vivace assai). Their expositions are nearly identical in length (94 and 95 measures, respectively); both feature primary themes that begin with virtually identical surface rhythms (♪ | ♩.   ♪ | ♫♫ ; the long note is embellished with a turn in Op. 33/5), and in both cases the opening rhythm recurs as an element of thematic elaboration and derivation. Also similar is the manner in which destabilized harmony just before the end of the exposition promotes open-ended connection across the structural divide; in either instance, the path will lead the second time around to a recollection of primary theme material in the key of G minor at the start of the development section. Finally, comparable strategies are evident in the way both movements end, passing a stepwise thematic gesture among different parts (descending in Op. 20/3, rising in Op. 33/5), then closing on a quizzical note rather than surging to a resonant conclusion (the contradictory, spirited outburst in the earlier work, mm. 267–68, has no counterpart in Op. 33/5).

Notwithstanding such uncanny resemblances, the two movements' expositions do betray marked differences in character and rhetoric as they unfold. There is nothing in Op. 20/3 comparable to the later work's paradoxical opening gesture—an unmistakable closing figure whose implications will be realized in various ways as the movement proceeds—nor is there anything in Op. 33/5 that quite resembles the earlier work's discontinuities and abrupt changes of topic, at least until the latter part of the exposition, where a striking resemblance materializes: in both works, a fortissimo exclamation intrudes on the scene (mm. 65–66 in Op. 20/3/i; m. 78 in Op. 33/5/i), planted in both cases on the exact same harmony: a B♭ major chord in first inversion, heavily scored in the ensemble's middle registers.

These analogous events—jarring non sequiturs that disrupt the expositions' course of action—pose riddles to be solved, and their consequences will be duly explored in the movements' recapitulations. Eventually, both will make amends by transforming their respective disturbances into agents of focused intensity. As described in the preceding chapter, the fortissimo exclamation in Op. 20/3 is ultimately converted into a grammatically coherent, goal-directed harmony: a diminished seventh chord that points urgently to a resolving tonic. Something equally persuasive occurs in Op. 33/5, where the loud chord (now marked forte) comes back transposed down a fifth, from B♭ to E♭, in keeping with the logic of recapitulation. Accompanying the tonal shift is the newly won stability of a low-register, root-position foundation; and the chord's function is now transformed to that of a lowered-submediant deflection following a pause on the dominant seventh (mm. 270–71). The surprise move from V^7 to $\flat VI$ at measure 272 acts as the springboard for a climactic derivative of the primary theme in which the weight of the event is magnified by double stops spanning middle and low registers.

New Ingredients: Perspectives on the "New, Quite Special Way"

Apart from the obvious formal and terminological innovations—the rondo and variation finales and the change of designation from minuet to scherzo—the chief novelties of Op. 33 reside in certain approaches to motivic development and ensemble play. Neither trait is foreign to Haydn's earlier works, and as far as basic principles are concerned, the new quartets are best regarded as a splendid sequel to previous accomplishments rather than an embodiment of something altogether new. Yet the true miracle of Op. 33 is not that Haydn builds so richly on his own precedents, but that he handles potentially complex materials with such a light touch, weaving them into movements whose guileless manner belies the ingenuity by which their often playful, rustic, or comic images are informed.

As in Mozart's contemporaneous piano concertos (K. 413–15), famously described by the composer in a letter of 28 December 1782 to his father, "there are passages here and there from which the connoisseurs alone can derive satisfaction; but these passages are written in such a way that the less learned cannot fail to be pleased, though without knowing why."[12] There is much that can be appreciated in the Op. 33 quartets on first hearing, by amateur and connoisseur alike, thanks to such virtues as narrative continuity, structural clarity, and disarming tunefulness; and yet these elements are typically interlaced with complicated motivic relationships, the wit of functional ambivalence, and the irony of undermined conventions. Here, perhaps, is the best argument for a genuinely "new, quite special way": the intersection of complexity and simplicity in works designed to be enjoyed from multiple vantage points and levels of sophistication.

Aspects of Motivic Process and Thematic Texture

The opening of the E♭ major quartet, Op. 33/2, recommends itself as a model of motivic concentration, notwithstanding the prevailing simplicity of melodic gesture and accompaniment (at least at the outset, where the latter consists merely of chord roots on the beat and afterbeat chord tones in the inner parts). An inverted form of the initial rising fourth recurs as early as the second half of measure 1 (see ex. 11.3a, in which the ideas are marked 1*m* and 2*m*); the rising triadic figure of measure 2 (3*m*) elaborates the first half of measure 1 and then joins

EXAMPLE 11.3 Op. 33/2/i

(a) mm. 1–4 (violin 1 only)

(b) mm. 12–15

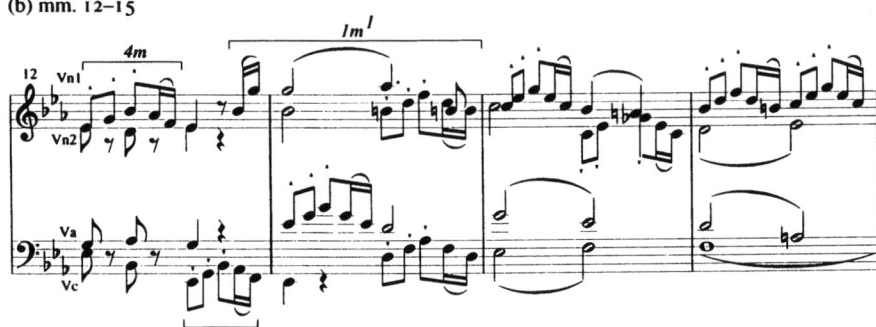

(c) mm. 19–21

(d) mm. 28–32

an inversion of the opening leap plus anticipation; the rhythm of measure 3 in its entirety rhymes with that of measure 1; and measure 4 brings the phrase to a close by combining 3m with a rhythmically altered replica of 2m. At least four motivic ingredients may thus be identified, and two of them, 1m and the composite 4m, will take on great urgency as the exposition continues. Development of 1m gets under way immediately (mm. 5–8), and the combined force of motivic elaboration and tonal transition is anticipated as early as measure 12, where the cello's impertinent echo of the first violin's closing gesture 4m begins a modulatory dialogue (ex. 11.3b). All four instruments now take up 4m in turn while inflected scale degrees begin to destabilize the harmony. Thus begins the journey into a new tonal orbit, spearheaded at first by the first violin's relentless development of 4m (mm. 15–18), but then expanded to encompass derivatives of 1m in all parts (mm. 19–20).

Meanwhile, the emphatic downbeat in measure 19 anticipates a structurally more salient event, an elided cadence in the new key at measure 21 (ex. 11.3c). The upbeat to this measure gives the impression of closing a tight circle by replicating, on the level of the dominant, the anticipatory leap of a fourth with which the movement had begun. Confirmation of the new key seems almost assured at this juncture, and yet forward motion persists in a rising sequence (derived from 4m, mm. 21–22), a quickening of the harmonic rhythm (mm. 23–24), and an explosion of triplet sixteenths (mm. 25–26) that will prepare for the ascent to a melodic climax (f^3 in m. 27) and a decisive cadence in measure 28. The path is now clear for a motivically saturated closing phrase comprising derivatives of 1m (mm. 29, 31–32) and 4m (m. 30; see ex. 3d).

Whereas Op. 33/2 greeted us with a fully formed, deceptively innocent tune at the outset, Haydn's strategy for Op. 33/3 is to draw our attention to motivic particles from the start, embedding them in a musical fabric that takes shape by degrees, eventually coalescing after several false starts. Only then are the motives' potentials realized as a central ingredient in the musical narrative. Measure 1 introduces a mere patter of inner-voice repeated notes to get things under way. The first violin then enters on a sustained pitch, as if warming up, before gaining momentum with a pair of embellished repeated notes; and at last the cello joins the action in measure 4. The group now seems to have come together in earnest; but signals get crossed almost immediately, and in fact the parts do cross: the first violin tumbles through two octaves; the cello mirrors this action all too vigorously, climbing two octaves, and thus the former ends up below the latter. After a half measure's pause, the whole process starts over, now a step higher, but with exactly the same result six measures later. A third try—repositioning the inner-voice repeated notes to a lower register and pitching them off key ($b\flat$ and d^1 rather than e^1 and c^2 or f^1 and d^2) gives the impression of finally loosening the primary theme's constraints, promoting continuity, and leading the way to the start of the transition.

Meanwhile, two distinct motives have arisen—the repeated-note idea of measures 2–3, the sixteenth-note turn figure of measure 5—and they will blossom as the exposition progresses. In measures 32–36, for example, the sixteenth-note gesture, detached from its original setting, is passed back and forth in dialogue and woven around variously developed reiterations of the repeated notes, whose rhythm has quickened from halves to quarters. As these two discrete portions of an opening idea play off each other simultaneously and in alternation, motivic congestion coincides with tonal change, and the texture becomes almost completely thematic.

Elsewhere among these works, we find prime examples of an even more tightly knit thematic interplay by which the functions of principal line and background, presented initially as separate strands, become intertwined to the point that distinctions between them almost dissolve. In a prime example, the beginning of the B minor quartet, Op. 33/1, the violins' opening move evinces whimsy and feigned simplicity. As if determined to skirt the responsibility of announcing the tonic minor key, they start with a fragment of melody and accompaniment that implies the relative major D. The deception lasts for a full two measures before the lower parts spring to life (see ex. 11.4). Here the cello turns the texture upside down by grasping the melody; simultaneously, the harmonizing upper parts clarify the tonal focus as they take up the repeated-note accompaniment. But this arrangement lasts only an instant before the balance of forces shifts once again: the cello, instead of assuming real melodic direction, hovers repetitively around the dominant note F♯, so that it begins to sound less like a melodic thread and more like a floor to the texture. Meanwhile, the first violin gains prominence by launching an arpeggiation to e^3, thus breaking away from the note-repetition pattern and capping the melodic line with an expressive high point. The phrase as a whole materializes as a dynamic process of give and take among parts, and the flow of motivic energy among them momentarily overrides any stable, hierarchic arrangement of melody and accompaniment.[13]

In first-movement sonata forms such as those considered above, motivic development is typically constrained by the imperatives of specialized themes and goal-directed strategies within a section. Elsewhere in the cycle, less complicated forms sometimes invite a more far-reaching motivic enterprise in which a single idea becomes the driving force for an entire section or even a whole movement, as in the unstoppable rondo finale of Op. 33/3, whose folk tune oscillates obsessively between two notes a third apart, variously skipping back and forth in eighths or moving in sixteenths to fill the space between those notes. Thus formed, the idea migrates to the inner voices as the second reprise begins. (When this happens, the first violin's repeated-note countermelody recalls in diminution the pitch, register, rhythm, and melodic decorations of the first movement's initial thematic idea.) The principal theme's traversal of the instruments climaxes with a harmonically destabilized rendition by the cello before the end of the refrain (mm. 15–18). The impression of tight motivic unity persists in the episodes, whose oscillating or neighbor-note figures derive more or less directly from the refrain's

EXAMPLE 11.4 Op. 33/1/i, mm. 1–4

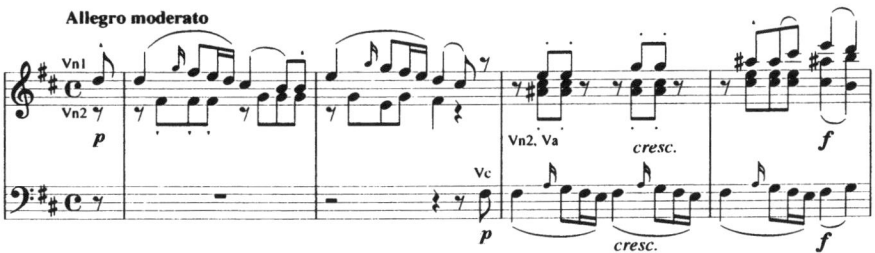

motive and its developments; and in each case, connection with the refrain is re-affirmed by direct quotations of its material in the episodes' open-ended second parts. Motivic ingenuity reaches a subtle but memorable apex in the transition from the end of the second episode to the final refrain. Propelled by an incessant rhythmic impulse, this passage develops the oscillating-third figure systematically in several stages: narrowing its range of motion to a diminished third (mm. 115–19), collapsing it to a series of repeated notes in a tense moment of melodic stasis (m. 120), then allowing the oscillation figure to reemerge by degrees, from a minor second (mm. 121–22), to a major second (mm. 123–24), and finally to a minor third (m. 125), at which point the return of the refrain is at hand.

Elements of Wit and Humor

The Op. 33/3 finale is one of many of this set's movements where a rapidly shifting thematic spotlight infuses the music with a spirit of lighthearted fun, and this in turn promotes an environment where comic and serious elements can coexist, clash, or become seamlessly intertwined with one another. The idea of a comic mode of expression is not new: there are earlier instances in which otherwise engrossing illusions of pathos or high drama are at least partially compromised by elements of parody, structural surprise, or some other discourse that confronts us with the composer's witty, scheming presence. But such traits nonetheless stand out among these works, whose inspired mixtures of comic and serious elements furnish precedents for later developments.

Especially pervasive in Op. 33 is the humor of incongruous juxtapositions, where divergent topics, gestures, or compositional techniques come face to face. In the process, certain tensions arise as one such element challenges the other's claim to our attention; each can have the effect of setting off the other in relief, and unexpected connections between them may be discovered. Examples include the improbable outbursts of solo figuration in the first movement of Op. 33/2 (mm. 25–28, 56–57, 83–86), which temporarily upstage the rustic tunefulness and conversational motivic play that otherwise prevail, and the confrontations of high spirits and sobriety in the alternating variation form of Op. 33/6/iv, whose ostensibly serious minor segments prove utterly powerless to tame the major theme's increasingly frothy variations.

Conventional formulas for beginning, ending, or connecting are part of a cherished stock-in-trade for the music of Haydn and his contemporaries, and their very familiarity recommends them as targets for comical treatment—through gross exaggeration, say, or manifestly inappropriate placement, sometimes with frankly baffling results. In the slow movement of Op. 33/5, Haydn manages to skewer his own inflated rhetoric with a single stroke. To all appearances, the punctuating tag (mm. 8–9) that concludes the opening ritornello seems dead serious as it traverses the tones of a minor tonic triad; and its solemn recurrence near the end seems to signal fulfillment of the movement's tragic destiny. But an impudent gesture transforms the mood at the last moment: together the ensemble leaps up an octave, embellishes the leap with a flippant grace note, then jumps back down to close on a unison pizzicato. With no more than a little help from the performers, these patently eccentric actions will annihilate the preceding measures' pomposity, and in so doing they will cast the entire movement in a freshly ambivalent light. Was the outpouring of impassioned sentiment merely a parody of tragic expression after all?[14]

The withering irony of Haydn's plucked strings is given more extended play at the end of the Op. 33/4 rondo. The close of a high-speed finale is an occasion to summon the ensemble's resources for a brilliant, full-volume peroration—a foolproof formula to signify the resolution of prior discord; and initially this seems to be what Haydn has in mind. The final refrain ends conclusively in measure 190, and a coda gets under way with a summarizing recall of the refrain's melody; but its progress sputters to a halt after six measures: a mystifying pause extends for a full measure; the ensemble then proceeds to mock its own inability to proceed, first by muttering an echo of the dissonant, off-tonic gesture that the interruption had left hanging, then teasing further with two more faint, fragmentary echoes in augmentation (mm. 200–202, 203–5), each sounded pianissimo and each separated by rests. Finally, as if to concede that nothing can be salvaged from the interruption and its consequences—and thus to abandon all pretense of a satisfying, room-filling noise at the close—the movement's action dissolves in a mincing parody of the refrain's closing sentence, intoned in a weightless pizzicato.

Thwarted Expectation

If the closing phrase of Op. 33/4/iv prompts a sigh of relief, this is because the prospect of a reassuring outcome had been so thoroughly confounded by the preceding disruptions: the broken-off phrase, the silences, and the progressive dismantling of the theme. The passage is one of several in this opus that catch us off guard by enlisting the performers' complicity in diverting the music from its course. To engage us in this manner as victims or coconspirators requires situations in which an expected outcome is strongly implied by stylistic norms, the particular musical context in question, or both. An antecedent phrase is normally followed by its consequent; the return to a rondo form's refrain implies continuation and completion of the structural unit to match its previous occurrence; and the approach to the conclusion of a fast-tempo finale leads us to expect the conventional apparatus of cadential repetition and headlong rhythmic continuity. The hilarity of exaggerated disruption and discontinuity in the last movement of Op. 33/2 (the "Joke") is sharpened by the fact that the course of events up to this moment has been so regular, predictable, and persuasively timed in accordance with a rondo's normal fluctuations between suspense and resolution.[15]

Although often comical in effect, Haydn's strategies for blocking expected outcomes can evoke an impressive range of responses, depending on the context in which they occur. In the Op. 33/5 scherzo, described earlier in connection with example 11.1, the silence at measure 8, supplanting the timely completion of a consequent phrase, transpires with unsettling intensity; and the stroke of surprise in the first movement of that work (m. 272), where a digression to the lowered submediant displaces a resolution to tonic, can be realized in performance as a moment of high drama (albeit complicated by the larger irony of this event: the fact that it realizes implications of a previously unexplained disruption in the exposition, the intruding B♭ major chord in m. 78).

A more antic, playful case of thwarted expectation dominates the first part of the Op. 33/1 scherzo. Regular building blocks at the start (2 + 2), combined with a triadic profile that rises to the dominant scale degree, strongly suggest a melodic continuation that will complete the upward arpeggiation to b² before descending to a cadence within a balancing four-measure phrase. As indicated by brackets above the staff in example 11.5, this is actually what happens, beginning on the upbeat to measure 9. But meanwhile, as the other ensemble members pursue a phraseology and thematic dialogue of their own, with imitative entries in measures 4 and 6, the first violin itself fastens obsessively on that dominant pitch, reiterating it in quarter notes, stretching it, then stammering it in a patch of frenzied bariolage, as if trying to shake loose from its grip, before all parts finally join in concert for the postponed consequent phrase of measures 9–12.

Haydn's penchant for undermining a normal order of events—whether to poke fun at conventional formulas, jostle the complacency of listeners who assume they know what will happen next, or enrich a musical design with the irony of unexpected connections or relationships—reveals itself in his approach to the start of the first-movement recapitulations of this set. None is without some kind of peculiarity at this normally unproblematical juncture, and there are instances in which destabilizing elements arise as both a structural surprise and a logical consequence of a primary theme's idiosyncrasies.

EXAMPLE 11.5 Op. 33/1/ii, mm. 1–12 (violin 1 only)

In a particularly memorable case, that of Op. 33/3/i, the preliminary, tapping eighth notes of the opening measure anticipate a theme that has not yet materialized, and an alert listener might be prompted to wonder how the recurrence of this unformed, accompanimental patter could make a convincing start to the recapitulation, given the structural weight and rhetorical importance that this event generally implies. The solution involves a premature return to the repeating eighth notes, and the measure where Haydn plants them actually coincides with the development section's anticipated point of furthest remove, a close in E minor on the downbeat of measure 108. That downbeat is made to elide with a tense, harmonically hollowed-out replica of the quartet's opening gesture, which now initiates a quick transition to tonic. The belated arrival of full-voice tonic harmony in measure 111 corresponds to the belated entry of the cello in measure 4 of the exposition. The moment of recapitulation is thus stretched to span the distance between initial thematic return (m. 108) and tonal resolution (m. 111); and in the process, Haydn both magnifies and transforms the significance of the opening theme's chief peculiarity—its special quality of becoming, of willing itself into being gradually in the course of the movement's opening measures. (Although it is executed with the special wit and agility that characterize Op. 33, this is not Haydn's first instance of an unstable, harmonically inflected return in which the reinstatement of tonic is momentarily postponed: a somewhat comparable situation may be found as early as the rounded binary minuet of Op. 2/6/ii, m. 21.)

～

That Haydn's contemporaries took due notice of the quartets' wit, novelty, and general appeal is evident from published accounts of early performances. The *Hamburgische unpartheyische Correspondent*, reviewing an August 1782 performance that included quartets from this opus, writes of their "splendid melody, exquisite harmony, unforeseen and surprising modulations and an abundance of new ideas never before heard," but mentions, significantly, that they require "execution by masters' hands." (The performers heard were members of a respected traveling quartet known to have given several concerts in Hamburg in 1782 and

1783 as well as in Berlin and Leipzig. The review identifies them by name: Schick, Triklir, Benda, and Hofmann.)[16]

A report in Cramer's *Magazin der Musik* on another Hamburg performance, this one a private concert on 17 November 1782, at which two of the quartets were played, notes that the audience was "extraordinarily moved and delighted";[17] and in that same year, Reichardt's *Musikalisches Kunstmagazin* offered a review of two Hummel publications—one consisting of six Haydn symphonies, the other comprising the Op. 33 quartets (Hummel's Op. 19)—which extols these works for the originality of their humor and their "liveliest and most pleasing wit."[18] A contemporaneous review in Cramer's journal echoes these comments in an account of the same two publications. Apparently referring specially to the quartets, the reviewer states that "[C. P. E.] Bach in Hamburg . . . expressed his utmost satisfaction with these works by Haydn, especially since Schick and Triklir performed them so splendidly."[19] The appearance of numerous early editions of the quartets further attests to their popularity, and an ample number of published arrangements of entire quartets or of individual movements—for flute quartet, keyboard trio, keyboard four hands, pairs of wind or string instruments, keyboard and violin, solo keyboard, or voice with keyboard accompaniment[20]—stands as further evidence of their enthusiastic reception.

Appreciation of Op. 33 among modern-day commentators, to some degree echoing such early critical reactions as those we have cited, has led to their being celebrated not only as quintessential examples of Haydn's art but also as crucial manifestations of late-eighteenth-century stylistic maturity. In this view, the composer's claim about their novelty stands as an emblem for the works' perceived historical importance.

For Sandberger, writing in 1900, the special uniqueness of Op. 33 resided in a phenomenon of "thematische Arbeit," which may be translated literally as "thematic work" or more idiomatically as "thematic development," or perhaps "thematicism." Described by Sandberger in terms of the *"mediation* between strict and free musical form," a species of transformed or reinvented counterpoint ("the child of the marriage between counterpoint and freedom"), which entails the *"organic development* of the motives," this technique was seen by him to have "taken possession of the string quartet" with Op. 33, so that *"the modern string quartet is invented."*[21] Sandberger's "thematische Arbeit" would thus seem to include motivically unified elaboration in the unfolding of a melodic line (as in our ex. 11.3), but also, and perhaps principally, those situations in which an entire texture is suffused with thematic significance. Sandberger's narrative has proved influential, as Webster noted in 1991 by remarking that it had "dominated musicological discourse for close to a century."[22] Its resonance can be sensed in Rosen's characterization of the opening of Op. 33/1 (quoted in ex. 11.4) as "a manifesto," representing "a revolution in style."[23] Sandberger's influence may likewise be felt in Finscher's positioning of Op. 33 as *"the* epoch-making work in which the string quartet achieved its first classical realization," the "goal of a development which had begun with Op. 1: string quartet style was discovered, the quartet defined as a genre."[24]

To designate Op. 33 as "the completion of a historical process"[25] is a questionable enterprise from several perspectives, and we should be wary of the consequences of such a view for our characterization of Haydn's achievement. Surely the quartets that precede Op. 33 have merits of their own: they need not be regarded merely as predecessors, as manifestations of an artistic crisis (as in scholarly critiques of Op. 20),[26] or as imperfect specimens of a genre not fully formed. And yet all three judgments are implied by assigning Op. 33 the privileged role of touchstone for compositional maturity in a process of eighteenth-century stylistic evolution.

It could perhaps be claimed that more than in any previous opus group, Op. 33 succeeds in engaging listeners in different ways simultaneously—inviting us to follow a tastefully ordered narrative but at the same time undermining that narrative with strokes of deception, humor, and irony. To a superlative degree, these quartets allow for both subjective involvement and objective contemplation—intimacy and distance—and their influence on Haydn's own later quartets is apparent in this regard.[27] But to say that "Haydn never again changed anything essential in this classical conception of the genre"[28] may risk being interpreted to mean that his subsequent endeavors were somehow lacking in technical innovation or fresh artistic inspiration. Rather than attempting to canonize Op. 33 as the climax of a historical process, it may be sufficient simply to recognize the stature of this set as a major landmark in Haydn's ongoing cultivation of the genre.

Op. 42 ([?1784–] 1785)

Haydn's letter to Artaria of 5 April 1784, cited in chapter 1, makes only brief, parenthetical mention of the obscure commission with which he was currently occupied. We learn simply that a group of three quartets has been requested by someone in Spain (Haydn does not actually specify "string quartets," so the instrumentation is not certain), that the works are "very short," that each consists of three movements, and that the project is half completed.[29]

That the lone Op. 42, published by Hoffmeister in 1786, had anything to do with this commission may seem doubtful at first glance. Not only does the piece have four movements, not three, but also the surviving manuscript[30] bears the date 1785—rather late, given the composer's assertion about being half finished with the quartets in question as of April 1784. The work's enigmatically small proportions are nonetheless suggestive, as is the fact that it has no known, surviving companions. The latter circumstance would seem to point to the likelihood of a commission from Hoffmeister, whose series of chamber-music publications, begun in 1785, did involve individual pieces: the fascicle which contained Op. 42, for example, included just this work, a quartet by Hoffmeister himself, and a quintet by Johann Sterkel.[31] But why the small size, which was not too likely to have been a stipulation of Hoffmeister's? (Mozart's K. 499, for example, also issued as part of the series, is certainly a full-size work.) If, as Webster has suggested, the surviving autograph represents a reworking of previously written material (which may possibly go back to a lost or abandoned Spanish commission),[32] then Haydn may have viewed Hoffmeister's publication series as a convenient opportunity to brush off an otherwise orphaned composition and turn it to profitable use.

How may this isolated work be situated within the oeuvre? The first movement's light textures and prevalent motivic ingenuity recall tendencies of the preceding opus, and there are certain procedural resemblances to the first-movement exposition of Op. 33's minor-key quartet (No. 1 in B minor), especially the recasting of opening material as a secondary theme in the relative major following a midpoint caesura. Op. 42's compact proportions may be cited as a resemblance to the previous group, although Haydn now takes this tendency to fresh extremes in the outer movements, both of which are shorter than any of their counterparts in Op. 33.

Traits that set Op. 42 apart from its immediate predecessors include the choice of an unusual first-movement tempo, andante ed innocentemente,[33] and an uncharacteristically narrow expressive range. Occasions for nimble ensemble play lighten the atmosphere to some extent in the outer movements, and the relative brightness of the minuet's D major is enhanced by upper-register melodic thrusts in the first violin. But the otherwise sober qualities suggest a closer affiliation with earlier quartets in minor, notably Op. 9/4 (D minor) and Op. 20/5 (F minor), than with the more recent, relatively high-spirited B minor Op. 33/1. Thematically prominent appoggiaturas lend a tinge of melancholy to the first movement, whose dominant pedal point of measures 90–93 supports a climax of muted intensity. Animated dialogue textures temper the accent on somber expression, however, and in each principal section, rapid exchange among parts almost takes on the quality of a game as performers must strive to time and balance the patterns of alternation.

The D major chord with which the first movement ends anticipates the major mode of the minuet that follows, where pervasive motivic development—virtually everything derives from the neighbor-note and scalar figures of measures 1 and 2—helps sustain an aura of concentration. A subdued D minor trio differs starkly in temperament from the principal dance, though its initial melodic gesture, which includes both an upper neighbor and a stepwise descent from the dominant A, may be heard as a balancing response to the minuet's opening idea.

The Adagio, cast in the submediant key of B♭ (like that of Haydn's previous D minor quartet, Op. 9/4), enhances the prevailing sobriety with its slow tempo, rich texture, and flowing legato lines. The manifest symmetry of the movement, framed by an opening twelve-measure theme and its recurrence (mm. 41–52), helps promote a measure of serenity and equilibrium. However, these qualities are disturbed by a singular event whose placement approximates the movement's golden section: at the end of a scalar descent in the first violin (m. 36), all parts come together on a whole-note unison G, thus transcending for a magical instant the otherwise ubiquitous elements of pulse and harmony.

Not unlike that of Op. 9/4, the finale makes allusions to strict style, in this instance by a declamatory principal subject that lends itself to imitative entries in the course of both first and second reprise. In a manner that calls to mind another minor-key finale, that of Op. 20/3 (mm. 32–35, 94–95), there are ghostly patches in which all small-note activity disappears. An undercurrent of tension informs the two spans in question (mm. 23–26, 76–81) as the music floats weightlessly through a series of half-note chords prior to an eventual drive to the close of the section.

To return to the matter of Haydn's letter to Artaria and its possible connection with Op. 42: although the simple fact that Op. 42 has four movements may argue against such a connection, it is not hard to imagine Haydn's revising the original idea to accommodate a minuet, once the decision was made to publish the work separately. Disparities between the minuet and the other three movements would seem to support this speculation: its lighter manner dilutes the gravity that would otherwise give the work a distinctly unified tone;[34] and the first violin's top d^4 far exceeds the more modest high points in the other movements. From this perspective, the minuet looks as though it might not have been part of the original plan; and it may also be perceived as an intruder in light of the work's overarching symmetries and proportional relationships. There are pointedly symmetrical features within each of the movements (not excluding the minuet, to be sure); but with the minuet subtracted, those elements also take on an intermovement dimension (see fig. 11.1, which represents a structural overview of first, third, and fourth movements).

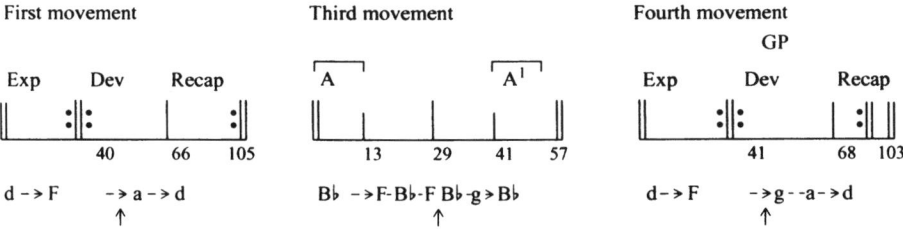

FIGURE 11.1   Op. 42: Overview of corresponding and symmetrically placed structural elements in first, third, and fourth movements (As indicated below the sketches, each "midpoint" arrow points to a crucial landmark near the middle of each movement.)

Symmetry is immediately apparent between the outer movements: both are in $\frac{2}{4}$ time, their lengths are nearly identical (at least with respect to measure count), and they correspond in other ways as well. In their respective expositions, the switch to the relative major takes place at approximately the same point, and the lengths of the two expositions are nearly identical (thirty-nine and forty measures, respectively). The first movement as a whole is conceived so that its exposition and recapitulation balance in size (thirty-nine vs. forty measures), and the development section is designed so that its virtual midpoint (m. 52) coincides with the first attainment of the movement's highest note, e^3, and the cello's simultaneous descent to low E, as the dominant of A minor, by far the lowest long-sustained pitch. The effect of a crux in the tonal design is thus reinforced by a moment of maximal registral expansion at the very heart of the form. In the finale, a general pause in measure 49 divides the movement in two nearly equal parts, and there are correspondences with the first movement (although not quite symmetrically placed) in addition to the basic proportional relationships noted above: the highest pitch, struck at measure 62, is also e^3, and this note occurs as part of a corresponding tonal event, the momentary establishment of A minor (mm. 60–65) before the return to tonic at measure 68.

As for the dance movement's own contributions to the theme of symmetrical proportion, measure 14, the midpoint of the minuet proper, marks the end of an extended stepwise descent in the first violin and the beginning of a long-range ascent to the closing peak. The diminutive trio is precisely symmetrical, not only in its 8 + 8 formal outline but also in its tonal profile: the opening and closing four-measure spans are squarely in tonic whereas the two middle ones, on either side of the double bar, occupy the relative major. Finally, the break between the two halves of the trio, the precise center of the movement, is marked for special emphasis by the fact that it negotiates the most extreme contrast in register, from the cello's lone, low F at the close of the first part to the first violin's likewise unaccompanied c^3 after the double bar.

Op. 42 remains a mystery, standing alone, written under circumstances that remain unclear, and with a certain mix of qualities—small dimensions and relative technical simplicity on one hand, seriousness of tone on the other—that set it somewhat apart from either preceding or following quartets. Hans Keller's characterization of the piece as "a miracle within the miracle that is [Haydn's] output of great string quartets" may be overdrawn,[35] but he is right to deplore its dismissal by commentators. As he notes, the piece is to be specially cherished by amateur performers for whom larger, technically more demanding quartets might be an excessively daunting challenge; and on purely musical grounds—motivic resourcefulness, complex and fast-changing ensemble work, satisfying symmetrical proportions balanced by the locally dynamic play of rhythmic, melodic, and harmonic forces—it merits recognition as a worthy member of the canon.

Op. 50 (1787)

By the year 1787, more than half a decade had passed since the completion of Op. 33. In light of Haydn's growing reputation as a composer of instrumental music, assisted by his own efforts in having works printed and performed both locally and abroad, it would seem that the time was more than ripe for him to reassert his stature as a master of the quartet. Among the proudest of his recent accomplishments were the six "Paris" symphonies, begun in 1785 and finished the following year, and to some extent Op. 50 may be understood as a complementary achievement, a superlative effort in a neighboring genre, although pointedly different in character from those brilliant, audience-pleasing works—and quite different also from the popularly successful Op. 33. Although the new opus made a fitting sequel to the preceding group in its accent on wit, motivic development, and spirited ensemble play, there is less of an inclination toward accessibility and breadth of appeal. Possibly with Mozart's recent accomplishment in mind (i.e., the six "Dedication" quartets), Haydn now seems more intent on reclaiming the quartet as a medium for connoisseurs. Regarding the works from this vantage point, we can see evidence of a return to the more stringent approach witnessed in Op. 20.

The earliest signs that a new project had begun come from a pair of letters from Haydn to his publisher, Artaria, in February 1787.[1] Writing on 11 February, he promises, "You will receive the quartet a week from tomorrow"; and on the 14th, "The quartet will follow soon."[2] Reference is made to a third quartet in a communication dated 7 March; then on 19 May he mentions a fourth in the series. Hopefully (and perhaps somewhat disingenuously), he claims on 10 June that a fifth quartet is almost finished and a sixth is about to follow. In fact, however, we learn in a letter from 21 June that neither the fourth nor the fifth had yet been sent.

In the meantime, plans were under way to supply the still-to-be completed opus group with a dedication. As early as 27 February, there had been mention of correspondence with Konstantin Jacobi, Prussian minister to the Viennese court, concerning the idea of dedicating a composition of Haydn's to Friedrich Wilhelm II. The king himself communicated with Haydn later in the spring (21 April), offering a ring as a token of appreciation for his having received copies of the Paris symphonies; and on 19 May, Haydn confided to Artaria that he felt "deeply in His Majesty's debt" and declared that he could think of no better way to show his "thankfulness to His Majesty (and also in the eyes of the whole world) than by dedicating these 6 quartets to him."[3] It is owing to this circumstance that the works were to become known as the "Prussian" quartets.

The decision to proceed with a royal dedication attests to the favor Haydn's art enjoyed in the highest circles of nobility and connoisseurship, and it reflects the importance the composer himself must have attached to the works now in progress: clearly he felt confident that the new quartets would be worthy of a sovereign's appreciation. The dedication was to be a mark of prestige and ennoblement, but it was musically impersonal: composition of the set was evidently under way prior to any specific plans for the dedication, so that the king's particular tastes and musical talents—he was an accomplished cellist—would not have been foremost in Haydn's mind. The cello participates vitally as an ensemble member throughout these works, but there are scarcely any places where that instrument could be said to shine as a royal soloist.[4]

Was Haydn somehow daunted by the prospect of a royal dedication? For whatever reason, work on the quartets progressed more slowly than previously predicted as spring changed to summer. A letter of 23 June states that he is sending the fourth quartet and mentions a fifth, yet completion of the fifth was to be seriously postponed. On 12 July Haydn reports sending the quartet to be designated as the sixth, but it is not until 16 September that he is able to send the fifth and to exclaim that "Now, thank God, I am very glad that I finished them at last."[5]

While the composer was keeping Artaria abreast of his progress, there was something afoot that the publisher apparently did not know: a plan to sell the same works to the London firm of William Forster, to whom Haydn wrote on 8 August, "I would like to inform you that I have composed six quartets . . . which I have not yet given to anyone."[6] Whether or not Forster believed the implied claim that he was first in line, he did accept the offer. He had Haydn sign a contract, and copies of all six quartets were duly sent to him on 20 September (i.e., just several days after the last to be completed had been forwarded to Artaria). The quartets arrived in London on 5 October and were soon issued as Op. 44, apparently before Artaria's edition. (The latter, published as Op. 50, was first advertised on 19 December.[7] Both the Viennese and London editions have the same ordering of quartets, identical to the traditional sequence, as do the four surviving autograph manuscripts and the authentic set for Forster.)[8]

In another troubling development, Artaria learned by October that manuscript copies of the quartets were in circulation. According to the composer Dittersdorf, copies were sold by subscription for six ducats apiece, and they apparently enjoyed wide distribution: one of the subscribers was Dittersdorf's patron in Silesia.[9] Artaria questioned Haydn, who responded by expressing astonishment at the "theft" and vigorously defended the integrity of his copyist. The composer went on to suggest that Artaria's copyist, "a rascal," had accepted a bribe from one Laurent Lausch, a Viennese copyist who profited from selling manuscripts of new works by leading composers, and he proposed that Lausch be made to appear before the mayor and reveal his source for the quartets.[10]

It was sometime in November that Artaria learned about the Forster edition, and when asked about this, Haydn chose to sidestep the issue in his letter of 22 November. However, less than a week later (27 November), he acknowledged that he had indeed granted publication rights to Forster. Having been caught, he shifted the blame to Artaria (as he had in the matter of the Op. 33 subscription project), suggesting in this case that the publisher might have prevented the situation from arising if he had sent the quartets several months earlier to his London associates, Longman & Broderip, and granted them the publication rights. "No one can blame me for attempting to secure some profit for myself," he now declares, "after the pieces have been engraved: for I am not properly recompensed for my works, and have a greater right to get this profit than the other dealers."[11]

Haydn's breathtaking lack of candor in this affair (and others to which it might be compared) seems rather at odds with the images of homespun probity in traditional accounts of the composer's life, personality, and philosophical outlook. Certainly he was shrewd in recognizing the international scope of his popularity and the profits to be gained from the sale of his music abroad. From this perspective he can scarcely be faulted for doing what was necessary to ensure that he reaped at least some of that gain for himself.[12] But to contemplate his behavior from still another perspective, might there be a meaningful connection between the ambivalent, contradictory facets of Haydn's business dealings and the penchant for artful deception witnessed in his music?

Until recently, the known authentic sources for Op. 50 consisted of the original Artaria print (for which Haydn is known to have seen proofs), the Forster print, the signed manuscript parts from which Forster's edition was prepared, a complete though scattered set, originally from Haydn's library, consisting of Nos. 1, 2, 4–6 and No. 3, and an incomplete set, Nos. 1, 2, 4–6.[13] But in 1982, autograph manuscripts for four of the six (Nos. 3–6) actually resurfaced in Australia (three of them, Nos. 3, 4, and 6, bearing the date 1787). Their owner turned out to have been the granddaughter of a retired British colonel who had acquired them at a London auction in 1851. The manuscripts have since been resold at auction to an anonymous collector.[14]

Overview of the Opus

As represented in table 12.1, there are marked digressions from some of Haydn's earlier practices but at the same time pointed resemblances to certain aspects of Op. 20 as well as Op. 33. Gone are several of the previous set's most outstanding novelties: the lightweight rondo finales, the transformation of the minuet into a high-speed caper, as in Op. 33/1 and 5, and the accompanying scherzo designation. Variation form, which had migrated to the end of the cycle in two of the Op. 33 quartets, finds its place once again as an interior slow movement, as in Op. 20/4/ii, and the reappearance of a sentimental, slow-tempo siciliana (in Op. 50/6/ii), comparable in essential respects to those of Opp. 9/1, 17/1, and 20/5, likewise suggests a partial reversion to earlier manners.

Different from either Opp. 20 or 33 is the choice of a single scheme for overall cyclic organization: fast-slow-minuet-fast. (As seen in a handful of previous works—Op. 20/2, 4, and 6; Op. 33/5 and 6—situating the slow movement in second place results in a concentration of intermovement contrast in tempo and character early in the cycle. The dance movement then mediates between the slow movement's self-absorption and the natural exuberance of the finale.) Other features of the opus reinforce this element of general similarity: all first movements are in a fast or moderately fast sonata form (as in Opp. 20 and 33, although not the previous groups), and this proves to be the only set subsequent to Opp. 9 and 17 with as many as five last movements in sonata form. With regard to tonal range, all but No. 4, in the rarely encountered F♯ minor, draw from an inner circle of familiar keys, with a typical bias toward the flat side, and this latter tendency is underscored by the fact that as many as half these quartets have slow movements in their home key's subdominant.

Balancing outward consistencies in design are many signs of an effort to give each work a distinctive profile. The first movements' opening gestures are especially revealing in this regard: no two are even remotely alike, several are virtually unprecedented in the strangeness of their sonority or melodic line, and all are heavily scented with implications for subsequent elaboration. That of Op. 50/1 surely ranks as one of the oddest. A succession of throbbing B♭s in the cello starts the movement in a state of half-comical mystery while the other parts bide their time. The low B♭s assure stability by anchoring the movement to tonic; but the hypnotic repetition also conveys a disquieting sense of detachment, suggesting indifference on the cellist's part either to the other ensemble members' initial silence or their eventual participation (the three upper parts enter on a dissonant chord in m. 3). The reiterated quarter notes maintain a distinct presence as the

TABLE 12.1 Summary statistics for Op. 50

Op.No.	Hob.No.	Movement			
		i	ii	iii	iv
50/1	III:44	B♭ ¢ Allegro SF 164	E♭ 6/8 Adagio Strophic var. 61	B♭ 3/4 Poco allegretto M/T 36(r)/28	B♭ 2/4 Vivace assai SF (irreg.) 245
50/2	III:45	C 3/4 Vivace SF 290	F ¢ Adagio. Cantabile Slow-mvt. 60	C 3/4 Allegro M/T 50/32	C 2/4 Vivace assai SF 232
50/3	III:46	E♭ 6/8 Allegro con brio SF (irreg.) 133	B♭ 2/4 Andante più tosto allegretto Strophic var. 137(r)	E♭ 3/4 Allegretto M/T 57/28	E♭ 2/4 Presto SF 203
50/4	III:47	F#m-F# 3/4 Spiritoso SF 184	A 2/4 Andante Alternating var. 100(r)	F#/F#m 3/4 Poco allegretto M/T 38/30	F#m 6/8 Allegro molto Fugue [Fuga] 87
50/5	III:48	F 2/4 Allegro moderato SF 170	B♭ 3/4 Poco adagio Slow-mvt. 47	F/Fm 3/4 Tempo di Menuet. Allegretto M/T 41/40	F 6/8 Vivace SF 133
50/6	III:49	D ¢ Allegro SF 154	Dm-D 6/8 Poco adagio SF 66	D 3/4 Allegretto M/T 32/54	D 2/4 Allegro con spirito SF 243

movement unfolds, sounding not only in the cello but migrating to other parts and thus emerging to prominence as a defining thematic property of the movement.[15]

One other memorable opening with which that of Op. 50/1 may be compared— its virtual opposite, in effect—is the unaccompanied treble line at the start of Op. 50/6: a dynamically accented, off-tonic attack, followed by a precipitous descent through the scale as the lower voices enter in harmony on the downbeat of measure 2. Derivatives of this restless idea figure prominently in the exposition, lending force to developmental passages, underscoring the tonal shock of a move to the lowered submediant in measure 38, and helping to motivate the rise to a melodic peak, f^3, in measures 42–43.

The theme of first-movement individuality is underscored by metrical variety. Years earlier, in Op. 20, Haydn had defied his own established custom by giving each slow movement a different time signature. He now takes a similar tack with respect to first movements. Triple time, rarely used for opening movements prior to this set, now appears twice (Nos. 2 and 4); and except for the thoroughly old-fashioned $\frac{3}{8}$, all the other possibilities (i.e., ¢, **c**, $\frac{2}{4}$, and $\frac{6}{8}$) are represented by one work each. Common time, the predominant choice in each of the four previous opus groups, thus loses its privileged status altogether.

Concomitant with the unprecedented range of meters is the exploration of new kinds of relationship between meter and surface rhythm. The alla breve signature, coupled with an unmodified allegro marking in Op. 50/1, designates a freshly streamlined type of motion in which triplet eighths replace the previous standard of eighths, sixteenths, and triplet sixteenths as favored subdivisions. Superseding the old moderato compound $\frac{4}{4}$ in spirit as well as notation, this approach involves not only the visual impact of larger note values on the page but also a more clearly defined hierarchy among quarter notes within the measure and a broadened sense of melodic trajectory and rhythmic momentum. The first movement of Op. 50/6, written in common time and marked allegro, adopts a similar pulse but differs from Op. 50/1/i by accommodating a wide variety of note values, including streams of sixteenths as well as tied whole notes, while nearly avoiding triplet eighths altogether.

As if to place the newer species of meter in perspective, Haydn also includes an opening movement in which basic elements of the older approach are retained. For the piece in question, Op. 50/5, he chooses a signature of $\frac{2}{4}$ rather than common time or alla breve, but familiar traits of the old common time are nonetheless pointedly on display: an allegro moderato tempo marking, a steady eighth-note impetus, embellishing thirty-second-note figures within the primary theme, and streams of triplet sixteenths in all of the movement's principal sections.

To feature a particular type of form, examining its potentials from different vantage points, had been a key item of Haydn's agenda in both Op. 20, with three fugues, and Op. 33, with its corresponding group of rondo finales. A related enterprise in Op. 50 may be seen in the choice of three slow-tempo variation forms among the second movements. One of the three, the Andante of Op. 50/4 (A major), comes close in form and spirit to an Op. 33 predecessor, the finale of No. 6 in D: both are in sharp keys, and both highlight the contrast between two modally opposed segments, subjecting both to variations that intensify the difference in character between them. The strophic variation design of Op. 50/3/ii (B♭), freer in form as well as more idiosyncratic in texture and ensemble play, resembles that of Op. 50/4 by incorporating a segment in the parallel minor, although here Haydn concentrates more on possibilities for coloristic variety than affective contrast. A rhythmically simple "walking" theme, presented as a querulous duet for tenor-range cello and low accompanying viola, sets the stage for textural diversity, successively engaging two, three, and four parts in the second reprise; and the minor theme that follows—more nearly a minor variation than a thematically contrasting idea—sustains the emphasis on variety of texture and timbre by having the instruments enter one by one in both first and second reprise. The appearance of a segment in minor directly following the theme would seem to imply the type of systematic, major-minor alternation seen in Opp. 33/6 or 50/4. But events unfold unpredictably here as Haydn restores major for good following the minor variation, separates second and third variations with an open-ended interpolation, and follows the final variation with a summarizing appendage over a tonic pedal.

The second movement of Op. 50/1 (E♭) proposes yet another way to juxtapose major and minor by embedding a minor version of the theme as the second of three variations within a relatively straightforward strophic design. The movement is further distinguished by an expansive, rhetorically varied coda, as in the magisterial D minor variations of Op. 20/4, and the recurrence of this idea in Op. 50/1 contributes to the sense of a privileged relationship between the two opus groups. The two variation-movement codas do in fact betray marked resemblances in procedure: both feature an early melodic high point, a descending sequence, and a soloistic flourish followed directly by a declamatory unison; and then, shortly before the end in both cases, an extravagant, wide-ranging arpeggio followed by a succession of eloquent pauses and an eventual descent to a quiet, lower-register cadence.

Markedly different in form, character, and ensemble technique are the three nonvariation slow movements, each of which proposes a different way to frame soloistic delivery within a sonata-related structure. The Adagio of Op. 50/2 resembles the Largo e cantabile of Op. 33/5 by parodying the manner of a concerto movement, complete with an opening ritornello before the first violin's principal entry. In a more collaborative approach, the slow movement of Op. 50/5 (the "Dream") unfolds as a pensive soliloquy in two parts, exposition and recapitulation, in which lower instruments support the first violin with richly scored support and commentary. Their voices, an almost continuous, subtly expressive presence, fall silent only for several brief moments of unaccompanied solo figuration (mm. 14, 17, 39, and 42). In Op. 50/6/ii, solo presentation and ensemble work are woven into the narrative conventions of a full-fledged sonata form: the lower voices, subordinate at the outset, gain prominence toward the end of the primary theme restatement (mm. 8–10) by echoing and elaborating on the first violin's nimble embellishment figures of measures 5–6. With the turn to the relative major at measure 11, first violin and inner parts engage as competing strands in the fabric for several measures before the first violin once again upstages the others, this time with goal-directed passagework (mm. 16–20). Finally, a closing phrase (mm. 22–25) helps rebalance the ensemble by temporarily passing the main thematic thread to the inner parts and enlivening the cello part with broken-chord acrobatics (anticipated in m. 20).

The Op. 50 dance movements, variously marked by peculiarities of ensemble technique, harmony, rhythm, and the relationship between minuet and trio, embody some of the group's most imaginative inspirations and deviations from stylistic norms. Much as in the previous set, although without recourse to the high velocity implicit in Op. 33/1 or 5, we find Haydn reveling in the use of a conventional form to frame elements of whimsy, feigned disorder, and distraction. In two cases, tonal derailments challenge customary minuet decorum. In Op. 50/4/iii (F♯ major), a plunge to the lowered submediant transpires five measures into the second reprise (mm. 13–14). The splash of color is magnified not only by double-stopped attacks in the inner voices but also by the first violin's simultaneous leap to a climactic f♯³, the highest note in the movement. As if reeling from the impact, the ensemble now comes together in unison, gropes upward chromatically toward the dominant, then reestablishes tonal order by progressing to a half cadence in measure 20. A more elaborate digression marks the second reprise of the minuet in Op. 50/3, which reaches well beyond customary limits in duration as well as tonal compass. A reassuringly solid cadence in tonic (E♭) marks the end the first part, but a melodic inflection to C♭ prefigures disturbance at the start of the second reprise. An excursion deep into flat territory now gets under way; and at the virtual midpoint of the form (m. 28), a cadence in the remote key of G♭ marks the point of furthest remove before a gradual return to the realm of tonic.

More pointedly at odds with dance-movement convention are the cases of metrical dissonance, related in principle to those witnessed in previous opus groups, in which surface patterns contradict the minuet's otherwise dependable triple pulse. In the trio of Op. 50/1, the combined effect of imitative entries at intervals of two beats (mm. 45–49), followed by the confusion of second-beat forzato accents (mm. 50–54), temporarily annihilates the underlying meter; and toward the end of the minuet proper in Op. 50/5, close canonic imitation between the violins collapses triple meter into a surrogate $\frac{2}{4}$. Hemiolic compression, in which a duple impulse temporarily overrides the triple measure, is not uncommon; but what proves uniquely eccentric here is the refusal of the dissonance to resolve:

the canonic passage flows directly into a resounding cadential formula whose chords, spaced two beats apart, obliterate any trace of the traditional dance step as they sustain the spurious duple meter.[16]

Temporal disturbance of a different sort haunts the spacious trio of Op. 50/6, whose extended second reprise may be identified as the longest in the repertory.[17] Here the music leads us into a state of timeless reverie, enhanced by a variety of rhythmic peculiarities: a drifting, syncopated principal line above a prolonged dominant pedal point (mm. 45–56, embellished with an upper neighbor in m. 55); a leisurely fermata (m. 56); harmonically static echo figures (mm. 73–76); and a pair of meditative general pauses, each lasting for a full two measures (mm. 67–68 and 77–78).

Marked contrasts between minuet and trio variously involve elements of texture, mode, and rhythmic impetus. However, to a greater degree than in any previous opus groups, differences between the two segments are mediated by explicit thematic connection. Closest of all with respect to melodic profile, and yet fraught with deep conflict in character, are the minuet and trio of Op. 50/5: the latter transforms the minuet's opening thematic gesture from an unaccompanied line to a four-part unison and steers it from major to minor. Thematic connections in several other dance movements are less pronounced, and also less saturated with elements of surprise: the trio of Op. 50/4 opens with a straightforward replica of the minuet's initial rhythmic figure (now assigned to the viola as principal melodic line), and the trio of Op. 50/3 recalls aspects of both rhythm and pitch from the beginning of the minuet proper.[18]

Among the finales of Op. 50, the fugue that closes the F♯ minor quartet stands in sharpest contrast to the more easygoing manner of Op. 33. The fugal premise obviously accentuates the individuality of the quartet to which it belongs, but its appearance also may be heard as part of a more general preoccupation with learned polyphony in this set. The other final movements are designed as fast or very fast sonata forms, all but one in $\frac{2}{4}$ time; and in this respect Haydn appears to be endorsing a return to pre–Op. 20 norms. And yet there are noticeable differences: the movements in question are generally longer and weightier than their counterparts in Opp. 9 and 17, and the finales of Nos. 1, 3, and 5 display rondo-like qualities (both thematic and structural, involving the presence of multiple returns to a refrain-like idea) that call to mind the rondo finales of Op. 33.

Rondo overtones are especially pronounced in the last movement of Op. 50/1, whose narrative is complicated by several well-marked recurrences of primary theme material, all in tonic, as it runs its course. The process begins with an early return at measure 109, just thirty-four measures into an eighty-eight-measure development section. A preparatory dominant pedal (mm. 103–8), stretched by fermatas and adorned with a soloistic flourish in the first violin—an improvisatory *Eingang*—obliges us to take notice and register this as an important juncture in the form. But tonic stability is short-lived, and modulatory activity resumes even before completion of a single primary theme phrase. Eventually, a prolonged dominant in measures 156–63 heralds a second return to tonic; and this time a full rendition of the opening theme (mm. 164–79) tells us that the recapitulation has begun in earnest. An abridged recall of transitional and secondary material follows, and when the closing theme returns, now restored to tonic, it feels as though the movement is ready to end. There is more to come, however: a two-measure pause intrudes, and this in turn provides a perfect foil for breaking the silence with yet another recollection of the opening theme prior to a decisive final cadence.

Motivic Process and Tonal Enrichment

Motivic development and elaboration, elements of key importance throughout the previous two opus groups, and in the lone Op. 42 as well, are explored with at least equal intensity in Op. 50. Typically, one or more ideas stated at the beginning— a pithy melodic gesture, rhythmic figure, striking sonority, or pattern of ensemble interaction—work their way into subsequent events whose outer appearance may prove quite dissimilar. The resulting designs, in which elements of contrast coexist with underlying connections, enjoy the cohesion of ubiquitous interrelationship without compromising a movement's narrative diversity.

A prime example, the finale of Op. 50/2, begins with a pair of ideas whose suggestions of comical banter and physical gesture invoke the manner of an opera-buffa ensemble (see ex. 12.1a): an upbeat leading to a string of repeated notes (1m) and a more animated, overlapping response (2m), colored by an echo of the initial upbeat figure in the cello. Implying both partnership and opposition, this opening premise invites lively discussion in which all voices will participate, either in dialogue with one another or else simultaneously, as part of rhythmically differentiated layers of activity.

As early as measure 8, a barrage of sixteenth notes in the cello signals the onset of heightened intensity as it elides with the end of the opening phrase. The first violin proceeds to reshape and elaborate the two featured ideas (1m and 2m), absorbing both and redirecting their motivic energies to the unfolding of a wide-ranging, extended line (mm. 9–22; see ex. 12.1b, which quotes from the start of the long phrase). Motivic play persists in the transitional activity that follows, largely through ensemble play involving variants of 1m and 2m; but the first violin's extended span of passagework, beginning in measure 30, proves to be thematically informed as well (see m. 34, for example, quoted in ex. 12.1c, where slurred sixteenth-note figures arise as an inversion of those first heard in m. 10).

Surface activity comes to a halt momentarily at measure 50; and now that a tonal plateau has been attained, new derivatives of 1m and 2m work simultane-

EXAMPLE 12.1 Op. 50/2/iv

(a) mm. 1–4

(b) mm. 8–10

(c) mm. 33–34

ously to underscore impressions of local contrast as well as overriding motivic cohesion (see ex. 12.1d). Elaboration assumes still another guise in the closing theme, begun in measure 59. As shown in example 12.1e, the first violin's recurrent, chromatically inflected descents (bracketed in mm. 60, 62, and 64) may be heard as embellished augmentations of the sixteenth-note figure in measure 58 (itself a permutation of the sixteenth-note figure of the original 2m).

The development section transforms the shape and rhetorical quality of 1m, substituting a wide downward leap for the long dominant note of measure 2 (ex. 12.1f). What had been proclaimed initially as an interrogative, open-ended gesture, inviting comment or response, is now recast into something more declara-

EXAMPLE 12.1 (continued)

(d) mm. 51–54

(e) mm. 58–68 (violin I only)

(f) mm. 87–90 (violin I only)

(g) mm. 224–27

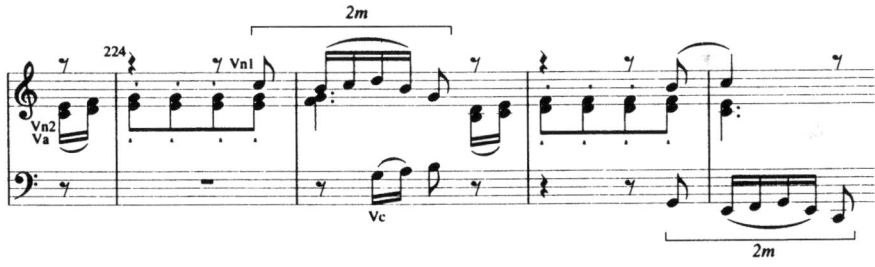

tive, more appropriate to the local task of signaling arrival in a key (A minor) and asserting its temporary predominance.

The layering and interaction of motivic particles evolves further in the recapitulation, seemingly in response to changing circumstances. Following the recurrence of the exposition's opening phrases, for example, the cello helps signify restored stability by prolonging a low dominant pedal (mm. 177–82). Meanwhile, the paired inner parts reaffirm their initial partnership by spinning a stepwise melodic arc from the material of 1m, and the first violin's simultaneous display of sixteenth notes contributes another layer of reinvention by recalling 2m and its derivatives. Eventually, Haydn crowns this showcase of motivic ingenuity by coming full circle and ending with a replica of the movement's opening measures, cunningly altered to bring about a thematically integral punctuation. As shown in example 12.1g, the harmony of measures 226–27 has been reversed—dominant seventh to tonic instead of tonic to dominant seventh as in measures 3–4—and Haydn underscores the switch by relocating 2m from the first violin to the cello, whose resonant low C will have the last word (the movement's final measures, 228–32, comprise a variant of mm. 224–27). The logic of the transformation is both simple and powerful: as motivic exploration and reiteration persist to the very end, a previously tensional, interrogative 2m, initially sounded by the first violin, is now tonally stabilized and grounded in the ensemble's lowest voice at the close.

Elsewhere we find Haydn taking a more audacious, electrically charged approach by attaching motivic importance to a chromatic inflection: a strategically placed disturbance that gives rise to conflict, drama, or tonal expansion through repetition, intensification, and development. Perhaps the clearest example comes from the first movement of Op. 50/5 (F major), in which a discordant pitch, embedded in the primary theme, has serious consequences. The unassuming violin duet with which the work begins is unproblematic tonally, but as an opening gesture it betrays tension and uncertainty. Where are the lower parts, whose entry will give the texture full resonance, shore up the tonal foundation, and permit the action to get under way in earnest? Refusing to accommodate or conform, the missing voices make their eventual appearance by echoing the violins' two-note iambic figure off key, on a unison C♯ in measure 5 (ex. 12.2a). The tonally dissonant figure quickly resolves up a half step to D, explaining itself as part of an extended cadential progression (mm. 5–8); but its intrusion had marked it for special motivic significance, and its recurrence in the following phrase, transferred to a high register and woven into a more extended, chromatic line (rising from c^3 in m. 12 to f^3 in m. 18), further points to its likely role as a harbinger of developments to come.

Suspicions that this might be the case are initially confirmed in a passage toward the end of the exposition (mm. 47–54) that plants an abbreviated replica of the primary theme's events within a chromatically rising bass line G–G♯–A just before a cadence in the dominant (C). But later on, past the double bar and into a volatile development, the potentially disturbing element is not so neatly contained. The section begins with an altered recurrence of the primary theme in the dominant; and on the upbeat to measure 74, listeners will understand the violins' repeated-note idea as the start of simple repetition of measures 70–73, where the same offending G♯ had resolved to A (see ex. 12.2b). But the performers who now play that pitch can see that a drastic change is under way. The

EXAMPLE 12.2 Op. 50/5/i

(a) mm. 1–8

(b) mm. 70–77

note has been respelled as Ab, and in this new guise it will act as a tonal pivot—a disruptive force on a higher order of magnitude, diverting the music from its expected course (a cadence in C) and planting us in the remote region of Eb as a platform from which the section's modulatory action will now proceed.

Although the recapitulation starts off on a reassuring note by supplying the violins' opening duet with a supportive bass (mm. 102–5), new complications soon arise. Mimicking the development section, the note C♯ becomes Db (mm. 110–11), claims new status as a locally consonant chord tone, and leads to a temporary overthrow of the reestablished tonic as it negotiates a shift to the key of Ab, down a fifth from the development section's move to Eb and three accidentals removed from the home key.

Experienced up to now as an agent of interruption and tonal expansion, the dissonant repeated-note idea eventually transforms itself into a factor of reconciliation. Early in the recapitulation, the paired chromatic pitches, still notated as Db and woven into an animated dialogue between upper and lower parts, supply the bass of an augmented sixth chord that will highlight a structurally decisive half cadence in tonic (mm. 118–19, repeated in mm. 120–21). Then, closer to the end of the movement, and following a tense moment of silence (mm. 142–43), the figure appears once again to help motivate the movement's rhetorical climax: a recurrence of measures 5–8, followed by an extended ascent to a dissonant local peak (mm. 155–58), a phrase that revels in the achievement of a unified ensemble sonority (mm. 159–65), and a final stretch of tonal resolution (mm. 166–70), colored by chattering triplet sixteenths in the first violin as the inner parts enjoy a last chance to recall the primary theme's opening gesture.[19]

Cyclic Integration

For the most part, cyclic cohesion in Haydn's quartets before Op. 50 tends to rest on close intermovement tonal relationship as well as such elements as agreeably balanced proportions and a convincing distribution of complementary tempos, meters, affective states, and the like. On occasion, most emphatically in Op. 20, we have seen Haydn transcend these factors with explicit schemes of intermovement connection, unification, and cyclic wholeness. Unlike Op. 20, the new quartets include no examples of run-on connection from trio to minuet, nor are there any open-ended situations comparable to the second-movement Capriccio of Op. 20/2, which segues to the following minuet without coming to rest on a full cadence. And yet there are tangible signs in Op. 50, most prominently in Nos. 4 and 6, of a concern for heightened cyclic integration as a vital component of a quartet's design.[20]

In Op. 50/4, the imposing presence of a closing fugue lends natural cohesion as an emblem of cyclic culmination. Its effect is rendered problematical, however, by the severity of a minor ending, which seems an unexpected outcome in light of preceding events: the resolution to major in the first movement's recapitulation and the further ascendancy of major in the dance movement (despite the turn to minor in the trio). Might a decisive affirmation of major have furnished a more persuasive sequel?[21] Less ambiguous aspects of culmination and summary include the sheer magnitude of the finale's peroration and the readily perceived connection of its subject to thematic material from previous movements.[22] In addition, the fugue revisits—and perhaps reconciles—the work's divergent tendencies toward difficulty and learned technique (as in the first movement's intense motivic development, the polyphonic textures of the second movement's minor-key segments, or the contrapuntal accent of the third-movement trio) and galant manners (as in the lyrical principal melody of the variation movement or the ingratiating simplicity of the minuet's opening measures). The finale accommodates both qualities by alternating between rigorous fugal procedure and less stringent passages in which rhythmic relationships among parts are more synchronized or homogeneous than independent, as in measures 39–45 or 62–72.

The last-mentioned passage, in which the first violin climbs to the highest pitch in the movement (g^3, m. 70), contributes to an impression of connectedness by recalling the force of related events from earlier in the cycle. The minuet's exhilarating high point (m. 13) resembles the finale's climax in general profile and sonority, with double-stopped chordal support and a downward arpeggiation from the melodic peak, and also in the choice of a comparably inflected harmony: ♭VI in the minuet, ♭II in the finale. Indeed, the brilliant D major chord of the minuet's measure 13, whose great prominence transcends that of any surrounding events, may be heard to connect with the last movement's G major sonority at measure 70 almost in the manner of a dominant resolving to its tonic. Similar connections may be drawn between the finale's climax and the first movement, whose recurrent principal idea, a triad-outlining unison, prefigures both the rhetorical emphasis of the finale's measure 70 and its arpeggiated melodic shape, with chord degrees traversed in the order 5–8–5–3.

The D major quartet, Op. 50/6, enjoys a measure of integration simply by its single-tonic format. More important, it exhibits the set's most straightforward instance of thematic connection between movements: embedded in a secondary theme of its finale (ex. 12.3a, mm. 182–85) is a paraphrase of the work's initial melodic line (ex. 12.3b). The announcement of this idea at the head of the opening movement had engendered friction and ambiguity on several counts: the first, unharmonized note, not part of the tonic triad, gave the impression of starting out in the middle of a theme rather than its beginning; and the exaggerated finality of the descent to tonic in measure 4 caused it to resemble a misplaced closing formula. True to the purpose of a finale in highlighting restored stability, the borrowed gesture is pointedly transformed. The opening attack is now harmonized as a chord tone of a temporarily tonicized submediant, and the descent to tonic, no longer functionally incongruous, serves to bring an eight-measure thematic statement to a satisfying close.[23] The original theme's chief peculiarities are thus turned to good account at last, enhancing rather than contradicting the implications of their position in the structure.

The work gains further integration through far-reaching consequences of the first movement's inflections to the note B♭: slipped into an embellishing figure in the cello (mm. 11–13), quietly sustained by the viola (m. 14), sounded loudly and much more prominently by the first violin late in the exposition (m. 39), then eventually raised to the status of a tonicized ♭VI in the recapitulation (mm. 129–34), the aberrant pitch haunts the closing measures of the movement as an unresolved melodic and harmonic disturbance—but also as a harbinger of the second movement's minor mode and the neighbor-note figure A–B♭–A of its primary theme (m. 1). Further echoes of the B♭ inflection resound in the dance-movement trio (m. 55), in which the cello makes a conspicuous move up a half step from a low A pedal point that had been held for a full ten measures, and in the finale, where both the B♭ and the dominant's lower neighbor, G♯—also a prominent feature of the opening Allegro—color the first violin's bariolage fireworks on the threshold of the recapitulation (mm. 139–41).

EXAMPLE 12.3 Op. 50/6 (violin 1 only): Thematic relationship between first and last movements

(a) iv, mm. 178–85

(b) i, mm. 1–4

Another connective thread, intertwined with the one just cited, concerns the
special prominence of the dominant note A, whose unifying influence is underscored by its thematic presence at the very beginning of the second movement,
minuet, trio, and finale. In each instance the first violin either strikes the A
immediately or else rises to it on the first downbeat; each time its importance is
reinforced by one or more repetitions; and it always prefaces a more or less immediate stepwise descent. The preoccupation with this pitch, either as a springboard or melodic center of gravity, climaxes with the colorful stream of bariolage
that yields ten rapid-fire iterations of the note at the start of the finale.

Finally to be considered are the cautionary inscriptions affixed to the close
of both second and third movements ("Sieg[ue] il Menuet"; then "Sieg[ue] Finale"). By prohibiting any momentary lapse in concentration that might otherwise accompany the full close between movements, these warnings affirm the
significance of multimovement cohesion as part of the work's overall character
and design.[24]

Wit and Temperamental Complexity

To describe Op. 50 in terms of gravity, intensity, and technical ambition would
seem appropriate in light of the quartets' concentration on motivic development,
polyphonic texture, challenging ensemble technique, and cyclic integration. And
yet these works are anything but dead serious, laced as they are with touches of
unexpected color, eccentric turns of phrase, pungent harmonic inflections, and

the like. Comic and serious elements complement and enrich one another's presence in circumstances likely to produce knowing smiles among those attuned to the composer's manner. The delights of the Op. 50/6 finale owe much to the incongruity of a truly bizarre sonority at the start of a movement otherwise controlled by a straightforward, well-disciplined narrative. And even in places where the music strikes a particularly serious tone—the outer movements of Op. 50/4, the exalted soliloquy of Op. 50/2/ii, or the pensive siciliana in Op. 50/6—there are distracting touches that lighten the mood.

Memorable cases of humor involve peculiar low-register sonorities in the cello. Some of these arise simply from the effort to spread thematic interest among different parts. But other situations witness the wholesale transformation of the instrument from dignified ensemble member to opera buffa character role, and still others highlight a paradoxical quality of the instrument's line, which naturally participates thematically but also must serve as textural foundation. Thus, the closing theme of Op. 50/5/iv (m. 45; m. 125 in the recapitulation) has the instrument transform an otherwise commonplace, reiterated pedal point into a querulous, low-pitched afterthought that parodies the first violin's neighbor-note figure from the opening theme and engages in bantering dialogue with the upper parts.

More elaborate mixtures of serious and comic involve passages that draw us into a game of anticipation, confounding predictions about how certain events will unfold, then rewarding us with unexpected outcomes that prove both logical and inevitable. For example, the peculiarity of the first violin's off-tonic attack at the start of Op. 50/6 proves justified when we discover how it helps bridge the gaps between principal sections: all that is needed for a seamless connection to the theme's chief points of recurrence—the repeat of the exposition, the start of the development, and the beginning of the recapitulation—is a patch of transitional figuration to link up with the primary theme's unaccompanied opening note. But Haydn complicates matters at the last of these junctures, the break between the intense culmination of the development and the start of the recapitulation. A sustained melodic peak in measure 102, the apex of a long rising line above an anticipatory dominant, forewarns of an imminent return (see ex. 12.4), but exactly where and how it will fall into place is unclear. A descending sequence begins, based on the quartet's opening measure; and as the pattern unwinds, the importance of measure 104 could pass almost unnoticed by listeners caught up in the mechanical rhythm of sequential repetition. The forzato accent is definitely a clue, especially if the performer helps out with an appropriate physical gesture. Still, it is only with the downbeat of measure 105 that we know for sure that the recapitulation has in fact already begun.

Haydn's penchant for ambivalence and reinterpretation—leading us to attach a particular meaning to an event and then switching without warning to another—is a trait that reaches new levels of sophistication in these works, and

EXAMPLE 12.4 Op. 50/6/i, mm. 100–106

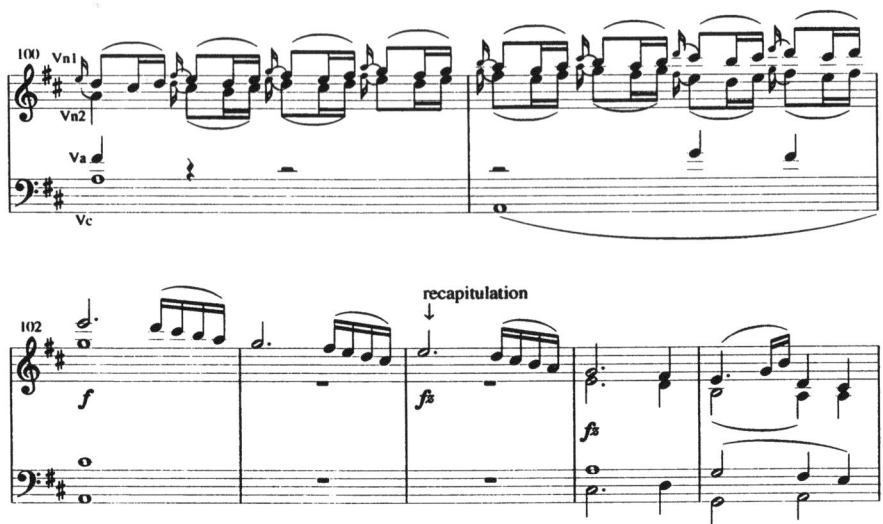

the means involved may seem deceptively unassuming on first encounter. In a memorable passage from Op. 50/2/i, a small, pungent detail acts as a powerful instrument of tonal surprise, temporarily changing the movement's course and extending its harmonic range in both the exposition and recapitulation. The process begins innocently enough with the first violin's inflection of a previously sounded chord tone D (as part of the local tonic of G) to a dissonant D♯ (m. 59; see ex. 12.5). Upward resolution to E seems necessary and inevitable, and this indeed comes about in measure 61. Meanwhile, the cello moves prematurely from B to C (m. 60), and the resulting change in harmony to an apparent C minor chord (spelled C–G–D♯) registers as a fleeting accident of voice leading. But after the phrase that encompasses these events starts to repeat, the first violinist discovers what only becomes apparent to everyone else after the fact: upon repetition, the D♯ has indeed been respelled as E♭. This notational switch affirms the note's reconfiguration as a locally stable chord member, and in this new guise it will act as a tonal pivot to the unexpected, remote key of A♭. As we realize only in retrospect, the note's need to resolve has magically vanished in the process, its dissonant energy absorbed by a luminous tonal transformation (Haydn recalls the crucial respelling at the analogous point in the recapitulation, m. 246, where G♯ becomes A♭).

Unusually rich in nuance and technical élan, even by Haydn's standards, Op. 50 stands out as a special achievement, firmly grounded in the composer's own precedents yet transcending them in important respects. What might have

EXAMPLE 12.5 Op. 50/2/i, mm. 58–66

prompted Haydn to undertake a new set of quartets at this point in his career—and to do so with a vengeance, as if striving hard to expand the horizons of his chamber-music technique? The fact that several years had elapsed since he had composed the attractive, superbly crafted Op. 33 might have been reason enough; but another stimulus, mentioned in passing earlier in this chapter, may be worth considering as well: Mozart's contemporaneous set of six brilliant quartets written during the few years preceding Op. 50 and published by Artaria in 1785 with a dedication to Haydn.

The sheer ingenuity of those works, distinctly Mozartian yet inspired by Haydn's example in matters of ensemble play, motivic process, and formal subtlety, had raised the genre to a new level of importance. Simply to pass over them in silence must have seemed out of the question, especially in light of the published dedication, with its formal recognition (if any were needed) of Haydn's standing as preeminent master of the quartet.

But if a musical response was called for, what form could it take? Given Haydn's self-acknowledged stature, pride, and sensitivity to criticism, this was hardly an occasion for parody, flattery, or the appearance of imitation. In a way, Mozart's path had been more clearly defined, notwithstanding the "long and laborious study" mentioned in the letter of dedication. Haydn's leadership was an established fact, and his example had evidently furnished Mozart with a deepened understanding of the medium's possibilities. Any response by Haydn would have to be more an assertion of artistic independence than an act of emulation or tribute.

Nonetheless, certain aspects of Op. 50 suggest that Haydn, whether consciously or not, may have been adapting aspects of his younger contemporary's idiom for his own use. To begin with, the broadened rhythmic stride felt in several of the opening movements signifies that Haydn has come to resemble Mozart more closely than before in matters of pace and surface activity. (To be sure, there are anticipations of a less crowded surface in several of Haydn's own earlier first movements, notably those of Op. 20/4 and Op. 33/3.) Added to this factor is a new inclination to enrich the flow of principal and subsidiary lines with chromatic inflections, sometimes in a way that seems intended to compensate for lesser amounts of rhythmic and figural detail in the course of a phrase.

These tendencies may owe as much to general trends of the time as to any exclusive influence of Mozart's; and yet there are circumstances in which Haydn's approach bears close resemblance to a Mozart trademark: the graceful technique of bridging a punctuation between phrases or themes with an even-paced connecting line, often unaccompanied, in which legato articulation and chromatic inflections convey an aura of effortless elegance and refinement. In the first movement of Mozart's C major quartet, K. 465, for example, the opening sentence of the Allegro ends with an inflected cadence in measure 30, and thematic action resumes in the next measure. Meanwhile, the first violin sustains both rhythmic momentum and linear interest by gliding through the octave and linking seamlessly with the downbeat of measure 31 (ex. 12.6a). A similar strategy on Haydn's part can be seen in example 12.6b, from late in the exposition of Op. 50/2/i: a half cadence in measure 83 marks the end of a daring tonal excursion (cited in connection with ex. 12.5), signals a point of restored equilibrium in the orbit of the dominant, and prepares for the start of a closing theme on the downbeat of measure 85. But action does not come to a halt. As in the passage

EXAMPLE 12.6

(a) Mozart, String Quartet in C, K. 465/i, mm. 29–32

(b) Haydn, Op. 50/2/i, mm. 81–86

from Mozart's K. 465, a suave, chromatically inflected descent animates the space between cadence and new thematic entry.

However Mozart-like in profile, this patch of connective tissue also owes much to Haydn's own motivic resourcefulness. The D–C♯–D of measure 84, framed on either side by comparably salient lower-neighbor figures, may be seen in a larger perspective as a variant, in diminution, of the neighbor-note figure introduced at the head of the primary theme. Likewise integral to the movement's fabric, and to this local environment in particular, is the underlying chromatic descent, which reverses the rising half steps of the opening phrase and bears comparable relationship to the dominant-key variant that gets under way at measure 85. Measure 84 is thus well interwoven with strands of chromaticism that unfold within the movement's primary and secondary themes. Furthermore, the connecting gesture we have been considering is not a unique event within the exposition. A similar idea had been introduced by the cello in measure 42 as a link from the transition to a new theme in the dominant. Its higher-register recurrence in measure 84 may thus be heard as a subtly intensified response to that earlier pivotal moment—positioned one step closer to the goal of a secure close in the dominant, and likewise both a signal of structural delineation and an emblem of Haydnesque unity and motivic concentration.

～

Apart from the deservedly popular "Frog," Op. 50/6, the quartets of this group have received relatively little attention from performers, listeners, and (at least until recently) commentators as well. This neglect is perhaps understandable in light of the works' absorption in structural and textural complexity, their unrelenting attention to motivic process, and certain peculiarities of their melodic idiom—variously severe and astringent, as in Op. 50/4/i; enigmatic and understated, as in Op. 50/1/i; or plainly eccentric, as in the quizzical Lombard rhythms and jarring accents of Op. 50/6/iii. On the whole, the first movements tend to be relatively cerebral and contrived, the slow movements more decorative than soulful, the dance movements more quirky and puzzling than ingratiating. Only in the finales (apart from the disturbingly intense fugue that caps Op. 50/4) can we savor something akin to the accessibility of Op. 33. But if the Op. 50 quartets seem short on popular appeal, they command highest respect for the inventiveness of their challenge to prevailing customs. They rival Mozart's contemporaneous works in proving the quartet's ascendancy as an aristocrat among instrumental genres, and, given the adroitness with which they embrace both serious and comic manners while transcending the limits of both, they set a formidable standard for subsequent accomplishments.

13

Op. 54/55 (1788)

On 22 September 1788, about a year after the completion of Op. 50, Haydn let it be known to Artaria that he had gotten wind of a certain business arrangement: "A few days ago I was told that you, my dear Sir, were supposed to have purchased from Herr Tost my very newest 6 quartets and 2 new symphonies."[1] (The symphonies in question were Nos. 88 and 89, and the middleman to whom Haydn refers was Johann Tost,[2] a former colleague of Haydn's who had served as leader of the second violins in the Esterházy orchestra from March 1783 to March 1788.) Although the reference to new quartets implies that such works did indeed exist, circumstances surrounding the transaction are not altogether clear: the alleged sale, whether already consummated or not, may have been based on a promise of compositions not yet delivered. Bearing on this last possibility is a somewhat earlier letter, of 10 August, in which a set of quartets is mentioned as a mere proposal: "Since I am now in a position where I need a little money," he confesses, "I propose to write for you, by the end of December, either 3 new quartets or 3 new pianoforte sonatas. . . . I shall then complete the other 3 quartets, or pianoforte sonatas, so that the edition will comprise half-a-dozen, as usual."[3] Was Haydn being coy, not letting on that the quartets were already under way, perhaps even finished? Or was he envisaging a subsequent project, not connected with the quartets mentioned in the September letter? In the absence of other evidence, it remains uncertain just when Haydn began the Op. 54/55 quartets or when they were completed, although to place them in the year 1788 seems reasonable.

Possibly through Tost's offices, an edition was eventually issued in Vienna without a publisher's name. Its two installments were sold by Artaria as advertised in the *Wiener Zeitung*, the first part on 1 July 1789, the second on 13 January 1790. Fueling suspicion that Artaria's firm was actually the publisher is the fact that the firm did print the two symphonies mentioned in Haydn's letter of

22 September, advertising them on 1 July 1789, the same day as the first set of quartets.[4]

Prior to the quartets' appearance in Vienna, there were business dealings elsewhere involving their sale and distribution. Haydn's letter of 5 April 1789 to Sieber in Paris reveals that Tost had taken the quartets, along with two symphonies, to the French capital. Rather dryly, he writes, "Now I would ask you to tell me candidly just how, and in what fashion, Herr Tost behaved in Paris. Did he have an *Amour* there? And did he also sell you the 6 quartets, and for what sum? Item, will the quartets and the 2 symphonies soon appear in print?"[5] Sieber's response is not known, but a letter from Haydn to Pleyel on 20 May 1801 implies an affirmative answer regarding the quartet transaction: here, Haydn reports that Sieber wishes to have a certificate verifying his purchase of "those particular 12 quartets" from Tost.[6] Although the compositions are not specified, Opp. 54/55 and 64 seem the most likely, as they are the only ones with which Tost's name is associated in the letters and documents. Sieber did, in fact, issue the works, advertising the first of two sets on 13 June 1789, and sometime in 1789 he also published the two symphonies.[7]

Meanwhile, it appears that quartets from the new series had become known through public performances in London, where they were eventually published by Longman & Broderip. Haydn had apparently supplied manuscript copies to a group known as the Professional Concert,[8] and from their London concert programs it is known that new quartets by Haydn were played from manuscripts at the organization's first and third concerts of winter 1789 (2 and 16 February).[9] The London firm then published the works in two parts, the first registered at Stationers' Hall on 7 July 1789 (to claim copyright) and advertised shortly thereafter on 7 August, the second registered on 12 March 1790.[10]

There are no extant completed manuscripts in Haydn's hand for the quartets,[11] nor is there any other evidence that might indicate how the composer intended to have them ordered and grouped for publication. As it happens, the early editions all present them as two sets of three each, and in the editions we have cited, the orderings within those sets are mostly different from one another. The pairs of opus numbers differ as well: 59/60 for the Viennese edition, 57/61 for Longman & Broderip, and 54/55 for Sieber; and whereas Sieber's opus numbers prevailed, it was the Viennese print whose ordering of quartets became standard when it was adopted for Pleyel's complete edition.

The designation "Tost quartets" derives less from Tost's involvement with their sale than from the mistaken belief that they had actually been dedicated to him. In Artaria's posthumous edition of fifty-eight Haydn quartets, the first violin part for each subset of this group bears a note which reads "Dediés á M^r. Doft";[12] but the designation has no known authentic basis. Possibly there may have been a confusion with Op. 64, which actually bore a dedication to Tost in the first printing of an edition by Kozeluch. In any event, there appears to be no evidence to support the claim, found throughout the literature, that the violin writing in these quartets was specifically influenced by Tost's violin technique.[13]

Another tradition associated with Op. 54/55 likewise seems groundless, however charming, namely the designation of Op. 55/2 as the "Razor."[14] The factual basis for the nickname involves a visit to Eszterháza in November 1789 by the London publisher John Bland. According to the earliest known version of the story (an allegedly firsthand account published in 1836), Bland came upon the composer while the latter was attempting to shave with an inadequate blade and heard him exclaim that he would give one of his best compositions for an English razor. Recognizing a business opportunity, Bland rushed to his inn, fetched the coveted instrument, and gave it to Haydn, who in honor of the vow put into his hands the manuscript of a quartet that Bland later published, and to which he referred as his "Razor Quartett."

But which composition was this? An account in Pohl's biography of Haydn, based on a later version of the story, identifies it as No. 5 of the "Tost" quartets,[15] and Pohl's statement was interpreted as a reference to Op. 55/2. Bland, however, did not publish Op. 54/55, and the belief that Pohl was referring to this quartet is further contradicted by the biographer's own article for Grove's *Dictionary of Music and Musicians* (1879), in which the piece is given as "Trautwein, No. 2": that is, the second quartet in a mid-nineteenth-century Berlin edition of the subsequent set, Op. 64, which Bland did in fact publish. According to Trautwein's sequence, which differs from the traditional numbering, this would mean that the work in question was the familiar "Lark," Op. 64/5. As for the other treasured object in the legendary trade, equally fitting as a symbol for the publisher's business acumen or the composer's wit, a relevant letter from Haydn to Bland, dated 12 April 1790, informs the publisher that he has "received the razors in good condition"[16]—an indication, perhaps, of a real connection between razors and the publication of Op. 64. The identity of an alleged "Razor" quartet remains unknown, however, although it may be significant that Bland chose to feature Op. 64/5 as the first in his series. This fact may have led Pohl to assume that the quartet thus favored must have been the one implicated in the exchange.

Given the closeness in time between Op. 50 and Op. 54/55, it is reasonable to expect similarities, and there are indeed points of connection between the two sets. The general impression, however, is that of a change in direction toward greater timbral brilliance and first violin virtuosity, qualities that partially override the distinctly chamber-like ensemble play featured in Opp. 20, 33, and 50. At least one contemporary critic was moved to imply that the works in Op. 54 were something other than "true quartets."[17] To make this generalization is perhaps to slight the works' nuances and to risk understating their diversity of character and expression, though the accent on solo technique is unmistakable nonetheless.

Can connections be drawn between the bold, *quatuor brilliant*[18] manner of Op. 54/55 and the circumstances under which the works were written? Although Tost's involvement with their sale in Paris and Haydn's own transactions with the Professional Concert in London suggest that the composer may have had his eye on the cosmopolitan environment of those foreign cities as he composed Op. 54/55,[19] it also seems clear from Haydn's negotiation with William Forster concerning Op. 50 that London, at least, was already in his purview with that earlier set. Correspondingly, the letter from August 1788 cited earlier indicates that Haydn had Artaria and the Viennese milieu at least partially in mind for the new venture, just as with Opp. 33 and 50.

Overview of the Opus

In fashioning these relatively extroverted quartets, Haydn exceeds his previous set with respect to the range of home keys and in fact reaches his outer limits for the repertory: E major on the sharp end of the spectrum, F minor on the flat side (see table 13.1). In no other set do we find a comparable spread (from four sharps to four flats) for principal tonalities. The inclusion of both A and E, keys that were identified in Haydn's day with brilliance,[20] seems noteworthy: this is the only group subsequent to Op. 20 that includes a quartet in either key; and none, apart from the very early works published as Op. 2, employs both as principal tonics (Op. 2/1 is in A, 2/2 is in E).

True to the accent on tonal brightness, minor keys are somewhat downplayed: for Op. 55/2, the set's obligatory minor quartet, Haydn not only ends the opening variations and the principal Allegro (here the second movement) in major, but casts the minuet proper and the finale in its entirety in major. Op. 54/2 (like Op. 55/2 a single-tonic work in which a scheme of modal alternation is naturally to be expected) does have an interior slow movement in a dark C minor, but minor harmony is not confirmed at its end: instead, a dominant chord leads without a break into the C major of the minuet. In fact, the only full closing cadences in minor in the entire opus are those of the Op. 54/2 and 55/2 dance-movement trios, and minor sonority is neutralized in the former instance by the choice of a closing unison rather than a chord with a minor third.

Added to the emphasis on sharp keys and major tonality are other signs of sanguine character, notably the preference for spirited tempos (allegro, vivace, or vivace assai) and streamlined surface activity for the opening sonata form movements (and for the second movement of Op. 55/2). All but two use Haydn's recently adopted, fast-paced alla breve with subdivisions mainly in eighth notes (Op. 54/2/i and 55/2/ii) or triplet eighths (Op. 54/3/i and 55/1/i, both recalling the rhythmic impetus of Op. 50/1/i). Different though no less forceful in rhyth-

TABLE 13.1 Summary statistics for Op. 54/55

Op.No.	Hob.No.	Movement			
		i	ii	iii	iv
54/1	III:58	G e Vivace assai SF 131	C $^6_8$ Allegretto SF 112	G $^3_4$ M/T 44/24	G $^2_4$ Vivace Rondo 193(r)
54/2	III:57	C ¢ Vivace SF 233	Cm $^3_4$ Adagio Rounded binary 35(r)	C/Cm $^3_4$ Allegretto M/T 46/26	C $^2_4$ Adagio–Presto–Adagio Nonstandard 140(r)
54/3	III:59	E ¢ Allegro SF 189	A $^3_4$ Largo. Cantabile Ternary var. 65	E $^3_4$ Allegretto M/T 38/22	E $^2_4$ Presto SF (irreg.) 218
55/1	III:60	A ¢ Allegro SF 174	D $^2_4$ Adagio. Cantabile Slow-mvt. 74	A $^3_4$ M/T 26/28	A ¢ Vivace Rondo (irreg.) 145
55/2	III:61	Fm-F $^2_4$ Andante o più tosto allegretto Alternating var. 202(r)	Fm-F $^4_4$ Allegro SF (irreg.) 180	F/Fm $^3_4$ Allegretto M/T 54(r)/38	F $^6_8$ Presto SF 118
55/3	III:62	B♭ $^3_4$ Vivace assai SF 197	E♭ $^4_4$ Adagio ma non troppo Strophic var. 82	B♭ $^3_4$ M/T 42/20	B♭ $^6_8$ Presto SF 103

mic character is the first movement of Op. 54/1, which resembles Op. 50/6/i in its combination of fast tempo, common-time signature, and mix of eighth- and sixteenth-note subdivisions.

Featured among the slow movements are three different kinds of variation: Op. 55/3/ii follows a strophic model (as in Op. 50/1/ii); Op. 55/2/i is a species of alternating variation (roughly comparable to that of Op. 50/4/ii); and one is new, the A B A¹ ternary variation (Op. 54/3/ii), which proves well suited to testing the first violinist's command of expressive embellishment. The other three slow movements, although different from one another in character and form, are comparable as vehicles for solo display: a sonata form (Op. 54/1/ii) with a lyrical but intense treble line that repeatedly climbs high above the staff; a rhapsodic piece in rounded binary form (Op. 54/2/ii) that sets off a rhythmically elastic, chromatically inflected first violin melody against the other instruments' sober, hymn-like delivery; and a concerto-like slow-movement form (Op. 55/1/ii), similar in principle to Opp. 33/5/ii and 50/2/ii, with an eight-measure ritornello to precede the soloist's first principal entry, and a pair of ensemble cadenzas that call to mind the accompanied cadenza of Op. 33/5.

The dance movements, perhaps less boldly original as a group than those of either Op. 33 or 50, are nevertheless rich in ensemble color, rhythmic play, harmonic interest, and formal intrigue. The opening of the Op. 54/3 minuet makes comical reference to the spare textures of early dance movements in which violins and lower parts, both in octaves, square off in two-voice counterpoint. The trio of Op. 55/1 introduces a stratospheric first violin descant, and the oddity of a pair of five-measure phrases in the Op. 54/1 minuet recalls the similarly peculiar 5 + 5 phrasing heard in the minuet of Op. 20/3. In the trio of Op. 54/1, Haydn exercises his penchant for metrical complication by implying a switch from $\frac{3}{4}$ to $\frac{3}{2}$ (mm. 53–56), and then accelerating to a series of virtual $\frac{2}{4}$ measures (mm. 57–58) before restoring triple time. Likewise memorable are the prolonged, bleak dissonances of the Op. 54/2 trio; the intense pathos of a dominant-ninth-chord climax in the Op. 55/2 trio (mm. 82–83); and the surge to a melodic peak of c^4 in the Op. 54/2 minuet. Two of the new dance movements revisit specific devices featured in the preceding set: the minuet of Op. 55/2 resembles that of Op. 50/1 by treating its first part to a varied reprise, this time involving contrapuntal enrichment in addition to the altered distribution of lines among the instruments; and the minuet and trio of Op. 55/3, like several of those in Op. 50, are connected thematically, in this case by way of an embellishing triplet figure at the end of the minuet that blossoms into a principal idea in the trio.

Among the finales, rondo form returns on two occasions, Op. 54/1 and 55/1. Although these last movements are instantly recognizable as examples of the genre, neither conforms to a straightforward alternation between refrain and episode as found in Op. 33/2, 3, and 4. In Op. 54/1, the order of events is normal at first—a rounded binary refrain followed by an episode in minor—but then becomes developmental and unpredictable once the first reprise of the returning refrain has sounded (mm. 66–73). The Op. 55/1 finale veers from the norms of rondo form right after the end of its first episode. At this juncture (m. 61), a long span dominated by fugal polyphony (mm. 61–107) deftly combines the functions of second episode and refrain, and in the process unites the two special finale types—fugue and rondo—that had been showcased in Opp. 20 and 33, respectively. Of the three finales in sonata form, that of Op. 54/3 digresses from sonata norms with a premature return to primary theme material in tonic (m. 95) and a subsequent dovetailing of development and recapitulation. Structurally more regular, and roughly comparable in character, the last movements of Op. 55/2 and 3 both make use of a presto tempo and $\frac{6}{8}$ meter as a basis for the play of contrast between galloping eighth-note rhythms and strands of virtuosic sixteenths. Standing apart from all the others is the unclassifiable Op. 54/2 finale, whose unique traits include stark differences in tempo, texture, and theme between outer and middle sections.

Aspects of Texture and Register; The Special Role of the First Violin

Of the quartets' sources of brilliance and rhetorical impact, none claims greater importance than the dominating presence of the first violin. The accent on treble-dominated sonority, different from the generally more collaborative textures of the preceding three opus groups, calls to mind precedents in Opp. 9 and 17, where the top part likewise often stood out conspicuously from the accompanying voices. The new works are quite different, however, in quality of motion and in the relationship between principal line and metrical impulse. As shown in example 13.1a, from the opening of Op. 9/3, a background of throbbing eighth notes establishes a moderate pace, while the first violin strides from one half-measure unit to the next, variously accentuating the downbeat or the middle of the measure with decorative figures in small note values. The opening phrase of Op. 54/1 (ex. 13.1b) is obviously related, but the pace has quickened, and the principal melody bounds more freely across the theme's temporal space: the long initial G, whose attack is enlivened by leaping grace notes, commands virtually the entire measure. The sixteenth notes crowding the last beat lend an updraft to measure 2, where repeated notes provide a long anacrusis to a galvanizing high D in measure 3, whose impact helps draw the phrase together as a single, unified gesture.

Embedded within the first violin flights that characterize this opus group are several ascents to a riveting high peak on the E string, and at least one passage in each of the quartets reaches somewhere in the range of c^4 to $d\sharp^4$. Extreme heights are not altogether new with Op. 54/55. The minuet of Op. 20/2 had gone up to c^4, and there were several comparable peaks in Opp. 42 and 50. But here they do

EXAMPLE 13.1

(a) Op. 9/3/i, mm. 1–3

(b) Op. 54/1/i, mm. 1–4

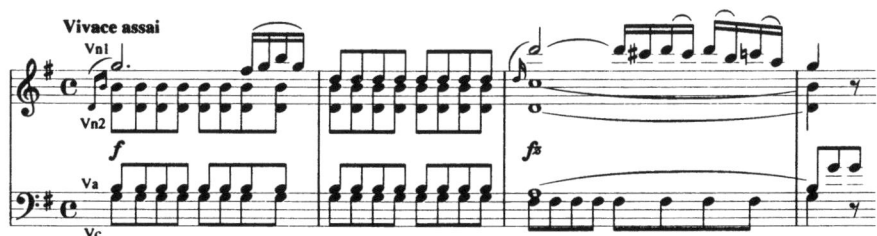

enjoy unprecedented emphasis, dramatizing brilliant high points and sparkling with soloistic intensity. Exemplifying the first violin climax, the finale of Op. 54/3 starts out in an atmosphere of suppressed energy, withholding the group leader's entry for a full nine measures as the second violin quietly unfolds a skittish principal theme in a middle to low register. The atmosphere brightens with the top part's entry in measure 10, and by measure 14 the line has ascended to e^3, two and a half octaves above the second violin's low point in measures 5 and 6. But only after the middle of the exposition, following a move to the orbit of the dominant and the shift in surface activity to steady sixteenths, does the first violin go higher, first to f♯^{3} (mm. 54 and 58), then finally, supported an octave below by the second violin, to a climactic d♯^{4} (m. 67) before retreating to a lower range and drawing the exposition to a close.

The first violin's propensity for high notes serves a more purely coloristic purpose in the trio of Op. 55/1. Here the second violin gamely carries the tune while the first violin, released from thematic responsibility, rises high above the others in a descant that attains c♯^{4} in both first and second reprise. The impression of an otherworldly sound-picture is reinforced by discontinuity near the end of the trio: as if awakening from a dream, all parts come to a sudden halt on the downbeat of measure 49, and the first violin, left hanging on c♯^{4}, now plummets more than three octaves to pick up the thread and finish with a closing phrase on the G string. The second violin's appropriation of the main line, allowing the first to indulge in figural display, is one of numerous such instances throughout the set, and the slow movement of Op. 54/2, with its haunting violin solo that flourishes above an unembellished theme, stands as the *locus classicus* for this device. (Although specially emphasized in Op. 54/55, the technique is not new here. The slow movement of Op. 20/5 is a prize example, and there are significant precedents among the earliest quartets.)

Helping to counteract the first violin's otherwise domineering manner, Haydn occasionally has other instruments participate on a more equitable basis by engaging them in animated dialogue (as in Opp. 33 and 50), by having them take part in embedded passages of fugal polyphony (an artifice encountered here for the first time among the quartets, in Op. 55/1/iv and 55/2/ii), or by exploring more novel effects of ensemble texture and register. Representing this last category, ironically, are the two notated cadenzas that adorn the slow movement of Op. 55/1 (mm. 28–33 and 61–67). Both times, the lower parts chime in once the first violin has begun the cadenza, thereby collapsing the space between solo foreground and background accompaniment, and transforming what had started out as a span of unhindered solo display into a group effort that draws on the entire ensemble—all together, in unison with the soloist in measures 30–32, then one by one, with independent (but rhythmically synchronized) lines of their own in measures 62–65.[21]

In addition, there are places where attention is directed to the cello as either an opposing force or a vehicle for expansion in ensemble color and thematic register. The finale of Op. 55/3, for example, had begun with a cascade of sixteenth notes in the first violin, joined in unison by the others in the second measure, and that instrument's predominance throughout the exposition had climaxed in an ascent to c^4 in measure 38, three measures before the double bar. But then, following an ethereal close to the exposition, the cello designates a point of dramatic reversal by leading with a gruff, earthbound note that initiates a quasi inversion of the top part's initial sixteenth-note descent, and the viola and second violin now proceed to fill in the newly opened space by joining in imitation.

Chromatic Harmony and Tonal Enrichment

Decorative and thematically salient inflections are often allied in Op. 54/55 with solo delivery and the drama of registral contrast, and there are passages in which chromatic embellishment pays dividends in the form of structural or motivic integration. A simple but elegant case, from the slow movement of Op. 54/3, involves Haydn's treatment of the closing cadence to the outer sections of this A B A¹ form. Whereas the cadence at the end of A (m. 24) stands virtually unadorned, apart from a turn on the preceding upbeat, the corresponding moment at the end of the form (m. 65, following a richly varied A^1) seems almost over-drawn with its rising chromatic line in thirty-second notes—a soloistic act of resis-tance to descent and closure. And yet this restless figure also can claim thematic credentials as the consequence of an earlier event, a pivotal chromatic descent in the cello, which occupies the midpoint of A (mm. 12–13) and A^1 (mm. 50–51) on the way to a prolonged, structurally important dominant (through m. 16; m. 54 in A^1). The decorated closing gesture of measure 65 transforms that idea, relo-cating it from the middle of the section to its end, promoting it from the bass line to the highest voice, quickening the rhythm, and reversing the direction so that the dominant note is approached from below rather than above.

On other occasions, Haydn enriches a theme with one or more foreign pitches whose latent energy enlivens the intrigue that follows. In Op. 55/3/i, a single half-step inflection—the E♮ that ends the opening unison statement—elicits an immediate response in the rising half steps of the cello (mm. 6–7) and paired violins (mm. 7–8; see ex. 13.2a). The viola, developing the gesture in mea-sures 20–23, adds an accented, destabilizing G♭ to the cello's previous E♭–E♮–F motion (ex. 13.2b). Later, past the midpoint of the exposition, a thematically more prominent rising line in the cello embodies an entire chromatic fourth from D to G within its stepwise ascent, highlighting the inflected pitches with accented syncopations (ex. 13.2c). A concomitant sense of tonal restlessness per-sists, and to some degree intensifies, as the exposition continues. Near the end of the section (mm. 60–64), Haydn complicates the process by causing the upward-striving gesture to reverse direction: a falling chromatic line in the cello (B♮–B♭–A) helps signal the impending close, and the event is underscored by long-sustained diminished seventh harmony above the B♮ prior to a continuation of the descent.

The chromatic-line idea evolves further as it joins a polyphonic elaboration of the primary theme early in the recapitulation (mm. 137–38). Here, the first vio-lin's extended series of rising half steps reaches all the way from D to B♭ (ex. 13.2d).

Chromatically enriched phrases such as those cited here have a larger-scale counterpart in movements with entire sections distinguished by exotic tonal paths or excursions to remote keys. In the second movement of Op. 54/1, an opening theme's melodic inflections foreshadow an astonishing sequence of tonal digres-sions that color both the exposition and recapitulation of this harmonically unique sonata form.[22] The process begins rather innocuously with embellishing scale degrees (C♯ in m. 4, D♯ in m. 7), then continues with the rhythmically more sus-tained inflection to B♭ (m. 10) and the rising and falling half-step figures that adorn the close of the phrase (mm. 11–12). Melodic chromaticism intensifies in the transition that begins in measure 21 (labeled T in fig. 13.1), where passages of undulating sixteenths become almost saturated chromatically (mm. 29, 31–32). And when the secondary theme begins in measure 34, tonal adventure gets un-derway in earnest: a rising line of half steps in the second violin (G through B♭ in mm. 35–37), joined below by the cello, succeeds in dislodging the theme from

EXAMPLE 13.2 Op. 55/3/i

(a) mm. 1–8

(b) mm. 20–23 (viola only)

(c) mm. 46–50 (cello only)

(d) mm. 137–40

the established G major as it leads to a cadence in B♭ (m. 39). Displaced to this remote tonal plane, the phrase repeats, thereby advancing another minor third to
land in D♭ (m. 44). It is now the first violin's turn to rise chromatically (mm. 45–47)
and thus to direct the tonal center to a restored G major as the end of the exposition draws near.

The full-fledged recurrence of these events in the latter part of the recapitulation, now transposed down a fifth, further widens the harmonic spectrum. The
impact of the strange migrations is enhanced by the overall symmetry and structural transparency by which they are framed: the exposition passes from tonic

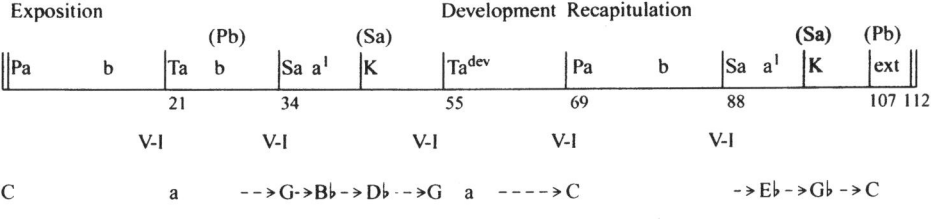

FIGURE 13.1 Op. 54/1/ii

through A minor on the way to the dominant; the brief development section, which draws on the exposition's transition phrase, mirrors that theme's previous tonal motion by progressing from A minor toward a restored home key; the return of the secondary theme in the recapitulation (which now follows directly on the heels of the primary theme) essentially comprises a transposed version of the exposition's corresponding events; and the full stop in the dominant at measure 54, a central pivot in the design, occurs just before the midpoint of the movement.

Encounters with alien tonal relationships, a recurrent feature of these quartets, are rendered with particular force when coupled with a movement's main theme: having established a principal key at the outset, and destined for comparably important service at the start of the recapitulation, an affirmative opening idea is a natural focus of structural weight. When that weight is unexpectedly displaced to a remote key, the result is likely to be a potent challenge to stability: the assertion of a new perspective, and thus a prime opportunity for color, drama, or intrigue. The second-movement Allegro of the "Razor," Op. 55/2, which exceeds all others in this set with respect to tonal range and emphasized contrast of key and mode, exemplifies the powerful coupling of theme and tonal excursion. The principal idea—marked for emphasis by long opening note values, a distinctive rising leap, and clear separation in register and rhythmic profile from its repeated-chord accompaniment—makes no fewer than fifteen appearances (not counting sectional repeats) encompassing eleven different pitch levels or keys: F minor, Gb, and Ab come into play in the exposition; Db, A (or Bbb), Bb, Eb, C minor, Eb minor, and Bb minor are all added in the fugal development section; and F major is eventually featured in the recapitulation. Tonal contrast arises early in the exposition. After an oddly final-sounding tonic cadence in measure 16 and a pregnant silence of nearly three measures, the primary theme's recurrence on Gb comes as a sudden break with the regime of tonic (although logically connected as a Neapolitan relationship) and a springboard for motion toward the relative major, which will eventually be secured by the recurrence of the opening theme in Ab at measure 41.

Events early in the development section build on the tonal shock of the exposition. After an initial statement of the opening theme in Db, the suspense of an extended pause once again precedes a surprise change of harmony, just as in the exposition—this time to B♭♭ (spelled A). The impact of local contrast proves comparably startling, as the thematic statement that now breaks the silence lies a half step above the unison A♭ with which the preceding phrase had ended. In effect, the A♭–B♭♭ juxtaposition approximates the earlier switch from F minor to G♭.

Tonal restlessness continues in the subsequent fugal elaboration, where almost every entry of the subject (based on the primary theme) transpires in a different key. This part of the design may be heard as a prolonged search for tonal restitution, for recovery from a fatal step into distant territory; and the eventual return to harmonic stability, which seems close at hand with the first violin's entry in F minor at measure 125, is perhaps only fully accomplished by the turn to F major in measure 145, following the dissolution of the fugal polyphony over a long dominant pedal point. The movement now proceeds with a recurrence of material from the latter part of the exposition, transposed from A♭ to F major.

Cyclic Novelty and Coherence

Although familiar conventions for movement type and cyclic design predominate in this opus group (an ebullient, fast-paced opening movement, an introspective soliloquy or other solo vehicle for contrast, a moderately fast dance movement, a high-speed finale), the general picture is complicated by two quartets whose unusual cyclic profiles mark them as special cases. The works in question, Op. 54/2 and 55/2, have single-tonic designs in which tonal constancy goes hand in hand with the play of contrast between major and minor, and in various respects they exhibit pronounced elements of cyclic cohesion, a tendency witnessed previously, most notably among quartets in Opp. 20 and 50, and cultivated here from fresh vantage points. In both works, integration complements—and in turn is nourished by—oddities of movement form and cyclic shape. At issue is a twofold premise: an impression of cyclic cohesion, from whatever source, can help compensate for perceived instability within a movement; but certain points of instability may themselves promote interdependence between movements by participating in some larger, intermovement scheme of connectedness.[23]

In Op. 54/2, the first movement's highly dramatized inflections to ♭VI (mm. 13, 138, and 185) prefigure the C minor realms explored in each subsequent movement, and a run-on connection between Adagio and minuet (like that witnessed in Op. 20/2) renders the work open-ended at its very core. The structural seam in question marks a threshold between two very different styles: a rhapsodic solo whose fluid rhythms and expansive melodic gestures conjure images of exoticism and passion, followed by a cultivated minuet, replete with signs of a temporarily restored equilibrium. But the dance movement itself turns out to have complications, including locally destabilizing ingredients that point to events elsewhere in the cycle. Important in this regard are the trio's reversion to minor, with dissonant harmonies whose air of unrest and yearning—including an uncanny anticipation of Wagner's *Tristan* chord at measures 66–67[24]—resonates with the mood of the Adagio, and the minuet's astonishing final measures (42–46): a dramatic unison ascent and richly scored final cadence with double stops in all three upper parts. Locally, this closing flourish helps maximize the impression of contrast between the minuet and the minor-mode trio, the latter beginning darkly with a low-register, arpeggiated unison, but its larger significance becomes apparent when it comes back at the end of the minuet's return. Here it works to define this moment as a major divide, separating all that precedes from the break with cyclic convention that will follow: a finale whose singular design easily ranks as one of the oddest in the repertory, but whose connections to prior events lend it weight as a species of cyclic culmination nonetheless.

How can this strange final movement be described? In simplest terms, it sandwiches a fleeting, perpetual-motion Presto between two ponderous Adagios: the former a rather long, compound section enriched by a temporary change of mode, the latter a relatively brief, summarizing recollection of the first. As represented in figure 13.2, the movement unfolds in discrete segments, each of which indicates the likelihood of a certain continuation. And yet the signals continually mislead. Conventional realizations of structural implications are denied, and listeners, drawn into a maze of thwarted expectations, must continually reinterpret the meaning of events after the fact. The finale has been examined from this perspective by Cone and Webster.[25] The account that follows draws on their insights as it surveys some of the chief anomalies as well as the underlying logic of the design.

- **A** (Adagio) **a**: 4 + 4 (mm. 1–8). Contradicting our initial anticipation of a high-speed refrain or primary theme announcement, the dark, slow-tempo opening could signify the start of a slow introduction (perhaps comparable to that of Mozart's contemporaneous G minor quintet, K. 516), although this device is not otherwise found in a Haydn quartet finale.

- Repeat of **a**. The literal repeat undermines the probability of a slow introduction, which would surely have progressed in some more continuous fashion toward the eventual change to a quick pace. Instead, the repeat leads us to deduce that this strain must be the first part of a closed, two-reprise form.

- **b b** (mm. 9–24): an eight-measure phrase-pair (4 + 4) followed by a virtually literal repeat. Armed with the evidence described directly above, we may be inclined to hear **b** as the start of a second reprise, and the cadence on the dominant in measure 16 helps reinforce this impression. What should happen now is a balancing response to complete the supposed binary or rounded binary form. But by presenting a repeat of **b** instead, Haydn obliges us to hear this unit as an intact, open-ended strain in and of itself: a first reprise, in

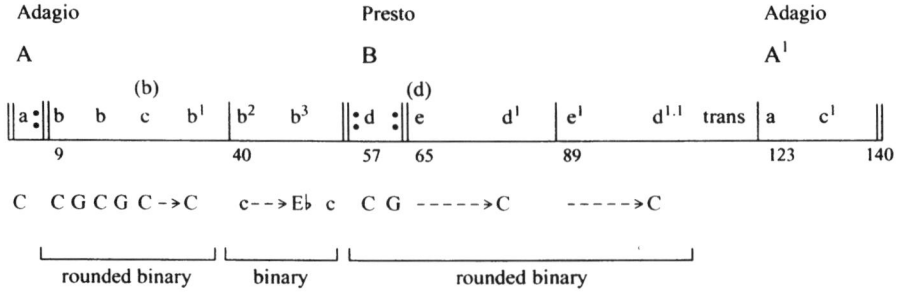

FIGURE 13.2 Op. 54/2/iv

other words, so that our previous theory about **a** (that *it* was a first reprise) proves no longer tenable. Was it an introduction after all?

- **c b¹**: 8 + 8 (mm. 25–40). The continuation—eight tonally unstable measures (**c**) ending on the dominant, followed by a tonally altered return to the material of **b** (**b¹**), confirms our revised interpretation of **b** and its repeat: **b** was indeed a first reprise, and the span encompassing **b b c b¹** works out as a fully closed, rounded binary form though without a repeat of the second part (see the brackets under the sketch).

- **b² b³** in C minor: 8 + 8 (mm. 41–56). The sentence **b²**, a minor-key transformation of **b** that progresses to the relative major, E♭, is balanced by **b³**, which moves back to tonic. The fact that **b³** ends on a half cadence rather than a full stop fuels suspicion that **b² b³** may be the middle section of a large, slow-tempo ternary design, and that the movement will eventually proceed with a recurrence (perhaps varied) of the rounded binary form recognized above (**b b c b¹**).

- **B** (Presto, mm. 57–122): closely similar in structure to the rounded binary design of measures 9–40 (**b b c b¹**),[26] but this time with a written-out repeat of the second part (**e d¹**). The tempo change at measure 57, the most jarring disturbance so far, requires us to revise all assumptions about preceding events while at the same time raising new questions. Could the Adagio have been an introduction to a fast-tempo finale after all? Conceivably, although this is rendered unlikely by the compact size of the rounded binary Presto, which turns out to be a mere fraction of the Adagio in playing time.

- **A¹** (Adagio) **a** (mm. 123–30): return to the adagio tempo and to the material of measures 1–8. It now appears that the movement will play itself out as a peculiar ternary form, with slow outer segments and a fast middle section, but the fact that Haydn goes back to the very opening, rather than just retrieving what we had come to understand as the Adagio's first principal section (the rounded binary form comprising **b b c b¹**), means that we must revise our notion of **a** as merely an introduction to the Adagio.

- c^1 (mm. 131–40). Once again, unforeseen events oblige us to alter our thinking: the cadence in measure 130 is followed not by a replica of the rounded binary section but by a derivative of that form's harmonically unstable middle section c (mm. 25–32). Ironically, this unanticipated span of transformed recurrence, now tethered to a tonic pedal, actually serves to ground the movement's harmonic action as the first violin negotiates a long descent to the close.

An object lesson in the mechanisms by which a series of events may be understood to cohere as a musical form, the movement also demonstrates cyclic integration by its allusions to earlier events and realization of long-range implications. In broadest terms, it serves to resolve principal harmonic issues: there are no further tonal shocks or digressions, as found in the first movement; the harmony has been cleansed of anything resembling the trio's dissonant sonorities; and the local assurance of conventional, transparent relationship within each of the finale's segments complements elements of tonal richness and unpredictability experienced in earlier portions of the work. Also significant is the juxtaposition of major and minor modes in the A section. Here, for the first time in this work, the two are placed side by side in a design that captures the contrast in color and mood as directly and succinctly as possible—through the simple transformation of a theme from major to minor.

Added to these harmonic factors are certain corroborating aspects of register and instrumental idiom. Gone from the finale are the piercing first violin climaxes that had marked both the first movement and the minuet. Instead, we can sense a gravitational pull that only occasionally permits the first violin to rise above the staff. At the same time, the cello gains new importance as a counterweight to the first violin and a source of tonal solidity. Its stately arpeggiations in the A section climb as high as f^2, and the resonance of its low C, more than three octaves below, enjoys special prominence: the two dozen occurrences of the pitch (concentrated toward the end, to be sure) exceed those of the rest of the quartet put together.

Final mention may be made of the first violin's downward motion from a climactic f^3, first struck at measure 121, then reclaimed at measure 133. From here the line makes a virtually stepwise descent to c^2 for a full cadence in measure 138, two measures before the end. Both the first movement and the minuet had left yawning gaps between their late melodic high points (mm. 218–19 and m. 44, respectively) and their lower-register conclusions, so that the finale's more gradual descent may be heard as a form of ultimate resolution, filling what had previously been experienced as empty registral space, and thus enhancing the impression of a satisfying conclusion.

Op. 55/2 in F minor, the set's other single-tonic work, complements Op. 54/2 by exploring modal contrast and transformation from an opposing perspective:

instead of the tension, harmonic complication, or pathos that may emerge when major is temporarily overtaken by minor, this work experiences a very different kind of journey as it progresses from minor to major, and in this respect it constitutes something of a watershed. Before this opus, Haydn's quartets in minor had ended in minor or at least adhered to minor until the final measures of the last movement (as in Op. 20/3); and with the recent exception of Op. 50/4, the first movements had likewise resisted wholesale capitulation to major.[27] From now on, however, minor tonality will be extinguished at some point well before the end of the work. Op. 55/2 is actually an extreme case, with the later portions of the first and second movements, the minuet proper, and the entire finale all in major.

Also complementary to Op. 54/2 is the manner in which the normal cyclic profile is inflected, for here the signal aberration—the reversed order of first and second movements—affects the start of the work rather than its conclusion. Can the special order of movements in Op. 55/2 be related to the larger agenda of a contest between minor and major? Haydn fashions the first movement's alternating variations so that the opposing modes represent separate yet interrelated domains. The form may be summarized as $A\ B\ A^1\ B^1\ A^2\ B^2$, in which the A and B portions are in minor and major respectively, and the last segment is stretched by a twelve-measure extension. The fact that the B theme begins by recalling the rising triadic figure of A, now ascending a half step higher ($c^2\ f^2\ a^2$ instead of $c^2\ f^2\ ab^2$) accentuates the effect of transformation. The F major theme materializes not merely as a contrasting element, but as a consequence of the initial idea, elevated to a new, more brightly illuminated plane, with the strife of salient dissonances, contrasts, and discontinuities yielding to a climate of serenity in rhythm, line, and texture.

The transformative relationship of B to A, established in the themes' initial presentation, is intensified in the variations that follow. The contrast between A^2 (mm. 117–42) and B^2 (mm. 143–90) proves especially telling in this respect, as a strident cantus firmus in octaves and its turbulent lower-range counterpoint (mm. 117–22; 133–41) yield to a peaceful F major in which the first violin's ethereal figures grace the cello's lyrical, high-register melody (mm. 151–74).

The second movement's tonal diversity makes a fitting sequel to this play of opposed yet interdependent forces. Its modulatory extravagance fills out the polarized, single-tonic landscape of the first movement with tonal abundance while forging a longer, harmonically varied path from minor to major. The attainment of tonic major is secured by measure 145, where the key signature changes, and is reaffirmed in measures 172–73 by the climactic rising half step from ab^3 to a^3, an event that calls to mind the first movement's crucial change from ab^2 to a^2 between its A and B themes.

The minuet, infused with the brightness of the second movement's close, upholds F major as principal tonic,[28] although its second reprise does embrace chromaticism and tonal variety. The trio connects explicitly with earlier phases of the cycle by reverting to minor, but there are other connections as well: the high point of db³ (mm. 82–83), climaxing a long span of chromatically charged motivic development, recalls both the peak of the first movement's opening minor segment (m. 20, likewise db³) and the principal theme of the second movement, measure 3, in which db³ arises as an expressive upper neighbor to the dominant note c³. Despite the late resurgence of minor that this trio signifies, the obvious fact that minor discourse is now relegated to the movement's middle segment, enclosed by the F major minuet, affirms its subordination to an increasingly prominent major.

The last movement certifies the ascendancy of major not merely by supplanting minor but by appropriating its tonal ingredients. Unlike the first movement's B theme (which is only modestly inflected), or the first reprise of the minuet (where the secondary leading tone B, first heard in measure 5, and the embellishing F♯ in m. 21 are the sole accidentals), the last movement displays chromatic inflections from the start, and the scale degrees of F major and F minor, so pointedly separated by the minor-major duality of the first movement, are now embraced in a theme that incorporates both. From the opening thematic idea (mm. 1–4, quoted in ex. 13.3a), only the respective seventh degrees of the two scales are missing (Eb, E♮). But can any more specific conclusions be drawn regarding the theme and its inflections? Spelling the accidentals as sharps—G♯ rather than Ab, C♯ rather than Db, and F♯ rather than the Neapolitan Gb—suggests a tonal order in which minor elements are not purged but disguised. Moreover, the fact that the accidentals in question are now metrically subordinated to their more heavily accented neighbors reinforces the impression of a tonal environment securely dominated by major despite the chromaticism.

Further elaborations of the chromatic theme at the start of the development section prove especially telling from a cyclic perspective (see ex. 13.3b). Here, the cello sounds an inverted variant of the primary theme's opening notes and engages the viola in close imitation. The imitative play is then joined by the violins in the next measure, and the net result is a texture that proves both completely thematic and completely saturated chromatically. In light of the work's long-range accumulation of chromatic tendencies, beginning with the opening movement's A theme, further advanced in the second-movement development section, then still more intensified in the second parts of both the major minuet and the minor trio, the concentration of half-step relationships here may be heard as a subtle yet satisfying culmination to a cyclic process of modal transformation and accommodation.

Viewing Op. 54/55 in the context of previous opus groups reinforces our impression of Haydn's fondness for continually shifting his vantage point. Op. 33 seemed well tailored to the tastes and ambitions of accomplished amateurs, with its blend of popular style, intricate motivic play, and high-spirited commentary

EXAMPLE 13.3 Op. 55/2/iv

(a) mm. 1–4

(b) mm. 55–59

on contemporary practices and listeners' assumptions. Op. 50, although hardly neglecting the quartet's capacity for humor, generally maintained an air of serious concentration while making few concessions to popular tastes or performers' technical limitations. Op. 54/55, by comparison, is a less intimate affair, suitable for professional performers and crafted with an eye toward audience appeal. Yet this is not to suggest some drastic contrast between the latest opus and its predecessors. Upholding his reputation as leading exponent of the quartet, Haydn would not disappoint those who admired subtlety and complexity. Nevertheless, he may well have sensed that to continue in the more esoteric vein of Op. 50 might have restricted the scope of his audience and identified his approach to the genre too closely with an exclusive realm of chamber-music artistry. Having thus struck a fresh balance in Op. 54/55 between private and public idioms, Haydn could have chosen to continue along this particular path. But nothing was more characteristic for him than a change of direction, and his next set of quartets would indeed be devoted to reaffirming such core string quartet values as intricate dialogue, timbral shading, and pervasive attention to compositional detail.

14

Op. 64 (1790)

To judge from the dated autograph manuscripts that survive for five of this group's quartets[1] (that of the G major quartet, Op. 64/4, is lost), it would seem likely that the entire set was completed within the year 1790, and thus prior to the composer's first visit to London, undertaken at year's end. Whether they all predate the crucial events that preceded the journey—the death of Haydn's patron in September of that year, the subsequent dismantling of the Esterházy musical establishment, and Salomon's proposal that Haydn accompany him to the British capital—cannot be determined for sure. But because nothing about the quartets themselves indicates that they were specially designed for public concert use, it seems probable that they were finished before such a prospect had come into question. Haydn took them along nonetheless, likely with opportunities for performance as well as publication in mind.

As early as 24 February of that first winter season in London, an ensemble led by Salomon presented a Haydn quartet—presumably one from the new opus, as the program specifies that the work was played from manuscript. The occasion was a concert of the New Musical Fund at the Pantheon. This performance was soon followed by several others, each in connection with a series of concerts produced by Salomon that winter and spring at the Hanover Square Rooms. In all, three quartets were performed: one at the second concert, one at the sixth and eleventh, and another at the eighth and ninth; allegedly the two that were repeated were done so "by particular desire,"[2] although lack of time to rehearse additional quartets may possibly have been a factor. Each work was designated a "New Quartetto," and all were probably played from manuscripts. During the 1792 concert season, quartets by Haydn were again presented, once in Salomon's regular series and twice at benefit concerts, with Salomon's group performing on both occasions.[3] The works performed may well have been from Op. 64. The relevant programs make no such distinction as "New Quartetto" or "MS," but the quartets had been published in London by early 1792, and they would probably no longer have been regarded as new.

Because there may have been as many as nine public performances involving one or another of the new works, we may assume that those presented were well received, despite the fact that they attracted relatively little notice in the news-papers. A *Morning Chronicle* report of Salomon's second concert in the 1791 sea-son merely states that Haydn's "new Quartetto is exceedingly beautiful, and was well executed." The critic was obviously more deeply impressed by that evening's presentation of the composer's Symphony No. 92, declaring it "a sublime com-position" and describing its merits in some detail.[4]

Meanwhile, the early publication history of Op. 64 began to unfold. As with Op. 54/55, Haydn appears to have sold these quartets to Tost, whose initiatives were evidently responsible for their publication by Sieber in Paris and probably also for the edition by Leopold Kozeluch's Magazin de Musique in Vienna.[5] (Kozeluch's edition appeared as a set of six, Op. 65, first advertised on 20 April 1791, whereas Sieber's was issued in two parts as Op. 64/65, advertised incorrectly as Op. 63/64 on 9 June 1791.) A third important print was briefly alluded to in the previous chapter in connection with the razor episode. This was Bland's Lon-don edition, which was given the single opus number 65, although it was pub-lished in two parts just like Sieber's print. It was announced as early as 10 June 1791, and registered shortly afterward at Stationers' Hall (the first set on 17 June, the second on 4 July), but it probably did not appear until 1792 (it was advertised on 22 February). Recalling the inscription on Longman & Broderip's edition of Op. 54/55, Bland's title page includes the phrase: "Composed by Guiseppe [sic] Haydn, and Performd [sic] under His Direction, at Mr. Salomon's Concert, The Festino Rooms Hanover Square." The traditional opus number 64, originally as-signed to Sieber's first set of three, was not applied to the entire set until the edi-tion issued by Pleyel in 1799–1800.

Curiously, none of the early editions we have cited preserves Haydn's own numbering of the quartets. Kozeluch's, which later became standard, comes close, merely reversing the last two quartets with respect to Haydn's sequence; and even though the order in Sieber's edition differs from Kozeluch's, the text proves closely enough related to suggest that both must derive from the same source, one containing revisions that may have originated with Tost. Bland's appears to have been based directly on the autograph manuscripts that Haydn took to Lon-don, but the second book of his two-part edition shows influences also from Kozeluch's readings.[6]

As noted in the previous chapter, the title page of Kozeluch's edition bears a dedication to Tost ("Composés et dediés a Monsieur Jean Tost par Monsieur Joseph Haydn"), and it is presumably for this reason that the set has traditionally been linked with his name (i.e., as the so-called second set of "Tost" quartets, Op. 54/55 having been the first). Taken at face value, the tribute in the Kozeluch edition appears to ring true, but can we be sure it actually originated with the composer? Haydn was off in London at the time and appears to have had no direct involvement in the transaction. Suspicions are further aroused by the fact that the dedication was removed in a reprinting of 1793, when Haydn was back in Vienna.[7] In any case, it is no more likely that these quartets were matched to Tost's attributes as a performer than were those of the preceding group.

Despite Haydn's apparent eagerness to have the Op. 64 quartets formally presented in a London concert hall, we need not assume that he regarded this as an ideal environment for the music, whose temperament actually suggests a retreat from the extroverted manner of Op. 54/55. With less in the way of soloistic writing and a heightened concern for textural subtlety, the new works recommend themselves as much to the players' own enjoyment as to appreciation by an audience.

By concentrating on the interaction of ensemble members, the Op. 64 quartets resemble those of Op. 50, where themes and their development often engaged all parts. And yet the atmosphere seems generally less learned than in that earlier set, less bent on challenging the mettle of listeners and performers, and instead more given to a veneer of tunefulness and a penchant for whimsical encounters between comic and serious styles. In these respects, the search for connections to previous opus groups takes us back to Op. 33, where textural novelty and motivic development coexisted with humor and images of rural music-making, and where the composer seemed to be addressing amateurs and connoisseurs in equal measure.

But to acknowledge the new quartets' return to certain chamber-music ideals is not to deny significant correspondences with Op. 54/55. Aspects of continuity as well as divergence between the two adjacent sets can be seen, for example, in the latter's persisting tendency to take the first violin to the top of its range. Often a source of drama and penetrating brilliance in Op. 54/55, the device is here sometimes directed toward purely coloristic purposes, as in Op. 64/6/iii, where the first violin's high staccato descant—a veritable sonic halo to the second violin's rustic melody below—goes all the way up to e♭⁴. A comparably lightened touch marks the latter set's approach to chromaticism, whose expressive potential is now mixed on occasion with a measure of humor or irony. The jaunty refrain of Op. 64/6/iv, for example, begins with a carefree, rising line (mm. 1–4), only to be chastened by an opposing force in unison (mm. 5–8), the mock-serious intent amplified by the ominous gesture of a chromatic descent from B♭ to F.

Overview of the Opus

One basic change in opus character from that of Op. 54/55 is apparent in the new quartets' choices for home keys, now limited to a range of three flats to two sharps (see table 14.1). All but one, B minor, belong to an inner circle of most favored tonalities among the quartets; and in light of other connections with Op. 33, it seems significant that these are the only opus groups whose home keys match exactly: C, G, D, B minor, Bb, and Eb. Moreover, a striking similarity marks the opening gestures of the two works in B minor: both begin in a state of tonal ambivalence, initially suggesting the relative major and clarifying the tonal picture only with the arrival of fully scored dominant harmony before the end of the first phrase. The degree to which opposite-mode relationships expand the tonal horizons within individual quartets is different, however, from Op. 33. In the later B minor work, for example, not only the dance-movement trio but also the entire slow movement and the latter part of the finale are in the parallel major (five sharps); and the middle section of Op. 64/3/ii, cast in the parallel minor, extends the tonal spectrum on the flat side to Eb minor (six flats).

A point of correspondence with Op. 33 (and Op. 42 as well) involves the return to a cyclic design by which the minuet-trio complex comes second rather than third (in Nos. 1 and 4). Can any significance be attached to this revisiting of an earlier approach to movement sequence? Although there appears to be no obvious rationale for a return to the older custom, the mere fact of its revival here may point to larger issues of opus character and profile. To locate the minuet second is normally to insert a buffer between a quartet's two weightiest movements, with the result that attention may likely focus on each as an end in itself. By contrast, placing a meditative Adagio, say, directly on the heels of a robust opening Allegro, so that feelings aroused by the first movement's kinetic energy are channeled in an utterly different direction, suggests the kind of dramatized contrast commonly associated with the symphony. The dance that follows typically has an uplifting effect, given the natural physicality of its rhythm and metrical impulse, and in this respect it mediates between the slow movement's introspection and the customary effervescence of the finale. This type of musical narrative appears to have been more or less in force among the quartets of the preceding set, apart from the cyclic anomalies of Op. 54/2 and 55/2. In Op. 64, however, much as in Op. 33, concern for a large-scale profile of this kind seems less pronounced, even among the quartets that do have a slow movement in second place.

In several of the new works, chamber-style intimacy is inscribed in the opening movement's metrical framework and quality of surface activity. Op. 64/2/i stands out especially in this respect, with its intricately shaped opening idea—unaccompanied, tonally ambivalent, and packed with motivic potential—which immediately fosters an atmosphere of concentration. The movement as a whole features the kinds of decorative rhythmic detail and motivic work typical of the now old-fashioned moderato common time (i.e., the so-called compound $\frac{4}{4}$) prevalent among the first movements of Opp. 9 and 17, and encountered also in Opp. 20 and 33. The first movements of both Op. 64/2 and 4 are indeed notated

TABLE 14.1 Summary statistics for Op. 64

Op.No.	Hob. No.	Movement			
		i	ii	iii	iv
64/1	III:65	C ¢ Allegro moderato SF 174	C/Cm $\frac{3}{4}$ Allegretto ma non troppo M/T 44/38	F $\frac{2}{4}$ Allegretto scherzando Strophic var. 129(r)	C $\frac{6}{8}$ Presto SF 110
64/2	III: 68	Bm e Allegro spiritoso SF 108	B $\frac{3}{4}$ Adagio ma non troppo Strophic var. 94(r)	Bm/B $\frac{3}{4}$ Allegretto M/T 42/20	Bm-B $\frac{2}{4}$ Presto SF 201
64/3	III:67	B♭ $\frac{3}{4}$ Vivace assai SF 170	E♭ $\frac{2}{4}$ Adagio Ternary var. 92(r)	B♭ $\frac{3}{4}$ Allegretto M/T 58/42	B♭ $\frac{2}{4}$ Allegro con spirito SF 245
64/4	III:66	G e Allegro con brio SF 99	G $\frac{3}{4}$ Allegretto M/T 32/28	C $\frac{2}{4}$ Adagio. Cantabile e sostenuto Ternary var. 93(r)	G $\frac{6}{8}$ Presto SF 179
64/5	III:63	D ¢ Allegro moderato SF 179	A $\frac{3}{4}$ Adagio. Cantabile Ternary var. 84	D/Dm $\frac{3}{4}$ Allegretto M/T 42/24	D $\frac{2}{4}$ Vivace Ternary var. 128
64/6	III:64	E♭ ¢ Allegro SF 144	B♭ $\frac{3}{4}$ Andante Ternary 72(r)	E♭ $\frac{3}{4}$ Allegretto M/T/T* 36/24/24	E♭ $\frac{2}{4}$ Presto Rondo 192

* There are two trios, the second a variant of the first.

in common time, although with faster tempo markings than the once-customary moderato or allegro moderato. Three others (Nos. 1, 5, and 6) adopt the alla breve signature, and yet only one of those, No. 6, sports an unmodified allegro: Nos. 1 and 5 are both designated allegro moderato, comparable in this respect to the opening movement of Op. 33/3, the first instance of this particular metrical type among the quartets' opening movements.

Also different from the concert-style manner of Op. 54/55 is the first movement of Op. 64/3, in $\frac{3}{4}$ time, which in certain outer respects appears to be a counterpart to that of Op. 55/3: the two share the same key (B♭), tempo (vivace assai), and meter; but there is a world of difference between them. The earlier piece opens with a succession of expansive, legato phrases, mainly in half notes and quarters, adds passages in eighth notes to lend motion toward structural goals, and only sporadically makes any use of smaller note values. Op. 64/3/i, by contrast, displays small note values and dense motivic detail from the start, and later passages are further enlivened by undercurrents of sixteenth-note figuration.

The slow movements of Op. 64, for the first and only time among the opus groups, are all conceived as some species of variation form (the ternary design of Op. 64/6/ii is a near-exception, with relatively little embellishment in the return). This peculiarity of the opus—its unique emphasis on a form type specially suited for reflection and decoration—may be added to our portrayal of a renewed commitment to an authentic chamber style. At the same time, however, there are pointed connections to the slow movements of the previous set, especially that of Op. 54/3: the slow ternary movements of Op. 64/3, 4, 5, and 6 all recall that earlier movement's three-part design, and there are resemblances in style and technique as well. The Adagio of Op. 64/5 resembles the previous opus group's eloquent first violin solos; the middle section of Op. 64/6/ii bears explicit resemblance to that of Op. 54/3/ii in setting an impassioned soliloquy against a background of continuously throbbing chords; and the slow third movement of Op. 64/4 recalls a certain sonority from the major-mode segments of the "Razor" quartet's variations, namely, the idyllic legato melody for first violin, supported by a simple bass line and keyboard-like, arpeggiated accompaniment in the inner parts.

All but one of the six slow movements indulge in varied repeats, drawing attention to delicate balances of sameness and difference by rescoring or embellishing one or both parts of embedded binary segments within a strophic or ternary form. In a particularly far-reaching engagement with the technique, the second movement of Op. 64/2 treats both parts of a binary theme to varied repeats before proceeding with three variations, all unimpeded by either literal or altered repeats, in which elements of both the theme and its varied strains are elaborated and intensified.

The dance movements are seemingly consistent in tempo—all are designated allegretto ("ma non troppo" in the case of Op. 64/1/ii)—but are actually quite varied in temperament. Along with the streamlined, measure-accented impulse of the minuets in Op. 64/2 and 5, we find examples of countryside yodeling (Op. 64/4, minuet and trio), courtly manners (Op. 64/1, minuet and thematically related trio), and a revisiting, in the Op. 64/5 trio (mm. 43–46, 61–64), of the minor-key chromatic-scale themes found among trios of the earliest quartets. Most unusual of all, the minuet of Op. 64/3 unfolds as a pure exercise in dance-movement eccentricity, with its quizzical pauses, metrically dissonant horn-call figures, and incongruous phraseology.

Last movements in Op. 64 tend to resemble those of the previous opus group, at least in general terms. Fast-tempo sonata forms, variously in $\frac{2}{4}$ and $\frac{6}{8}$, are common to both, and the single rondo finale of the new set, Op. 64/6/iv, recalls that of Op. 54/1, with similar attention to elements of surprise and glittering ensemble work. The galvanizing effect of fugue, contrived to occupy the very core of the rondo finale in Op. 55/1, finds a worthy counterpart in the fugal middle section of a ternary form in Op. 64/5/iv.

Most of the Op. 64 finales call to mind the spirit of opera buffa with their spans of unstoppable rhythm, contentious dialogue, and stealthy entries or exits. They are also leavened by comical end games, not unlike those of the Op. 33 rondos. In Op. 64/6, for example, pauses and false starts near the end resemble those of Op. 33/4 as they conjure a mischievous force intent on sabotaging the conclusion. The comedy of unraveling closure begins as early as measure 146, five measures into what had begun as a normal recurrence of the refrain. Here the theme's progress degenerates into a sequence of motivic particles (mm. 146–48); then, as if trying to get back on track, or perhaps to shake loose from a cycle of hapless repetition, the ensemble unleashes a unison barrage of sixteenth notes— but then soon becomes sidetracked by an inflection to the lowered submediant (mm. 155–60). The struggle to recapture an elusive main thread resumes in measures 162–77; and in a new strategy that now materializes—an effort to gain a fresh foothold on the theme by casting certain of its ingredients in augmentation—we can hear an explicit resemblance to that earlier rondo (Op. 33/4/iv, mm. 200–205). This last endeavor evidently succeeds, and the way is clear for a final burst of energy that will restore the refrain's opening measures at full speed (mm. 183–86) before liquidating in a unison scale and a cadential flourish (mm. 189–92).

Aspects of Texture and Ensemble Play

Although the Op. 64 quartets share with those of Op. 33 a bent for motivic exchange and shared thematic responsibility, one aspect of this tendency more closely resembles instances of learned style in Opp. 42, 50, and 54/55: the occasional recourse to imitative polyphony, most prominently in the fugal middle section of Op. 64/5/iv, where the continuous elaboration of a subject systematically engages all members of the ensemble. Other, less strictly regulated patterns of imitation lend structural coherence and textural diversity as they point to an ideal of cooperative relationship among the performers. In the Op. 64/1 trio, for example, the viola (whose voice was conspicuously absent from the opening of the minuet) announces the theme, a minor-mode derivative of the minuet's rising arpeggio figure, and the second violin responds. The viola picks up the thread again (now down a third), but this time the first violin replies, and the full ensemble now proceeds toward a cadence in the relative major. After a patch of sequential development at the start of the second reprise, the first violin recalls the main theme in tonic and the viola answers (mm. 69–72), and it is only now, ten measures from the end of the trio, that the cello completes the picture with a thematic statement of its own.

Unusual sonorities, planted on several occasions at the start of a movement, awaken heightened attention to textural nuance and instability. In the opening measures of Op. 64/1, for example, Haydn pairs the first violin with the viola, withholding the second violin and limiting the cello to a few supporting chord roots. Too fragile and eccentric a premise to be sustained for long, the odd scoring raises issues—the exclusion of an ensemble member, unoccupied registral spaces, the inherent edginess of a barely harmonized texture—that will be addressed as the exposition unfolds, with corrective actions gaining structural and expressive weight accordingly: notably the robust, filled-out sonorities for important thematic statements and structural punctuations, and the reassuringly solid texture of the closing theme (mm. 55–60), in which the three lower parts lend harmonious support to the first violin's melody. Events in the recapitulation may be viewed in a similar light (the second violin is missing at the outset here as well), although the play of contrast between delicate and full-voiced sonority is subject to further development in this final section.

In a way that specially recalls Op. 33, there are choice examples of principal lines and accompaniments that shade imperceptibly into one another. The opening phrase-pair in the Op. 64/1 minuet (quoted in ex. 3.3) epitomizes this sleight of hand. More frequently encountered are Haydn's porous, fragmentary textures in which melody and accompaniment are clearly distinguished, one or the other being subject to constant change in the hands of dialoguing voices. The secondary theme of Op. 64/3/i (first heard in mm. 33–42, then revisited in the development section, mm. 87–96) exemplifies this technique by engaging the accompanying second violin and viola in a pattern of continuous alternation, and the first violin's lyrical sound-image is further complicated by the momentary rests distributed among different parts as the phrases unfold.

In a reversal of this relationship between dialoguing strands of accompaniment and an unbroken principal line, a playful three-way exchange in the Op. 64/6/i development section scatters a thematic figure among first violin, viola, and cello while anchoring the texture to a continuous accompaniment of oscillating eighth notes in the second violin (mm. 68–83). As each of the participating instruments takes up the four-note motto in turn, the unpredictability of the figure's migrations underscores the instability of ongoing modulation, and listeners will readily find themselves caught up in the game of trying to guess where the idea will appear next.

Lyricism and Popular Style

Woven into Op. 64's abundance of styles, textures, and ensemble colors are instances of straightforward melody and accompaniment whose rhythmic impulse and harmonic simplicity seem rooted in popular song and dance. The lilting cadence of the Op. 64/3/i secondary theme, although not its complicated accompaniment, exemplifies this tendency, as do the secondary or closing themes of several last movements, notably those of Op. 64/1 (mm. 31–38), 2 (mm. 47–52, 174–79), and 4 (mm. 39–46, 126–33). The charm of a bucolic scene, encountered almost as if by accident amid the bustle of a sonata form finale, is especially well drawn in the last of these cases. The movement had begun in a state of nervous energy, with repetitive melodic figures, tiratas, and stretches of repeated eighth-note pulsation in the bass. This restless motion had led to a mid-exposition caesura at measure 38, highlighted by a rising unison arpeggio on the dominant of the new key. The theme now heard stands out as a musical oasis, a momentary patch of singsong, first violin melody comprising a rhyming pair of legato phrases. The equanimity is relative, of course, and the fleeting impression of rustic simplicity is rendered fragile by counteracting elements: staccato arpeggiations in the background, the altered scoring of the accompaniment's second phrase, and a new surge of activity as the rate of harmonic change doubles in measures 46–47.

 Impressions of popular dance resound in the trios of Op. 64/2, 4, and 6, each of which invokes images of a fiddler and his band. That of Op. 64/6 seems a close relative to the Ländler-style trio in Op. 33/2, also in E♭, but without the earlier work's antic portamentos and glissandos; it compensates, however, with a coloristic thrust of its own, the very high first violin part in the second trio—actually a variant of the first, marked "per la seconda volta, caso mai se piacesse a replicarlo" in Haydn's manuscript. (Early editions differ in the interpretation of this circumstance, variously leaving out the original trio and giving only the one with the high descant, having the minuet proper recur twice, once after each version of the trio, or else regarding each of the two parts of the alternate version as a varied reprise.)[8] In the trio of Op. 64/4, whose broken-chord theme was foreshadowed by the minuet proper, allusions to folk style include the rolling eighth-note motion of the principal line, the lower instruments' pizzicato, and the elemental simplicity of the harmony. But along with these emblems of homespun music-making comes the contrivance of a phrase rhythm in five-measure units (see ex. 14.1). The second reprise settles temporarily into a more regular phrasing (essentially 2 + 2 + 4), before closing with a replica of the opening 5 + 5 configuration and thus restoring the temporal artifice with which the trio had begun.[9]

EXAMPLE 14.1 Op. 64/4/ii, mm. 33–42

No account of the melodious, idyllic side of Op. 64 can fail to mention the opening movement of the group's best-known quartet, the "Lark." The theme in question bespeaks a more urbane manner than that of the trios' country dance tunes, but it compares with them—even outdistances them—as a model of undiluted melodic expression. Serenely prepared at the outset by an eight-measure vamp, the theme presents a succession of three lyrical phrases (ex. 14.2). If the repeats are taken, it will be heard a total of eight times, for Haydn showcases the melody with a full statement in the development (in the subdominant) and two recurrences in the latter part of the movement (extended by one measure in its last statement), in addition to placing it near the head of the exposition. Here for once is a principal first-movement theme fashioned to exist as a melody in its own right and not a wellspring for development, and as such it belies Haydn's customary practices. Yet the theme proves well suited to the medium's capacity for clear, vocally inspired projection, and its lyricism resonates with moments of pastoral or rustic character heard elsewhere in the opus, especially, as noted earlier, among the finales and dance-movement trios.

Peculiarities of Surface Rhythm and Phrasing

Complementing the patches of rustic simplicity and predictability are cases of novelty and surprise involving either sudden change in surface activity or the interruption of a regular, established phrase rhythm. Whether playing for humor

EXAMPLE 14.2 Op. 64/5/i, mm. 8–20 (violin 1 only)

or intrigue, such temporal oddities generally explain themselves as purposeful ingredients of a larger design, however disruptive locally.

In the first movement of Op. 64/6, a barrage of triplet eighth notes, first unleashed in measures 20–23, then resumed in measure 36, promises to drive the latter part of the exposition toward a close in the dominant. But several measures before the double bar, Haydn brakes the momentum, redirecting attention from surface energy to the pungent accent of an exposed appoggiatura that extends for more than two beats before resolving in a stepwise descent to the end of the measure (see ex. 14.3). The resulting four-note figure (Bb–A–G–F) then begins to repeat, first literally (m. 42), then in diminution, as it progresses through two stages of acceleration: all eighths in measure 43, and then a frenzy of sixteenths in measure 44. As this fresh wave of activity arises, it becomes apparent that the very agent of thwarted progress—the long appoggiatura and subsequent descent—has turned out to be the motivating element for a rush to the exposition's final goal. The overwrought quality of the passage may be heard as a kind of parody, highlighting the phenomenon of rhythmic acceleration that we normally experience over a much longer span, and compressing it into a last-minute scramble near the end of the section. (A parallel series of events, transposed down a fifth, ends the recapitulation.)

When temporal contrast coincides with tonal inflection, the withdrawal of surface activity may suggest a skimming of the music's froth to reveal a hidden stratum of harmonic color and suspense. The finale of Op. 64/3 highlights this phenomenon with its startling change of rhythm and harmony at three crucial points in the course of the movement. The first occurs in the midst of the exposition, where motion into the dominant, propelled by a flow of sixteenth notes begun in measure 26, seems nearly accomplished by measure 35. But the point of dominant arrival yields no caesura and no easing of harmonic tension: instead, it marks the start of a long anacrusis, whose intensity increases by degree as the volume drops to piano (upbeat to m. 42), then pianissimo (upbeat to m. 45). Finally, the music seems almost to freeze as the cello rises from G to Ab, the viola descends simultaneously from E to Eb, and all four parts proceed in a tonally inflected stream of long note values. The resumption of dominant seventh har-

EXAMPLE 14.3 Op. 64/6/i, mm. 41–45 (violin 1 only)

mony and renewed surface energy at measure 53 confirms the significance of the passage as a rhetorical parenthesis or aside—a mysterious, fleeting digression from the main line of thought. Too important an event to pass without further consequences, the slow-motion episode and its suspenseful preparation recur in the midst of the development (mm. 91–110) and once again in the recapitulation (mm. 162–81) to complete the pattern of tonal enrichment and rhythmic stasis as a centerpiece to each of the form's principal sections.[10]

Moments of pure silence—one step beyond Haydn's temporary cessations of pulse and surface activity—stand out on occasion in these works, sometimes in ways that remind us specifically of Op. 33, although there is nothing so outrageous as the exaggerated pauses that mark the end of Op. 33/2/iv. A measure or so of rest in all parts, cunningly placed to take listeners by surprise, may work to command attention, stir us from any complacency that a predictable flow of events may have induced, and thus make way for the change to another phase of action. Such a scheme marks the outset of the development section in Op. 64/1/iv, where an echo of the exposition's closing figure suggests an impasse. More than a measure's worth of silence magnifies the dilemma but also gives the ensemble a chance to regroup and develop a new line of argument (a series of imitative entries) from a fresh tonal perspective (the lowered submediant). A more prolonged span of silence-driven suspense, fraught with comical indecision, marks the beginning of the development section in Op. 64/4/iv (m. 67): here a secretive, tonic-minor recall of the opening measures sets off a series of false starts as the ensemble vacillates between rise and fall, loud and soft, harmony and unison, taking up and discarding several keys before eventually getting back on track (m. 83) after a total of eight interrupting pauses within the opening sixteen measures of the section.

Related in principle to the surface interruptions and changes of pace are Haydn's departures from a previously established pattern of phrase lengths. Scarcely unique to Op. 64, the technique does stand out here as a means of unsettling the discourse for structural or expressive purposes. The themes in three of the variation movements, for example, are inflected by the substitution of a five-measure phrase for a normally expected continuation in two- and four-measure units: Op. 64/1/iii, beginning of the second reprise (mm. 9–13); Op. 64/2/ii, also the beginning of the second part (mm. 17–21); and Op. 64/4/iii, an extended consequent phrase within the first reprise (mm. 5–9). Especially memorable is the extended reach from four measures to five in the second of these cases, that of

Op. 64/2/ii. Conspicuously placed as an aberration in the midst of an otherwise symmetrical design (‖ 4 + 4 : ‖ : 5 + 4 : ‖), the phrase encompasses several expressive gestures—a prolonged dominant pedal point, a descent by half steps in the melody, a chromatically inflected move to a half cadence—that contribute to a subtly nuanced climax in the design of the theme and a corresponding point of emphasis in each of its varied recurrences.

When planted at the beginning, an oddly formed, five-measure phrase may have particularly disruptive consequences—unless its destabilizing force is immediately constrained by a complementary phrase of the same length, as in the Op. 64/4 trio quoted in example 14.1. In the opening of the Op. 64/2 minuet (shown in ex. 14.4a), the out-of-countenance element is easy to identify: the figure that comprises measure 3, which stubbornly repeats measure 2, has the result of displacing the end of the phrase to measure 5. The impulse signified by this reiterating one-measure unit, embedded in the middle of the initial phrase, will repeatedly threaten to spin out of control as the dance continues. The result is a "veritable orgy"[11] of expanded phrase lengths, affecting the rest of the first reprise—whose consequent phrase stretches for nine measures to the double bar—and the second reprise in its entirety, whose return begins by charging through a seven-measure variant of the opening phrase (quoted in ex. 14.4b).

Finally, a well-turned pattern of phrase contraction merits notice. The last movement of Op. 64/1 begins with a normally balanced pair of four-measure phrases, and the stability of this structure is reaffirmed when a corresponding phrase-pair returns to start the recapitulation, the consequent phrase now enhanced by sixteenth-note diminutions. But in a summarizing variant near the end of the movement (mm. 99–104), two statements of a three-measure idea (a shrunken version of the original mm. 5–8) initiate a progressive dismantling of the theme, in which a pair of two-measure units (mm. 105–8, recalling mm. 1–2) dwindles further to a pair of one-measure pianissimo echoes (mm. 109–10), thereby capping the illusion of the movement's turning in on itself, evaporating, or disappearing into the distance.

Structural Idiosyncrasies

Whereas the Op. 64 quartets' interior movements involve few surprises with regard to overall structure, most of the outer sonata form movements display unusual license and unpredictability of relationship between principal sections. One type of aberration results from the extra reassertion of primary theme material—climactic, valedictory, or simply redundant—in the latter part of the form, whereas an opposite anomaly involves the suppression of a portion of secondary or closing material from the recapitulation. The latter situation is noteworthy in light of the customary practice of bringing back important secondary-key material in tonic, presumably in the interest of restoring a movement's tonal equilibrium.

EXAMPLE 14.4 Op. 64/2/iii (violin 1 only)

(a) mm. 1–5

(b) mm. 27–33

Digressions from this convention arise most conspicuously in two first movements (Nos. 2 and 3) and two finales (Nos. 1 and 2). No single explanation covers all cases, yet each may be seen as part of the set's tendency to sustain unpredictable, developmental action deep into the latter part of a sonata form movement. Table 14.2, selective and representative rather than fully comprehensive, outlines major instances of thematic suppression, displacement, and redundancy that characterize this opus. Sonata form peculiarities comparable to some of those listed may be found elsewhere in the repertory, but their concentration in Op. 64 is unique.

The additional recurrences of primary theme material vary in nature and complexity, perhaps the simplest being the wittily transformed recall of an opening gesture near the end of the Op. 64/4 finale. Starting at measure 170, the first violin retrieves the movement's opening melody an octave higher than at the outset, as if poised for a climactic ascent. It then breaks loose in a shimmering arpeggiation that soars to the quartet's highest note, d^4 (mm. 174–75), before falling to the low G string to complete the thematic reference. In so doing, it encompasses nearly the entirety of the instrument's registral space within these culminating events.

Most outstanding of all such recurrences is that of the "Lark," whose first movement embraces a full-blown, second return to the main theme within an expanded recapitulation. How can this idiosyncrasy be explained? The movement's main impression—the heart of its unique personality—resides in its image of pure, lyrical serenity. Pitched high above the beat-marking staccato of the lower instruments, the opening melody stands almost completely aloof from other, relatively unsettled phases of the exposition. Its recurrence just after the double bar helps establish this point in the form as a structural landmark while furnishing a springboard for the developmental activity to follow. Development proves sufficiently intense and extended for the well-prepared return at measure 105 to sound convincing as the point of recapitulation; and the fact that subsequent

TABLE 14.2 Digression from customary recapitulation procedures in Op. 64, including instances of supplementary recurrence of primary theme material or the omission of secondary or closing material

---

Op. 64/1/i

P material, embedded within an extended K, elaborated polyphonically in the recapitulation, mm. 152–65.
S material of mm. 26–54 substantially omitted from the recapitulation.

Op. 64/1/iv

S/K material of mm. 31–38 omitted from the recapitulation; replaced by closing material, mm. 99–108, derived from P.

Op. 64/2/i

Material derived from P (partially recalling mm. 9–10) interpolated and elaborated within the recapitulation's reconfigured S area, mm. 92–97.
S material of mm. 20–25 partially supplanted by new and P-related material in the recapitulation, mm. 79–191. A portion of S material from mm. 26–33 is excised, but other elements are recalled, notably the leaping half-note figures of mm. 28–29; in addition, mm. 98–101 elaborate the harmony of mm. 32–33.

Op. 64/2/iv

P material (transformed from minor to major, mm. 158–73) largely supplants S in the recapitulation.
S mm. 21–46, substantially omitted from the recapitulation.

Op. 64/3/i

S material of mm. 33–42, recalled in the development section, mm. 87–96, omitted from the recapitulation.

Op. 64/3/iv

P recalled literally following K in the recapitulation (mm. 226–35); P derivatives conclude the movement (mm. 236–45).

Op. 64/3/i

Opening of P recalled in mm. 85–86.
1S (mm. 16–22), derived from P, omitted from the recapitulation; 2S (mm. 23–32) substantially omitted in the recapitulation, though portions are recalled and elaborated.

Op. 64/4/iv

P material recalled and elaborated as an interpolation within K (mm. 148–56), and then as a sequel to K (mm. 170–77).

Op. 64/5/i

P theme recapitulated twice (mm. 105–16, 142–54).

Op. 64/6/i

P-derived material (with elements of S) interrupts K in the recapitulation (mm. 123–34).
Opening gesture of S (mm. 25–26), derived from P, absorbed in the recapitulation by the canonic elaboration of P begun in m. 102 (mm. 108–12 correspond to mm. 26–30).

elaborations stay squarely in tonic confirms that interpretation. Tonally, this is no premature return or false start, destined to be interrupted by a resumption of modulatory action, but rather the return proper, dedicated to reinstating the home key.[12] Yet a distinct edginess emerges as the secondary and closing themes fail to recur intact in the measures that follow (117–41). From this perspective, the return to the "Lark" melody once again at measure 142 may be heard as a second try, a renewed attempt to impose order and guide the movement to a satisfying conclusion through the return of exposition material.

Ultimately, the theme's double return, with open-ended ensemble action in between, may simply be a matter of arbitrary thematic privilege, the melody reasserting its status as the movement's predominant feature. The design that results, however strange when viewed against the larger backdrop of Haydn's sonata form customs, proves less puzzling in the context of this opus group, with its recurrent topic of deviation from stylistic norms for recapitulation.

As for the inclination to suppress altogether the recall of secondary or closing material, thus bypassing the practice of tonal restoration, each of these cases proves to be a rule unto itself, although most involve some large-scale, end-weighted strategy whose implementation overrides the recognized imperative of thematic return in tonic. The most provocative of all such aberrant designs, that of Op. 64/3/i, was discussed in chapter 4. The finale of Op. 64/1, relatively uncomplicated by comparison, also exemplifies the idea of a momentum-driven agenda that avoids any direct parallel with the exposition as it draws to a close. The movement opens on a note of suppressed intensity, with pairs of urgently repeated staccato eighth notes to head the main theme, then releases energy in streams of sixteenth notes and forays into a higher register by which the dominant key is attained. Late in the exposition and well after the new key has been established, a fresh idea is heard (m. 31): a relatively relaxed theme whose tunefulness stands opposed to the preceding commotion. Such a melodically distinctive idea, well grounded in the dominant key, would seem to require a corresponding statement in tonic prior to the end of the recapitulation. But Haydn evidently has in mind a dynamic trajectory whose impetus will cause surface motion to persist without major interruption—and without any reference to the contrasting theme—as the latter part of the movement runs its course.

Questions of Cyclic Integration

The general emphasis on surface detail in Op. 64 appears to go hand in hand with a retreat from the large-scale sweep of cyclic integration as witnessed on occasion among previous opus groups. Subtle but intriguing signs of intermovement cohesion may nevertheless be cited as evidence of a persisting concern for this aspect of quartet design. Op. 64/2, for example, like Op. 54/2 and 55/2, is a single-tonic work; and just as in the "Razor," a scheme of modal contrasts and juxtapositions ends with the triumph of major over minor. Woven into the later phases of this process (i.e., the third and fourth movements) is a pattern that interlaces points of modal change with moments of thematic resemblance: the minuet's initial gesture (quoted as ex. 14.5a)—a dominant upbeat, ascent from tonic to third scale degree, then a descending step—is replicated in major at the start of the trio (ex. 14.5b); and another version of that same gesture, restored to minor, launches the finale, now stretched and reshaped to encompass a four-measure phrase (ex. 14.5c).

Having reached across the boundary between the last two movements, the scheme of modal alternation and thematic resemblance culminates in the transformation of the finale's primary theme idea from minor to major at measure 158 (ex. 14.5d). Integration is further enhanced by the promotion of the dance movement's dominant upbeat to a salient thematic ingredient in the finale, where it evolves into a pair of eighth notes. This version of the idea leaves its imprint on virtually every thematic event that follows, and at two critical points in the form—the transitional passage at the end of the exposition (mm. 60–64, quoted in ex. 14.5e) and the similarly designed anacrusis to the point of change from minor to major (mm. 154–57)—the original upbeat impetus is elaborated with particular intensity as a repetitive dialogue between the first violin and the three lower parts. Given these developments, the retrieval of the figure once again at the close (quoted in ex. 14.5f) may be heard as an ironic transformation, the anacrusis now reconfigured as a kind of envoi, but also as the fulfillment of a certain long-range melodic implication: each of the rising gestures cited in example 14.5a–d had begun to traverse the tonic octave, reaching the third degree by the end of the first measure, then rising to the fifth degree at some point within the first phrase (m. 4 of the minuet, m. 3 of the trio, m. 2 of the finale). But we do not experience the satisfaction of a complete, octave-spanning arpeggiation (1–3–5–8) until the end of the last movement (mm. 193–95, reiterated an octave higher in mm. 195–99).[13]

Other kinds of cyclic coherence may be sensed in Op. 64/5, mainly through similarities of structure and procedure among the second, third, and fourth movements: each unfolds as a ternary form whose central, minor-mode portion derives at least in part from its opening section. The middle part of the Adagio cantabile develops that movement's opening melodic figure; the third-movement trio begins by echoing the lower instruments' scalar gesture from the end of the minuet (that gesture itself imitates a recurrent rising line first articulated in mm. 3–4); and the initial counterpoint to the finale's D minor fugue subject grows directly out of the opening section's perpetual-motion theme.

An aspect of integration that embraces this quartet in its entirety arises from an impression of progressive change in texture, rhythmic activity, and melodic process from one movement to the next. The work begins soloistically, at a mod-

EXAMPLE 14.5 Op. 64/2 (violin 1 only in a–d)

(a) iii, mm. 1–2

(b) iii, mm. 43–44

(c) iv, mm. 1–4

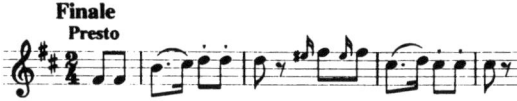

(d) iv, mm. 158–61

(e) iv, mm. 60–64

(f) iv, mm. 193–201

erate pace, with broad expanses of thematic statement and recurrence whose accompaniments engage rhythmic values no smaller than the quarter note, and it ends with an intensely developmental, whirlwind Vivace that sustains an unstoppable patter of sixteenth notes virtually throughout. Bridging the distance between these disparate musical realms, the slow movement enlivens the rhythmic surface and engages in motivic development as well as embellishment. The dance movement further intensifies the motivic impetus, trades the previous movements' soloistic textures for a more balanced ensemble (thereby helping prepare for the finale's four-voice polyphony), and presents a trio whose flowing surface rhythm anticipates the finale's headlong flight.

∾

How can we best take the measure of this opus as a stage in Haydn's encounter with the genre? The set as a whole—unsurpassed by Haydn, as Rosen proposes, in its "mature power and variety"[14]—is superbly original in many respects. Yet its originality resides more in fresh approaches to enduring customs than in any tendency to branch out in new directions; and in this view, Op. 64 clearly resists familiar models of evolution or linear progress. Apart from the insistent challenge to certain thematic conventions of sonata form, there are few radical innovations or signs of stylistic advancement. None of these works are longer, technically more difficult, or richer harmonically than their predecessors within the repertory, at least not in any particularly striking way. Instead, perhaps to a greater extent than in any previous opus, we find Haydn looking over his shoulder, taking the opportunity to revisit ideas previously explored.

Op. 64 shies away from both the drama and brilliance of Op. 54/55 and the more learned pretensions of Op. 50. The formalities of strict style are only moderately emphasized, apart from the polyphonic adventure of the Op. 64/5 finale; and elements of theatrical surprise, virtuosic display, and emotional intensity are generally downplayed in favor of an idiomatic chamber style, characterized by changeable textures and nuanced relationships among parts. Like Op. 33, these works seem ideally suited to private use as vehicles for musical discourse among performers for their own edification and enjoyment. And yet they have sufficient eloquence, expressive depth, and melodic attractiveness to gratify the composer's ever-growing audience of admiring listeners.

However satisfying, the approach that Op. 64 represents is one that Haydn chose not to sustain in the quartets that followed. The accent on popular appeal persists in the next series, Op. 71/74, but the ideal of intimate conversation will be compromised as Haydn embarks once again on a different path, this time toward a musical style more attuned to the theater or concert stage than to the drawing room.

15

Op. 71/74 ([?1792–] 1793)

To draw connections between the character of the Op. 71/74 quartets and the circumstances under which they were written is a temptation hard to resist. Conceived in the wake of the monumental first series of symphonies for London, Nos. 93–98, these works are marked by brilliance, clarity, and a specific concert-related trademark: the introductory, "noise-killing" events[1] with which each begins. Points of resemblance between the quartets and the symphonies that preceded them may be viewed from two vantage points, neither necessarily excluding the other. On the one hand, we can picture Haydn being inspired by his London experience to try to capture the drama of the public arena, thereby inviting performers and listeners to experience the paradox of using a private medium to invoke sound-images of the concert hall. On the other hand, the public inclinations of these works may be viewed as a practical change of course with respect to the more intimate manner of Op. 64: whether suited to concert performance or not, quartets from the preceding set had been presented that way during Haydn's first London season. A return engagement afforded another opportunity to display such works before London audiences, but this time they would be explicitly designed with a public venue in mind.[2]

That Haydn himself connected Op. 71/74 with London seems apparent from the fact that the works are actually listed (as "6 Quartettes") in his catalogue of compositions written during the course of his first visit there.[3] And yet it is unlikely that any were actually written before his return to Vienna in 1792. Autograph manuscripts for all six survive, and all are dated: four of them specify the year 1793 unambiguously, but the case is not so clear with Op. 71/1 and 2, because Haydn scratched out the original last digit of their dates, presumably a "2," and replaced it with a "3." But even if those two were written as early as the previous year, the fact that none of the six is notated on English paper weighs against the possibility that any were undertaken while the composer was still in England.[4]

Haydn began his second journey to the British capital in February 1794, and it was not long after his arrival that quartets from Op. 71/74 were being played in Salomon's concert series.[5] (The concerts were held in the Hanover Square Rooms, allegedly designed to accommodate an audience of eight hundred, although five hundred apparently was the norm.)[6] As documented by contemporary newspaper notices, Salomon's second, fifth, seventh, and eighth concerts all included new quartets. However, as with Op. 64 in Salomon's 1791 season, several of these performances were repeats: the fifth concert repeated the second concert's quartet, whereas the eighth repeated that of the seventh. (For the 1795 season, there appear to be no further references to Haydn quartet performances. Salomon suspended his concerts, and the composer joined forces with the Opera Concert, which favored vocal and orchestral music.) The quartets presented in the 1794 season may have made a more vivid impact than their Op. 64 predecessors, or perhaps audiences and commentators had become more accustomed than before to the inclusion of such works on Salomon's programs. In any event, the newspaper reports are at least somewhat more detailed than those for the earlier season's performances, citing matters of technical difficulty as well as artistic merit and bestowing praise on Salomon and the other performers in addition to the composer.[7]

Surviving accounts suggest that the new public-performance endeavor was successful, limited as it was with respect to the actual number of concerts and works performed. But once again it is instructive to compare critical assessments of Haydn's quartets with reports of symphony performances. Audiences and critics may have been impressed by a quartet's "variety, gaiety, and the fascination of its melody and harmony," but a symphony seemed capable of inspiring near-ecstasy, with "absolute shouts of applause," and cries of "Encore, encore! encore!" resounding throughout the hall.[8]

Notwithstanding the apparent centrality of the Hanover Square enterprise, there is no reason to assume that Haydn intended the Op. 71/74 quartets solely for concert use. In fact, license to enjoy them in the traditional manner of chamber music is virtually inscribed on the title page of the earliest editions, which bear the name of the dedicatee, Count Apponyi, a leading connoisseur of the day. The count allegedly paid Haydn one hundred ducats for the privilege of having the quartets to himself for a year prior to their general availability through publication,[9] and it was not until sometime in 1795 that prints of the first three of these works were undertaken (and only in 1796 did the latter three finally appear). The London firm of Corri, Dussek & Co. came first, publishing an edition of the first three and assigning them the opus number 72.[10] Given that Haydn had close personal ties with Dussek,[11] this print was presumably based on authentic material (the evidence suggests copies, very likely the parts used in performance, rather than the autographs). The edition was advertised on 14 October as "new music published this day," along with Dussek's arrangement of all three works for keyboard trio.[12] The print may have appeared, however, as early as April or May: in a letter of 6 October 1795 from the music amateur and middle-man Gaetano Bartolozzi (1757–1821) to Artaria, the writer expresses surprise that the quartets had not yet appeared in Vienna, indicating that they had been published in London more than five months before. In the same letter, Bartolozzi informs Artaria that he is sending a package to Artaria's agents in Hamburg that includes prints of the quartets and one of Dussek's arrangements.[13] Artaria did proceed to publish the three quartets, evidently drawing on the Corri, Dussek edition as a basis, although there are revisions and other differences. The publication was announced, with the opus number 73, on 21 October.[14]

The next year, both Corri, Dussek and Artaria followed through with publications of the remaining three quartets. These were advertised in February and April, respectively, both bearing the opus number 74. On 1 March 1796, Bartolozzi sent a copy of the new Corri, Dussek print to Artaria, as he had with the previous set the year before. This time, Artaria's text proved to be independent of the British print that had preceded it. Although both firms' editions appear to have been based on authentic copies, neither seems to have been derived from the autographs.[15]

The sequence of the works within both these editions is the same, and it corresponds to the traditional order; but Haydn's own intentions in this regard are not known: the autograph manuscripts, unlike those of Op. 64, are not numbered. As for the traditional opus numbers, we have seen that the number 74 had become attached to the quartets of the second set in prints issued by Corri, Dussek and Artaria; but it was Pleyel, in editions of both sets that preceded the 1801 *Collection complette*, who coined the designation Op. 71/74.[16]

Overview of the Opus

A notable resemblance between this group and Op. 64, and therefore Op. 33 as well, is the relatively narrow spectrum of principal home keys (see table 15.1). As in both those previous sets, and the later Op. 76 also, the range extends merely from three flats to two sharps. For no obvious reason, home keys with flats are specially favored (here there are four; all other sets from Op. 9 through Op. 76 include either two or three); also curious is the inclination to cast slow movements in the home key's dominant—less common on the whole (Haydn chose the subdominant more frequently) but found on four occasions here. This may simply be understood as a counterweight to the flat-side bias with respect to home keys, but another rationale suggests itself: to the extent that a dominant relationship denotes tension and forward-directed motion, as opposed to the subdominant's inherent relaxation,[17] then choosing the dominant for a quartet designed with concert performance in mind can be read as an antidote to the reduced

TABLE 15.1 Summary statistics for Op. 71/74

Op.No.	Hob.No.	Movement i	ii	iii	iv
71/1	III:69	**B♭** c Allegro SF 155	**F** $\frac{6}{8}$ Adagio Ternary 57	**B♭** $\frac{3}{4}$ Allegretto M/T 40/30	**B♭** $\frac{2}{4}$ Vivace SF 235
71/2	III:70	**D** e Adagio–Allegro SF 125	**A** $\frac{3}{4}$ Adagio. Cantabile SF (irreg.) 77	**D** $\frac{3}{4}$ Allegro M/T 28/20	**D** $\frac{6}{8}$ Allegretto–Allegro Rondo-var. hybrid 117
71/3	III:71	**E♭** $\frac{2}{4}$ Vivace SF 315	**B♭** $\frac{2}{4}$ Andante con moto Alternating var. 136	**E♭** $\frac{3}{4}$ M/T 47/36	**E♭** $\frac{6}{8}$ Vivace Rondo (irreg.) 142
74/1	III:72	**C** e Allegro SF 155	**G** $\frac{3}{8}$ Andantino (grazioso) SF 174	**C/A** $\frac{3}{4}$ Allegro M/T 60/52	**C** $\frac{2}{4}$ Vivace SF 285
74/2	III:73	**F** ¢ Allegro spiritoso SF 260	**B♭** $\frac{2}{4}$ Andante grazioso Strophic var. 115(r)	**F/D♭** $\frac{3}{4}$ M/T 41/37	**F** $\frac{2}{4}$ Presto Sonata-rondo 289
74/3	III:74	**Gm-G** $\frac{3}{4}$ Allegro SF 197	**E** ¢ Largo assai Ternary var. 64	**G/Gm** $\frac{3}{4}$ Allegretto M/T 34/40	**Gm-G** e Allegro con brio SF 146

level of energy that naturally accompanies a second movement's slow tempo and subdued temperament.

The dominant-key second movements extend the tonal range just one step to the sharp side (i.e., to A, the key of Op. 71/2/ii), but the compass is further widened by a practice new to this set, the digression to remote, third-related keys for several interior portions of the cycle: in addition to the distant E major for the slow movement of Op. 74/3, the dance movement of Op. 74/1 (in C) has a trio in A, while that of Op. 74/2 (in F) has a trio in Db. (Additionally, the parallel minor of Bb major is recognized with temporary changes of key signature in the course of both Op. 71/3/ii and 74/2/ii.)

The Op. 71/74 quartets' readiness to assume a public facade and play to an audience is signaled at the outset by their galvanizing initial gestures. Collectively the most striking novelty of the set, these admonishments to settle down and pay attention can be heard either as a practical response to the challenge of performing chamber music in a concert hall, or else as a stroke of ironic commentary on a real or imagined concert environment, with its singular encounter between chamber performers on display and a large, relatively anonymous audience. Viewed either way, they act to arouse curiosity, generate implications to be fulfilled, and thereby elevate the importance of the music that follows. (What follows in most instances is a movement built for speed and brilliance, with a greater emphasis than in any previous opus group on a particular kind of modern, first-movement common time, as seen in Opp. 50/6, 54/1, and 64/4, in which an accent on velocity and rhythmic diversity involves generous quantities of sixteenth-note figuration.)

The most elaborate, expressively charged of the opening moves is that of Op. 71/2, whose gravity and portent suggest a diminutive, mock-symphonic introduction. The multiple-stopped tonic and dominant chords of measures 1 and 2 stake out a tonal domain; a semblance of four-part polyphony, intoned in a stately adagio tempo, establishes performers' individual presence; and the switch to a fast tempo and loud dynamics on the upbeat to measure 5 registers as a stirring moment of release as the instruments enter the fray with overlapping statements of their plunging octave exclamation. In addition to acting as a foil for the Allegro, the slow introduction serves an organic purpose by anticipating key elements of the first movement's primary theme, thus forging a link to the start of the movement proper and ennobling that theme as a vehicle of motivic transformation. The connections are subtle but telling. The downward octave leaps in measures 1 and 2 (bracketed above the staff in ex. 15.1a) anticipate the primary theme's initial melodic action, where the lower note sounds on the beat. The cello's opening descent through a fourth to a sustained, accented leading tone foreshadows a similar gesture in the first violin, measure 6 (bracketed in ex. 15.1b). Finally, the cello's move to a root-position dominant in measure 8 may be heard as a consequence of both the initial bass-line descent and the cello's succession

EXAMPLE 15.1 Op. 71/2/i

(a) mm. 1–2

of pitches in measure 2, G–F♯–E–D–A, now shifted half a beat to occupy a stronger metrical position (ex. 15.1c).

In starkest contrast to the Op. 71/2 introduction, the first movement of Op. 71/3 is prefaced by a single tonic chord. The startling compression of this event has been compared with the matched pair of chords that opens Beethoven's Third Symphony, likewise in E♭.[18] Notated to occupy one isolated beat, this musical lightning bolt clears the air for the exposition's delicate opening phrase, and it serves as a validating precedent for subsequent resonant chords, notably in measures 42–43, to mark an important caesura, and again at the very end of the movement. But the loud opening stroke also may be interpreted tongue in cheek: the work that begins with this awesome sonority turns out to be the least pompous, most nearly chamber-like of the group; and one of its choicest moments arises as a belated reference to the initial impact—the shockingly outsized chords attached to the end of the second movement (not unrelated in principle to the famous hammerstroke of Symphony No. 94, from the first set of London symphonies). Struck forte with multiple stops in the upper parts, the chords are bound to arouse listeners with a start as they annihilate the reverie of an otherwise gentle conclusion.

Op. 74/1 expands the introductory gesture from a single chord to two—a loudly proclaimed dominant seventh and its resolution, likewise separated from the Allegro proper by a general pause. The top part, moving from a sustained leading tone to tonic, anticipates the prominent rising half steps of the primary theme; and as the movement progresses, several other measure-long swaths of tension-laden, dominant harmony—always preceding a structural landmark, as in measures 17, 51, and 148—stand as reminders of the opening call.

Still more expansive, and also more closely integrated with the main body of the movement, is the brusque harmonic succession I–ii$^6_5$–I$^6_4$–V^7–I declaimed at the start of Op. 71/1. It invites us to savor the irony of a standard closing formula cast in the role of an introduction, and it anticipates similar progressions that do in fact serve as structural punctuations. In addition, there are passages that echo its salient features—strongly directed harmonic progression, march-like staccato, and downward melodic motion from dominant to tonic—as if bending to the force of this original proposition. The primary theme, for example, incorporates both the initial descent from F to B♭ and (in the inner-voice accompaniment) the opening measure's detached articulation. A varied replica of the entire five-chord gesture, transposed to the dominant and simplified to the progression I–V^7–I–V^7–I (mm. 68–69), serves not only to punctuate the close of the exposition but also to mimic the opening measures' role by introducing the repeat (and the development section, the second time around, as the latter likewise begins with a reference to primary theme material).

Finally to be considered are the opening calls in Op. 74/2 and 3, both of which bear directly on thematic action in the first movement proper. At the head of Op. 74/2, a robust, fanfare-style unison furnishes a model for the exposition's primary and (closely related) secondary themes. The comparable-size curtain-raising gesture in Op. 74/3 likewise acts as a thematic wellspring. Separated from the subsequent action by a long general pause (mm. 9–10), it cannot be mistaken for the primary theme per se, and it does not come back in the recapitulation. Yet Haydn does affirm its structural importance by including it within the repeat, and its key ingredients—the rhythmically homogeneous unison, the leap upward from first beat to second, and the repeated-note figures—are all variously absorbed within the material that follows. Furthermore, the original melodic motive in its entirety is treated to more than a dozen measures of elaboration (mm. 83–95) in the course of the development section.

True to the prevailing theme of public style and the attendant imperatives of clarity and (apparent) narrative simplicity, the first movements tend to dwell on a distinctive primary theme and its derivatives. Nearly all sprout secondary ideas drawn from opening thematic material, and principal milestones are typically emphasized by suspended surface action, decisive cadential formulas, or other emphasized punctuations and signs of arrival.

With respect to the relationship between exposition and recapitulation, there are two first movements, those of Op. 74/2 and 3, in which the latter section adheres relatively closely to the original order of events; and in Op. 71/3, the correspondence between outer sections proves reasonably transparent despite various points of abbreviation, elaboration, and replacement. Differences are more pronounced among the other three, whose recapitulatory liberties to some extent resemble those witnessed in Op. 64. Here they may be read not only as a

challenge to formal convention, however, but also as part of an effort to drama-
tize the form and maintain a firm hold on an audience's attention.

In Op. 71/1, the recapitulation's omissions serve to alleviate redundancy (since
primary and secondary themes are closely related) and to sustain a large-scale
rhythm of alternation between ritornello-like thematic statements and intervening display. In Op. 71/2, the return of a mere four measures of primary theme
material (mm. 71–74) suffices as a sign of recapitulation, and much of the original transition is obliterated by a fortissimo outburst: a developmental foray that
intensifies the initial falling octave idea by reversing its direction and reshaping
the instruments' pattern of imitative entries into a rising sequence (mm. 75–78).
Balancing these acts of surprise and compression is a redoubled emphasis on the
contrasting theme first heard in measures 39–46 (elaborated in mm. 93–96, then
recalled intact in mm. 104–11).

More pointedly theatrical is the recapitulation in the first movement of
Op. 74/1, which displays a phenomenal series of novelties, rhetorical strokes,
and surprises: a drastically altered transition that startles by treating a gnarled
version of the movement's opening idea to canonic imitation (mm. 105–10); a
moment of contrast in surface activity (mm. 128–31) in which the harmony
veers to the lowered submediant (A♭); an outburst in a momentarily tonicized
A♭ (mm. 132–34); and a final, climactic recall of primary theme material, now
in unison (mm. 149–52), shortly before the close.

For the slow movements, all now in second place, Haydn builds on the previous group's diverse approaches to variation: Op. 74/2/ii features a strophic design enriched by a variation in minor; Op. 71/3/ii unfolds as a species of alternating variation whose order of events becomes unpredictable after the first
three segments; Op. 71/1/ii and 74/3/ii are ternary forms in which the third part
varies the first (variation is minimal in the former but proves quite intense in the
latter); and Op. 71/2/ii is a sonata form that mimics ternary variation procedure
by adorning the recapitulation with a wealth of melodic embellishment. Variation likewise comes into play in the other slow-movement sonata form, that of
Op. 74/1: here the recapitulation's opening phrase displays a favorite decorative
technique of Haydn's (as seen in the first variation of Op. 64/1/iii, for example)
by consigning the principal melody to a lower member of the ensemble, while
the first violin performs a descant in small note values.

The dance movements, diverse in character as well as pace, include two minuets (Op. 71/2 and 74/1) whose combination of fast tempo and unrelenting surface motion recalls precedents from among the Op. 33 scherzos, notably those of
Nos. 1 and 5. Op. 71/1 and 74/3, by contrast, uphold the Op. 64 preference for a
more self-possessed allegretto; and the unmarked minuets of Op. 71/3 and 74/2
seem best suited for temperate speed in light of their beat-oriented rhythmic impetus. Several of the minuets display rustic qualities, notably those of Op. 71/3,
which highlights a foot-stomping repeated-chord figure; Op. 74/1, with leaping-
octave pedal points; and Op. 74/2, whose pizzicato chords in the final phrase

lend an idyllic, strumming sound to the first violin's lilting arpeggios. By contrast, a more cultivated manner characterizes two of the trios: Op. 71/3, with a graceful, recurrent turn figure; and Op. 74/3, enriched by chromaticism and a hint of polyphony.

On the whole, the minuet-trio complexes resemble those of Op. 54/55 by tending more often to confirm dance-movement expectations than to destabilize with elements of comedy, eccentricity, or exaggeration, as found to at least some degree in most other opus groups. And yet here, as in Op. 54/55, there is no lack of novelty. In addition to the remote tonal juxtapositions of Op. 74/1 and 2, we find an instance of odd phrasing in the Op. 71/2 minuet. If we discount the solo cello's downward-bound arpeggio at the opening, the entire dance unfolds in nine-measure units: ‖ 9 : ‖: 9 + 9 : ‖.[19] And the first reprise of Op. 71/1 (ex. 15.2) is marked by the peculiar reharmonization of a repeated six-measure phrase (4 + 2). Curiously, this case of musical irony, a second phrase whose melody retraces that of the first while the harmony proceeds to a new key, revisits a much earlier minuet, that of Op. 20/3 (quoted in ex. 10.5). In fact, correspondences are so close as to suggest that Haydn may have had the earlier quartet at least half-consciously in mind as a model. The tonic keys of both minuets (G minor and B♭) have the same signature; the reharmonization device gains pungency in both instances from unusual phraseology; and the phrases themselves bear curious similarities, highlighting the pitches D and B♭ at the outset and ending with decorated descents from F to D.

The last movements call to mind many precedents among previous quartets in their rhythmic vitality and concentrated motivic development. Among the three cast in sonata form, Op. 71/1, 74/1, and 74/3, Haydn colors the fast pace with whimsy—for example, the false starts, interruptions, and frenzied climax of the development section in Op. 74/3—and structural enrichment, notably the late deflection to the remote key of D♭ in Op. 71/1 and the form-stretching interpolations of Op. 74/1 and 3. The other three finales incorporate aspects of rondo form, though with closer ties to the irregular last-movement designs of Opp. 54/55 and 64 than to the more predictable rondo structures of Op. 33. In Op. 71/3, a rustic-sounding refrain, complete with oom-pah-pah accompaniment, plants us in familiar rondo terrain, but then both form and style are complicated by excursions to the realm of fugal polyphony. The two remaining rondo-related finales are best described as hybrids or mixtures: rondo procedures compete with a ternary variation principle in Op. 71/2/iv, whereas the finale of Op. 74/2 combines certain rondo elements, including a rounded binary refrain, with the overall outlines of sonata form.

Nearly all the finales adhere to simple harmonic schemes (Op. 71/1 is the exception), with the impression of bedrock tonal solidity being especially pronounced in Op. 71/3 and 74/1. Tonal reassurance and simplicity in these final movements may be reckoned as part of a basic cyclic strategy: anchoring the principal action to a home key and its closest relatives helps signal long-range

EXAMPLE 15.2 Op. 71/1/iii, mm. 1–12

resolution and impending close. Indeed, most of the finales meet expectations of cyclic culmination in other ways as well, building to a climax of surface energy (most pointedly in Op. 71/2, whose change of tempo from allegretto to allegro marks the start of a dash to the end), summarizing with thematically charged interpolations before the close (as in Op. 74/1 and 3), or drawing the ensemble's forces together in a thematically neutralized but rhythmically unstoppable drive to the final cadence (Op. 71/2 and 3).

Sonority

Given the apparent aim of these quartets to put the medium itself on display, as it were, it is not surprising to find a degree of timbral diversity readily equaling if not surpassing that of the preceding several opus groups. Typically, moments of vivid sonority form an integral part of a movement's design, even while standing out as memorable events in their own right. In Op. 74/1/iv, for example, Haydn transforms the repetitive, solidifying function of a closing theme into the skirl and drone of a bagpipe, with a chromatically inflected melody in octaves above sustained, double-stopped sonorities in the lower instruments. Less topically explicit cases include the varied return in Op. 74/3/ii, with its unearthly bowed tremolo, sounded pianissimo in all four parts (mm. 49–50), and the final segment of the alternating variation design in Op. 71/3/ii, where the cello temporarily drops out (mm. 90–96), and the upper parts are left to wander through a shower of staccato sixteenth notes (the passage is repeated, with an extension, in mm. 99–108).

A more virtuosic spirit informs passages in which the instruments compete for attention with brilliant figuration, simultaneously or in close succession. Instances include the closing measures of both exposition and recapitulation in Op. 74/1/i, where broken-chord flourishes are taken up by each ensemble member in turn, and the tumultuous D minor episode in Op. 71/2/iv, in which instruments alone or in various combinations scramble through patches of rapid-fire passagework (mm. 22–29). Elsewhere, disciplined polyphony comes to the fore, as in the recapitulation of Op. 74/1/i: following a cadence and momentary rest in the upper parts (m. 104), the violins reenter with a canon at the fifth, and the lower instruments respond three and a half measures later with their own version of the canonic phrase, abbreviated and metrically displaced. Instances of fugue-related technique—initiated by the switch from four-part texture to a lean, portentous sound of two voices declaiming as subject and countersubject—bestow textural diversity and heightened intensity on the finales of Op. 74/1 and 2 as well as that of Op. 71/3.

Added to the strokes of instrumental color and intricate ensemble work (especially, though not exclusively, in last movements) are Haydn's devices for magnifying the quartets' powers of delivery. Most obvious in this respect are the multiple-stopped chordal accents by which the music springs to life at the outset in Op. 71/1, 71/3, and 74/1; but many interior passages project with unusual intensity as well, and not only through exaggerated mass or dynamics. More subtle strategies come into play in situations such as that quoted in example 15.3, from late in the exposition of Op. 71/2/i. At measure 33, the first violin initiates a gradual pulling together of the ensemble prior to an eventual confirmation of the dominant key. By measure 36, the event seems more than ready to be consummated as the group shapes itself into a relatively dense choir of rhythmically synchronized voices. But the awaited cadence is averted (m. 37), and an extra measure of chromatically thickened transition intervenes, marked by an even more tightly compressed ensemble, before tonal stability is at last secured. Now, as if holding onto something too precious to abandon—or perhaps rhetorically too important to allow for immediate dispersal among the voices—the players retain a semblance of their close, rhythmically coordinated spacing as a new theme unfolds (m. 39–40). Only in measure 41 does the register expand, in preparation for a liberating burst of surface activity in measure 42.

Among the most electrifying passages are those that command a four-part unison—usually loud, melodically sharp-edged, and often brimming with surface-rhythmic energy. But Haydn makes a surprise move in the first movement of Op. 74/1 (C major) by reducing the volume of unison sonority to a suspenseful murmur the first time it appears, just beyond the threshold between exposition and development section. Here a strangely quiet, chromatically charged transformation of the primary theme's opening call forewarns of serious consequences as it negotiates a modulation to the distant region of Eb major: a link has been forged between the principal theme and the implied unanimity of unison texture, but only as a dark, tonally ambivalent aside. The weight of a tonally decisive unison is correspondingly enhanced when it finally arrives in measures 149–52, just before the end of the movement. All signs have pointed to a straightforward analogy with the end of the exposition, and thus to a direct path from the cli-

EXAMPLE 15.3 Op. 71/2/i, mm. 33–42

mactic dominant trill of measure 148 to the cascading arpeggiations that precede the final cadence. Instead, a full-voice, unison return to the opening idea suddenly materializes—a shocking interruption, but also a satisfying moment of resolution, for even as it revives the memory of a disturbing episode (i.e., the start of the development), it releases the suppressed energy of that earlier event in a tonally grounded acclamation just before the movement's closing flourish.

Expanded Harmonic Resources

The potential forces of sonority and ensemble work notwithstanding, no other resource available to Haydn could rival the sudden deflection to a remote chord or key as a source of drama. Although the local impact of such an event is generally paramount, it may involve larger implications as it destabilizes the tonal environment in which it occurs; and as Haydn amply demonstrates in this opus group, some rationale—an overarching strategy of which the disturbance turns out to be an integral part—can often be detected, as in the development section of Op. 74/2/i. The second ending to the exposition, following a firm close in C, introduces a wrenching tonal shift to A major just before a statement of the opening theme in that distant key. Locally, this event dislodges the movement's course from the tonic-dominant axis and thus prepares for a new phase of action. But it also participates in a logical scheme of temporal organization and tonal relationship. Ingredients of the plan include a balancing move toward the end of the development section to the key of E♭, a polar opposite to A in the circle of fifths (m. 153), and a general pause at measure 130, the exact midpoint of the movement. The silence of this pivotal moment is broken by a recurrence of the primary theme idea transposed to C minor, the modal opposite of the dominant, and a key whose tonic note lies equidistant from those of A and E♭, the remote keys by which the main portion of the development is framed. An additional touch merits notice: the migration of the theme to the cello at the point of modulation to E♭—a moment of textural reversal to match the image of tonal polarity within the structure of the development section.

The move to a remote key at the start of a development, as in Op. 74/2, is mitigated to some extent by the fact that destabilizing events are naturally to be expected at this point in the form. Encountered elsewhere, a far-flung digression may prove more surprising, as in the slow movement of Op. 74/1 (G major), whose fatal step into alien territory could not reasonably have been anticipated. At measure 94, Haydn hails the start of the recapitulation with a G major triad whose heavy scoring and forzato accent seem to augur well for a full restoration of the home key. But the return to tonic proves not so conclusive after all. The recapitulation proceeds normally at first, and the full cadence that had coincided with the start of a closing phrase in the exposition (m. 51) comes back on schedule, in tonic, at measure 133. But where is the closing idea? Instead of staying on track and hastening to the end, the ensemble gives the impression of holding progress in check, first by dwelling on recollections of the movement's opening phrase, then freezing altogether as the resolution of a chromatically inflected appoggiatura plants us in the maximally distant region of C♯ minor (m. 148), a tritone away from the home key of G major. The mystery of prolonged suspense deepens as the tonal detour stretches to encompass a patch of primary theme development (mm. 149–53). Things fall into place at last in the next measure, as the cello ascends from C♯ to D (a telling climax to the movement's pervasive theme of accentuated melodic dissonances that resolve up or down by semitone) prior to an eventual resolution to tonic in measure 156 and the retrieval of the long-awaited closing phrase at last (m. 168).

Turning to the instances of remote tonal juxtaposition in the Op. 74 dance movements (No. 1 in C, No. 2 in F), we find elements of accentuated local contrast as well as integration. In the first of these cases, Op. 74/1/iii, the surprise shift from C to A at the start of the trio stands out as an opposing force, a relationship that counters the quartet's tendencies elsewhere to steer toward the flat side. This way of hearing the event scarcely lessens the tonal shock, which is intensified by its close proximity to the minuet's own move to A♭, even more distant from tonic on the flat side, at the start of its second reprise (m. 15). And yet there are similarities of theme and gesture that help compensate for the tonal diffusion. To begin with, the first violin's pattern of rising thirds by which the minuet's momentary tonal shift unfolds (A♭–C–E♭, mm. 15–17) may be heard as an expansion of the rising scale steps E–F–G from the movement's first three measures. In addition, the rising chromatic semitone in the principal line between the minuet's close on C and the first violin's C♯ at the start of the trio recalls the rising half-step motion from the end of the minuet's first reprise (in G) to the start of the second (in A♭). Finally, the trio's initial stepwise ascent from third to fifth scale degree above a repeated-note tonic pedal constitutes an unmistakable reference to the minuet's own combination of rising melodic line and static bass.

The trio of Op. 74/2/iii, cast in the warm tones of D♭ major, bears no obvious thematic connection to the minuet proper. However, the enharmonically equivalent pitch C♯ had figured there as a conspicuous dissonant element—underscored by long note values and forzato accents in measures 4 and 21, and thus prominent enough to be heard as a foreshadowing of the trio's foreign key.

Questions of Cyclic Cohesion

Although the emphasis on tonal stability sensed in most of the Op. 71/74 finales may be heard as an emblem of large-scale resolution, and hence a species of cyclic culmination, there are few other palpable sources of intermovement cohesion such as those found at least sporadically among previous works. For the first time since Op. 9, there are no single-tonic quartets; there are no run-on connections, apart from the transitional passages between trio and recurring minuet in Op. 74/1 and 2; and there is little in the way of significant, unconcealed thematic or procedural resemblance between movements. From this perspective, we could almost speak of a special emphasis on intermovement contrast through disparities in tempo, character, or sonority; and the impression that a movement might inhabit a sound-world of its own, substantially independent of its neighbors, would seem to be enhanced by the cases of high-profile remote relationship—potentially an affirmation of uniqueness and distance from customary tonal procedures within a cycle. But as we have seen among quartets of other opus groups, most notably

Opp. 50 and 54/55, peculiar events in one movement may resonate with those in another, thereby countering the centrifugal forces of local novelty or eccentricity with elements of cyclic interrelatedness.

In Op. 74/1/i, for example, Haydn widens the range of tonal play by turning to the flat side at two crucial moments: early in the development section, where the opening thematic idea comes back in Eb, then late in the recapitulation, where it participates in a climactic shift to Ab. As if responding to these events, or perhaps simply animated by a similar impulse, the second movement, in G, swerves to Eb, that key's own lowered submediant, for a prominent statement of opening-theme material early in the development section. Similarly, the move to Ab at the start of the minuet's second reprise, however astonishing at the moment of its occurrence, may be heard as a sequel to the quartet's previous tonal adventures.

More intriguing are the cyclic riddles posed by the "Rider" quartet, Op. 74/3, whose chief tonal oddity, the distant slow-movement key of E major, challenges Haydn's own entrenched norms of key relationship. Endowed with the gravity of a very slow tempo and marked for special intensity by vivid dynamics and coloristic ensemble effects, the Largo assai stands apart as a luminous gem within the larger design. Impressions of isolation and discontinuity are balanced, however, by a network of connections with tonal action elsewhere in the work. Table 15.2a helps demonstrate this by identifying favored, structurally important keys in each of the four movements. As represented in table 15.2b, all the keys in question but three (B, F minor, and Ab) are balanced by their modal opposites either within a movement, between one movement and the next, or both.

Seen from this vantage point, the tonal relationship between first and second movements can be rationalized as a modally upside down version of the conventional pairing of a major tonality (e.g., G major) with its relative minor (E minor); and the plausibility of this notion is reinforced by the conspicuous presence of those very two keys: G major in the first-movement recapitulation, E minor in the middle section of the slow movement. C major, the ultimate goal of the slow movement's middle section, stands in close relationship to G; but it also connects with its modal opposite, C minor, whose main appearance in the first movement (mm. 96–109) straddles the form's midpoint.

Also important from a cyclic perspective is the evolving relationship between G minor and G major—a narrative of modal rivalry that informs the first, third, and last movements. In accordance with what has become Haydn's regular practice for an opening movement in minor, a switch to the parallel major occurs well before the end of the recapitulation, so that a state of near-equilibrium is achieved between the minor tonic at the start of both exposition and recapitulation and an emergent major prior to the movement's close. But a dynamic surprise in the last measure, a pair of massive G major chords, gives rise to new questions: overdrawn with respect to their immediate surroundings, they seem intent

TABLE 15.2 Intermovement tonal connections in Op. 74/3

(a) Prominently featured keys in movements i–iv

i: Exp.: Gm B♭		Dev.: Cm A♭			Recap.: Gm G			
ii: A: E B | E		B: Em C			A¹: E B | E			
iii: Min.: G D | G		Trio: Gm Dm | B♭ Gm			Min: G D | G			
iv: Exp.: Gm B♭		Dev.: A♭ Fm B♭m			Recap.: Gm G			

(b) Distribution of modal pairs represented in (a)

G minor:	i		iii	iv
G major:	i		iii	iv
B♭ major:	i		iii	iv
B♭ minor:				iv
E major:		ii		
E minor:		ii		
C major:		ii		
C minor:	i			
D major:			iii	
D minor:			iii	

on commanding a view of the cycle as a whole and prefiguring the more decisive modal reversals to come. (The first movement does in fact possess one other out-sized harmonic event to which these chords may be compared: the fortissimo dominant and diminished seventh chords of mm. 126–27, the latter sustained by a fermata, that preface the recapitulation. These chords also may be heard to anticipate a later momentous occurrence—a tumultuous, rhythmically animated version of the diminished seventh leading up to the finale's recapitulation at m. 88.)

The minuet, apparently building on the strength of those larger-than-life chords at the end of the first movement, unfolds in a bright G major. The minor mode is relegated to a dynamically subdued trio, and yet it does enjoy new importance by encompassing an entire closed form. The finale sustains the contest of opposite modes by giving G minor an outspoken role at the start of both the exposition and the recapitulation: the primary theme's melody stretches upward for two octaves from the first violin's open G string while enjoying the firm support of tonic and dominant harmony. Minor discourse comes to a halt under the weight of a pair of fermatas in measure 99, the twelfth measure of the recapitulation, and the path is now clear for a decisive switch to G major. The work eventually concludes with two multiple-stopped G major chords to echo those heard at the end of the opening Allegro.

Other events in the finale contribute to a general picture of cyclic summation through recollections of previous ideas. Thus, the key of the lowered second scale degree, A♭, which had been featured prominently toward the end of the first-movement development section (mm. 110–14) returns with elevated impor-tance in the finale as the first emphasized tonal area of this movement's develop-ment (confirmed in m. 59). And as mentioned earlier in passing, the explosive diminished seventh outburst of measures 84–87, with cavernous octave Cs in the cello, explicitly recalls the first movement's diminished seventh of measure 127, likewise situated to mark the boundary between development and recapitulation.

The argument for cyclic cohesion may be further extended to include a rare case of intermovement thematic resemblance—understated to be sure, but none-theless significant in the context of this quartet's other cohesive properties. As shown in example 15.4a, a well-emphasized leap of a sixth (1m) characterizes the first movement's jaunty contrasting theme (introduced in B♭ at m. 55 and re-capitulated in G major starting at m. 169, as quoted in ex. 15.4b). In bringing back that rising sixth, the finale transplants it from a prancing triple meter to a more stable common time and awards it pride of place within the principal theme (ex. 15.4c, m. 3). The sixth is now narrowed from major to minor in order to ac-commodate a temporarily reinstated minor tonic and is thus poised for further transformation. As seen in example 15.4d, the finale's secondary theme, begun on the upbeat to measure 19, attaches the primary theme's triadic opening figure (marked 2m in ex. 15.4c and d) to a rhythmically altered version of the now-familiar upward leap; and as it proceeds, this freshly derived theme will spin out another variant of the leap—restored to its original size but now situated so that the high note falls on the downbeat as a local melodic peak (ex. 15.4e). Finally, when the secondary theme comes back in the recapitulation, where it will initiate the turn to G major, we may recognize the leap to B on the downbeat of measure 105 (ex. 15.4f) as a relative of the jump from D to B♭ in measure 3 (ex. 15.4c), now stretched from minor to major and transposed an octave higher. If so, might it not also be appreciated as another sign of cyclic cohesion—of coming full circle—by calling to mind the first movement's transformation from minor to major (ex. 15.4b), where that particular leap had first appeared?

∽

Our discussion of the Op. 71/74 quartets has emphasized traits that render them suitable for concert use, or at least for conveying sound-images suggestive of pub-lic performance. But such qualities, however prominent, scarcely lessen the stature of these works as superlative examples of Haydn's string quartet idiom. Hallmarks of that idiom—conversational dialogue, decorative figuration, intricate motivic development, and the like—are much in evidence, however tempered by tenden-cies toward simplicity of melodic profile and outspoken delivery. The fast-tempo development sections accommodate relatively dense motivic processes (as in Op. 71/3/i, mm. 127–46, a passage that engages all instruments simultaneously

EXAMPLE 15.4 (violin 1 only) Points of thematic resemblance in Op. 74/3/i and iv

(a) i, mm. 55–58

(b) i, mm. 169–72

(c) iv, mm. 1–3

(d) iv, mm. 19–20

(e) iv, mm. 23–24

(f) iv, mm. 104–5

in the development of primary- and closing-theme motives), slow movements sometimes indulge in richly decorated line and accompaniment, and the minuets and trios provide a typically Haydnesque forum for ensemble play.

In certain respects, Op. 71/74 may be appreciated as a relatively stable plateau in Haydn's approach to the genre, with structural types from preceding opus groups passing in review, framed within quartets that adopt a consistent cyclic order and that avoid such idiosyncrasies as run-on connections between movements and single-tonic formats. But indications that Haydn has chosen to limit his scope to tried-and-true techniques are countered by aspects of novelty in harmony and sonority—most notably in cases of juxtaposed third-related keys and in the resonant sonorities of the introductory gestures and subsequent landmarks. Whether such traits were motivated specifically by the prospect of public performances in London and elsewhere can only be guessed, although clearly there are signs of a general effort to extend the quartet's reach, enhance its versatility, and expand its capacity for the play of topical associations. The mingling of public and private domains that Haydn achieves here appears to have furnished a basis for his subsequent quartets, though not in any way that would suggest the persistence of fixed formulas for style or design. Instead, we find him choosing once again to challenge some of his own customary practices in the endeavors that followed: a full set of six quartet masterpieces in Op. 76, two additional, comparably original and ambitious works published as Op. 77, and the late, partially completed Op. 103.

16

Op. 76 ([?1796–] 1797)

It is from the correspondence of Silverstolpe that we find earliest mention of what would turn out to be the composer's last complete series of quartets. In a letter of 14 June 1797,[1] the Swedish diplomat describes the privilege of being able to sit beside the master at the keyboard, hear him play through "violin quartets," which he found to be "more than masterly and full of new thoughts," and to observe their scoring. Of crucial importance to the identification of these works is Silverstolpe's mention that the music had been ordered by "a certain Count Erdödi" whose name is in fact linked to Op. 76. (Haydn evidently received a fee of one hundred ducats from the count, whose generosity was later acknowledged by a dedication in Artaria's edition of the set.) Just how many of the quartets had been finished by this time remains unclear, although the entire opus was presumably completed within the year.[2] In September, at least one of the new quartets enjoyed an early hearing as part of a festive occasion at Eisenstadt: a report in the *Wiener Zeitung* of 7 October speaks of a newly composed quartet, and the diary of Joseph Carl Rosenbaum reports that "new quartets by Haydn were played, [one of them] based on the song *Gott erhalte Franz den Kaiser*," that is, Op. 76/3.[3]

As with Count Apponyi and Op. 71/74, the agreement with Erdödy stipulated that publication be withheld for a certain period of time.[4] Thus, it was not until 1799 that printed editions began to appear, most significantly those of Longman, Clementi & Co. in London and Artaria in Vienna. Both were prepared from material supplied by the composer himself, as indicated in his correspondence,[5] and both present the quartets in the same order.

In several respects, the story of the works' sale and publication parallels that of Op. 71/74: an initial time lapse to honor the terms of the commission; arrangements for publication in London, followed closely by a corresponding agreement with Artaria in Vienna; and the now-customary practice in both cases of issuing the set in two parts consisting of three quartets each. (Haydn's wording in his letter of 12 July 1799 to Artaria suggests that he himself regarded the set as a group of six compositions,[6] and yet it is also clear from his letters that he readily acquiesced to the idea of a divided publication.)[7] This time there was another factor in play, however. True to his propensity for complicated business arrangements, Haydn had entered into an agreement in 1796 with Frederik Augustus Hyde, a partner in the firm of Longman & Broderip (and its successors), the terms of which would result in his being compromised financially if someone else were to come out with an edition in advance of the London publisher.[8] At first, the matter proceeded as planned: the London print of the first three quartets, designated by the opus number 76, was registered at Stationers' Hall on 13 June 1799 and advertised two days later; and it was on 17 July that Artaria first advertised his counterpart, published as Op. 75.[9] Haydn, uncertain as to where matters stood abroad, feared that his London publisher might have delayed printing the first three quartets with the ultimate intention of publishing all six together. If this turned out to be the plan, and if Artaria were to come out with both sets of three in the meantime, Haydn might face the prospect of losing seventy-five pounds on each; and as he explained in an anxious mid-August letter to Artaria, it was to guard against this unhappy outcome that he had chosen temporarily to withhold from his Vienna publisher the last quartet of the second set.[10] In the end, Artaria's edition of the second set, published as Op. 76, did in fact precede Longman, Clementi's: it was advertised on 7 December 1799. Longman, Clementi's, although announced as forthcoming in January 1800, was not advertised until 25 April of that year.[11] This edition bore the same opus number 76 that the London firm had assigned to its edition of the first three, so that the two prints combined represent the first instance of the traditional numbering (i.e., the opus number 76 to encompass all six works).

The autograph manuscripts, which were probably given to Erdödy, appear not to have survived. However, there are autograph drafts for the slow movement of Op. 76/3, both for string quartet and keyboard. Authentic copies in score for three of the quartets, Nos. 2, 4, and 6, also exist.[12]

The commission from Erdödy came at a time when Haydn was otherwise preoccupied with vocal music: the yearly project of writing a mass for Princess Maria Hermenegild Esterházy's name day had begun in 1796, The Creation was now in progress, and we learn from Silverstolpe's letter that other vocal pieces were being composed as well. It is easy to imagine that the connections to song, aria, and learned-style traditions found in Op. 76 may owe something to that circumstance. But this would only partially account for the astonishing abundance of musical invention in the new quartets, with their formal novelties, technical demands, and elaborations of procedures familiar from previous opus groups. In part because of their diversity, these works can boast of an especially attractive surface and a corresponding breadth of appeal. There are few instances of tragic expression or deep pathos (as in the preceding two sets, all slow movements are in major) and only limited indulgence in frank comedy, and yet the variety of mood and character is exceptional.

From this vantage point, it is worth considering the expanding circles of the composer's admirers, their maturing musical tastes, and their competency as listeners and amateur performers. Haydn may well have felt pulled in different directions in response to their expectations, tempted to acknowledge the enduring popularity of earlier works still in circulation by adopting tried-and-true strategies, but also inclined to recognize growing sophistication among musical consumers by accommodating their thirst for novelty and acknowledging their familiarity with the idiosyncrasies of his art.

Given such an environment, it is reasonable to suppose a desire on Haydn's part not merely to entertain his admirers—rather, to inspire and instruct them through his many-faceted engagement of the musical resources at hand.[13] Can such a deeper purpose be sensed beneath the quartets' play of changing colors, textures, and moods? Different from either the subtle artistry of Op. 64 or the more popular accent in Op. 71/74 is a certain rhetorical intensity, a quality that encompasses the drama of emphasized contrasts in rhythm, dynamics, and sonority, the spaciousness of widened tonal horizons, the rigor of relentless motivic development, the volatility of minor-key discourse (the point of departure in no fewer than four of the twelve outer movements), and also the purity of an unembellished melodic line. Notwithstanding splendid examples of lighthearted wit and humor, an elevated tone prevails, sustained by forms marked for clarity, coherence, and a fine-honed sense of direction. This last-mentioned trait stands out especially in movements that embody cumulative, developmental, or endweighted designs—not a new phenomenon here, yet newly emphasized in ways that breathe fresh life into conventional forms while continuing to provide reliable structural foundations.

An early review of the initial Artaria edition, comprising the first three quartets in the series, praised their beauty and originality,[14] and a more detailed, resounding endorsement, underscoring the composer's affinity for the medium and his ability to coax inspiration from available materials, was recorded by Burney in his letter to Haydn on 19 August 1799: "I had the great pleasure of hearing your new *quartetti* (*opera* 76) well performed before I went out of town, and never received more pleasure from instrumental music: they are full of invention, fire, good taste, and new effects, and seem the production, not of a sublime genius who has written so much and so well already, but of one of highly-cultivated talents, who had expended none of his fire before."[15]

Burney's encomium justifiably celebrates the novelty of these works, which variously display forms, tonal schemes, and melodic procedures different from anything encountered before among the quartets. And yet just as with most of the previous sets, there are ample signs of continuity with past efforts, and especially with the immediately preceding opus. An explicit connection is recognizable at the very outset: the call to attention that prefaces the exposition of Op. 76/1/i clearly belongs to the same family of audience-taming chordal sonorities that had adorned the opening measures of Op. 71/1, 71/3 and 74/1. Much as in the previous opus, consequences of this initial gesture resound in the music that follows. For example, a variant of the opening progression, texturally varied and extended by two chords, realizes its potential as a sign of conclusion by marking the end of the exposition and recapitulation. In both locations, an enlivened scoring transforms the originally solid chords into arpeggios that cascade through the ensemble, thus serving both to summarize and unite the movement's opposing sonorous forces—a fully consolidated ensemble versus the dispersion of line and figure among the instruments.

Other suggestions of a rhetorically magnified, public temperament abound, some evidently stemming from the introductory-gesture idea, others not. The startling G minor unison that heads the Op. 76/1 finale recalls that of the first movement in Op. 74/3 (also in G minor). Likewise introductory in spirit, although functionally integrated as part of the exposition proper, are the electrifying dominant-to-tonic chordal exclamations at the head of the Op. 76/5 finale and the menacing, threefold exclamation in C minor with which the last movement of Op. 76/3 begins its journey. In the latter part of the exposition of Op. 76/3/i (mm. 30–31), a furious barrage of chordal impacts and high-register arpeggiations gives rise to one of the noisiest sonorities in the repertory; and in Op. 76/5/i, an initially subdued, pastoral theme turns out to have been a deceptively peaceful backdrop for subsequent hailstorms of sixteenth- and thirty-second-note activity as the movement unfolds.

As in the preceding set, a conservative choice of principal keys (G, D minor, C, B♭, D, E♭) furnishes a solid, familiar base for ventures into remote terrain, notably the second movement of the D major quartet, Op. 76/5, which reaches out to the major mediant, the rare key of F♯, for its tonic, and the suggestively labeled "Fantasia" of Op. 76/6, based on the lowered submediant (C♭, although actually notated as B). Especially peculiar in the latter case is the absence of a key signature at the outset, understandable in light of the extraordinary range of remotely related keys traversed within the first half of the movement.

An Overview of the Opus

As shown in table 16.1, formal novelty stands at the forefront on two occasions: the first movements of Nos. 5 and 6. Neither adheres to the practice of beginning with a large-scale sonata form, and in fact, both movements feature variation-based procedures. A comparison may be drawn in this regard with two much earlier works, Opp. 9/5 and 17/3, whose opening variations replaced the customary

TABLE 16.1 Summary statistics for Op. 76

Op.No.	Hob.No.	Movement			
		i	ii	iii	iv
76/1	III:75	G ¢ Allegro con spirito SF 225	C $\frac{2}{4}$ Adagio sostenuto SF 95	G $\frac{3}{4}$ Presto M/T 40/34	Gm-G ¢ Allegro ma non troppo SF 200
76/2	III:76	Dm ¢ Allegro SF 154	D $\frac{6}{8}$ Andante o più tosto allegretto Ternary var. 67(r)	Dm/D $\frac{3}{4}$ Allegro M/T 37/43	Dm-D $\frac{2}{4}$ Vivace assai Sonata-rondo 267
76/3	III:77	C ¢ Allegro SF 121	G ¢ Poco adagio. Cantabile Strophic var. 104	C/Am $\frac{3}{4}$ Allegro M/T 56/44	Cm-C ¢ Presto SF 188
76/4	III:78	Bb ¢ Allegro con spirito SF 188	Eb $\frac{3}{4}$ Adagio SF/Slow-mvt. 74	Bb $\frac{3}{4}$ Allegro M/T 50/55(r)	Bb ¢ Allegro ma non troppo–più allegro–più presto Rondo-var. hybrid 175(r)
76/5	III:79	D $\frac{6}{8}$ Allegretto–Allegro Nonstandard 127(r)	F# ¢ Largo. Cantabile e mesto SF 97	D/Dm $\frac{3}{4}$ Allegro M/T 32/33	D $\frac{2}{4}$ Presto SF (irreg.) 291
76/6	III:80	Eb $\frac{2}{4}$ Allegretto–Allegro Strophic var. 227	B $\frac{3}{4}$ Adagio Nonstandard [Fantasia] 112	Eb $\frac{3}{4}$ Presto M/T* 60/96	Eb $\frac{3}{4}$ Allegro spiritoso SF 166

*The designation for trio is "Alternativo."

305

sonata form, but not with Op. 55/2, where the normal order of first and second movements was simply reversed. As described in chapter 7, the two Op. 76 movements resemble one another in their novel combination of variation and fugue; and unlike the earlier instances in Opp. 55/1/iv, 55/2/ii, 64/5/iv, and 71/3/iv, with their centrally located slices of polyphony, here the fugal apparatus arises later, as part of end-weighted designs that gather momentum as they progress, surmounting customary formal constraints along the way.

The remaining first movements are large-scale sonata forms whose motivic detail (especially in Nos. 1, 2, and 3) competes for attention with outbursts of sonority and brilliant figuration. Notwithstanding general similarities, each proves unique in its manner of borrowing from recognized prototypes. Op. 76/1, for example, adopts a modern-style alla breve: a fast quarter-note impetus prevails, and there are no notated rhythmic values smaller than the eighth note either in thematic lines or their accompaniments. In contrast, the first movement of Op. 76/4 (B♭), notated in common time, showcases the nervous energy of sixteenth notes. Such action is not emphasized from the start, however. In keeping with a favored practice of Haydn's, deluges of sixteenths are held in reserve for later phases of the exposition's narrative, and this gives rise to a paradox: Op. 76/4/i is marked Allegro con spirito, but the promise of exuberance is destined to be fulfilled not in the primary theme, nor in the related secondary theme, both of which move serenely in longer note values, but in subsidiary patches of transition, developmental elaborations, and closing flourishes.

The first movement of Op. 76/3 revels in a different kind of paradox: the contradictory mix of old-fashioned, chamber-like qualities—including a persistent eighth-note surface rhythm, half-measure thematic units (variously situated on the downbeat or the middle of the measure), and embellishing details in triplet sixteenths and thirty-second notes—and the overt concert-style embrace of inflated sonorities and stunning climaxes in register, dynamics, and surface activity.

A retrospective eighth-note impetus likewise informs the first movement of the D minor quartet, Op. 76/2 (the "Fifths"). But instead of the more pointed disparities of style and rhythmic pacing encountered in Op. 76/3, here the multilayered common time has an explicit unifying purpose: variously engaging different levels of rhythmic activity, from half note to sixteenth, it assists in articulating the movement's complex motivic action (further discussed below) with clarity and persuasion.

More than in most previous opus groups, the slow interior movements constitute a forum for variety of character and design. The three variation-based structures all are radically different from one another. Op. 76/2/ii is a richly colored ternary design marked by the quaint charm of pizzicato accompaniment in the first reprise, ubiquitous development in a modulatory middle section, and an extraordinary display of melodic-outline variation in its final part. By contrast, the Emperor's Hymn movement of Op. 76/3 is a uniquely pure, structurally transparent example of cantus firmus variation in which the famous tune remains virtually unchanged throughout. Divergent from either of these approaches is the Fantasia of Op. 76/6, whose first half concentrates on thematic repetition as a basis for far-reaching harmonic excursion; Haydn's choice to dispense with a key signature for this portion of the form underscores the impression of a challenge to basic principles of tonal constancy. Keys traversed, following an opening statement in the local tonic of B (or C♭), include C♯ minor, E, G, and B♭ (i.e., a complete rising sequence of keys a minor third apart) before a brief return to B and an additional thematic statement in A♭. (At m. 60, a key signature of five sharps finally appears, and the focus of interest shifts from harmonic color to the rigor of fugal polyphony, with the elaboration of a subject based on the opening phrase. The rest of the movement's 112 measures remain tied to the orbit of B major.)

The other three slow movements, all in sonata form, include two (those of Op. 76/1 and 4) that resemble earlier examples of Haydn's aria- or concerto-like manner, complete with high-register figural work, great leaps, and points of contrast between solidly scored ensemble phrases and intervening stretches of solo figuration. Both are problematic structurally. The former complicates the underlying sonata model with multiple, ritornello-like recurrences of an opening idea, including two in tonic (mm. 49 and 72), whereas the latter confronts us with a case of genuine formal ambivalence. Following the end of the exposition in the dominant (B♭) at measures 29–30, a four-measure transition over a pedal leads to an altered version of the primary theme in E♭ minor, the tonic key's minor twin (m. 35, close to the midpoint of the form). Although this may be heard as the start of a recapitulation of sorts, there is a degree of instability in the measures that follow, and there are no functionally unequivocal, metrically accented tonic sonorities in root position. This degree of tonal assurance will be reserved for the next structural landmark, an elided cadence at measure 52 that introduces a variant of the opening theme in the home key. The fact that the movement confounds simple stereotypes need hardly interfere with our appreciation of its satisfying coherence: an initial journey from tonic to dominant, a thematically salient detour through the parallel minor, eventual restoration of tonic major, and further elaboration of exposition material within the orbit of tonic in the latter part of the form.[16]

The remaining slow movement in sonata form, that of Op. 76/5, stands apart from the others by its startlingly remote key (F♯) and its tempo indication, whose qualifier "mesto" underscores the distance from concert-room theatrics as it conjures a realm of melancholy reflection. Virtually everything about the music itself resonates with the implications of the movement's rare tonal center[17] and expressive marking, including a plangent main theme; a long, contemplative development section; and a tendency to gravitate toward middle-range sonority and subdued rhythmic activity.

The minuets and trios display an extraordinary wealth of dance-movement antics and novelties. Striking peculiarities include cases of offbeat accent and metrically dissonant surface patterns (Op. 76/5), extreme contrast between the movement's two segments (Op. 76/2, in which the trio's burst of D major chords resounds on the heels of the minuet's two-part polyphony in minor), elided boundaries (the second ending to the Op. 76/4 minuet, which connects seamlessly with the start of the trio), and structural enigma (the mystery of an embedded binary form within the second reprise of the Op. 76/3 trio). The minuets of Op. 76/1 and 6 bear the extreme tempo marking presto, and particularly in the former instance, the combination of measure-level pulse and supercharged rhythmic impetus seems to eclipse the traditional minuet topic altogether. A truly demonic tone prevails in the canonic minuet of Op. 76/2, whose hard-driving momentum owes less to sheer velocity than to the unrelieved two-part texture, with upper and lower parts locked in octaves throughout.

Featured among the minuet portions of the dance movements are rounded binary designs, such as that of Op. 76/6, in which an intensely elaborated second reprise partakes of the progressively developed, end-weighted tendencies that characterize the opus group as a whole. Altogether unique is the Op. 76/6 trio, the only one in the repertory to escape the customary two-reprise model. Labeled Alternativo, this contrapuntal tour de force proposes a simple tonic scale, variously rising and falling, for its basic subject. It then follows a plan in which various arrangements of imitative entries form the governing principle of organization: as represented in figure 16.1, there are three imitative cycles based on descending scales (D), alternating with three in which the scale ascends (A). Each begins quietly with either the cello or the first violin, and in each case but the first, the appearance of a resonant four-voice texture, marked forte, signals the conclusion of the cycle.[18] The plan as a whole, extending to ninety-six measures, is by far the longest span in the repertory to be controlled by a single key without modulation. And in this connection it is worth noting that a directive in Elssler's authentic copy actually gives performers the choice of stopping at the end of either the first or the second thirty-two-measure segment if they find the entire trio too long.[19]

The finales in Op. 76 are distinguished by motivic ingenuity, expressive weight, and narrative complexity. All are impressive in size, if not consistently or dramatically longer, say, than those of Op. 71/74. Only one forgoes the inherent complications of sonata procedure in favor of a simpler design. The exception, the rondo-variation of Op. 76/4, is a close relative of Op. 71/2, complete with a tonic-minor episode and eventual change to a quickened tempo, although here the race to the end is compounded by a second phase of accelerated tempo, più presto, on the heels of the earlier più allegro.

Op. 76/5/iv exhibits a customary last-movement blend of duple meter, presto tempo, sonata form, and nearly unstoppable rhythmic drive; but it exceeds the norms of its genre by the impact of its initial tonic-dominant oscillation figure, the nervously darting theme that follows, and the hauntingly repetitive, staccato open-fifth sonorities in eighth notes that underlie and connect principal thematic statements and their elaboration. The resulting rhythmic juggernaut, to which

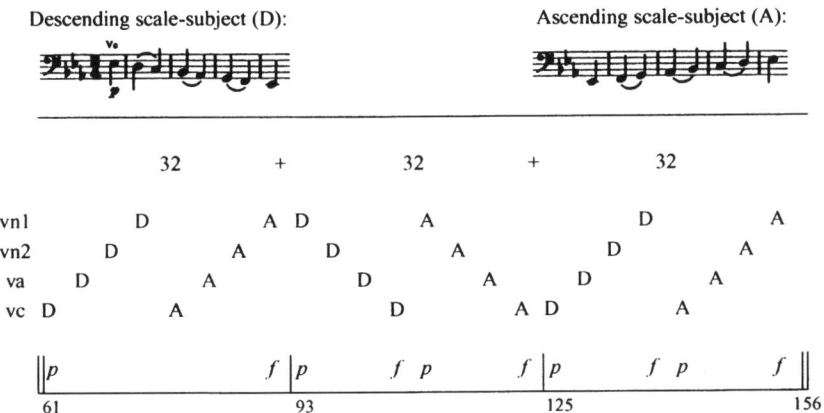

FIGURE 16.1 Op. 76/6/iii, Alternativo

all the above elements contribute, provides a context for strokes of drama and surprise: the arresting combination of harmonic derailment and thwarted rhythmic drive at measures 70–72, where a long, galloping upbeat collides with a block of minor-inflected half notes; the screeching ascent to a registral ceiling (e⁴) at measure 110, propelled by the maximal energy of soaring sixteenth-note passagework begun in measure 102; the exalted, full-voiced deceptive resolution (V⁷ to ♭VI, m. 126) just where a repeat of the exposition was expected (this is the only fast-tempo sonata form among the quartets without an exposition repeat); and the added burst of energy that greets the start of the recapitulation at measure 193, where a new layer of frantic sixteenth notes in the second violin accompanies the return of the opening fanfare.

The last movement of Op. 76/6, different from that of No. 5 in many ways, may be heard as a study in contraries with respect to the outwardly more conventional idiom of its immediate neighbor. Instead of opening with a pattern of synchronized harmonic, rhythmic, and melodic action, perfectly aligned with the duple measure, this ¾ finale (the only one of its kind up to this point in the repertory) gets off to a perplexing start: a descending staccato scale fragment, begun on the upbeat, straddles the bar line, displaces a lone, accompanying chord to the middle of the first measure, and thereby signals the onset of an all-out comedy of metrical contradiction. Highlights include the confusion of competing hemiolic patterns in upper and lower parts (mm. 13–14, 17–18); metrically displaced imitation (for example, mm. 21–23); a stretto-like pattern of motivic repetition whose telescoping effect adds local propulsion while overriding the bar line (mm. 26–28); and a span of astounding metrical play in the development. Here, beginning at measure 71, an open-ended stream of staccato eighth notes in the first violin heeds neither the bar line nor any other recognizable, surrogate meter. Instead, its winding line conspires with the lower parts' sporadic, punctuating chords to define nonregular groupings based on the beat-level pulse rather than the measure. As shown in figure 16.2, durational units articulated by line and accompaniment grow progressively shorter in measures 71–75, in the course of harmonic motion from C minor to F minor (five beats, four, three, then two); likewise, the patterning in measures 75–78 accelerates from four beats to three, then two. Motion stabilizes with a series of four-beat units from the end of measure 78 into measure 82, before stretching out to six and seven beats along the path from F minor to A♭ major, whose dominant is finally reached on the downbeat of measure 87.[20] In a manner that anticipates the rhythmic artifice of Stravinsky, Haydn builds his changeable durations directly from the beat. Any sensation of regular meter temporarily disappears, and the music offers us no alternative but to substitute the irregular (but well calculated) chordal accents for points of emphasis otherwise identified with the bar line.

Common to three of the finales, those of Op. 76/1, 2, and 3, is a dramatized, end-weighted model by which elements of darkness and conflict give way to visions of unity and reconciliation in the end. Crucial to achieving this shared outcome is the ultimate ascendancy of major over minor, as witnessed in several previous sonata forms in minor, beginning with Op. 50. All three of these final movements are in fact cast in minor at the outset—a normal enough premise for the D minor quartet but a striking novelty in each of the other two, where the sudden encounter with minor tonality comes as a profound disturbance: a deflection from major clarity and assurance that must be rectified as the movement unfolds. The initial emblems of minor discourse are different in each case—a turbulent unison in No. 1; an exotically inflected, folk-style melody in No. 2; a ferocious chordal exclamation in No. 3—and in each instance the minor foundation persists at least through the early part of the recapitulation. But then there comes a suspenseful, revelatory moment, marked by dominant harmony and prolonged or followed by a fermata that prepares us to cross the threshold into a major realm in which minor forces are variously banished or transformed.

Sonority and Ensemble Play

Although Haydn's favored sonorities and ensemble configurations in Op. 76 resemble those of previous opus groups, the sheer variety of texture and timbre here is outstanding, enriched as it is by intensified versions of familiar strategies as well as new ways of tailoring the medium's sound resources to particular musical processes.

Haydn's customary fondness for showcasing the first violin as a soloist remains in force, especially in two of the slow-movement sonata forms—Op. 76/1/ii (complete with notated cadenzas near the close of the exposition, mm. 30–32, and re-

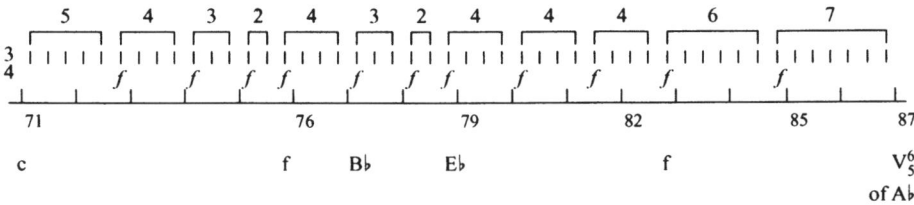

FIGURE 16.2 Op. 76/6/iv, mm. 71–87 (Explanation of symbols: Vertical strokes mark the beats, and brackets delineate melodic patterns. The dynamic marking *f* designates the occurrence of accompanying chords in the lower parts, all marked forte in the score.)

capitulation, mm. 88–90) and Op. 76/4/ii—and in the ternary variation design of Op. 76/2/ii, whose passages of thirty-second notes sometimes reach high above the treble staff. In all but the last quartet of this series, the occurrence of extremely high peaks bestows piercing brilliance on points of color and rhetorical emphasis. (Haydn's highest violin note of all, f⁴, is attained in Op. 76/5/i, m. 36.)

The ensemble's other voices make do with less scintillating moments, but none are ignored altogether, and the two lower instruments both enjoy unusual degrees of eloquence. The viola's elaboration of the main theme in the Op. 76/5/ii development section has been identified as "the deepest viola solo in all Haydn",[21] and there are moments throughout the set when the cello part brims with character and timbral interest. In Op. 76/1/ii, for example, fleeting snippets of dialogue between the ensemble's highest and lowest members create an indefinable blend of humor and melancholy. More ominously, the cello becomes rasping and strident at the start of the development section in Op. 76/6/iv, transforming the otherwise light-stepping principal theme into a ponderous, baritone-range tirade. Comparably distinctive, although by no means unique to this opus, are the cello's recurrent passages of rumbling figuration near the ends of sections or movements, variously depicting an ineluctable gravitational pull, a state of near-exhaustion, or else final murmurings amid an encroaching silence.

As in all previous opus groups, Haydn portrays ideal images of ensemble equality by allocating a motive or imitative subject to each member in turn; but Op. 76 excels in this regard, creating seamless thematic fabrics in which all members participate alike (as in the D minor minuet of Op. 76/2, by far the longest canon in the repertory), or passing ideas from one part to another methodically as if to contemplate them from different angles. Perhaps the most unexpectedly contrived arrangement of this sort is the opening of the Op. 76/1/i exposition: following the introductory hammerstrokes, the solo cello leads off with what almost sounds like a fugue subject, to judge from the beat-marking rhythmic stride and customary motion from tonic to dominant (see ex. 16.1). The viola now enters with the semblance of a tonal answer, approximating the cello's rhythm and melodic profile as it duly returns from dominant to tonic. Meanwhile, however, the cello has

EXAMPLE 16.1   Op. 76/1/i, mm. 3–18

ceased to play, so there is no evolving fugal texture but rather a thoroughly ex-posed, concentrated dialogue spotlighting the two lower parts in turn while the violins look on in silence—surely among the strangest of the quartets' opening presentations. Subsequent entries prove equally systematic and no less baffling. As the second violin takes up the subject (in its original tonic-to-dominant form), the cello actually does chime in with a countersubject; but again progress comes to a halt once the subject has run its four-measure course; those who were play-ing now drop out, and it is left for the first violin and viola to complete this per-fectly logical, skeletal parody of learned procedure by sounding the answer ver-sion of the subject and its counterpoint, respectively.[22]

Motivic Work and Thematic Continuity

No previous opus group better exemplifies Haydn's penchant for open-ended motivic process and homogeneous continuation to guide the progress of themes, sections, or entire movements. Accentuating this quality almost to exaggeration are situations whose fixation on a peculiar sound or process tests the capacity of performers and listeners—or the medium itself—to concentrate unwaveringly on a featured musical idea. The oversized Alternativo of Op. 76/6 stands out espe-cially in this regard, with its narrowed focus on a fixed tonal center, an elemental, ubiquitous thematic figure, and single compositional procedure. Although shorter, even counting binary repeats, the canonic minuet of Op. 76/2 proves no less obsessive, given the uniformity of its octave-bound, two-part texture, canonic premise, and concomitant surface continuity. From a purely motivic perspective, the category of single-minded obsession also includes the fast-paced minuet of Op. 76/1, where variants of a basic motive inhabit nearly every measure.

It is natural for Haydn to temper a movement's motivic or thematic consistency with elements of diversity that help freshen and enrich the texture; and the deft balancing act that results is a specialty of this opus. The task is accomplished with a peculiarly tight logic in the first movement of Op. 76/4 (the "Sunrise"), whose close resemblances between primary and secondary themes are countered by equally vivid points of contrast that work to enhance the form's tonal polarity and spatial symmetry. As the quartet begins, the "sunrise" melody traces a two-fold ascent, supported first by tonic harmony, then by a dominant seventh, before lighting on a full cadence in measure 12 (ex. 16.2a). Later, after a half cadence in the new key to mark the midpoint of the exposition, a derivative of the opening theme unfolds in the dominant, thereby projecting the dual harmonic focus on a higher order of magnitude. But here the sense of a larger-scale polarity—between keys rather than chord functions—is enhanced by a transformation of the original theme's countenance: both the texture and the principal melody itself are turned upside down.[23] The theme is assigned to the cello, whose line actually starts on the original pitch level but now winds downward (ex. 16.2b). The topic of reversal is then further enhanced by a turn from major to minor, timed to coincide with the elided cadence that punctuates the end of the theme (m. 44).

The primary theme's recurrence at the start of the recapitulation naturally reinforces the architectural balance of the form. But the return is also marked by a change in rhetorical significance. The theme had been veiled at the beginning of the movement by a quiet, uniform dynamic level, in keeping with its role as a deceptively placid, understated point of departure; but here it claims new assertiveness as the bearer of tonal recovery. A crescendo now underlies both phrases, and the chords that punctuate the phrases resonate with double and triple stops. Also subject to change in accordance with altered circumstances is the return of the principal idea in its secondary theme guise (m. 142): no longer an emblem of tonal opposition, the line now rises and falls in a blend of the preceding versions' directional tendencies (see ex. 16.2c; here, as indicated by the bracketed figures x and y, the opening gesture explicitly conflates those of the exposition's primary and secondary themes). Moreover, it is no longer pinned to the bottom of the texture as an antithesis to the first violin's opening statement. Rather, starting with the upbeat to measure 146, it wanders among the inner voices as well, thereby further dissolving the exposition's polarities.

So potent are the forces of relationship and derivation in Op. 76 that they sometimes spill over from one work to another, as in the opening measure of

EXAMPLE 16.2 Op. 76/4/i

(a) mm. 1–12

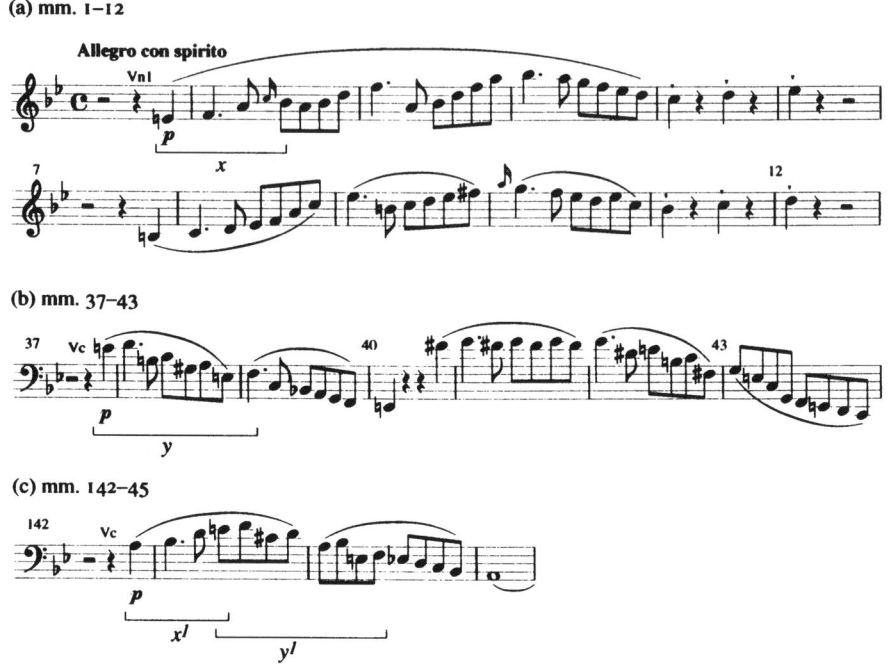

(b) mm. 37–43

(c) mm. 142–45

Op. 76/6/ii, which replicates that of Op. 76/4/ii, pitched an augmented fifth higher but otherwise nearly identical in line, rhythm, and harmony (see ex. 16.3a and b). Although possibly a case of accidental self-borrowing, the resemblance may readily be heard as a deliberate effort to explore divergent paths from a given point of origin.[24] The two movements do indeed part company as early as the second measure, and yet they resemble one another in the sheer intensity with which the initial lower-neighbor idea is pursued: featured in both works as a recurrent principal idea, it makes more than two dozen appearances in each, not counting inversions.

Less explicit, yet nonetheless resonant with implications for opus-group character, are the motivic similarities among first-movement principal themes in three adjacent quartets, Nos. 1, 2, and 3. As shown in example 16.4a through c, all begin with rhythmically simple motives characterized by interlocking intervals in descending sequence.

In Op. 76/1/i, the opening subject's taut construction, with its nested sequential patterns (interlocked thirds in m. 3, embedded within a succession of falling arpeggiated triads), represents a protean force, continually subject to renewal and reshaping as it lends continuity among contrasting phrases and themes within all main sections. At measure 19, for example, the top part's primary theme con-

EXAMPLE 16.3

(a) Op. 76/4/ii, mm. 1–2   (b) Op. 76/6/ii, mm. 1–2

tinuation grows directly from the subject (see ex. 16.5), yet it changes continuously, tightening the thirds to seconds (m. 23) and enlivening the surface rhythm (m. 24), shortly before bringing this phase of elaboration to a halt with punctuating staccatos in measure 26; but those staccatos themselves now become a generative force, yielding a phrase with salient features that derive from elements in the initial theme and its previous elaborations, notably the slurred falling thirds, triadic figures in sequence, and falling, slurred octave (mm. 27–32).

Motivic connections in Op. 76/3/i are comparably pervasive and likewise enriched by processes of transformation. Melodic and rhythmic variants of the opening interlocked-thirds motto[25] insinuate themselves as motivating elements in every theme group and almost every phrase, and, as seen in the excerpt quoted in example 16.6b, they participate in strategies of formal articulation and long-range relationship as well. Here, just beyond the middle of the exposition, a motivically charged phrase in the dominant closes with a derivative of the opening five-note gesture (mm. 25–26, marked *x* in ex. 16.6a). The elision to a new theme at measure 26, energized by a burst of sixteenth notes in the accompaniment, creates a link between two contrasting phrases. But there is a deeper connection as well, for the new idea takes shape as a variant of the opening motto's answering figure (*y*). In effect, the miniature antecedent-consequent relationship of measures 1–2 now takes on higher-level meaning as a unifying model for the connection between themes in the latter part of the exposition.

EXAMPLE 16.4

(a) Op. 76/1/i, mm. 3–4   (b) Op. 76/2/i, mm. 1–2   (c) Op. 76/3/i, m. 1

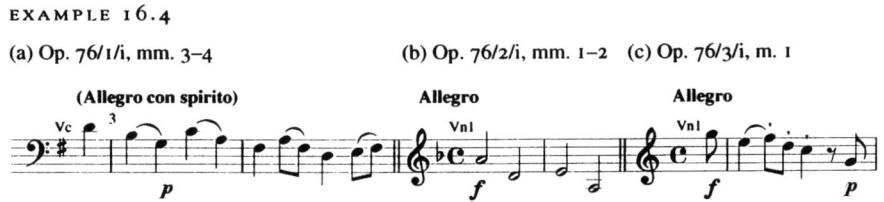

EXAMPLE 16.5　Op. 76/1/i, mm. 19–32 (violin 1 only)

Of the leading, interlocked-interval motives quoted earlier in example 16.4, the plainest, but also the most intensively worked out, is that of Op. 76/2. The first violin's stark announcement of interlocked fifths in long note values sounds as ripe for development as a fugue subject, and in fact, much of the movement will be consumed by fugally derived techniques, including diminution, inversion, and stretto, all woven into the thematic and developmental substance of a large-scale sonata form.[26] Example 16.7a focuses on a portion of the process as it unfolds in the exposition (mm. 20–26). Here a variant of the subject, newly reshaped to climb sequentially rather than fall, becomes implicated in a strategy involving threefold diminution—half note to quarter, quarter to eighth, eighth

EXAMPLE 16.6　Op. 76/3/i

(a) mm. 1–2 (violin 1 only)

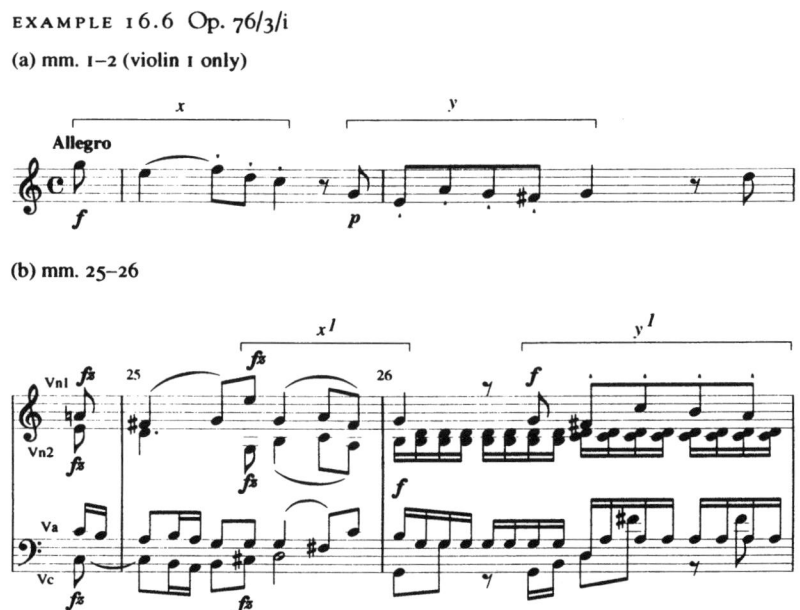

(b) mm. 25–26

EXAMPLE 16.7 Op. 76/2/i

(a) mm. 20–26 (violin 1 only)

(b) mm. 67–69

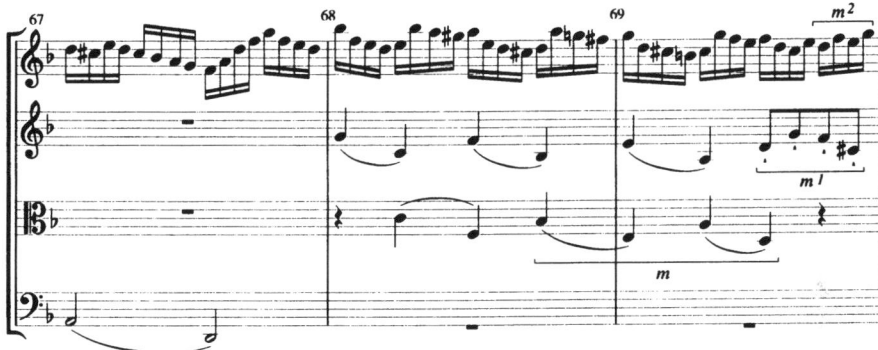

(c) mm. 72–75

to sixteenth (mm. 21–24)—the interlocked thirds of measures 23–24 constituting inversions of the motive, diminished intervallically as well as rhythmically.
In the process, momentum builds to a mid-exposition crisis (mm. 25–26), where
an abrupt return to the half-note pace of the subject combines surface disruption
with an impression of seamless motivic continuity.

   True to Haydn's fondness for schemes of progressive elaboration, the development section generates related designs of still greater complexity and motivic
resourcefulness. In a variant of the logic encountered in the Op. 76/4/i exposition, the new section begins with an inversion of both texture and subject: a pair

of rising fifths in the cello, accompanied from above. Multiple reiterations of the falling-fifth idea in half notes dominate much of the action in the nine measures that follow (mm. 59–67), and the stage is thus set for an extraordinarily dense span of elaboration (see ex. 16.7b): the inner parts take up the two-note figure, treating it to canonic imitation in diminution (m. 68); and in the middle of measure 69, the moment at which the canon dissolves coincides with the sounding of motivic derivations on each of the smaller levels of diminution simultaneously— eighth notes in the second violin, sixteenths in the top part.

Meanwhile, we find that derivatives of the subject have traversed the sonic spectrum from low cello (m. 67) to first violin (end of m. 69), while simultaneously a series of progressively smaller diminutions in surface rhythm has followed the same path through the instruments, from half notes (cello) to quarters (inner parts), and then eighths and sixteenths in second and first violins respectively. In the latter phases of the process, increasing rhythmic diminution coincides with shrinking interval size—from the inner parts' fifths in quarter notes, to the second violin's fourth and diminished fourth in eighths, to the first violin's still faster-paced major and minor thirds in sixteenths (end of m. 69 through m. 70). Then, at measure 72, close to the very heart of this 154-measure form, the accumulated energy of overlapping motivic layers climaxes in a passage of close imitation that saturates the texture with recollections of the opening motive in half notes (ex. 16.7c).

Issues of Cyclic Integration

The concentration of formal novelty, motivic intrigue, and harmonic daring in Op. 76 naturally gives rise to questions of cyclic profile: To what extent do a movement's unsettling deviations from structural or stylistic norms compensate by nurturing intermovement relationships or other unifying forces? Although the evidence varies from one work to another, there appear to be sufficient signs of cyclic cohesion—if not outright unity or structural integration—for us to consider this factor as part of the opus group's character.

The case for integration in Op. 76/6, for example—easily one of the most peculiar cycles in the repertory, with radically nonstandard elements in three of its movements—would seem to be particularly elusive. As in Op. 76/5, the slow movement comes on the heels of an unusual, end-weighted form and likewise stands apart by virtue of an unaccountably remote key—to which is now added the novelty of startling shifts in tonal focus and an utterly unpredictable form. Nothing about the preceding movement, with its staid adherence to the tonic key and its close relatives, could be said to foreshadow this turn of events—nothing, that is, except for its insistent recurrences of the foreign note C♭ as an enigmatic, passing detail of the opening movement's theme. First heard in the cello just before the cadence in measure 8, it recurs as a melodic inflection in the first violin in the course of the second reprise (mm. 24–25). In this guise, it insinuates itself in each of the theme's variations, and it turns out to be the last accidental heard prior to the end of the movement (mm. 209–10). The sound of B major (C♭ enharmonically respelled) has thus been slyly prepared by the time the Fantasia gets under way, and a point of connection between the two seemingly disparate movements has therefore been drawn. But another palpable source of integration may be considered as well, one that embraces the entire cycle: an obstinate and (for Haydn) unusual preoccupation with melodic repetition.[27] Manifestations include the first-movement theme's recurrences as a cantus firmus, the unadorned restatements in different keys that mark the first part of the Fantasia, the hypnotically repetitive descending and ascending scales of the third-movement Alternativo, and in the finale the nearly literal, subdominant transposition of the primary theme's opening measures, which form a structural milestone in the latter part of the development section.

Evidence of cyclic coherence proves more abundant in the first three quartets of the series, with their dramas of transformation from minor to major. In Op. 76/2, as in previous single-tonic quartets, modal play stands out as an all-encompassing cyclic theme, though the first-movement emphasis on learned-style severity and *Sturm und Drang* theatrics keeps the tonic major out of the picture. D major eventually materializes as a quiet, self-effacing presence in the first section of the ternary Andante but grows into something more formidable in the extended, varied return, energized by torrents of thirty-second notes, rhetorically amplified by harmony-sustaining fermatas, and expanded in its upper range by a whole octave. The dance movement virtually reverses the second movement's modal scheme, giving pride of place to the D minor canonic minuet and relegating D major to the trio. But the latter key gains new strength here, not only by the rough-hewn energy of its D major hammerstrokes (beginning on the upbeat to m. 43), but also by the attainment of the quartet's highest peak, d^4, in the final measure of the trio. The resurgence of D major in the last movement, following the change of key signature at measure 180, recapitulates the dynamic profile of its journey up to this point by starting out quietly, gradually gaining strength, and finally blossoming in full-volume triplet figuration, unison arpeggiation, and multiple-stopped harmony.

In addition to these mode-related phenomena, an intimation of cyclic unity may be gleaned from a certain thematic resemblance between the two otherwise diametrically opposed interior movements: as shown in example 16.8, the idyllic theme of the second movement, which traverses the third and fifth scale degrees (*x* in ex. 16.8a) before falling gracefully through the dominant octave (*y*), is both mirrored and transformed by the minuet's assertive staking out of D minor territory, stepping from first to third degree and back (*x¹* in ex. 16.8b), then thrusting to the tonic note an octave above (*y¹*).

EXAMPLE 16.8 Op. 76/2 (violin 1 only)

(a) ii, mm. 1–2

(b) iii, mm. 1–3

The most elaborate cyclic scheme among these works is doubtless that of the G major quartet, Op. 76/1, in which elements of an overarching narrative may be traced through each movement. The plot begins with the first movement's early juxtaposition of sharply opposed elements: the forceful impact of double- and triple-stopped chords at the outset followed by the comically exaggerated change to a lone, ambling subject in the cello. The play of extremes is rejoined later in the first-movement exposition, where a passage of stormy unison arpeggiation in minor (mm. 56–63) yields to an idyllic sound-picture in major (mm. 73–80): a four-square, folk-like melody (designed as if to express a six-note scale, without a leading tone), accompanied by a gentle, idealized version of a rustic drone.

The second movement bestows a more elevated tone on the theme of contest between rival forces, introducing a hymn-like theme, then yielding to operatic-style delivery after measure 16. A harmonic crisis at measure 28, where G minor momentarily supplants G major, recalls a similar event in the first-movement exposition (m. 54). Restoration of major now takes the form of a brilliant, high-register cadenza that articulates the tones of a G major chord prior to a recurrence of the opening phrase in a well-established dominant key. Modal restlessness and vivid topical contrast resurface in the third movement, whose presto, rounded binary minuet (which takes a brief but emphatic turn toward G minor) envelops a relaxed, countrified trio, complete with pizzicato accompaniment, that recalls the spirit of the first movement's bucolic theme.

The G minor finale, having begun with the troubled unison shown in example 16.9a, makes the expected turn toward Bb, the relative major (m. 18). But the new key will eventually be overridden by a deflection to its own parallel minor (m. 54), and from this remote space yet another key will materialize—Db, the rela-

EXAMPLE 16.9 Op. 76/1/iv (violin 1 only)

(a) mm. 1–6

(b) mm. 139–46

(c) mm. 181–84

tive major of B♭ minor, distant from the home key by a diminished fifth—before a locally more stable B♭ major is recaptured to end the section. The development begins by denying the restoration of B♭ major and reinstating B♭ minor instead, and the pervasive theme of modal opposition now leads further afield: the key of A♭ major, attained at measure 90 as relative major of F minor (which in turn had arisen as the dominant of B♭ minor), is fatally undermined by its parallel minor as early as measure 93. Then, for a span of four haunted, static measures (98–101), poised to hover over the finale's midpoint, Haydn sustains D♭ minor harmony (as iv of A♭ minor), as distant a point as can be imagined from the quartet's tonal center of G major: a diminished fifth away and in the opposite mode. Motion resumes with an enharmonic sleight of hand (notationally foreshadowed by the viola's E in mm. 98–101, which stands for F♭ as the third of the D♭ minor chord) that enables a skip to the sharp side (A major in m. 102, initially perceived as VI of D♭ minor, i.e., B♭♭); and the path is now clear for a sequence of descending fifths that will lead back to G minor for the start of the recapitulation (m. 122).

At this juncture, the dominance of a usurping G minor is once again reaffirmed, but only temporarily: seventeen measures into the recapitulation, a pause on a dominant chord heralds the change of signature to G major (m. 138) and the appearance of a peaceful theme (ex. 16.9b) that transforms the G minor declaration with which the movement had begun—major rather than minor, harmonized rather than unison, soft rather than loud, elevated to a higher register and sounded legato in contrast to the initial lower-range staccato—while nonetheless preserving basic elements of the original rhythm and melodic profile.

With this event the movement has gained a decisive foothold in major, although another modal reversal is in store: the logically ordained return of that secondary theme from the exposition which had moved from B♭ to B♭ minor, and which will now undergo a corresponding switch from G major to G minor. At last, following a half cadence and a full measure's rest (mm. 179–80), the air clears for good with a wondrous sequel to the earlier transformation, a theme that recalls the rustic episodes of the first and third movements while scoring a final multifaceted stroke of reversal (see ex. 16.9c). Surmounting the frightful character of the opening unison by the inviting sound of a simple tune with plucked accompaniment, the new melody not only vitiates dark forces but symbolically embraces them by turning the original figure upside down and changing the harmony from minor to major. Finally, an exalted flourish, triumphantly recalling the first movement's opening chords, brings the quartet to a close.

To understand Haydn's final complete quartet opus as a model of synthesis and culmination—a fully formed embodiment of the composer's will to innovate as well as revisit and reinvent—is certainly tempting. Could there have been a deliberate plan to have the fruits of past accomplishments pass in review, interwoven with fresh exploration? Perhaps the composer had nothing more special in mind than casting an unusually wide net, capitalizing on the popularity of previous works by absorbing elements of their style, and leading his admirers to higher realms of sophistication while at the same time creating works that could be rendered convincingly on the concert stage as well as in a more intimate setting. This seems a plausible explanation, and it furnishes a suitable premise for appreciating Haydn's valedictory accomplishment in the medium, the two complete quartets published as Op. 77, and the two movements ultimately printed as Op. 103.

17

Op. 77 (1799) and Op. 103
([?1802–] 1803)

In early spring 1799, following the public premiere of *The Creation* in Vienna, readers of the Leipzig *Allgemeine musikalische Zeitung* would have had occasion to learn not only that Haydn had embarked on a new oratorio, *The Seasons*, but also that he was engaged in writing a set of six quartets "for the Hungarian Count K."[1] That the journal's correspondent deemed the latter item newsworthy is in itself a telling reflection of the public interest that now attached to the medium and its preeminent master. Yet how much time Haydn was able to devote to the new commission is questionable, given the obligations and commitments with which he was currently saddled.[2]

During the course of the year, Haydn did manage to complete two of the promised six quartets, as we know from the autographs, both dated 1799.[3] Under circumstances that are not clear, work on the commission then stalled, and there appears to be no documented reference to the project on anyone's part for a long time thereafter.[4] Not until the summer of 1801, well after the completion of *The Seasons* (premiered that April) does the matter arise as a topic of concern. In a letter to Härtel of 4 July, Griesinger, whose correspondence with the Leipzig publisher makes frequent mention of the composer's activities and plans, helpfully identifies the patron (the anonymous "Count K.") who had commissioned the quartets: Prince Lobkowitz, a member of the *Gesellschaft der Associirten*, which under the leadership of Gottfried van Swieten had sponsored the late oratorios' first performances; and several weeks later, on 24 July, he claims that four have been completed.[5] Another document from this time, Hoffmeister's letter of 11 July to Ambrosius Kühnel,[6] paints a more sober picture by reporting, correctly, that Haydn had finished just two of the quartets. Hoffmeister then specifies the composer's intention to supply two more works in one and a half years and the remaining two in three years. Three years! It is true that there were competing projects, including the never-to-be-realized fulfillment of a promise made several years earlier to Count Moritz von Fries (1777–1826) for a set of quintets. Nonetheless, this would seem to be a long time to allocate for the quartets' completion.

Whether or not they were willing to confront the fact, friends and close associates must have known by now that all was not right with Haydn. The composer himself had confessed as much in a painfully sad letter that accompanied the score to *The Creation*, sent to Breitkopf & Härtel more than two years earlier, in which he complained of weakened memory, nervous exhaustion, and consequent bouts of deep depression.[7]

Haydn himself apparently clung for a time to the hope of finishing the commission. This may be inferred from a report of Griesinger's in January 1802, which explains that although Haydn had wanted to wait until all six quartets were finished before proceeding with publication, he had agreed to have the two completed ones printed.[8] In March of that year, Griesinger mentions a modification of this plan: Artaria will wait until a third quartet is completed.[9] This goal proved untenable, however, and Haydn consented after all to having the two completed quartets published as a pair. They were issued as such by Artaria in September of that year (advertised on 11 September) and published shortly afterward by Breitkopf & Härtel (advertised on 6 October), in accordance with a prior agreement between the two firms.[10] Both editions bore the opus number 77 and a dedication to Prince Lobkowitz.

The larger project, although not abandoned, continued to languish. References in Griesinger's correspondence indicate that a third quartet was at least on the composer's mind during the autumn of 1802,[11] but a fragmentary draft of a letter from Haydn to his brother, dated 22 January 1803, confesses that for the past five months he has been unable to accomplish anything.[12] Griesinger, for his part, continued to make sporadic mention of the quartet as a work in progress but was not able to report much in the way of concrete results.[13] We find him striking a vaguely optimistic tone in writing to Härtel at the start of the next year (4 January 1804): "At present he is working in good moments on quartets." Later that month (25 January), he actually asserts that Haydn "is finished with the Allegro, an Andante and variations, and the Minuet and Trio of his quartet; only another Allegro is wanting."[14] Sketches survive that evidently represent plans for both outer movements,[15] but this was clearly too sanguine an account, and in fact Griesinger revised this claim in a letter from 22 August of that year, acknowledging that there were only two completed movements. A year later, on 21 August 1805, he conceded that "his shell, alas, continues to get more fragile and every little raw breeze annoys him. He has given up hope of being able to complete the quartet he has begun."[16] The work was thus destined to remain a fragment, comprising merely a pair of interior movements completed in 1803.[17] Finally, in 1806, this last major effort of Haydn's was issued as a two-movement entity: on 28 March, Haydn granted Breitkopf & Härtel exclusive rights to the work,[18] which was to be dedicated to Count Fries,[19] and Griesinger forwarded the autograph score to the firm on 2 April. The edition appeared some six months later, and an advertisement in the *Allgemeine musikalische Zeitung* (15 October) made note of the composer's request that this piece be known as his swan song, his last farewell.[20]

Meanwhile, a bargain was struck with Pleyel, who was eager to be the first to issue the quartet in Paris, and whose edition, advertised as early as 12 September, evidently preceded Breitkopf & Härtel's. Another early print seemingly based, like Pleyel's, on a copy of the autograph, was that of Clementi's firm in London, issued by the end of 1806 or thereabouts.[21] Curiously, Artaria's print did not appear until well into the next year (advertised on 27 May 1807). Its particular significance resides in its title page: omitting the dedication to Fries, it identifies the work as "3.me et Dernier Quatuor [3rd and Last Quartet] . . . Oeuvre 77,"[22] thus confirming the work's true origin as one of the quartets for Lobkowitz. As for the opus number 103, this designation appears to have originated with the edition by André in Offenbach.[23]

$\sim$

These last quartets form a complex and multifaceted sequel to Op. 76. Readily measuring up to Haydn's own standards for the genre, the two quartets of Op. 77 resemble their immediate predecessors with respect to size, richness of invention, and expressive range, and the two movements of Op. 103 are comparably impressive. Any attempt to characterize the works as a group is obviously hampered by the set's incompletion, and the true scope of what Haydn was planning remains unknowable. But is it possible to hazard a guess about the direction in which he was headed? The accelerated pace of the minuets and the choice of remote keys for interior portions of the cycle indicate an effort to expand on featured traits of the two previous groups (see table 17.1). But in other respects there are signs of retrenchment and consolidation. The outer movements of the Op. 77 quartets are all cast as relatively transparent (if not always predictable) sonata forms; the slow movements of all three quartets are based on tried-and-true models (sonata, strophic variation, and ternary form); and the dance movements, though hardly deficient in novelty, conform to Haydn's existing, flexible norms with respect to overall size, proportion, and rounded binary procedure within both minuet and trio. By comparison with either Opp. 71/74 or 76, there are fewer passages of loud, dense texture; and at the other end of the sonic spectrum, there is no recourse to the transparency of pizzicato accompaniment. With respect to harmonic action within movements, there are no tonal adventures quite so radical or diverse as those of the Op. 76/6 Fantasia or the Op. 76/1 finale. Curiously, given the incorporation of fugue-related passages in each of the past several opus groups, Haydn now chooses to bypass the topic of fugal polyphony altogether.

The absence of fugal procedure may be read as one of several signs of an altered concept of movement design in these last quartets, one that tends to avoid the kinds of dramatized, end-weighted forms encountered in Op. 76 in favor of

TABLE 17.1 Summary statistics for Opp. 77 and 103

Op.No.	Hob.No.	Movement			
		i	ii	iii	iv
77/1	III:81	G ¢ Allegro moderato SF 189	E♭ ¢ Adagio SF 90	G/E♭ $\frac{3}{4}$ Presto M/T 81(r)/100(r)	G $\frac{2}{4}$ Presto SF 282
77/2	III:82	F ¢ Allegro moderato SF 172	F/D♭ $\frac{3}{4}$ Presto M/T/Coda* 78/40/9	D $\frac{2}{4}$ Andante Strophic var. 129	F $\frac{3}{4}$ Vivace assai SF 195
103	III:83	B♭ $\frac{2}{4}$ Andante grazioso Ternary 112	Dm/D $\frac{3}{4}$ Menuet ma non troppo presto M/T 46/40		

*Coda = transition.

relatively balanced, more nearly symmetrical structures, as in the ternary slow movement of Op. 103, with its straightforward, undecorated return. One partial exception must be noted, however: in the finale to Op. 77/2, Haydn interrupts an otherwise unproblematic recapitulation with a tongue-in-cheek parody of a rhetorical climax (mm. 155–71). The interpolated passage begins as a span of intensified elaboration, but progress comes to a standstill in measure 166 on dominant seventh harmony. A moment of silence clears the air, and the first violin reenters with a melodic figure that recalls Papageno's panpipes in Mozart's *Die Zauberflöte* (ex. 17.1). Meanwhile, the cello, as if unable to resist a chance for low comedy, mutters asides from below—far below, so that a chasm of more than four octaves yawns between the two dialoguing parts. Here the composer appears to be spoofing several of his own favored conventions in a single stroke: the (sometimes profoundly serious) dialogue between outer parts, the daring thrust to a high peak, and the inflated rhetoric of interpolation within the course of a final section.

Contrary to the lightminded character of this initial example, many other passages may be cited as evidence of extraordinary technical ingenuity, relational complexity, and Haydnesque wit at its most sophisticated. The opening measures of Op. 77/2/i furnish a concise example (quoted as ex. 17.2). The opening statement appears to comprise a pair of four-measure phrases. Or does it? It is true that a full close underlies the first violin's descent to F in measure 4, but the upward-turning figure that lays claim to this measure is more than a mere embellishment to the phrase ending. A variant of the bracketed three-note idea first sounded in measure 2, elaborated in measure 5, spun out further in the form of a rhythmically diminished, rising sequence in measure 6, then sounded again to complete the octave in measure 7, it constitutes a generative cell in its own right, proving in retrospect to have been the start of a new line of thought. The span in question (mm. 1–8) may be parsed in several different ways accordingly: 4 + 4, with measure 4 anticipating the motivic thrust of an intensified answering phrase; 3 + 5,

EXAMPLE 17.1 Op. 77/2/iv, mm. 167–71

EXAMPLE 17.2 Op. 77/2/i, mm. 1–8 (violin 1 only)

with an elision at measure 4 to mark the start of a new, extended phrase; or even 5 + 3, by which measure 5 marks the end of a sprawling opening phrase, followed by a relatively pithy response that recalls the initial scalar descent and triadic figure in reverse order as it rushes to complete the sentence by measure 8. Taken together, these multiple interpretations highlight the theme's elusive quality of friction between balanced and disruptive forces, and hence its suitability as the start to a complex musical narrative.

Op. 77/1 and 2: A Comparative Overview

Notwithstanding general similarities in style and procedure, the two complete works represent divergent paths within Haydn's string quartet idiom: an extroverted manner in Op. 77/1, marked by vivid contrast within and between movements, as opposed to a more private, nuanced chamber style in Op. 77/2. Op. 77/1, like several of its G major predecessors, most notably Op. 54/1, leans toward concert-style energy and brilliance. The opening movement's alla breve time signature and beat-marking pulse furnish the metrical basis for a scheme in which swaths of triplet-eighth figuration dominate the action between variants of a more deliberately paced, march-like theme and its derivatives. Moving to a very different terrain, the Adagio transpires in a solemn E♭ major and proceeds to highlight the first violin as an ardent solo voice, with extravagant passagework, chromatically inflected melodic gestures, and a climb to b♭^{3} (m. 28), the quartet's highest peak so far. The first violin maintains its prominence in the minuet (marked presto), with waves of eighth-note figuration and ecstatic, register-crossing leaps, including the widest of all to be found among the quartets, from d^4 in measures 75–77 to the open G string on the downbeat of measure 78. The trio provides only partial relief with its brittle melodic line and urgent quarter-note pulse, periodically intensified by a shudder of repeated eighths. The finale sustains the minuet's spirit of temporal overdrive and technical showmanship with the help of its own presto tempo marking, a vigorous eighth-note pulse within the $\frac{2}{4}$ measure, and virtually unimpeded surface activity. Added to these familiar last-movement traits is the impetus of propulsive unisons, angular melodic lines with metrically unsettling leaps, fast-moving dialogue, and soloistic fireworks in the first violin.

Op. 77/2, generally less brilliant and more inclined to distribute thematic material among the ensemble's voices, begins with a movement that actually shares its counterpart's meter and tempo marking. The temporal framework proves altogether different, however: rather than anything comparable to the G major quartet's streamlined apparatus of quarter-note pulse and airborne triplet eighths, this opening movement displays a dense rhythmic fabric with multiple strata of activity and an accent on thematic detail, decoration, and motivic development. Haydn further differentiates the work from its neighbor by placing the dance movement second, thereby reviving a practice last witnessed on two occasions in Op. 64 (Nos. 1 and 4). In this instance, a fast-paced, antic minuet offers comic relief from the first movement's attention-absorbing detail while at the same time confronting us with complexities of its own, mostly involving repetitive, two-beat figures whose insistent presence results in an almost constant tug of war between the notated meter and a contrary duple impulse.

A mellow, distant-key trio temporarily resolves the metrical dilemma in favor of a thoroughly regular $\frac{3}{4}$, whereas duple meter comes truly into its own with the stately $\frac{2}{4}$ time of the variation-based third movement. Here an accent on decorative detail enhances the prevailing chamber-music atmosphere, notwithstanding the first violin's brilliant figural display that dominates the second variation (mm. 74–104). Conversational exchange and textural nuance are especially pronounced in the developmental episode of measures 59–73 (between the first and second variations), where all parts engage in spinning a web of thematic fragments and derivations.

The persistence of a chamber-music spirit in the finale owes much to the movement's syncopations and other rhythmic complexities, factors that help train our attention on details within the phrase. The rare choice of $\frac{3}{4}$ time itself (anticipated, to be sure, by the last quartet of Op. 76) is a willful departure from the presto duple-meter convention, and the showcasing of topical color—the recurrent polonaise pattern and its accompanying rough-hewn drone—completes the picture of stylistic opposition to the outwardly more conventional, public façade of Op. 77/1.

Remote Tonal Relationships

By stepping outside the circle of closest relationships to tonic for both their slow movements and dance movement trios, the Op. 77 quartets draw on tendencies witnessed in Op. 71/74 (remote-key trios in Op. 74/1 and 2; remote slow movement in Op. 74/3) and Op. 76 (distant slow movements in Nos. 5 and 6). But only once before, and in a different genre, had Haydn chosen remote keys for both slow movement and trio (Symphony No. 99 in E♭, with the former in G and the latter in C).[24] Impressions of tonal discontinuity are accentuated in both of the new quartets by the fact that the interior foreign keys materialize with so little warning. From this perspective, the startling first measure of the F major quartet's finale seems almost like an act of desperation: a loud tonic chord, sustained for two beats, then cleanly separated from the exposition that follows, with the apparent purpose of eradicating the previous movement's foreign tonality and reinstating the home key in a single stroke.

Tonal usage in Op. 77/1 is distinguished by the single-minded focus on the lowered submediant as a contrasting center, and also by the special way in which this key is showcased in the dance-movement trio. It has been noted that among G major movements in works by Haydn, Mozart, and Beethoven, E♭ harmony sometimes stands out with great prominence as a surprise substitute for tonic at a crucially important cadence late in the form (as in the first-movement recapitulation of Op. 33/5, m. 272).[25] Dramatized V to ♭VI progressions are scarcely the exclusive property of this key; yet something about G major specially invites their occurrence, and the abrupt but seamless shift from G to E♭ in the Op. 77/1 dance movement may be heard as an overblown extension of this phenomenon: a second ending to the minuet elides with the start of the trio by substituting a deceptive resolution (V[7] to ♭VI) for the standard full close, and Haydn now prolongs the new harmony as an elevated tonal plateau until the eventual appearance of the note C♯ turns the provisional tonic E♭ into an augmented sixth chord (E♭–G–B♭–C♯), thereby obliging it to resolve to D (m. 174) as V of G in preparation for the return. The relationship between the dance's two segments is thus transformed. Rather than constituting a separate formal unit, the trio is configured as an interpolated tonal digression within the frame of the minuet proper. Ironically, then, the shift to ♭VI arises as both a disruption—a tonal surprise—and a source of cohesion in which the trio is tightly bound to the minuet as part of a single tonal arch. By extension, the choice of E♭ for the second movement may be understood as a further promotion of the lowered submediant: a higher-level endorsement of this privileged relationship within the sphere of G major.

The Logic of Symmetry and Balanced Proportions

In relinquishing the evolving narratives of Op. 76, with their extended returns, fugal apotheoses, minor-to-major transformations, and the like, the last quartets gravitate not only to relatively simple models of symmetry, as in the slow movement of Op. 103, but also to more complex schemes of opposition, parallelism, or pivotal change. In Op. 77/1/i, for example, an elision at measure 27 designates both a mid-exposition arrival in the dominant and the start of a secondary theme that begins as a variant of the opening idea, with the texture now turned upside down: the principal line passes from first violin to cello, and the inner-voice accompaniment is heard above.

The plan thus far resembles that of Op. 76/4/i, with its mid-exposition inversion of texture. But the play of opposing elements has only begun: it resumes just after the start of the development section, where the tonal center shifts abruptly from the dominant to the subdominant, a diametrically opposed tonal center and the point of departure for a developed statement of the primary theme. The modulatory action that follows parallels the tonal direction of the exposition, and we land at measure 87, not quite halfway through the movement, right back in the key of G major. What happens now might be perceived as a species of false recapitulation, although the theme heard here is a recollection not of the movement's opening idea but its texturally inverted relative (i.e., its secondary theme version). Modulatory action now continues, and the rightful primary theme is eventually reunited with tonic to initiate the recapitulation (m. 128). Logically enough, this final section will avoid the redundancy of restating an already recapitulated secondary theme.[26]

If the first-movement design of Op. 77/1 may be said to turn mainly within a tight circle of close relationships in which the home key itself passes close to the very heart of the form, then the opening movement of Op. 77/2 attains the virtual opposite: an adventurous tonal scheme whose path leads to a mystified corner of the tonal landscape, just beyond the movement's midpoint, in what surely counts as one of the most precarious, suspenseful moments in the repertory.

The motivic vehicle for this tour de force derives from a transitional figure first sounded by the second violin in measures 20–21 (bracketed in ex. 17.3a). References to this idea resurface early in the development (mm. 70–71, shown in ex. 17.3b), and they become increasingly insistent. By measure 84, a condensed version of the motive takes hold as an all-consuming preoccupation (ex. 17.3c). Incessant reiterations of the figure reach an impasse as the violins echo the lower parts' statement on E♭ (mm. 92–93, quoted in ex. 17.3d), heard here as the dominant of A♭ minor. A discreet yet momentous change now comes about through the magic of enharmonic notation. As Haydn took care to specify in his score, the respelled pitch on the upbeat to measure 94 (D♯) must sound the same as the preceding E♭ ("l'istesso tuono"); but differences in rhythm and articulation signal a change in tonal complexion—actually a reversal of relationship between the two alternating pitches. The lower pitch, freshly energized by eighth-note activity in measures 94–95, no longer conveys the inertia of a locally stable point of reference (as did the previous E♭). Instead, it has become a powerfully directed leading tone (D♯), alternately drawn to and deflected from the upper note, now spelled E, whose altered significance solves the tonal dilemma: rather than a

EXAMPLE 17.3 Op. 77/2/i

(a) mm. 20–21 (violin 2 only)

(b) mm. 70–71 (violin 1 only)

(c) m. 84 (violin 1 only)

(d) mm. 91–95

hovering, inflected appoggiatura, it now constitutes a local, metrically accentuated tonic whose appearance marks the start of a path to the recapitulation. Meanwhile, tonal transformation is duly ratified by the harmonizing entry of other parts in measure 95, where stability of pitch must be ensured by having the first violin play on the open A string ("das leere A"), as Haydn instructs in the autograph manuscript.[27]

The Incomplete Op. 103

"Gone is all my strength; old and weak am I." The song quotation that the ailing composer chose for his visiting card was a sad acknowledgment of advancing frailty. Affixed to the print of Haydn's very last quartet, it stood as a touching reminder of the reason for the work's incomplete state, and its message seems especially painful in light of the undiminished mastery that informs the two finished movements.

In setting out to write this work in D minor—a favored minor key, shared by Opp. 9/4, 42, and 76/2—Haydn was obviously not content to inscribe his impending loss of mental and physical powers on a composition of modest proportions and technical means. Rather, he seemed intent on defying the ravages of age and illness by equaling and even exceeding his previous accomplishments.

The Andante grazioso, cast in Bb major, stands out as the longest of the quartets' ternary slow movements, purely in terms of measure count, and its middle section proves uniquely bold harmonically: extending Haydn's normal reach from the start, this portion of the form begins not in the parallel minor of Bb but in that key's submediant, Gb. After a modulation to the dominant (Db), the developmental action that follows experiences a drastic change in tonal orientation, although not one that is immediately apparent to listeners without score in hand: the darkening of the harmony to Db minor turns out in retrospect, through the chasm-crossing power of enharmonic respelling, to have accomplished a jump to the sharp side of the tonal spectrum (C♯ minor). This becomes the start of a modulatory route that will end up on the dominant of the relative minor (G minor) just before the principal section returns. Early in this process, a phrase that straddles the midpoint of the movement presents a full-voiced thematic statement in E major, locally the relative major of C♯ minor but significant from a larger perspective as a polar opposite, remote by a diminished fifth from the movement's home key.[28]

The Op. 103 minuet, marked "ma non troppo presto," proves altogether different in tone from the scherzo-like manner of the Op. 77 dance movements. A model of *Sturm und Drang* theatrics, it highlights an array of unsettling forces: offbeat accents, forzato exclamations, diminished seventh chords, chromatically inflected counterpoint, extended phrases suffused with dissonant harmony, a gasping general pause, and a startling climax of rhythm, line, and dynamics right before the close, where the first violin's three-octave plunge from a^3 prefaces the stepwise surge to a peak of d^3 (quoted in ex. 17.4a).

Some of these features hark back to a much earlier minuet, that of Op. 9/4/ii, also in D minor and likewise bent on transcending customary dance manners in favor of dramatic intensity. In both cases, minor harmony prevails with special tenacity, the first reprise ending in the dominant minor rather than the relative major. Similar, too, although not unusual for a minuet in minor, is the trio's change to a gentler manner in the parallel major. (An additional affinity between Opp. 103 and 9/4, and Op. 42 as well, may be recognized in the choice of the submediant, Bb, for the slow movement.)

The minuet's closing fortissimo outburst presents something of a puzzle. Its intensity seems oversized, even for this stormy context; and by its very promi-

EXAMPLE 17.4 Op. 103

(a) ii, mm. 44–46

(b) i, mm. 109–12

nence, it calls to mind a no less stunning gesture at the end of the preceding movement, shown in example 17.4b. Here the shock is even greater in light of the even-tempered character of that movement's outer sections—not to mention the divergence from Haydn's more common tendency to descend toward the close of his slow movements and end softly: the first violin's fortissimo g^3 on the downbeat of measure 111 is the movement's highest pitch, and (apart from the second violin's open D and A strings in mm. 69–70) the final measures display the movement's only multiple-stopped chords.

What could Haydn have been striving for with such intensity? It seems significant that the second of these two exaggerated, rising gestures complements the first in several specific ways: a scalar ascent versus rising arpeggiations; slurred versus staccato articulation; concentration on the first violin versus sonority distributed among lower and upper parts; and a backdrop of dominant harmony within a minor key versus a precadential swath of the subdominant in major. These correspondences and antitheses impose a degree of interrelatedness between the two movements, perhaps enhancing their credibility as members of a freestanding, two-movement entity. At the same time, the very fact that both movements end with such powerful, inexplicably marked events points up the missing context that the outer movements would have provided. Assuming a first movement and finale that measured up to the dynamism of the two inner portions, it would appear that Haydn had something particularly formidable in mind, perhaps a bold demonstration of undiminished strength—to himself and to the world at large—even as he faced imminent collapse from inside.[29]

~

As a consequence of the afflictions that darkened the last years of Haydn's career, Lobkowitz had to make do with an unfinished commission, Haydn's publishers were denied the satisfaction of even a half set of completed works to issue, and Griesinger was left with unfulfilled promises. Might it also be said that the oeuvre was deprived of a crowning masterpiece? That there was a genuine oeuvre in question—not merely an extant profusion of manuscript copies and printed editions, but a comprehensive legacy to be revered—is attested by Pleyel's publication of the *Collection complette,* whose first, 1801 edition represented virtually all the quartets, and then some, through Op. 76. To undertake such a project was to celebrate this body of works as an epochal accomplishment and thus to enhance its biographical, artistic, and cultural resonance. The dedication to Napoleon only confirmed the monumentality of Pleyel's enterprise.

Doubtless there were reasons enough to go ahead with the edition—the dawn of a new century, accumulating evidence that the master's career was drawing to a close—despite the fact that the *Collection complette* was still manifestly incomplete, lacking the two quartets of Op. 77 and whatever new compositions might still be coaxed from Haydn's pen. Although Op. 77 and the unfinished Op. 103 would eventually be added to subsequent editions, for the time being both the *Collection* and the Lobkowitz commission were works in progress.

The temporary absence of Op. 77 notwithstanding, Pleyel's edition served an important practical purpose in offering fresh access to works not readily available otherwise. (In accordance with standard practices of the time, it consisted of separate performing parts, not scores.) But how satisfactory were such parts for gaining access to the inner workings of Haydn's compositional technique? Could an admiring connoisseur readily enjoy the satisfaction of deep understanding without actually being able to see the interaction of musical lines on a page? Evidently in response to a demand for this privilege, Pleyel conceived the novel idea of printing works by Haydn as pocket scores, to be read while listening or else pondered at leisure. Word of the public's enthusiasm for the concept apparently reached Haydn through the Berlin composer Friedrich Heinrich Himmel (1765–1814), who was in Vienna in the autumn of 1802, following travels to London and Paris, and who presented Haydn with copies of several of Pleyel's recently issued scores (three quartets and one symphony). Reportedly, amateurs and connoisseurs in the French capital carried the quartet scores about and read them during performances. "One can't imagine anything more beautiful and elegant," Haydn later exclaimed in a letter to the publisher. "Heaven reward you for your pains!"[30]

Haydn's letter to Pleyel also mentioned the complete edition in parts, and here his words betray not only gratitude but also a keen awareness of his own exalted stature: referring to the edition's appearance, Haydn declares that Pleyel "will be remembered for them forever." Even more intriguing is a remark that Griesinger reported to Härtel in November of the preceding year: "Haydn is very pleased with it [the edition] not only because of the beautiful paper and print, but because one would be able to observe his gradual progress in the art [stufenweises Fortschreiten in der Kunst] through the apt [chronological] arrangement."[31] The quartets were thus understood by Haydn himself as both an enduring object of veneration and a window on the secrets of his craft. His acknowledgment of this circumstance would seem to sanction (or at least anticipate) an enterprise such as ours, and yet it need not be read as license to search for the path to an artistic pinnacle or to designate a point of final stylistic maturity. As Griesinger wrote to Härtel in the spring of 1806, in connection with plans for the publication of Op. 103, the art of music knew no boundaries, and the composer saw that "what could yet be accomplished in music was far greater than what has been achieved so far. Ideas often come to him by which his art might be much further advanced, but his physical limitations do not allow him to proceed with their realization."[32]

Viewed in this light, might Haydn's final effort be regarded not as a valedictory masterpiece in the making, but simply part of an ongoing exploration of the genre's potentials with no particular destination in sight? If so, then perhaps we could extend this line of thought by drawing an analogy between Haydn's "Fortschreiten in der Kunst" and the relentless thematic process that often informs his individual quartet movements, sometimes with a will that vitally resists the forces of closure.[33] Like his penchant for open-ended development in the unfolding of a musical idea, Haydn's lifelong endeavor as a composer of string quartets readily conveys the impression of unlimited possibility. In attempting to address both aspects of this phenomenon, surveying the repertory in its entirety as well as probing the mechanisms of individual works, we have admittedly just scratched the surface of a boundlessly complex topic. But in doing so we hope to have at least been able to illuminate something of the quartets' technical foundations and to point the way to further understanding of their significance.

Notes

Introduction

    1. Koch, *Musikalisches Lexikon*, 1210.

    2. Particularly significant in this regard are the views argued by Webster in "Haydns Opus 9 und Opus 17"; "Eighteenth Century"; and *"Farewell" Symphony*, 335–66.

Chapter 1

    1. Gotwals, *Two Contemporary Portraits*, 9–10 (Griesinger, *Biographische Notizen*, 8–10).

    2. Translated in Landon, *Chronicle and Works*, 2:397–99 (Bartha, *Briefe*, 76–78). The sketch, in the form of a letter, was supplied by Haydn for the publication *Das gelehrte Oesterreich*.

    3. Griesinger, using a musical incipit, identifies this quartet as the work that came to be known as Op. 1/1, but there is no evidence to support his choice. For Griesinger's account, see Gotwals, *Two Contemporary Portraits*, 13 (Griesinger, *Biographische Notizen*, 13).

    4. Johann Georg Albrechtsberger (1736–1809). The brother in question was Anton Johann, born in 1729. See Landon, *Chronicle and Works*, 1:228–30.

    5. See Webster and Feder, *New Grove Haydn*, 9, which proposes a range of ca. 1755–60; see also Feder, *Haydns Streichquartette*, 26.

    6. In "Towards a History," 228, Webster suggests that the existence of Bohemian manuscripts for the Richter quartets indicates that they may possibly date from before the composer's move to Mannheim in 1747.

    7. The contract, dated 1 May 1761, is given in translation in Landon, *Chronicle and Works*, 1:350–52 (Bartha, *Briefe*, 41–44).

    8. Parker, *String Quartet*, 235–38; Heartz, *Music in European Capitals*, 969–71.

    9. Heartz, *Viennese School*, 474; Brown, "Preface," viii.

    10. Hickman, "Nascent Viennese String Quartet," 199.

    11. Monk, "Introduction," vii–viii. For additional commentary on Asplmayr's Op. 2, see Krummacher, "Haydn—Gründer des Streichquartetts?" 24–27.

    12. On the temporary change in Haydn's compositional activity, see Webster, "Chronology," 34.

13. Heartz, *Viennese School*, 324. For more on the question of why Haydn resumed string quartet production at this juncture, see Webster, "Chronology," 30, and Somfai, "Haydn's String Quartet Autographs," 6.

14. For relevant discussion of the composers and their works, see Levy, "*Quatuor Concertant*" (a summary of musical sources is given on pp. 397–403), and Parker, *String Quartet* (esp. 127–78). With respect to raw quantity, Levy counts some two hundred composers whose works appeared in the Parisian market during the final three decades of the eighteenth century (7).

15. The new contract is translated in Landon, *Chronicle and Works*, 2:42–43 (Bartha, *Briefe*, 83–84).

16. Haydn used the phrase, and variants thereof, in correspondence with Johann Caspar Lavater (3 December 1781) and other potential subscribers.

17. See, for example, Blume, "Haydns künstlerische Persönlichkeit," 543–47, and Finscher, *Studien*, 266–69. Finscher identifies Op. 33 as "*the* epoch-making work in which the string quartet achieved its first classical realization" (Webster's translation in "*Farewell*" *Symphony*, 345). Parker provides a useful overview of scholarly positions on the significance of Op. 33 in *String Quartet*, 1–6.

18. Walter, "Zum Wiener Streichquartett," 301–5. Walter proposes that Hoffmeister's publication of Mozart's String Quartet in D, K. 499, may have been part of the same initiative.

19. Landon, *Chronicle and Works*, 2:490 (Bartha, *Briefe*, 136). On the larger question of the dissemination of Haydn's music in Spain, see Feder, "Manuscript Sources," 133–34; Solar-Quintes, "Las relaciones"; and Landon, *Chronicle and Works*, 2:588–90.

20. According to Michael Kelly's *Reminiscences*, cited in Landon, *Chronicle and Works*, 2:491.

21. Anderson, *Letters of Mozart*, 2:891 (Bauer and Deutsch, *Mozart: Briefe*, 3:404). For perspectives on Haydn's Op. 33 as an inspiration for the Mozart quartets, see Cherbuliez, "Bemerkungen"; Blume, "Haydn und Mozart"; LaRue, "Haydn-Dedication Quartets"; and Bonds, "Sincerest Form of Flattery?"

22. See the description of the manuscripts and the summary of Mozart's textual revisions in John Irving, *Mozart: The "Haydn" Quartets*, 14–18.

23. Walter, "Zum Wiener Streichquartett," 305.

24. See Walter, "Zum Wiener Streichquartett," 308, 311–12.

25. Translated from Feder and Saslav, *Kritischer Bericht*, 14. Hickman gives the advertisement's date as 19 February 1791 ("Flowering of the Viennese String Quartet," 160n5).

26. Landon, *Chronicle and Works*, 2:737, 741, 745 (Bartha, *Briefe*, 228, 235–36). The addressee was the wife of the physician Peter Leopold von Genzinger.

27. See the account in Landon, *Chronicle and Works*, 2:748–56. See also Jones, *Oxford Composer Companions: Haydn*, 351.

28. Woodfield, "Bland," 234–35, 239. See also Landon, *Chronicle and Works*, 2:751–52.

29. For discussion of the phenomenon of "concert character" in Op. 71/74, see Somfai, "London Revision."

30. See Webster and Feder, *New Grove Haydn*, 38, 124–25.

31. Hickman cites a total of close to two hundred quartets brought out by Viennese composers between 1788 and 1800 ("Flowering of the Viennese String Quartet," 157).

32. Hickman, "Flowering of the Viennese String Quartet," 158–72; Parker, *String Quartet*, 52–54.

33. Sigismund Neukomm, for example, lists forty-six of these settings in a catalogue of his own works, and to Fredrik Samuel Silverstolpe he allegedly claimed some seventy. See Angermüller, "Neukomm und seine Lehrer," 39, and Mörner, *Wikmanson*, 404.

34. Landon, *Chronicle and Works*, 4:468 (Bartha, *Briefe*, 319–20).

35. Gotwals, *Two Contemporary Portraits*, 40 (Griesinger, *Biographische Notizen*, 39).

36. Landon, *Chronicle and Works*, 5:344 (Biba, *Eben komme ich von Haydn*, 247–48). In nearly all references to Griesinger's letters, we cite Biba's edition as the source for the German texts; Landon's translations are based on Olleson's earlier, less inclusive edition.

37. Griesinger's letter incorrectly identifies the poet as Gellert.

38. See Walter, "Kritischer Bericht," 182, 206, 217.

39. Beer and Burmeister, "'in betreff des geizigen Carakters von Haydn,'" 44.

40. For a concise account, see Tyson and Landon, "Who Composed Haydn's Op. 3?" The question of the authorship of Op. 3 is scrutinized in greater detail in Somfai, "Zur Echtheitsfrage," and in Unverricht, *Die beiden Hoffstetter*, 12–22.

41. Jones, *Oxford Composer Companions: Haydn*, 157 (Feder, "Aus Roman Hoffstetters Briefen," 201). The composer's name is spelled variously with one "f" or two in the literature.

Chapter 2

1. See, for example, Drabkin, "Corelli's Trio Sonatas" and *Reader's Guide*, 11–16. See also Geiringer, "Rise of Chamber Music," 521–31, 548–52.

2. Finscher, *Studien*, 44–89.

3. Webster offers a meticulously documented portrayal of the repertory in "Towards a History" (on soloistic performance, see 231–35; on evidence against basso continuo use, see 243–46).

4. Webster, "Towards a History," 215–27.

5. Webster, "Bass Part" (1977), 416.

6. See Feder, "Haydns frühe Klaviertrios," 315.

7. The question of improvised embellishment in the quartets has received scant attention in the literature. Although some passages may invite embellishment, particularly when literal repeats are involved, there are grounds for objecting to such liberties: in a contemporary document that transmits Haydn's advice for a planned performance of the *Missa in tempore belli*, the composer is reported to have urged that the singers must avoid any manner of embellishment, as this would lead only to disfigurement. The letter in question is discussed and quoted in Feder, "Manuscript Sources," 126–27. See also Feder, *Haydns Streichquartette*, 114.

8. "Singing allegro" designates "a song-like melody set in quick tempo" (Ratner, *Classic Music*, 19). For further discussion of the term and the question of its application to Haydn's quartets, see Seedorf, "Saitengesänge," 26–33.

9. Much has been written on Haydn's ethnic background, the popular- and folk-music practices to which he is likely to have been exposed, and the sources of his melodic borrowings. Important contributions include Schmid, *Buch von Vorfahren*; Cushman, "Haydn's Melodic Materials"; and Schroeder, "Melodic Source Material."

10. In the discussion that follows, Steblin's *Key Characteristics* serves as a principal point of reference, esp. Appendix A: "Catalogue of Characteristics Imputed to Keys," 221–308. Contemporary writers whose descriptions of keys are summarized include Galeazzi, Grétry, Junker, Ribock, Knecht, Koch, Rousseau, Schubart, and Vogler.

11. Of Haydn's quartets in F (Opp. 2/4, 17/2, 50/5, 74/2, 77/2), only one, Op. 50/5, has an opening gesture that seems at all in agreement with later-eighteenth-century descriptions of the key as "silent," "lonely," "gentle," "calm," and the like; and Galeazzi's contrary mention of "shrill" in connection with this key bears little correspondence to Haydn's practice.

12. Webster, pondering the significance of F♯ minor as a home key, emphasizes its status as something exceptional, representing "a remote and inhospitable part of the musical universe" (*"Farewell" Symphony*, 116). As he notes, it is found as a home key in just three instances: the quartet, the "Farewell," and the Piano Trio, Hob. XV:26 (332).

13. This aspect of late-eighteenth-century musical practice is given detailed treatment in Ratner's *Classic Music* and Allanbrook's *Rhythmic Gesture in Mozart*.

14. On this aspect of Haydn's art, see Bonds, "Origins of Musical Irony."

15. Eventually, Haydn's contemporaries may have come to understand a certain variety of quiet ending to a quartet as a convention in its own right. Sutcliffe, noting Pleyel's cultivation of "the soft, wry, comic ending," suggests that it might be regarded as a Viennese specialty ("Haydn, Mozart and Their Contemporaries," 196).

16. This often-discussed aspect of Haydn's art has been closely examined in Wheelock's authoritative *Haydn's Ingenious Jesting* and Paul's comprehensive "Wit, Comedy, and Humour" (represented in concise form in his article "Comedy, Wit, and Humor"). See also Ballstaedt, "'Humor' und 'Witz.'"

17. Ribeiro, *Letters of Burney*, 1:400n72.

18. Sutcliffe, "Haydn, Mozart and Their Contemporaries," 203.

19. See Wheelock, *Haydn's Ingenious Jesting*, 10–13. For other perspectives on Op. 33/2/iv and its famously eccentric ending, see Schöllhorn, "Haydn und Tieck," also Danuser, "Ende als Anfang."

Chapter 3

1. Levy, "*Quatuor concertant*"; Hickman, "Flowering of the Viennese String Quartet"; Parker, *String Quartet*.

2. Schwindt-Gross, *Drama und Diskurs*; Moe, "Texture in the String Quartets"; Drabkin, *Reader's Guide*. Also to be noted is Moe's subsequent essay, "Texture in Haydn's Early Quartets."

3. Ribeiro, *Letters of Burney*, 400n74, 400.

4. Parker, *String Quartet*, 72.

5. Drabkin cites this phrase from a related perspective in *Reader's Guide*, 34–35. For further discussion of the particular issue raised here, see Rosen, *Classical Style*, 116–17.

6. See Raab, *Funktionen des Unisono*, 31–111, and Levy, "Texture as a Sign," 507–30.

7. This distinctive paired-octave texture is featured in the following minuets from the earliest quartets: Opp. 1/1/iv (mm. 1–4, 8–9, 19–22), 1/3/iv, 1/4/iv (mm. 1–8, 17–26), 1/6/iv, 2/1/iv (mm. 3–4, 17–20), 2/2/ii (mm. 1–2, 4–8, 17–18, 20–22), 2/4/iv (mm. 1–2), and 2/6/iv, with lower parts partially in unison (mm. 1–6, 9–14, 21–26). For more on Haydn's early "2 + 2" minuet textures, see Moe, "Texture in Haydn's Early Quartets," 13–15.

8. In one instance, the trio of Op. 20/6, Haydn instructs all three performers in question (violin 1, viola, and cello) to play on their lowest strings throughout. See Drabkin, *Reader's Guide*, 38–39, for mention of this and other examples.

9. The device is indicated notationally by alternating stem directions for the succession of notes involved. An early, subtle, yet distinctly thematic instance colors the Op. 2/2/iv minuet.

Chapter 4

1. For a pertinent discussion, see Rosen's *Sonata Forms*, 16–27.

2. See Broyles, "Organic Form"; Dunsby, "Formal Repeat"; MacDonald, "To Repeat or Not to Repeat"; and Smyth, "'Balanced Interruption.'"

3. The phenomenon is examined in close detail by Hepokoski and Darcy in "Medial Caesura."

4. This categorization is expounded in Larsen, "Sonata Form Problems," 274–75.

5. Hepokoski and Darcy, "Medial Caesura," 118–19.

6. See Andrews, "Submediant in Haydn's Development Sections," 465–66. Among the 219 relevant development sections Andrews examined (i.e., those of movements in major keys), only forty-three failed to have "an important part, including at least one significant cadence," in the submediant.

7. Ratner, *Classic Music*, 225–27.

8. Koch, *Introductory Essay*, 200 (*Versuch*, 3:307–9). The passage in question is part of the theorist's description of the first Allegro of the symphony. See also Rosen, *Sonata Forms*, 37, 155–57.

9. On the notion of the false recapitulation in sonata form, see Rosen, *Sonata Forms*, 156–57, and Caplin, *Classical Form*, 277n58 (with further bibliographical references). Bonds offers a wide-ranging discussion of the phenomenon in "Haydn's False Recapitulations." Also pertinent is the discussion of the so-called medial return in Hoyt, "'False Recapitulation,'" summarized on 337–41.

10. Caplin, *Classical Form*, 139.

11. See LaRue, "Bifocal Tonality: An Explanation" and "Bifocal Tonality in Haydn Symphonies." The unmediated progression from V of vi to I between development and recapitulation occurs only in certain fast-tempo outer movements.

12. Koch, *Introductory Essay*, 201 (*Versuch*, 3:311); Churgin, "Francesco Galeazzi's Description (1796) of Sonata Form," 196; Kollmann, *Essay*, 5. See also Ratner, *Classic Music*, 217–18.

13. Caplin, *Classical Form*, 161–63; Ratner, *Classic Music*, 229; Webster, "Sonata Form," 693–94. See also Larson, "Recapitulation Recomposition."

14. For related examples, see 9/3/iv, 17/4/i, and 33/1/i.

15. See the pertinent inquiry into Haydn's "redundancy principle" in Haimo, *Haydn's Symphonic Forms* (esp. 5–7, where the principle is defined).

16. Koch, *Introductory Essay*, 201 (*Versuch*, 3:311).

17. Rosen, *Sonata Forms*, 106, 289–93.

18. Koch, *Introductory Essay*, 201 (*Versuch*, 3:311).

19. Cone, *Musical Form and Musical Performance*, 77. For a critique of Cone's idea and its reverberations, see Hepokoski, "Beyond the Sonata Principle."

20. Hepokoski, "Beyond the Sonata Principle," 120–30.

21. Bonds, "Haydn's False Recapitulations," 225–27.

22. The phenomenon of the coda has been approached from various angles by different scholars. Relevant studies include Neubacher, *Finis Coronat Opus*, and Smyth, "Codas in Classical form." See also Caplin, *Classical Form*, 179–91; Rosen, *Sonata Forms*, 297–352; Ratner, *Classic Music*, 230–31; and Webster, "Sonata Form," 694–95. Neubacher cites several instances in which the word was actually used by Haydn (130–50) and offers his own definition (142–44).

23. This list essentially corresponds to that given in Neubacher, *Finis Coronat Opus*, 148.

24. On the technical distinction between "small" and "large" forms, as indicated by Joseph Riepel and elaborated by Koch, see Sisman, "Small and Expanded Forms," 446–59.

25. On the sonata without development, see Webster, "Sonata Form," 697, and Caplin, *Classical Form*, 216–17. See also Rosen, *Sonata Forms*, 106–12, where two ambivalent cases are given interpretations that differ from ours: Op. 17/3/iii, whose thematic interest and tonal diversity in measures 46–54 suggest true development, and Op. 76/4/ii, in which measures 35–51 could be heard as a development section. Two movements not mentioned by Rosen (Opp. 33/5/ii, 55/1/ii) are analogous to Op. 50/2/ii, which Rosen recognizes as an instance of the form. Op. 33/6/ii, also omitted by Rosen, is partially similar in design.

26. See Rosen, *Sonata Forms*, 28–29, where this pattern is described and identified as "the almost invariable form of the outer parts of the operatic aria da capo" after 1720.

Chapter 5

1. There are exceptions to the rule of the single, closed, two-reprise trio: Op. 64/6 has an optional variant of the trio; several trios have an interrupted, open-ended second reprise; and one trio has a form that bears no close resemblance to the two-reprise model (Op. 76/6).

2. Wheelock examines the phenomenon of humor and novelty in Haydn's minuets, with particular attention to the symphonies, in *Haydn's Ingenious Jesting*, 55–89.

3. For discussion of Haydn's use of the term, see Russell, "Minuet, Scherzando, and Scherzo."

4. See the related discussion of Haydn's ballroom dances, "folk-like" as well as courtly, in Wheelock, *Haydn's Ingenious Jesting*, 61–63. See also Lowe, "Falling from Grace," 182–87.

5. The collections listed are included in *JHW*, 5/1 (*Tänze und Märsche*). Information on dating comes from the list of works in Webster and Feder, *New Grove Haydn*, 101–2. For discussion of circumstances under which the ballroom dances were written and performed, see Thomas, "Studien zu Haydns Tanzmusik."

6. On distinctions between the minuet's dance step, on the one hand, and the allemande (or German dance) and its relatives, on the other, see Allanbrook, *Rhythmic Gesture*, 33–36, 59–66.

7. Dance movements in instrumental cycles are not necessarily to be understood as derivatives, variants, or deviations with respect to a hypothetical "standard" represented by a ballroom tradition. By the late eighteenth century, the influence may just as well have flowed in the opposite direction. See Russell, "Unconventional Dance Minuet" and "Minuet Form and Phraseology." See also Jones, "Minuets and Trios," 81.

8. In no instance are there separate tempo markings for trios, despite the fact that the latter sometimes seem to require a different tempo in accordance with certain stylistic or topical cues. See Saslav, "Tempos," 97–102, 152–58.

9. On this elusive yet well-recognized phenomenon, see Rosen, *Classical Style*, 330–41. See also Schroeder, *Haydn and the Enlightenment*, 58–59.

10. Trios conforming to this scheme of abbreviated, rounded binary return are those of Opp. 1/1/iv, 2/1/iv, 9/5, 20/4, and 33/3. In the rounded binary trio of Op. 64/5, the second reprise is actually shorter than the first.

11. On uses of the familiar term "Ländler," see Allanbrook, *Rhythmic Gesture*, 63–64. See also Wheelock, *Haydn's Ingenious Jesting*, 70–72, and Carner, "Ländler."

12. See Drabkin, *Reader's Guide*, 103–4, for further discussion of connections between the Op. 20/2 minuet and trio.

13. Discussed in Webster, *"Farewell" Symphony*, 160–62.

14. For further commentary on this trio, see Rosen, *Sonata Forms*, 118–20.

15. The Op. 64/3 minuet is discussed from a different perspective in Levy, "'Something Mechanical Encrusted on the Living,'" 236–38. See also Agawu, *Playing with Signs*, 40–41.

Chapter 6

1. Sisman's *Classical Variation* explores many ramifications of the topic, with particular emphasis on connections between variation procedure and eighteenth-century traditions involving the teaching and practice of rhetoric. This chapter complements her study by focusing specifically on questions of form and style in variation movements within the Haydn quartet repertory.

2. Table 6.1 purports to be virtually comprehensive with respect to the specified categories, corresponding closely, although not exactly, to the lists of variation movements given in Sisman, *Classical Variation*, 265–70. An exact tally proves elusive: there are borderline cases, and there are several movements that defy easy categorization.

3. For several reasons, the term "alternating variation" seems preferable to the commonly used but potentially confusing "double variation." See Sisman, *Classical Variation*, 150–51, and the detailed discussion in "Tradition and Transformation."

4. Bach, *Essay*, 165–66 (*Versuch*, 1:132–33).

5. Translated from the German as given in Sisman, *Classical Variation*, 278–79.

6. See Brown, *Haydn's Keyboard Music*, 219–20.

7. Sisman, *Classical Variation*, 111–12.

8. For relevant discussion, see Sisman, *Classical Variation*, 69–71.

9. Further commentary is offered in Sisman, *Classical Variation*, 195.

10. For additional, related discussion, see Sisman, *Classical Variation*, 138–42. See also Drabkin, *Reader's Guide*, 133–37.

Chapter 7

1. The Op. 20 fugues are given detailed treatment in Drabkin, *Reader's Guide*, 51–68. See also Kirkendale, *Fugue and Fugato*, 141–45; an appendix to the German edition contains fugue diagrams not included in the translation (312–13).

2. Kirkendale, *Fugue and Fugato*, 140.

3. See Kirkendale, *Fugue and Fugato*, 142.

4. Kirkendale describes the "pathotype" formula as consisting of "the fifth formed by first and fifth degrees, and the diminished seventh which lies a semitone outside these notes. Characteristic is the leap of the diminished seventh, nearly always descending, with the leading note accented" (*Fugue and Fugato*, 91).

5. On the exceptional and problematical aspects of F♯ minor, including specific comments on this instance of the key, see Webster, *"Farewell" Symphony*, 332–34. See also Sutcliffe, *String Quartets, Op. 50*, 88, 94.

6. See Webster, *"Farewell" Symphony*, 333, and Sutcliffe, *String Quartets, Op. 50*, 90–93.

7. Kirkendale, *Fugue and Fugato*, 145.

8. For relevant background, see Cole, "Vogue of the Instrumental Rondo."

9. On Haydn's usage of ¢ meter, see Saslav, "Tempos," 70–76.

10. For further discussion of the movement—its theme, the variation procedures employed, and intramovement relationships involved in the incorporation of fugal technique—see Sisman, *Classical Variation*, 176–81.

11. See Brown, *Haydn's Keyboard Music*, 221–29, for a portrayal of the stylistic context in which the Fantasia and Capriccio may be understood.

12. According to an annotation by Landon and Barrett-Ayres in Haydn, *Streichquartette: Quartetto d-Moll Op. 42, Hob. III:43*, 13 (see also the note on 14).

13. For further discussion of Op. 33/2/iii from a somewhat different perspective, see Sisman, *Classical Variation*, 103–5.

Chapter 8

1. Gotwals, *Two Contemporary Portraits*, 13 (Griesinger, *Biographische Notizen*, 13).

2. Concerning this evidence and the issue of chronology, see Webster and Feder, *New Grove Haydn*, 5–10, and Landon, *Chronicle and Works*, 1:228–30. See also Feder, "Vorwort," viii–ix (*JHW*, 12/1); Biba, "Nachrichten zur Musikpflege," 38–39 (but cf. Heartz, *Viennese School*, 260); and Webster, "Chronology," 36–42.

3. Webster, "Chronology," 35.

4. One, at the Österreichische Nationalbibliothek in Vienna, represents Op. 1/2 and 6; the other, at the Széchényi National Library in Budapest, is a compilation of six quartets (Opp. 1/1, 2, 4, 6, and 2/1, 6), of which two (Opp. 1/2, 2/1) are marked with Haydn's corrections. For descriptions of these and additional sources, see Feder, *Kritischer Bericht*, 10–11, and Landon, *Chronicle and Works*, 1:253.

5. Finscher, *Studien*, 159–60. See also Landon, *Chronicle and Works*, 1:575.

6. The grouping described accords with the hypothesis advanced by Webster in *New Grove Haydn*, 9, by which these works may have been composed in three phases: Op. 1/1–4, 6, and Op. 0 (earliest), Op. 2/1 and 2 (last), and Op. 2/4 and 6 (some time in between). Concerning the *Entwurf-Katalog*, see Feder, *Kritischer Bericht*, 8–9, and Larsen, *Three Haydn Catalogues*.

7. See Landon, *Chronicle and Works*, 1:230.

8. See the discussion of this movement in Webster, "Freedom of Form," 527–28.

9. Translated from Unverricht, *Geschichte des Streichtrios*, 156 (cf. Landon, *Chronicle and Works*, 2:132).

10. As argued by Heartz, "'Von dem wienerischen Geschmack,'" 78–80. See also Heartz, *Viennese School*, 443–46.

11. The relevant passage is given in translation in Heartz, *Viennese School*, 257; Unverricht (*Geschichte des Streichtrios*, 156) provides the original German. At issue, presumably (and certainly in the interpretation of commentators on the quartets who have cited the 1766 Hamburg critique and the Viennese response), is the specific technique by which the violins, sounding in octaves, proceed in two-voice counterpoint with the lower instruments, likewise in octaves (see Feder, *Haydns Streichquartette*, 30–31, and Heartz, *Viennese School*, 255–56). That related arrangements may have been at issue with respect to quartets, that is, those in which upper or lower parts are in unison rather than octaves, is possible; in this regard, see the

discussion of trios in Unverricht, 156–58. Such textures are not easily described on paper, and the critics' precise meaning is not always clear.

12. See Finscher, *Studien*, 48, 150. See also Moe, "Texture in Haydn's Early Quartets," 18–20.

13. On Haydn's predilection for the last of these items, as exemplified in Op. 1/1/i, see Georgiades, "Zur Musiksprache der Wiener Klassiker," 33–38.

14. Landon, *Chronicle and Works*, 2:130.

15. Gerber, *Historisch-biographisches Lexikon*, 1:611.

16. Reichardt, *Vertraute Briefe*, 2:28.

17. For example, Reichardt, *Musikalisches Kunstmagazin*, 1:205 (the relevant passage is translated in Heartz, *Viennese School*, 261).

Chapter 9

1. The copies are held by the library of the Gesellschaft der Musikfreunde in Vienna (see Webster, "Chronology," 20; concerning their dating, see 33).

2. See Brook, *Breitkopf Thematic Catalogue*, 418.

3. The listings for Opp. 9 and 17 appear, respectively, on pages 2 and 6 of Haydn's catalogue, where Haydn uses the label "Divertimento a quatro" for Op. 9/4, and "a 4tro" (and variants) for Op. 17 and the remainder of Op. 9 (see Larsen, *Three Haydn Catalogues*). Arguments concerning the dating of Op. 9 derive from Webster, "Chronology," 30–34; Feder, "Vorwort," vi (JHW, 12/2); and Feder, *Haydns Streichquartette*, 34.

4. As described in Hoboken, *Werkverzeichnis*, 1:385. Like the authentic copies of the two Op. 9 quartets, this source also resides in the Gesellschaft der Musikfreunde library.

5. See Johansson, *Hummel*, 1:29, 84; Johansson, *French Music Publishers' Catalogues*, 140; and Feder, "Vorwort," vi (JHW, 12/2).

6. Feder, *Haydns Streichquartette*, 39, and Heartz, *Viennese School*, 331–32.

7. See Rosen, *Sonata Forms*, 299–301.

8. See Grave, "Metrical Displacement" and "Common-Time Displacement."

9. See Heartz, *Viennese School*, 333.

10. See Webster, *"Farewell" Symphony*, 152–55.

Chapter 10

1. Stockhausen, *Critischer Entwurf*, 464–65, quoted from Heartz's translation (*Viennese School*, 348–49) of an excerpt in Unverricht, *Geschichte des Streichtrios*, 94.

2. Landon, *Chronicle and Works*, 2:399 (Bartha, *Briefe*, 77).

3. A description of the manuscripts, held by the Gesellschaft der Musikfreunde library in Vienna, is given in Feder and Gerlach, *Kritischer Bericht*, 9–10, 31–32. Autograph sketches for the third movement of Op. 20/3, at the Széchényi National Library, Budapest (*Kritischer Bericht*, 10), are transcribed in JHW, 12/3; Somfai discusses them in "'Ich war nie ein Geschwindschreiber.'"

4. See Larsen, *Three Haydn Catalogues* (*Entwurf-Katalog*, 5).

5. The different shades of ink are described in Feder and Gerlach, *Kritischer Bericht*, 9, and the papers in Webster, *"Farewell" Symphony*, 299n30.

6. Feder and Gerlach, "Vorwort," vii. Here Feder and Gerlach caution that this grouping does not necessarily represent the order of composition, although Webster ("*Farewell*" *Symphony*, 299) believes it most likely does, in light of the documentary evidence.

7. Details on the editions come from Feder and Gerlach, "Vorwort," vii–viii, and *Kritischer Bericht*, 17–18.

8. Feder and Gerlach give the full texts of these advertisements, followed by an evaluation that raises questions about the extent of Haydn's involvement in the editing process (*Kritischer Bericht*, 28–29).

9. Heartz, *Viennese School*, 337–40.

10. Perhaps most prominent in this regard are the Symphonies Nos. 45 and 46, both from 1772. For relevant discussion, see Webster, "*Farewell*" *Symphony*, 13–112, 267–87.

11. Webster, "*Farewell*" *Symphony*, 295.

12. The novel features of this movement, including the long coda, are examined in Sisman, *Classical Variation*, 138–42.

13. Feder, *Haydns Streichquartette*, 51, describes this as a "finger-snapping" effect.

14. Despite the apparent connection between the minuet's suggestive title and its salient metrical dissonance, the only feature that resembles the conventions of the *style hongrois* is the emphasis on *pesante* accents (Bellman, "*Style Hongrois*," 97–98).

15. For a detailed discussion of this passage and its accompanying inscription, see Drabkin, *Reader's Guide*, 78–79.

16. Translated from Gerber, *Neues historisch-biographisches Lexikon*, 2:576.

17. For further information on Beethoven's copy and Brahms's corrected score, see Feder and Gerlach, *Kritischer Bericht*, 14 and 19, respectively; Brahms's bequest of the autograph to the Gesellschaft der Musikfreunde is discussed on page 9.

Chapter 11

1. Landon, *Chronicle and Works*, 2:454 (Bartha, *Briefe*, 106). Our quotations from the letter modify Landon's translation. Regarding the works' time of origin, there are references in Hoboken and elsewhere to a dating of 1778–81, but these are based on a set of forged letters. See Webster, "Chronology," 29–30n25.

2. The total was determined by Feder, who reproduces one of the three surviving letters in "Vergessener Haydn-Brief," 115. The other two are given in Bartha, *Briefe*, 106–7, and all three are translated in Landon, *Chronicle and Works* 2:454–55.

3. Landon, *Chronicle and Works*, 2:453, modified (Bartha, *Briefe*, 104); the enclosure (Bartha, *Briefe*, 104–5) is omitted by Landon.

4. Landon, *Chronicle and Works*, 2:464 (Bartha, *Briefe*, 115). For the announcement and related correspondence, see *Chronicle and Works*, 2:461–64 (*Briefe*, 109–15).

5. There is, however, a keyboard arrangement of the finale to Op. 33/5 in Haydn's hand at the Städtische Musikbibliothek in Leipzig (see Feder and Gerlach, *Kritischer Bericht*, 25). The arrangement is published in *JHW*, 12/3.

6. Feder and Gerlach, "Vorwort," vii. See also the *Kritischer Bericht*, 20, for a brief description of the source.

7. In other words, the quartets in the Melk copy are numbered 1, 2, 3, and 5, and the works in question correspond to the first, second, third, and fifth quartets in the Artaria print, which in turn correspond to the quartets numbered 5, 2, 1, and 6 according to the familiar

numbering. Description and facsimile of the fragment are given in Feder, "From the Workshop," 169. See also Feder, "Nachricht," 136.

8. For details on the editions, see Feder and Gerlach, "Vorwort," vii, and *Kritischer Bericht*, 22, 24.

9. See Landon, *Chronicle and Works*, 2:455–56.

10. Webster and Feder, *New Grove Haydn*, 64, referring to the "light, even popular style" heard in Symphonies Nos. 53, 61–63, 66–71, 73–75.

11. The melody is quoted in Feder, *Haydns Streichquartette*, 61.

12. Anderson, *Letters of Mozart*, 2:833 (Bauer and Deutsch, 4:245–46).

13. Rosen discusses the opening of Op. 33/1/i from a similar perspective in *Classical Style*, 116–17.

14. See Sutcliffe, *String Quartets, Op. 50*, 23.

15. See Wheelock, *Haydn's Ingenious Jesting*, 10–12.

16. Translated from Finscher, *Studien*, 268, which also discusses the traveling quartet (268–69). Finscher gives as his source of information the "Hamburgische Correspondent" (17 August 1782), presumably the *Staats- und Gelehrte Zeitung des Hamburgischen unpartheyischen Correspondenten*, which we have likewise abbreviated.

17. Translated from *Magazin der Musik* 1 (1783): 153.

18. Translated from Reichardt, *Musikalisches Kunstmagazin*, 1:205; cf. Finscher, *Studien*, 268–69, and Landon, *Chronicle and Works*, 2:466–67.

19. Translated from *Magazin der Musik* 1 (1783): 260; cf. Finscher, *Studien*, 129, and Landon, *Chronicle and Works*, 2:582.

20. See Hoboken, *Werkverzeichnis*, 1:398–99.

21. For an incisive discussion of Sandberger's argument, with translated quotations from his essay, see Webster, "*Farewell*" *Symphony*, 341–47. The quotations from Sandberger's "Zur Geschichte" are taken from the translated passages in Webster, 342. See also Landon and Jones, *Haydn*, 196.

22. Webster, "*Farewell*" *Symphony*, 343.

23. Rosen, *Classical Style*, 116.

24. See Finscher, *Studien*, 379. The quotations are taken from the translated passage in Webster, "*Farewell*" *Symphony*, 345.

25. Webster, "*Farewell*" *Symphony*, 345. The phrase is Webster's, describing Finscher's view of the historical significance of Op. 33.

26. See Webster, "*Farewell*" *Symphony*, 344.

27. See Bonds, "Origins of Musical Irony," for a detailed discussion of Haydn's "ironic distance" from the vantage point of contemporary writings.

28. Finscher, *Studien*, 267. The quotation is from the translated passage in Webster, "*Farewell*" *Symphony*, 345.

29. Landon, *Chronicle and Works*, 2:490 (Bartha, *Briefe*, 136).

30. At the Staatsbibliothek in Berlin.

31. Walter, "Zum Wiener Streichquartett," 300–305.

32. Webster, "Chronology," 28–29.

33. The tempo designation on the autograph manuscript was originally "Allegretto ed Innocentemente"; the "Allegretto" was later struck out and replaced by "Andante" (see Hoboken, *Werkverzeichnis*, 1:402).

34. It must be noted that the opposite argument also could be made: that without the contrasting mood and sonority of the minuet, the cycle as a whole would have lacked adequate affective diversity.

35. Keller, *Great Haydn Quartets*, 82.

Chapter 12

1. Throughout the literature, there are intimations of a connection between the Op. 50 works and Haydn's references to quartets in his correspondence with Artaria from spring 1784, principally the letter of 5 April (Webster, "Chronology," 28n1, gives a sampling of citations in the literature, to which Sutcliffe's more recent comments may be added [*String Quartets, Op. 50*, 30]). Webster (28) argues cogently that the notion of Haydn's having begun Op. 50 as early as 1784 is inconsistent with his normal quartet-writing procedure.

2. Landon, *Chronicle and Works*, 2:688, 689 (Bartha, *Briefe*, 157, 158).

3. Landon, *Chronicle and Works*, 2:693 (Bartha, *Briefe*, 167). For further information concerning the dedication, see the summary in Sutcliffe, *String Quartets, Op. 50*, 30–32.

4. Previous writers have nonetheless drawn a connection between the nature of the Op. 50 cello parts, such as they are, and the cello-playing dedicatee. For further discussion, see Rosen, *Classical Style*, 123, and Sutcliffe, *String Quartets, Op. 50*, 66.

5. Landon, *Chronicle and Works*, 2:698, modified (Bartha, *Briefe*, 178).

6. Landon, *Chronicle and Works*, 2:697 (Bartha, *Briefe*, 177). In the same letter, Haydn also prevaricates by making this claim with respect to his Paris symphonies, whose publication by Artaria was under way at the time. See the discussion of this affair in Sutcliffe, *String Quartets, Op. 50*, 33–36.

7. Discussion of the editions is based on Hoboken, *Werkverzeichnis*, 1:405, 409.

8. See Feder, *Haydns Streichquartette*, 67.

9. This claim was made in a letter from Dittersdorf to Artaria on 18 August 1788, and although it does not refer to the quartets by opus number, it is more likely a reference to Op. 50 than to Op. 33, issued by the publisher in 1782. Landon translates the relevant passage in *Chronicle and Works*, 2:699n6 (for the German text, see Badura-Skoda, "Dittersdorf," 47).

10. Landon, *Chronicle and Works*, 2:699 (Bartha, *Briefe*, 179–80).

11. Landon, *Chronicle and Works*, 2:701, modified (Bartha, *Briefe*, 182–83).

12. The point is affirmed by Feder, who cites the absence of copyright laws as self-evident justification for Haydn's action (*Haydns Streichquartette*, 66–67).

13. The various manuscripts are housed at the British Library in London (those for Forster and all but No. 3 of the set from Haydn's library) and the Széchényi National Library in Budapest (No. 3 of the latter set and the remaining incomplete set). See Landon, *Chronicle and Works*, 2:625.

14. For a detailed discussion of the story of the autograph manuscripts, see Sutcliffe, *String Quartets, Op. 50*, 37–47. See also Kartomi, "Haydn Autograph Manuscripts."

15. For an interpretation of this movement's peculiar opening theme and the realization of its implications in subsequent appearances, see Levy, "Gesture, Form, and Syntax," 357. See also Sutcliffe, *String Quartets, Op. 50*, 67–70, 75–76.

16. The passage in question is examined in Grave, "Metrical Dissonance," 193–95.

17. Purely in terms of measure count, the second reprise of the Op. 77/1 trio is longer, but this is only because the repeat is written out.

18. Instances of thematic resemblance between minuet and trio in Op. 50 are examined in Sutcliffe, *String Quartets, Op. 50*, 56–60.

19. The role of the C♯ is examined from a similar vantage point in Sutcliffe, *String Quartets, Op. 50*, 94.

20. Sutcliffe emphasizes the integrative role of the Op. 50 finales in presenting a "direct response to preceding events" (*String Quartets, Op. 50*, 54).

21. Regarding the peculiarity of having the work end in minor, following a dance movement in which the minuet proper was in major (implying a conclusion in major), see Webster, "Farewell" Symphony, 333.

22. Sutcliffe describes thematic connections between the fugue subject and each of the preceding movements in *String Quartets, Op. 50*, 90–93.

23. See Sutcliffe, *String Quartets, Op. 50*, 102.

24. Sutcliffe, *String Quartets, Op. 50*, 100.

Chapter 13

1. Landon, *Chronicle and Works*, 2:709 (Bartha, *Briefe*, 193).

2. On Tost's business dealings see Gerlach, "Tost," 345–46, and Landon, *Chronicle and Works*, 2:81–82.

3. Landon, *Chronicle and Works*, 2:708–9 (Bartha, *Briefe*, 191–92).

4. Hoboken, *Werkverzeichnis*, 1:160, 162, 412.

5. Landon, *Chronicle and Works*, 2:719, modified (Bartha, *Briefe*, 204–5).

6. Landon, *Chronicle and Works*, 5:58 (not in Bartha, *Briefe*).

7. Hoboken, *Werkverzeichnis*, 1:413 (concerning the quartets), and Gerlach, "Tost," 348 (concerning the symphonies).

8. Landon (*Chronicle and Works*, 2:598, 635) surmises that the manuscript on which the edition was based was one that Haydn had sent to the performing organization as part of his agreement with them.

9. McVeigh, "The Professional Concert," 75–76; see also 11.

10. Hoboken, *Werkverzeichnis*, 1:413.

11. The autograph materials consist of undated fragments, rather substantial, for Op. 54/1 and 3 (Staatsbibliothek, Berlin). See Webster, "Chronology," 26–27, and Landon, *Chronicle and Works*, 2:635.

12. Hoboken, *Werkverzeichnis*, 3:43.

13. For example, Keller (*Great Haydn Quartets*, 130), Barrett-Ayres (*Haydn and the String Quartet*, 230), and Landon (*Chronicle and Works*, 2:636, 638). Cf. Feder (*Haydns Streichquartette*, 76) and Gerlach ("Tost," 348), both of whom call attention to the erroneous tradition.

14. The following discussion of Op. 55/2, Op. 64, and the question of the "Razor" quartet derives principally from Woodfield's detailed account in "Bland," 238–44.

15. Pohl, *Haydn*, 2:235.

16. Landon, "Four New Haydn Letters," 216.

17. Feder, *Haydns Streichquartette*, 76–77.

18. The phenomenon of the *quatuor brilliant* is described in Hickman, "Flowering of the Viennese String Quartet," 165–68. See also Finscher, "Zur Sozialgeschichte," 37–39.

19. See Levy, "*Quatuor Concertant*," 1–41, for descriptions of the Parisian milieu. The role of the quartet in late-eighteenth-century London is concisely portrayed in Parker, *String Quartet*, 37–40.

20. See the relevant information furnished in Steblin, *Key Characteristics*, especially her discussion of theorists' articulations of the "sharp-flat principle" (103–33) and the summary assessments by eighteenth-century writers of the character of the two keys in question: E major (252–53) and A major (288–89).

21. This instance of a notated cadenza invites comparison with not only Op. 33/5/ii, mm. 41–51, but also with Mozart's "Hoffmeister" quartet, K. 499 (third movement, mm. 98–101), which may possibly have provided a model for Op. 55/1/ii.

22. On the apparent connection between this movement's harmonic peculiarity and the notorious introduction to Mozart's "Dissonant" quartet, K. 465, see Esch, "Haydns Streich-quartett Op. 54/1 und Mozarts KV 465." That Mozart's introduction was in turn inspired by the peculiarities of the opening theme of Haydn's Op. 33/3 is proposed by Bonds in "Sincer-est Form of Flattery?" 380–84.

23. Similar views are elaborated in Webster, "*Farewell*" *Symphony* (see esp. 204–6), and Haimo, *Haydn's Symphonic Forms* (for example, 120–21, 267). For a nuanced, skeptical cri-tique of both, see Hoyt, "Haydn's New Incoherence."

24. Cited by Feder in *Haydns Streichquartette*, 79. Although spelled differently and posi-tioned one octave higher than in the beginning of the *Tristan* prelude, the chord is otherwise identical in pitch and spacing.

25. Cone, "Uses of Convention," 282–84; Webster, "*Farewell*" *Symphony*, 300–308. See also Spitzer, "Haydn's Quartet Finales," 113–16. The description offered here essentially agrees with Webster's depiction of multiple stages of "expectation and reversal" (301).

26. Spitzer identifies the fast segment, measures 57–88, as a species of variation of mea-sures 9–40 ("Haydn's Quartet Finales," 114).

27. Like the finale to Op. 20/3, the first movements of Opp. 17/4 and 42 both switch to major shortly before the close.

28. The phenomenon of a major-key minuet is not an uncommon occurrence within the repertory of Haydn's minor-key quartets: it happens in five of the twelve works in question. In every other instance, however, the minuet either follows a slow movement with a contrasting tonal center (Opp. 50/4/iii, 74/3/iii), or the minuet comes second, following a first movement that sustains the minor mode until just before the end (Opp. 17/4, 42).

Chapter 14

1. Described in Feder and Saslav, *Kritischer Bericht*, 10–13. The locations are as follows: Royal College of Music, London (No. 1), private collection (No. 2), Rychenberg-Stiftung, Winterthur (No. 3), Library of Congress, Washington, DC (No. 5), Musashino Academiae Musicae, Tokyo (No. 6). There are also autograph sketches for the first movement of No. 5, described in *Kritischer Bericht* (11) and published in *JHW*, 12/5.

2. Landon, *Chronicle and Works*, 3:73, 81.

3. Relevant announcements, programs, and reviews for 1791 and 1792 are cited and ex-cerpted in Landon, *Chronicle and Works*; see esp. 3:48, 60, 65, 70, 73, 80–81 for 1791, and 146–48, 171 for 1792.

4. Landon, *Chronicle and Works*, 3:60; Landon's identification of the symphony is discussed in 3:54–55.

5. See Feder, "Vorwort," vii (*JHW*, 12/5). A further reminder of Tost's connection with this opus and his special business arrangement with Haydn takes the form of a notation on the autograph to No. 2: "Haydn's Quart. Op. 65 Belonging to Mʳ Todt [*sic*] of Vienna." The hand is not Haydn's, but it has been suggested that it might be Bland's (Feder and Saslav, *Kritischer Bericht*, 13).

6. Details concerning the editions come from Feder and Saslav, *Kritischer Bericht*, 13–14, 16–18, 21–23.

7. See Gerlach, "Tost," 358.

8. See Feder and Saslav, *Kritischer Bericht*, 45.

9. Feder offers further commentary in *Haydns Streichquartette*, 89.

10. A precedent for this particular kind of drastic temporal contrast may be found in the last movement of Mozart's String Quartet in A, K. 464 (development section, mm. 114–21), which in turn may possibly have been inspired by the coda of Haydn's Op. 20/5/i. It is known that Beethoven was influenced directly by the Mozart quartet in writing the finale to his Op. 18 No. 5; but he may have been thinking about this Haydn movement as well: whereas Mozart states his hymn-like phrase once in the midst of the development, Beethoven, like Haydn, embeds the arresting event in each principal section. For another view of the phenomenon as it appears in Mozart's K. 464, see Bonds, "Sincerest Form of Flattery?" 396.

11. The description is Keller's: "Asymmetry . . . is one of the most fertile elements of the minuet, whose first part reveals a 5 + 9-bar scheme: the most regular of dance forms transformed into a veritable orgy of irregularity!" (*Great Haydn Quartets*, 154).

12. For further commentary on the twofold return of the primary theme, see Grave, "Concerto Style," 93–95. Viewing the movement from a somewhat different perspective, Feder argues the case for calling the return at measure 105 a false reprise ("Haydn: Streichquartett D-Dur, op. 64, Nr. 5," 76).

13. For relevant discussion of the phenomenon in question (i.e., the eventually realized implication of an arpeggiated ascent through the octave), see Meyer's discussion of triadic melodies in *Explaining Music*, 157–65.

14. Rosen, *Classical Style*, 140.

Chapter 15

1. See Somfai, "London Revision," 167–69.

2. See Landon, *Chronicle and Works*, 3:456, 458.

3. The contents are given in Landon, *Chronicle and Works*, 3:316–17.

4. Feder, "Vorwort," vii (*JHW*, 12/5). See Feder and Saslav, *Kritischer Bericht*, for a description of the six complete autographs (49–53), various autograph sketches and fragments (53–54), and the authentic copies of Op. 74/2 and 3 (54). The complete autographs are in the Staatsbibliothek, Berlin.

5. For citations of the relevant programs, see Landon, *Chronicle and Works*, 3:235, 242, 245, 246.

6. McVeigh, "The Professional Concert," 3, 5.

7. Reviews are quoted in Landon, *Chronicle and Works*, 3:236, 236n1, 242, 245.

8. From newspaper accounts of a string quartet performance on 17 February 1794 and a performance of Symphony No. 100 on 7 April 1794 (Landon, *Chronicle and Works*, 236, 247).

9. Feder, "Vorwort," vii (*JHW*, 12/5). The arrangement with Count Apponyi is explained in a letter of Count Rasumovsky's, cited in Steinpress, "Haydns Oratorien," 83; see also comments on 84.

10. For details on the edition, see Feder and Saslav, *Kritischer Bericht*, 54–55, 65–66.

11. Jan Ladislav Dussek had played under Haydn's direction at Salomon's concerts, and his father was a friend of Haydn's. See Landon, *Chronicle and Works*, 3:62, 138.

12. Only one of these is known, that for Op. 71/1. On the title page it bears the inscription "as performed at Mr Salomon's concert, Hanover Square" (Feder and Saslav, *Kritischer Bericht*, 55).

13. The letter is excerpted in the original Italian in Landon, *Chronicle and Works*, 3:457.

14. For information on the edition, see Feder and Saslav, *Kritischer Bericht*, 56, 65–66. Here, Artaria's placement in the *Wiener Zeitung* is correctly identified as an announcement of a forthcoming edition, and not an advertisement of one that has already been published, as had previously been reported (cf. Hoboken, *Werkverzeichnis*, 1:424). This explains why Artaria would have had sufficient time to base his edition on Corri, Dussek's. (Compare the wording of the announcement [*Kritischer Bericht*, 56] with the advertisement for the second part [*Kritischer Bericht*, 60]).

15. Feder and Saslav, *Kritischer Bericht*, 59–60, 66–67.

16. See Feder and Saslav, *Kritischer Bericht*, 58–61.

17. See the relevant discussion in Rosen, *Classical Style*, 23–24. See also Hatten, *Musical Meaning*, 43.

18. Keller, *Great Haydn Quartets*, 190.

19. Feder calls attention to this peculiarity in *Haydns Streichquartette*, 93.

Chapter 16

1. Landon, *Chronicle and Works*, 4:255 (Mörner, *Wikmanson*, 318).

2. See Walter's speculation on the time of origin and completion in "Vorwort," vii. See also Webster, "Chronology," 25–26.

3. Excerpts from both accounts of the festivities are translated in Landon, *Chronicle and Works*, 4:259–60. See also Walter, "Vorwort," vii.

4. The fee and terms regarding publication are mentioned in Silverstolpe's letter (Mörner, *Wikmanson*, 318).

5. See Haydn's letters to Artaria of 12 July, 20 July, and 15 August 1799 in Landon, *Chronicle and Works*, 4:475, 478, 481–82 (Bartha, *Briefe*, 325, 328, 332–33).

6. Landon, *Chronicle and Works*, 4:475 (Bartha, *Briefe*, 325).

7. The inherent logic of the two-part grouping has been pointed out by Somfai: Nos. 1–3 all have sonata form opening movements and finales that progress from minor to major, for example. He suggests that the order in the authentic editions corresponds to the order of composition and thus implies that Haydn had such a scheme in mind from the start ("Opus-Planung," 109).

8. The contract in question, which stipulated that Haydn write a certain number of works over a five-year period, is photographically reproduced and transcribed in Rosenthal, "Con-

tract." According to the contract, Haydn received a predetermined fee from his London publisher for each type of work he wrote. For quartets, the fee was £75 for three, and therefore a total of £150 for six works.

9. Walter, "Kritischer Bericht," 180–81, 182. The text and date of Artaria's first advertisement (which appeared as part of an announcement for the set as a whole) are given on 180. (Concerning the date on which Longman, Clementi's edition was registered at Stationers' Hall, see Hoboken, *Werkverzeichnis*, 1:432, given by Walter as his source.)

10. Landon, *Chronicle and Works*, 4:481–82 (Bartha, *Briefe*, 332–33).

11. Walter, "Kritischer Bericht," 180–81, 182.

12. The drafts are located at the Österreichische Nationalbibliothek, Vienna (string quartet), and the Staatsbibliothek, Berlin (keyboard); the authentic copies are at the Széchényi National Library, Budapest. See Walter, "Kritischer Bericht," 179–80, 221. Walter (179) describes further relevant autographs at the Österreichische Nationalbibliothek, which are published in facsimile, along with the draft for strings, in Haydn, *Gott! erhalte Franz den Kaiser*.

13. Schroeder explores the question of Haydn's interaction with his late-eighteenth-century audiences and the potentially edifying purposes of his art in *Haydn and the Enlightenment*.

14. *Allgemeine musikalische Zeitung* 1 (1798–99): 850.

15. Landon, *Chronicle and Works*, 4:483.

16. For further commentary, see Rosen, *Sonata Forms*, 111–12.

17. Late-eighteenth-century commentators place the key of F♯ major "on the outer limits of the musical world" (Heinse, 1795), describe it as "hard because it is overloaded with accidentals" (Grétry, 1797), and cite its association with "a strange, lofty pride" (Cramer, 1786). See Steblin, *Key Characteristics*, 270.

18. For further commentary, see Sisman, *Classical Variation*, 183–84, and Kirkendale, *Fugue and Fugato*, 148.

19. Walter, "Kritischer Bericht," 202.

20. See Grave, "Metrical Dissonance," 196–201; on the related phenomenon in Stravinsky, see Toorn, *Stravinsky*, 64. See also Cooper and Meyer, *Rhythmic Structure*, 98–99.

21. Keller, *Great Haydn Quartets*, 224.

22. See the related discussion in Levy, "Texture as a Sign," 505–6.

23. McCaldin, "First Movements," 54.

24. This case may be compared with one found among the so-called Auenbrugger sonatas, published in 1780 (Hob. XVI:35–39 and 20): the opening gestures in the first movement of No. 39 (in G) and the second movement of No. 36 (in A) are nearly identical. Haydn remarked in a letter of 25 February 1780 to Artaria, "In order to anticipate the criticism of some half-wits, I find it necessary to add the following on the back side of the title page, underlined: NOTICE: <u>In these six sonatas there are two single movements in which several measures show the same idea. The composer has done this intentionally to demonstrate different methods of treatment</u>" (trans. in Brown, *Haydn's Keyboard Music*, 24 [Bartha, *Briefe*, 90]; the two movements in question are discussed on 320). For further discussion of the opening measures of Op. 76/4/ii and 6/ii, see Keller, *Great Haydn Quartets*, 230.

25. Somfai observes that the opening five-note idea "underlies the whole movement as a quasi *cantus firmus*" and proposes that its pitches have symbolic significance, representing a musical spelling of the initial letters to the opening words of the Emperor's Hymn: "Gott erhalte Franz den K[C]aiser" ("'Learned Style,'" 328–29).

26. See Somfai's detailed discussion of motivic process in this movement in "'Learned Style,'" 336–49. Of particular interest are the connections drawn between techniques in this movement and those outlined in the discussion of fugue in J. G. Albrechtsberger's *Gründliche Anweisung zur Composition* (Leipzig, 1790).

27. Sisman, *Classical Variation*, 185.

Chapter 17

1. *Allgemeine musikalische Zeitung* 1 (1798–99): 446; excerpt translated in Landon, *Chronicle and Works*, 4:454.

2. See Landon, *Chronicle and Works*, 4:466, 470 (Biba, *Eben komme ich von Haydn*, 26–27, 31).

3. The two autographs reside in the Széchényi National Library, Budapest, along with authentic copies; all are described in Walter, "Kritischer Bericht," 203–4. Both autographs have been published in facsimile editions: Haydn, *String Quartet in G* and *String Quartet in F*.

4. Landon (*Chronicle and Works*, 4:490, 501) proposes that an entry in Rosenbaum's diary for 13 October 1799 in Eisenstadt refers to the quartets of Op. 77: "We went to the castle to hear the quartets"; the composer, however, is not identified, nor the number of quartets specified.

5. Biba, *Eben komme ich von Haydn*, 87, 89.

6. Beer and Burmeister, "'in betreff des geizigen Carakters von Haydn,'" 44.

7. Landon, *Chronicle and Works*, 4:468 (Bartha, *Briefe*, 319–20).

8. Biba, *Eben komme ich von Haydn*, 132–33.

9. Landon, *Chronicle and Works*, 5:222 (Biba, *Eben komme ich von Haydn*, 153).

10. Walter, "Kritischer Bericht," 205, and "Vorwort," x.

11. Letters of 27 November and 18 December 1802 (Biba, *Eben komme ich von Haydn*, 173, 181).

12. Landon, *Chronicle and Works*, 5:252 (Bartha, *Briefe*, 419).

13. Letters of 18 June and 2 November 1803 (Biba, *Eben komme ich von Haydn*, 195, 211).

14. Landon, *Chronicle and Works*, 5:282, 283, modified (Biba, *Eben komme ich von Haydn*, 215, 220).

15. Extant sketch pages are described in Walter, "Kritischer Bericht," 215–16, and "Vorwort," xii–xiii, and in Jones, "A Newly Identified Sketchleaf."

16. Landon, *Chronicle and Works*, 5:293, 336 (Biba, *Eben komme ich von Haydn*, 227, 243).

17. The privately owned, dated autograph (described by Walter in "Kritischer Bericht," 215) is on loan to the Pierpont Morgan Library in New York.

18. As reported in Walter, "Vorwort," xi–xii.

19. Apparently at Griesinger's urging (see his letter of 27 November 1802 to Härtel [Biba, *Eben komme ich von Haydn*, 173]), probably in compensation for Haydn's not having written the quintets promised to Fries.

20. *Allgemeine musikalische Zeitung* 9 (1806–7), *Intelligenz-Blatt* I:2.

21. Concerning the Pleyel and Clementi editions, see Walter, "Vorwort," xiv, and "Kritischer Bericht," 216–18.

22. See Walter, "Kritischer Bericht," 216.

23. This opus number appears only on the André and Simrock editions, Simrock's deriving from André's. See "Kritischer Bericht," 216–18.

24. Haimo, "Remote Keys," 244–45.

25. See Webster, *"Farewell" Symphony*, 172.

26. See Rosen, *Classical Style*, 74, and *Sonata Forms*, 288. See also Hepokoski, "Beyond the Sonata Principle," 131–32.

27. For further discussion, see Somfai, "Bold Enharmonic Modulatory Model."

28. Here a connection may be drawn with the finale of Op. 76/1/iv, in which a tonal trajectory likewise led to the home key's polar opposite (in this instance, an extended span of Db minor harmony) precisely at the movement's halfway point.

29. Artistic rivalry between Haydn and Beethoven is a possibly relevant factor. See Webster, "Falling-out," 26, and Landon, *Chronicle and Works*, 4:502–8, 5:281–82.

30. Landon, *Chronicle and Works*, 5:235, 238 (Biba, *Eben komme ich von Haydn*, 169, Bartha, *Briefe*, 415, respectively).

31. Landon, *Chronicle and Works*, 5:84, modified (Biba, *Eben komme ich von Haydn*, 106).

32. Our translation from Olleson, "Griesinger's Correspondence," 51. See also Landon, *Chronicle and Works*, 5:344.

33. See Edwards, "Nonsense of an Ending."

Bibliography

Agawu, V. Kofi. *Playing with Signs: A Semiotic Interpretation of Classic Music*. Princeton: Princeton University Press, 1991.

Allanbrook, Wye Jamison. *Rhythmic Gesture in Mozart: "Le nozze di Figaro" and "Don Giovanni."* Chicago: University of Chicago Press, 1983.

Allgemeine musikalische Zeitung. Ed. Friedrich Rochlitz et al. 52 vols. Leipzig, 1798–1865.

Anderson, Emily, trans. and ed. *The Letters of Mozart and His Family*. 2d ed. 2 vols. Prepared by A. Hyatt King and Monica Carolan. London: Macmillan, 1966.

Andrews, Harold L. "The Submediant in Haydn's Development Sections." In *Haydn Studies* (1981), 465–71.

Angermüller, Rudolph. "Sigismund Ritter von Neukomm (1778–1858) und seine Lehrer Michael und Joseph Haydn: Eine Dokumentation." *Haydn-Studien* 3 (1973–74): 29–42.

Artaria, Franz, and Hugo Botstiber. *Joseph Haydn und das Verlagshaus Artaria, nach den Briefen des Meisters an das Haus Artaria & Compagnie dargestellt*. Vienna: Artaria, 1909.

Bach, Carl Philipp Emanuel. *Versuch über die Wahre Art das Clavier zu spielen*. 2 vols. 1753–62. Reprint. Leipzig: VEB Breitkopf & Härtel, 1969. Trans. and ed. William J. Mitchell as *Essay on the True Art of Playing Keyboard Instruments*. New York: W. W. Norton, 1949.

Badura-Skoda, Eva. "Dittersdorf über Haydns und Mozarts Quartette." In *Collectanea Mozartiana*, ed. Cordula Roleff, 41–50. Tutzing: Schneider, 1988.

Baker, James M. "Chromaticism in Classical Music." In *Music Theory and the Exploration of the Past*, ed. Christopher Hatch and David W. Bernstein, 233–307. Chicago: University of Chicago Press, 1993.

Ballstaedt, Andreas. "'Humor' und 'Witz' in Joseph Haydns Musik." *Archiv für Musikwissenschaft* 55 (1998): 195–219.

Bandur, Markus. *Form und Gehalt in den Streichquartetten Joseph Haydns: Studien zur Theorie der Sonatenform*. Pfaffenweiler: Centaurus, 1988.

———. "Plot und Rekurs—'eine gantz neue besondere Art'? Analytische Überlegungen zum Kopfsatz von Joseph Haydns Streichquartett op. 33, Nr. 1 (Hoboken III:37)." In *Haydns Streichquartette*, 62–84.

Barrett-Ayres, Reginald. *Joseph Haydn and the String Quartet*. New York: Schirmer Books, 1974.

Bartha, Dénes. "Thematic Profile and Character in the Quartet-Finales of Joseph Haydn (A Contribution to the Micro-Analysis of Thematic Structure)." *Studia Musicologica* 11 (1969): 35–62.

———, ed. *Joseph Haydn: Gesammelte Briefe und Aufzeichnungen.* Kassel: Bärenreiter, 1965.

Bauer, Wilhelm A., and Otto Erich Deutsch, eds. *Mozart: Briefe und Aufzeichnungen. Gesamtausgabe.* 7 vols. Kassel: Bärenreiter, 1962–75.

Beer, Axel, and Klaus Burmeister. "'in betreff des geizigen Caracters von Haydn'—Ein Brief Franz Anton Hoffmeisters als Quelle zur Musik- und Verlagsgeschichte der Zeit um 1800." *Die Musikforschung* 50 (1997): 36–47.

Bellman, Jonathan. *The "Style Hongrois" in the Music of Western Europe.* Boston: Northeastern University Press, 1993.

Berger, Christian. "Die Lust an der Form, oder: Warum ist Haydns Streichquartett op. 33,5 'klassisch'?" In *Rezeption als Innovation: Untersuchungen zu einem Grundmodell der europäischen Kompositionsgeschichte. Festschrift für Friedhelm Krummacher zum 65. Geburtstag,* ed. Bernd Sponheuer et al., 121–34. Kassel: Bärenreiter, 2001.

Biba, Otto. *"Eben komme ich von Haydn . . .": Georg August Griesingers Korrespondenz mit Joseph Haydns Verleger Breitkopf & Härtel, 1799–1819.* Zurich: Atlantis, 1987.

———. "Nachrichten zur Musikpflege in der gräflichen Familie Harrach." *The Haydn Yearbook* 10 (1978): 36–44.

Bloxam, M. Jennifer. "A Sketch for the Andante Grazioso of Haydn's String Quartet 'Opus 103.'" *The Haydn Yearbook* 14 (1983): 129–43.

Blume, Friedrich. "Haydn und Mozart." In Blume, *Syntagma Musicologicum,* 570–82.

———. "Joseph Haydns künstlerische Persönlichkeit in seinen Streichquartetten." *Jahrbuch der Musikbibliothek Peters* 38 (1931): 24–48. Repr. in Blume, *Syntagma Musicologicum,* 526–51.

———. *Syntagma Musicologicum: Gesammelte Reden und Schriften,* ed. Martin Ruhnke. Kassel: Bärenreiter, 1963.

Bonds, Mark Evan. "Haydn, Laurence Sterne, and the Origins of Musical Irony." *Journal of the American Musicological Society* 44 (1991): 57–91.

———. "Haydn's False Recapitulations and the Perception of Sonata Form in the Eighteenth Century." Ph.D. diss., Harvard University, 1988.

———. "The Sincerest Form of Flattery? Mozart's 'Haydn' Quartets and the Question of Influence." *Studi Musicali* 22 (1993): 365–409.

———. *Wordless Rhetoric: Musical Form and the Metaphor of the Oration.* Cambridge, Mass.: Harvard University Press, 1991.

Brook, Barry S., ed. *The Breitkopf Thematic Catalogue: The Six Parts and Sixteen Supplements, 1762–1787.* New York: Dover, 1966.

Brown, A. Peter. "The Chamber Music with Strings of Carlos d'Ordóñez: A Bibliographic and Stylistic Study." *Acta Musicologica* 46 (1974): 222–72.

———. "Joseph Haydn and C. P. E. Bach: The Question of Influence." In *Haydn Studies* (1981), 158–64.

———. *Joseph Haydn's Keyboard Music: Sources and Style.* Bloomington: Indiana University Press, 1986.

———. "Preface." *Carlo d'Ordonez: String Quartets, Opus 1,* vii–xiii. Madison, Wisc.: A-R Editions, 1980.

Brown, A. Peter, and James T. Berkenstock, in collaboration with Carol Vanderbilt Brown. "Joseph Haydn in Literature: A Bibliography." *Haydn-Studien* 3 (1973–74): 173–469.

Brown, Clive. *Classical and Romantic Performance Practice, 1750–1900*. Oxford: Oxford University Press, 1999.

Broyles, Michael. "Organic Form and the Binary Repeat." *The Musical Quarterly* 66 (1980): 339–60.

Caplin, William E. "The Classical Cadence: Conceptions and Misconceptions." *Journal of the American Musicological Society* 57 (2004): 51–117.

———. *Classical Form: A Theory of Formal Functions for the Instrumental Music of Haydn, Mozart, and Beethoven*. New York: Oxford University Press, 1998.

Carner, Mosco. "Ländler." In *The New Grove Dictionary of Music and Musicians*, 2d ed., ed. Stanley Sadie and John Tyrrell, 14: 222–23. London: Macmillan, 2001.

Cherbuliez, Antoine. "Bemerkungen zu den 'Haydn'-Streichquartetten Mozarts und Haydns 'Russischen' Streichquartetten." *Mozart-Jahrbuch 1959*, 28–45.

Churgin, Bathia. "Francesco Galeazzi's Description (1796) of Sonata Form." *Journal of the American Musicological Society* 21 (1968): 181–99.

———. "Harmonic and Tonal Instability in the Second Key Area of Classic Sonata Form." In *Convention in Eighteenth- and Nineteenth-Century Music*, 23–57.

Cole, Malcolm S. "Sonata-Rondo, the Formulation of a Theoretical Concept in the 18th and 19th Centuries." *The Musical Quarterly* 55 (1969): 180–92.

———. "The Vogue of the Instrumental Rondo in the Late Eighteenth Century." *Journal of the American Musicological Society* 22 (1969): 425–55.

Cone, Edward T. *The Composer's Voice*. Berkeley: University of California Press, 1974.

———. *Musical Form and Musical Performance*. New York: W. W. Norton, 1968.

———. "The Uses of Convention: Stravinsky and His Models." *The Musical Quarterly* 48 (1962): 287–99. Repr. in Cone, *Music: A View from Delft. Selected Essays*, ed. Robert P. Morgan, 39–54. Chicago: University of Chicago Press, 1989.

Convention in Eighteenth- and Nineteenth-Century Music. Essays in Honor of Leonard G. Ratner. Ed. Wye J. Allanbrook, Janet M. Levy, and William P. Mahrt. Stuyvesant, N.Y.: Pendragon, 1992.

Cooper, Grosvenor W., and Leonard B. Meyer. *The Rhythmic Structure of Music*. Chicago: University of Chicago Press, 1960.

Cushman, David Stephen. "Joseph Haydn's Melodic Materials: An Exploratory Introduction to the Primary and Secondary Sources Together with an Analytical Catalogue and Table of Proposed Melodic Correspondence and/or Variance." Ph.D. diss., Boston University, 1972.

———. "Sources of Haydn's Melodic Material." In *Haydn Studies* (1981), 377–80.

Danuser, Hermann. "Das Ende als Anfang: Ausblick von einer Schlussfigur bei Joseph Haydn." In *Studien zur Musikgeschichte. Eine Festschrift für Ludwig Finscher*, ed. Annegrit Laubenthal, 818–27. Kassel: Bärenreiter, 1995.

Demaree, Robert W., Jr. "The Structural Proportions of the Haydn Quartets." PhD. diss., Indiana University, 1973.

Deutsch, Otto Erich. "Theme and Variations, with Bibliographical Notes on Pleyel's Haydn Editions." *The Music Review* 12 (1951): 68–71.

Dies, Albert Christoph. *Biographische Nachrichten von Joseph Haydn, nach mündlichen Erzählungen desselben entworfen und herausgegeben*. 1810. Modern ed., Horst Seeger. Berlin: Henschel, 1959.

Drabkin, William. "Corelli's Trio Sonatas and the Viennese String Quartet: Some Points of Contact." In *Studi Corelliani V. Atti del quinto congresso internazionale (Fusignano, 9–11 settembre 1994)*, ed. Stefano La Via, 119–41. Florence: Olschki, 1996.

————. *A Reader's Guide to Haydn's Early String Quartets.* Westport, Conn.: Greenwood, 2000.

Dunsby, Jonathan. "The Formal Repeat." *Proceedings of the Royal Musical Association* 112 (1986–87): 196–207.

Dworschak, Fritz. "Joseph Haydn und Karl Joseph Weber von Fürnberg: Die ersten Streich-quartette—Schloss Weinzierl—Johann Georg Albrechtsberger und der Melker Kreis." *Unsere Heimat* 5 (1932): 187–204.

Edwards, George. "The Nonsense of an Ending: Closure in Haydn's String Quartets." *The Musical Quarterly* 75 (1991): 227–54.

————. "Papa Doc's Recap Caper: Haydn and Temporal Dyslexia." In *Haydn Studies* (1998), 291–320.

Engel, Hans. "Haydn, Mozart und die Klassik." *Mozart-Jahrbuch 1959*, 46–79.

Esch, Christian. "Haydns Streichquartett op. 54/1 und Mozarts KV 465." *Haydn-Studien* 6 (1986–94): 148–55.

Feder, Georg. "Apokryphe 'Haydn'-Streichquartette." *Haydn-Studien* 3 (1973–74): 125–50.

————. "Aus Roman Hoffstetters Briefen." *Haydn-Studien* 1 (1965–67): 198–201.

————. "Die beiden Pole im Instrumentalschaffen des jungen Haydn." In *Der junge Haydn: Wandel von Musikauffassung und Musikaufführung in der österreichischen Musik zwischen Barock und Klassik. Bericht der Internationalen Arbeitstagung des Instituts für Aufführungspraxis der Hochschule für Musik und darstellende Kunst in Graz, 29.6–2.7.1970*, ed. Vera Schwarz, 192–201. Graz: Akademische Druck- und Verlagsanstalt, 1972.

————. "Bemerkungen zu Haydns Skizzen." *Beethoven-Jahrbuch* 9 (1973–77): 69–86.

————. "Die Eingriffe des Musikverlegers Hummel in Haydns Werken." In *Musicae Scientiae Collectanea. Festschrift Karl Gustav Fellerer zum siebzigsten Geburtstag am 7. Juli 1972*, ed. Heinrich Hüschen, 88–101. Cologne: Volk, 1973.

————. "From the Workshop of the Haydn Edition," *The Musical Times* 123 (1982): 166–69.

————. "Haydn's Corrections in the Autographs of the Quartets Opus 64 and Opus 71/74." In *The String Quartets of Haydn, Mozart, and Beethoven*, 99–110.

————. "Haydns frühe Klaviertrios: Eine Untersuchung zur Echtheit und Chronologie." *Haydn-Studien* 2 (1969–70): 289–316.

————. *Haydns Streichquartette: Ein musikalischer Werkführer.* Munich: Beck, 1998.

————. "Haydns Streichquartette—Erlebnis und Interpretation." In *Internationales musikwissenschaftliches Symposium "Haydn & Das Streichquartett,"* 9–15.

————. "Joseph Haydns Skizzen und Entwürfe: Übersicht der Manuskripte, Werkregister, Literatur- und Ausgabenverzeichnis." *Fontes Artis Musicae* 26 (1979): 172–88.

————. "Joseph Haydn: Streichquartett D-Dur, op. 64, Nr. 5 ('Lerchenquartett')." In *Werkanalyse in Beispielen*, ed. Siegmund Helms and Helmut Hopf, 70–81. Regensburg: Bosse, 1986.

————. *Kritischer Bericht. Joseph Haydn: Frühe Streichquartette* (JHW, 12/1). Munich: Henle, 1973.

————. "Manuscript Sources of Haydn's Works and Their Distribution." *The Haydn Yearbook* 4 (1968): 102–39. Trans. of "Die Überlieferung und Verbreitung der handschriftlichen Quellen zu Haydns Werken (Erste Folge)." *Haydn-Studien* 1 (1965–67): 3–42.

————. "Nachricht über die Krakauer Haydn-Autographen." *Haydn-Studien* 5 (1982–85): 135–36.

————. "Similarities in the Works of Haydn." In *Studies in Eighteenth-Century Music*, 186–97.

————. "Textkritische Methoden: Versuch eines Überblicks mit Bezug auf die Haydn-Gesamtausgabe." *Haydn-Studien* 5 (1982–85): 77–109.

————. "Ein vergessener Haydn-Brief." *Haydn-Studien* 1 (1965–67): 114–16.

————. "Vorwort." *Joseph Haydn: Frühe Streichquartette*, vii–xi (JHW, 12/1). Munich: Henle, 1973.

————. "Vorwort." *Joseph Haydn: Streichquartette "Opus 9" und "Opus 17,"* vi–vii (JHW, 12/2). Munich: Henle, 1963.

————. "Vorwort." *Joseph Haydn: Streichquartette "Opus 64" und "Opus 71/74,"* vii–x (JHW, 12/5). Munich: Henle, 1978.

————. "Zur Textkritik von Haydns Streichquartetten." *Concerto* 2/6 (1985): 25–31. Also in *Festschrift Arno Forchert zum 60. Geburtstag am 29. Dezember 1985*, ed. Gerhard Allroggen and Detlef Altenburg, 131–41. Kassel: Bärenreiter, 1986.

Feder, Georg, and Sonja Gerlach. *Kritischer Bericht. Joseph Haydn: Streichquartette "Opus 20" und "Opus 33"* (JHW, 12/3). Munich: Henle, 1974.

————. "Vorwort." *Joseph Haydn: Streichquartette "Opus 20" und "Opus 33,"* vii–ix (JHW, 12/3). Munich: Henle, 1974.

Feder, Georg, in collaboration with Gottfried Greiner. *Kritischer Bericht. Joseph Haydn: Frühe Streichquartette* (JHW, 12/1). Munich: Henle, 1973.

Feder, Georg, and Isidor Saslav, in collaboration with Warren Kirkendale. *Kritischer Bericht. Joseph Haydn: Streichquartette "Opus 64" und "Opus 71/74"* (JHW, 12/5). Munich: Henle, 1991.

Fillion, Michelle. "Sonata-Exposition Procedures in Haydn's Keyboard Sonatas." In *Haydn Studies* (1981), 475–81.

Finscher, Ludwig. "Corelli, Haydn und die klassischen Gattungen der Kammermusik." In *Gattungen der Musik und ihre Klassiker*, ed. Hermann Danuser, 185–95. Laaber: Laaber, 1988.

————. "Joseph Haydn und das italienische Streichquartett." *Analecta Musicologica* 4 (1967): 13–37.

————. *Joseph Haydn und seine Zeit*. Laaber: Laaber, 2000.

————. *Studien zur Geschichte des Streichquartetts*. Vol. 1. *Die Entstehung des klassischen Streichquartetts. Von den Vorformen zur Grundlegung durch Joseph Haydn*. Kassel: Bärenreiter, 1974.

————. "Zum Begriff der Klassik in der Musik." *Deutsches Jahrbuch der Musikwissenschaft*, 11 (1966): 9–34.

————. "Zur Sozialgeschichte des klassischen Streichquartetts." *Gesellschaft für Musikforschung. Bericht über den Internationalen Musikwissenschaftlichen Kongress Kassel 1962*, ed. Georg Reichert and Martin Just, 37–39. Kassel: Bärenreiter, 1963.

Fischer, Wilhelm. "Zur Entwicklungsgeschichte des Wiener klassischen Stils." *Studien zur Musikwissenschaft* 3 (1915): 24–84.

Forschner, Hermann. *Instrumentalmusik Joseph Haydns aus der Sicht Heinrich Christoph Kochs*. Munich: Katzbichler, 1984.

Geiringer, Karl. *Haydn: A Creative Life in Music*. 3d ed. Berkeley: University of California Press, 1982.

————. "The Rise of Chamber Music." In *The New Oxford History of Music*. Vol. 7. *The Age of Enlightenment: 1745–1790*, ed. Egon Wellesz and Frederick Sternfeld, 515–73. London: Oxford University Press, 1973.

Georgiades, Thrasybulos. "Zur Musiksprache der Wiener Klassiker," *Mozart-Jahrbuch 1951*, 50–59. Repr. in Georgiades, *Kleine Schriften*, 33–43. Tutzing: Schneider, 1977.

Gerber, Ernst Ludwig. *Historisch-biographisches Lexikon der Tonkünstler*. 2 vols. 1790–92. Reprint. Graz: Akademische Druck- u. Verlagsanstalt, 1977.

———. *Neues historisch-biographisches Lexikon der Tonkünstler*. 4 vols. 1812–14. Reprint. Graz: Akademische Druck- u. Verlagsanstalt, 1966.

Gerlach, Sonja. "Johann Tost, Geiger und Grosshandlungsgremialist." *Haydn-Studien* 7 (1996–98): 344–65.

Gmeiner, Josef. *Menuett und Scherzo: Ein Beitrag zur Entwicklungsgeschichte und Soziologie des Tanzsatzes in der Wiener Klassik*. Tutzing: Schneider, 1979.

Gotwals, Vernon. "The Earliest Biographies of Haydn." *The Musical Quarterly* 45 (1959): 439–59.

Gotwals, Vernon, trans. and ed. *Haydn: Two Contemporary Portraits*. Madison: University of Wisconsin Press, 1968. Trans. of Georg August Griesinger, *Biographische Notizen*, and Albert Christoph Dies, *Biographische Nachrichten*.

Grasberger, Franz. *Die Hymnen Österreichs*. Tutzing: Schneider, 1968.

Grave, Floyd. "Common-Time Displacement in Mozart." *The Journal of Musicology* 3 (1984): 423–42.

———. "Concerto Style in Haydn's String Quartets." *The Journal of Musicology* 18 (2001): 76–97.

———. "Metrical Displacement and the Compound Measure in Eighteenth-Century Theory and Practice." *Theoria* 1 (1985): 25–60.

———. "Metrical Dissonance in Haydn." *The Journal of Musicology* 13 (1995): 168–202.

Grave, Floyd, and Margaret Grave. *Franz Joseph Haydn: A Guide to Research*. New York: Garland, 1990.

Griesinger, Georg August. *Biographische Notizen über Joseph Haydn*. 1810. Modern ed., Franz Grasberger. Vienna: Kaltschmied, 1954.

Griffiths, Paul. *The String Quartet*. New York: Thames and Hudson, 1983.

Haimo, Ethan. "Haydn's Altered Reprise." *Journal of Music Theory* 32 (1988): 335–51.

———. *Haydn's Symphonic Forms: Essays in Compositional Logic*. Oxford: Clarendon, 1995.

———. "Remote Keys and Multi-Movement Unity: Haydn in the 1790s." *The Musical Quarterly* 74 (1990): 242–68.

Hase, Hermann von. *Joseph Haydn und Breitkopf & Härtel: Ein Rückblick bei der Veranstaltung der ersten vollständigen Gesamtausgabe seiner Werke*. Leipzig: Breitkopf & Härtel, 1909.

Hatten, Robert S. *Musical Meaning in Beethoven: Markedness, Correlation, and Interpretation*. Bloomington: Indiana University Press, 1994.

Haydn, Joseph. *Briefe an Artaria: Eine Auswahl*. Facsimile ed. Eisenstadt: Verein Internationale Joseph-Haydn-Stiftung Eisenstadt, 1993.

———. *Frühe Streichquartette*. Ed. Georg Feder, in collaboration with Georg Greiner. *Joseph Haydn Werke*. Ser. 12, vol. 1. Munich: Henle, 1973.

———. *Gott! erhalte Franz den Kaiser und Streichquartett Op. 76, Nr. 3: Variationensatz*. Facsimile. Ed. Günter Brosche, with commentary. Graz: Akademische Druck- u. Verlagsanstalt, 1995.

———. *Streichquartette "Opus 9" und "Opus 17."* Ed. Georg Feder. *Joseph Haydn Werke*. Ser. 12, vol. 2. Munich: Henle, 1963.

———. *Streichquartette "Opus 20" und "Opus 33."* Ed. Georg Feder and Sonja Gerlach. *Joseph Haydn Werke*. Ser. 12, vol. 3. Munich: Henle, 1974.

———. *Streichquartette "Opus 64" und "Opus 71/74."* Ed. Georg Feder and Isidor Saslav, in collaboration with Warren Kirkendale. *Joseph Haydn Werke*. Ser. 12, vol. 5. Munich: Henle, 1978.

———. *Streichquartette "Opus 76," "Opus 77" und "Opus 103."* Ed. Horst Walter, with preparatory work by Lars Schmidt-Thieme. *Joseph Haydn Werke*. Ser. 12, vol. 6. Munich: Henle, 2003.

———. *Streichquartette. Urtext-Ausgabe*. Ed. Reginald Barrett-Ayres and H. C. Robbins Landon. 68 vols. Vienna: Doblinger, 1982–88.

———. *String Quartet in G, 1799, Hoboken III:81*. Facsimile. Ed. László Somfai, with commentary. New York: Belwin-Mills, 1972.

———. *String Quartet in F, 1799, Hoboken III:82*. Facsimile. Ed. László Somfai, with commentary. New York: Belwin-Mills, 1972.

———. *Tänze und Märsche*. Ed. Günter Thomas. *Joseph Haydn Werke*. Ser. 5, vol. 1. Munich: Henle, 1995.

Haydn the Innovator: A New Approach to the String Quartets. Ed. David Young. Todmorden, United Kingdom: Arc Music, 2000.

Haydn Studies. Ed. W. Dean Sutcliffe. Cambridge: Cambridge University Press, 1998.

Haydn Studies. Proceedings of the International Haydn Conference, Washington, D.C., 1975. Ed. Jens Peter Larsen, Howard Serwer, and James Webster. New York: W. W. Norton, 1981.

Haydns Streichquartette: Eine moderne Gattung. Ed. Heinz Klaus Metzger and Rainer Riehn. Munich: Boorberg, 2002.

Heartz, Daniel. "Ditters, Gluck und der Artikel 'Von dem wienerischen Geschmack in der Musik.'" *Gluck Studien* 1 (1989): 78–80.

———. *Haydn, Mozart and the Viennese School, 1740–1780*. New York: W. W. Norton, 1995.

———. *Music in European Capitals: The Galant Style, 1720–1780*. New York: W. W. Norton, 2003.

Hepokoski, James. "Beyond the Sonata Principle." *Journal of the American Musicological Society* 55 (2002): 91–154.

Hepokoski, James, and Warren Darcy. "The Medial Caesura and Its Role in the Eighteenth-Century Sonata Exposition." *Music Theory Spectrum* 19 (1997): 115–54.

Hickman, Roger. "The Flowering of the Viennese String Quartet in the Late Eighteenth Century." *The Music Review* 50 (1989): 157–80.

———. "Haydn and the 'Symphony in Miniature.'" *The Music Review* 43 (1982): 15–23.

———. "The Nascent Viennese String Quartet." *The Musical Quarterly* 67 (1981): 193–212.

———. "Preface." *Leopold Kozeluch: String Quartets, Opus 32 and Opus 33*, vii–xiv. Madison, Wisc.: A-R Editions, 1994.

Hoboken, Anthony van. *Joseph Haydn: Thematisch-bibliographisches Werkverzeichnis*. 3 vols. Mainz: B. Schott's Söhne, 1957–78.

Hoyt, Peter A. "The 'False Recapitulation' and the Conventions of Sonata Form." Ph.D. diss., University of Pennsylvania, 1999.

———. "Review-Essay: Haydn's New Incoherence." *Music Theory Spectrum* 19 (1997): 264–84.

Hughes, Rosemary. *Haydn String Quartets*. 1966. Reprint. Seattle: University of Washington Press, 1969.

Hunter, Mary. "Haydn's London Piano Trios and His Salomon String Quartets: Private vs. Public?" In *Haydn and His World*, ed. Elaine Sisman, 103–30. Princeton: Princeton University Press, 1997.

Internationales musikwissenschaftliches Symposium "Haydn & Das Streichquartett," im Rahmen des "Haydn Streichquartett Weekend," Eisenstadt, 1.-5. Mai 2002. Referate und Diskussionen. Ed. Georg Feder und Walter Reicher. Tutzing: Schneider, 2003.

Irving, Howard. "Haydn and Laurence Sterne: Similarities in Eighteenth-Century Literary and Musical Wit." *Current Musicology*, no. 40 (1985), 34–49.

Irving, John. *Mozart: The "Haydn" Quartets.* Cambridge: Cambridge University Press, 1998.

———. "Reading Haydn's Quartets." In *Haydn the Innovator*, 11–31.

Johansson, Cari. *French Music Publishers' Catalogues of the Second Half of the Eighteenth Century.* Stockholm, 1955.

———. *J. J. & B. Hummel: Music Publishing and Thematic Catalogues.* Stockholm, 1972.

Jones, David Wyn. "Haydn's Music in London in the Period 1760–1790. Part One." *The Haydn Yearbook* 14 (1983): 144–72.

———. "Minuets and Trios in Haydn's Quartets." In *Haydn the Innovator*, 81–97.

———. "A Newly Identified Sketchleaf for Haydn's Quartet in D Minor, 'Op. 103.'" *Haydn-Studien* 8 (2000–2004): 413–17.

———, ed. *Oxford Composer Companions: Haydn.* New York: Oxford University Press, 2002.

Joseph Haydn. Bericht über den Internationalen Joseph Haydn Kongress. Wien, Hofburg, 5–12 September 1982. Ed. Eva Badura-Skoda. Munich: Henle, 1986.

Joseph Haydn: Tradition und Rezeption. Bericht über die Jahrestagung der Gesellschaft für Musikforschung, Köln 1982. Ed. Georg Feder, Heinrich Hüschen, and Ulrich Tank. Regensburg: Bosse, 1985.

Kartomi, Margaret J. "Haydn Autograph Manuscripts Verified in Melbourne: String Quartets Opus 50 Nos. 3–6, of 1787." *Musicology* 7 (1982): 139.

Keller, Hans. *The Great Haydn Quartets: Their Interpretation.* New York: Braziller, 1986.

Kiem, Eckehard. "'. . . vielleicht zu überbieten, aber nicht zu übertreffen': Zeitartikulation in Haydns Quartett op. 50, I." *Musik & Ästhetik* 5 (2001): 5–24.

Kirkendale, Warren. *Fugue and Fugato in Rococo and Classical Chamber Music.* Rev. 2d ed., trans. Margaret Bent and the author. Durham, N.C.: Duke University Press, 1979. Trans. of *Fuge und Fugato in der Kammermusik des Rokoko und der Klassik.* Tutzing: Schneider, 1966.

Koch, Heinrich Christoph. *Musikalisches Lexikon.* 2 vols. 1802. Reprint. Hildesheim: Olms. 1964.

———. *Versuch einer Anleitung zur Composition.* 3 vols. 1782–93. Reprint. Hildesheim: Olms, 1969. Vol. 2, part 2, and vol. 3 trans. Nancy Kovaleff Baker as *Introductory Essay on Composition: The Mechanical Rules of Melody, Sections 3 and 4.* New Haven, Conn.: Yale University Press, 1983.

Kollmann, Augustus Frederic Christopher. *An Essay on Practical Musical Composition.* 1799. Reprint. New York: Da Capo, 1973.

Konold, Wulf. "Normerfüllung und Normverweigerung beim späten Haydn—am Beispiel des Streichquartetts op. 76, Nr. 6." In *Joseph Haydn: Tradition und Rezeption*, 54–73.

———. *The String Quartet. From Its Beginnings to Franz Schubert.* Trans. Susan Hellauer. New York: Heinrichshofen, 1983. Trans. of *Das Streichquartett. Von den Anfängen bis Franz Schubert.* Wilhelmshaven: Heinrichshofen, 1980.

Krummacher, Friedhelm. "Haydn—Gründer des Streichquartetts? Anmerkungen zu frühen Quartettsätzen." In *Internationales musikwissenschaftliches Symposium "Haydn & Das Streich- quartett,"* 17–42.

———. *Das Streichquartett.* Vol. 1. *Von Haydn bis Schubert.* Laaber: Laaber, 2001.

Landon, H. C. Robbins. "Four New Haydn Letters." *The Haydn Yearbook* 13 (1982): 213–19.

———. *Haydn: Chronicle and Works.* Vol. 1. *Haydn: The Early Years, 1732–1765.* 1980. Reprint. London: Thames and Hudson, 1994.

———. *Haydn: Chronicle and Works.* Vol. 2. *Haydn at Eszterháza, 1766–1790.* 1978. Reprint. London: Thames and Hudson, 1994.

———. *Haydn: Chronicle and Works.* Vol. 3. *Haydn in England, 1791–1795.* 1976. Reprint. London: Thames and Hudson, 1994.

———. *Haydn: Chronicle and Works.* Vol. 4. *The Years of "The Creation," 1796–1800.* 1977. Reprint. London: Thames and Hudson, 1994.

———. *Haydn: Chronicle and Works.* Vol. 5. *Haydn: The Late Years, 1801–1809.* 1977. Reprint, with supplementary addenda. London: Thames and Hudson, 1994.

———. "Haydniana (II)." *The Haydn Yearbook* 7 (1970): 307–19.

———. "Johann Peter Salomon—'Er brachte Haydn nach England.'" In *Joseph Haydn und Bonn,* ed. Ingrid Bodsch, in collaboration with Otto Biba and Ingrid Fuchs, 131–41. Bonn: Stadt Museum Bonn, 2001.

———. "More Haydn Letters in Autograph." *The Haydn Yearbook* 14 (1983): 201–5.

———. "On Haydn's Quartets of Opera 1 and 2: Notes and Comments on Sondheimer's *His- torical and Psychological Study.*" *The Music Review* 13 (1952): 181–86.

———, trans. and ed. *The Collected Correspondence and London Notebooks of Joseph Haydn.* Fairlawn, N.J.: Essential Books, 1959.

———, trans. and comp. "18th and 19th Century Newspaper Articles Regarding Haydn and Contemporaries." *The Haydn Yearbook* 21 (1997): 77–87.

Landon, H. C. Robbins, and David Wyn Jones. *Haydn: His Life and Music.* Bloomington: In- diana University Press, 1988.

Larsen, Jens Peter. *Handel, Haydn, and the Viennese Classical Style.* Trans. Ulrich Krämer. Ann Arbor, Mich.: UMI Research Press, 1988.

———. "Haydn and Mozart." In Larsen, *Handel, Haydn, and the Viennese Classical Style,* 117–22. Trans. of "Haydn und Mozart." *Österreichische Musikzeitschrift* 14 (1959): 216–22.

———. *Die Haydn Überlieferung.* 1939. Reprint. Munich: Kraus, 1980.

———. "Sonata Form Problems." *Studia Musicologica* 9 (1967): 115–39. Repr. in Larsen, *Han- del, Haydn, and the Viennese Classical Style,* 269–79. Trans. of "Sonatenform-Probleme," in *Festschrift Friedrich Blume zum 70. Geburtstag,* ed. Anna Amalie Abert and Wilhelm Pfannkuch, 221–30. Kassel: Bärenreiter, 1963.

———, ed. *Drei Haydn Kataloge in Faksimile.* 1941. 2d facsimile ed. as *Three Haydn Catalogues [Drei Haydn Kataloge].* New York: Pendragon, 1979.

Larson, Steve. "Recapitulation Recomposition in the Sonata-Form First Movements of Haydn's String Quartets: Style Change and Compositional Technique." *Music Analysis* 22 (2003): 139–77.

LaRue, Jan. "Bifocal Tonality: An Explanation for Ambiguous Baroque Cadences." In *Essays on Music in Honor of Archibald Thompson Davison by His Associates,* 173–84. Cambridge, Mass.: Harvard University Press, 1957. Repr. in *The Journal of Musicology* 18 (2001): 283–94.

———. "Bifocal Tonality in Haydn Symphonies." In *Convention in Eighteenth- and Nineteenth-Century Music*, 59–73.

———. *Guidelines for Style Analysis*. 2d ed. Warren, Mich.: Harmonie Park Press, 1992.

———. "The Haydn-Dedication Quartets: Allusion or Influence?" *Mozart-Jahrbuch 1991*, 1:518–21. Repr. in *The Journal of Musicology* 18 (2001): 361–73.

———. "A Haydn Specialty: Multistage Variance." In *Joseph Haydn*, 141–46.

———. "Multistage Variance: Haydn's Legacy to Beethoven." *The Journal of Musicology* 1 (1982): 265–74. Repr. in *The Journal of Musicology* 18 (2001): 344–60.

———. "Significant and Coincidental Resemblance between Classical Themes." *Journal of the American Musicological Society* 14 (1961): 224–34. Repr. in *The Journal of Musicology* 18 (2001): 268–82.

Lester, Joel. *The Rhythms of Tonal Music*. Carbondale: Southern Illinois University Press, 1986.

Levy, Janet M. "Gesture, Form, and Syntax in Haydn's Music." In *Haydn Studies* (1981), 355–62.

———. "The *Quatuor Concertant* in Paris in the Latter Half of the Eighteenth Century." Ph.D. diss., Stanford University, 1971.

———. "'Something Mechanical Encrusted on the Living': A Source of Musical Wit and Humor." In *Convention in Eighteenth- and Nineteenth-Century Music*, 225–56.

———. "Texture as a Sign in Classic and Early Romantic Music." *Journal of the American Musicological Society* 35 (1982): 482–531.

Lichtenstein, Osnat. "Haydn's Quartets Op. 20: The Interrelation of the Main Sections in the Sonata-Form First Movements." Ph.D. diss., Bar-Ilan University, 1996.

Löher, Burckhard. *Strukturwissenschaftliche Darstellung der ersten und letzten Sätze der sechs Streichquartette op. 76 von Joseph Haydn*. 2 vols. Münster, 1983.

Lowe, Melanie. "Falling from Grace: Irony and Expressive Enrichment in Haydn's Symphonic Minuets." *The Journal of Musicology* 19 (2002): 171–221.

MacDonald, Hugh. "To Repeat or Not to Repeat." *Proceedings of the Royal Musical Association* 111 (1984–85): 121–38.

Magazin der Musik. Ed. Carl Friedrich Cramer. 2 vols. 1783–86. Reprint. Hildesheim: Olms, 1971.

McCaldin, Denis. "The First Movements [of Haydn's String Quartets]." In *Haydn the Innovator*, 33–56.

McCreless, Patrick. "Music and Rhetoric." In *The Cambridge History of Western Music Theory*, ed. Thomas Christensen, 847–79. Cambridge: Cambridge University Press, 2002.

McVeigh, Simon. *Concert Life in London from Mozart to Haydn*. Cambridge: Cambridge University Press, 1993.

———. "The Professional Concert and Rival Subscription Series in London, 1783–1793." *R. M. A. Research Chronicle* 22 (1989): 1–135.

Meyer, Leonard. *Explaining Music: Essays and Explorations*. Berkeley: University of California Press, 1973.

Moe, Orin, Jr. "Texture in Haydn's Early Quartets." *The Music Review* 35 (1974): 4–22.

———. "Texture in the String Quartets of Haydn to 1787." Ph.D. diss., University of California at Santa Barbara, 1970.

Monk, Dennis. "Introduction." *Franz Asplmayr: Six Quatuors concertants, Opus 2*, vii–x. Madison, Wisc.: A-R Editions, 1999.

Mörner, C.-G. Stellan. *Johan Wikmanson und die Brüder Silverstolpe: Einige Stockholmer Persönlichkeiten im Musikleben des Gustavianischen Zeitalters*. Stockholm, 1952.

Neubacher, Jürgen. *Finis Coronat Opus. Untersuchungen zur Technik der Schlussgestaltung in der Instrumentalmusik Joseph Haydns, dargestellt am Beispiel der Streichquartette. Mit einem Exkurs: Haydn und die rhetorische Tradition.* Tutzing: Schneider, 1986.

Olleson, Edward. "Georg August Griesinger's Correspondence with Breitkopf & Härtel." *The Haydn Yearbook* 3 (1965): 5–53.

Parker, Mara. *The String Quartet, 1750–1797: Four Types of Musical Conversation.* Aldershot, United Kingdom: Ashgate, 2002.

Paul, Steven E. "Comedy, Wit, and Humor in Haydn's Instrumental Music." In *Haydn Studies* (1981), 450–56.

———. "Wit, Comedy, and Humour in the Instrumental Music of Franz Joseph Haydn." Ph.D. diss., Cambridge University, 1980.

Pohl, Carl Ferdinand. *Joseph Haydn.* 3 vols. Leipzig: Breitkopf & Härtel, 1875–1927 (vol. 3 completed by Hugo Botstiber with material left by Pohl).

Raab, Armin. *Funktionen des Unisono, dargestellt an den Streichquartetten und Messen von Joseph Haydn.* Frankfurt am Main: Haag & Herchen, 1990.

———. "Haydn-Bibliographie 1991–2001." *Haydn-Studien* 8 (2000–2004): 79–214.

———. "Unisono bei Wolfgang Amadeus Mozart und Joseph Haydn: Eine satztechnische Ausnahmesituation als Kriterium des Personalstils?" *Mozart-Jahrbuch 1991,* 1:522–28.

Radant, Else, ed. "The Diaries of Joseph Carl Rosenbaum (1770–1829)." *The Haydn Yearbook* 5 (1968): 7–158.

Ratner, Leonard G. *Classic Music: Expression, Form, and Style.* New York: Schirmer Books, 1980.

Reichardt, Johann Friedrich. *Musikalisches Kunstmagazin.* 2 vols. Berlin, 1782–91.

———. *Vertraute Briefe, geschrieben auf einer Reise nach Wien und den Österreichischen Staaten zu Ende des Jahres 1808 und zu Anfang 1809.* 2 vols. 1810. Modern ed., Gustav Gugitz. Munich: Müller, 1915.

Ribeiro, Alvaro, ed. *The Letters of Dr. Charles Burney.* Vol. 1. 1751–1784. Oxford: Clarendon, 1991.

Ritzel, Fred. *Die Entwicklung der "Sonatenform" im musiktheoretischen Schrifttum des 18. und 19. Jahrhunderts.* 3d ed. Wiesbaden: Breitkopf & Härtel, 1974.

Rosen, Charles. *The Classical Style: Haydn, Mozart, Beethoven.* Expanded ed. New York: W. W. Norton, 1997.

———. *Sonata Forms.* Rev. ed. New York: W. W. Norton, 1988.

Rosenthal, Albi. "The Contract between Joseph Haydn and Frederick Augustus Hyde (1796)." In *Studies in Music History Presented to H. C. Robbins Landon on His Seventieth Birthday,* ed. Otto Biba and David Wyn Jones, 72–81. London: Thames and Hudson, 1996.

Rothstein, William. *Phrase Rhythm in Tonal Music.* New York: Schirmer Books, 1989.

Russell, Tilden A. "Minuet Form and Phraseology in *Recueils* and Manuscript Tunebooks." *The Journal of Musicology* 17 (1999): 386–419.

———. "Minuet, Scherzando, and Scherzo: The Dance Movement in Transition, 1781–1825." Ph.D. diss., University of North Carolina, 1983.

———. "The Unconventional Dance Minuet: Choreographies of the Menuet d'Exaudet." *Acta Musicologica* 64 (1992): 118–38.

Salzer, Felix. "Haydn's Fantasia from the String Quartet, Opus 76, No. 6." *The Music Forum* 4 (1976): 161–94.

Sandberger, Adolf. "Zur Geschichte des Haydnschen Streichquartetts." *Altbayerische Monatsschrift* 2 (1900): 41–64. Repr. in Sandberger, *Ausgewählte Aufsätze zur Musikgeschichte*, 2 vols., 1921, 1:224–65. Reprint. Hildesheim: Olms, 1973.

Saslav, Isidor. "The *alla breve* 'March': Its Evolution and Meaning in Haydn's String Quartets." In *Haydn Studies* (1981), 308–14.

———. "Tempos in the String Quartets of Joseph Haydn." D. Mus. diss., Indiana University, 1969.

Schletterer, Hans Michael. *Joh. Friedrich Reichardt: Sein Leben und seine musikalische Thätigkeit.* 1865. Reprint. Walluf bei Wiesbaden: Sändig, 1972.

Schmid, Ernst Fritz. *Joseph Haydn: Ein Buch von Vorfahren und Heimat des Meisters.* Kassel: Bärenreiter, 1934.

Schmidt, Leopold. "Joseph Haydn, Volksgesang und Volkslied." In *Joseph Haydn und die Literatur seiner Zeit*, ed. Herbert Zeman, 25–33. Eisenstadt: Institut für Österreichische Kulturgeschichte, 1976.

Schmidt-Thieme, Lars. *Die formale Gestaltung von Exposition und Reprise in den Streichquartetten Haydns.* Frankfurt am Main: Lang, 2000.

Schöllhorn, Johannes. "Haydn und Tieck—eine Begegnung in der 'verkehrten Welt' des Streichquartetts. Das *Streichquartett op. 33 Nr. 2 Es-Dur (Hob. III:38)* von Joseph Haydn." In *Vier Vorträge zur Wienerklassik*, ed. Dominik Sackmann, 81–99. Wilhelmshaven: Heinrichshofen, 1997.

Schroeder, David P. *Haydn and the Enlightenment: The Late Symphonies and Their Audience.* Oxford: Clarendon, 1990.

———. "Melodic Source Material and Haydn's Creative Process." *The Musical Quarterly* 68 (1982): 496–515.

Schwindt, Nicole. "Haydn, Fux und das 'Kaiserlied' als cantus-firmus-Variation." *Musiktheorie* 17 (2002): 231–43.

Schwindt-Gross, Nicole. *Drama und Diskurs: Zur Beziehung zwischen Satztechnik und motivischem Prozess am Beispiel der durchbrochenen Arbeit in den Streichquartetten Haydns und Mozarts.* Laaber: Laaber, 1989.

Seedorf, Thomas. "Saitengesänge: Instrumentale Kantabilität in Haydns Streichquartetten." In *Haydns Streichquartette*, 3–39.

Seidel, Wilhelm. "Haydns Streichquartett in B-Dur op. 71 Nr. 1 (Hob. III:69): Analytische Bemerkungen aus der Sicht Heinrich Christoph Kochs." In *Joseph Haydn: Tradition und Rezeption*, 3–13.

Seifert, Herbert. "Die langsamen Sätze der späten Streichquartette Joseph Haydns." In *Colloquium. Die Instrumentalmusik (Struktur—Funktion—Ästhetik)*, Brno 1991, ed. Jiří Vysloužil and Petr Macek, 51–61. Brno: Masarykova Univerzita, 1994.

Sisman, Elaine R. *Haydn and the Classical Variation.* Cambridge, Mass.: Harvard University Press, 1993.

———. "Haydn's Variations." Ph.D. diss., Princeton University, 1978.

———. "Small and Expanded Forms: Koch's Model and Haydn's Music." *The Musical Quarterly* 68 (1982): 444–75.

———. "Tradition and Transformation in the Alternating Variations of Haydn and Beethoven." *Acta Musicologica* 62 (1990): 152–82.

Smyth, David. "'Balanced Interruption' and the Formal Repeat." *Music Theory Spectrum* 15 (1993): 76–88.

———. "Codas in Classical Form: Aspects of Large-Scale Rhythm and Pattern Completion." Ph.D. diss., University of Texas at Austin, 1985.

Solar-Quintes, Nicolás A. "Las relaciones de Haydn con la casa de Benavente." *Anuario musical* 2 (1947): 81–88.

Somfai, László. "A Bold Enharmonic Modulatory Model in Joseph Haydn's String Quartets." In *Studies in Eighteenth-Century Music*, 370–81.

———. "'Ich war nie ein Geschwindschreiber. . .': Joseph Haydns Skizzen zum langsamen Satz des Streichquartetts Hoboken III:33." In *Festskrift Jens Peter Larsen, 14. VI. 1902–1972*, ed. Nils Schiørring, Henrik Glahn, and Carsten E. Hatting, 275–84. Copenhagen: Hansen, 1972.

———. "An Introduction to the Study of Haydn's String Quartet Autographs (with Special Attention to Op. 77/G)." In *The String Quartets of Haydn, Mozart, and Beethoven*, 5–51.

———. "'Learned Style' in Two Late String Quartet Movements of Haydn." *Studia Musicologica* 28 (1986): 325–49.

———. "The London Revision of Haydn's Instrumental Style." *Proceedings of the Royal Musical Association* 100 (1973–74): 159–74.

———. "Opus-Planung und Neuerung bei Haydn." *Studia Musicologica* 22 (1980): 87–110.

———. "Zur Echtheitsfrage des Haydn'schen 'Opus 3.'" *The Haydn Yearbook* 3 (1965): 153–65.

Somfai, László, et al. "Problems of Authenticity—Op. 3." In *Haydn Studies* (1981), 95–106.

Sondheimer, Robert. *Haydn: A Historical and Psychological Study Based on His Quartets*. London: Bernoulli, 1951.

Spitzer, Michael. "Haydn's Quartet Finales and Cyclical Closure." In *Haydn the Innovator*, 99–120.

———. "Haydn's Reversals: Style Change, Gesture and the Implication-Realization Model." In *Haydn Studies* (1998), 177–217.

———. "The Retransition as Sign: Listener-Oriented Approaches to Tonal Closure in Haydn's Sonata-Form Movements." *Journal of the Royal Musical Association* 121 (1996): 11–45.

Steblin, Rita. *A History of Key Characteristics in the Eighteenth and Early Nineteenth Centuries*. Ann Arbor, Mich.: UMI Research Press, 1983.

Steinbeck, Wolfram. *Das Menuett in der Instrumentalmusik Joseph Haydns*. Munich: Katzbichler, 1973.

Steinpress, Boris. "Haydns Oratorien in Russland zu Lebzeiten des Komponisten." *Haydn-Studien* 2 (1969–70): 77–112.

Stockhausen, Johann Christoph. *Critischer Entwurf einer auserlesenen Bibliothek für die Liebhaber der Philosophie und schönen Wissenschaften*. 4th ed. Berlin, 1771.

Stowell, Robin, ed. *The Cambridge Companion to the String Quartet*. Cambridge: Cambridge University Press, 2003.

The String Quartets of Haydn, Mozart, and Beethoven: Studies of the Autograph Manuscripts. A Conference at Isham Memorial Library, March 15–17, 1979. Ed. Christoph Wolff. Cambridge, Mass.: Harvard University Press, 1980.

Strunk, W. Oliver. "Haydn's Divertimenti for Baryton, Viola, and Bass (after Manuscripts in the Library of Congress)." *The Musical Quarterly* 18 (1932): 216–51.

Studies in Eighteenth-Century Music. A Tribute to Karl Geiringer on His Seventieth Birthday. Ed. H. C. Robbins Landon and Roger E. Chapman. New York: Oxford University Press, 1970.

Sutcliffe, W. Dean. "Haydn, Mozart and Their Contemporaries." In *The Cambridge Companion to the String Quartet*, ed. Robin Stowell, 185–209. Cambridge: Cambridge University Press, 2003.

———. *Haydn: String Quartets, Op. 50.* Cambridge: Cambridge University Press, 1992.

Suurpää, Lauri. "Continuous Exposition and Tonal Structure in Three Late Haydn Works." *Music Theory Spectrum* 21 (1999): 174–99.

Szabolcsi, Bence. "Joseph Haydn und die ungarische Musik." *Beiträge zur Musikwissenschaft* 1/2 (1959): 62–73. Repr. in *Bericht über die Internationale Konferenz zum Andenken Joseph Haydns. Budapest, 17–22 September 1959*, ed. Bence Szabolcsi and Dénes Bartha, 159–75. Budapest: Akadémiai Kiadó, 1961.

Telesco, Paula J. "Forward-Looking Retrospection: Enharmonicism in the Classical Era." *The Journal of Musicology* 19 (2002): 332–73.

Tepping, Susan E. "Fugue Process and Tonal Structure in the String Quartets of Haydn, Mozart, and Beethoven." Ph.D. diss., Indiana University, 1989.

Thomas, Günter. "Griesingers Briefe über Haydn: Aus seiner Korrespondenz mit Breitkopf & Härtel." *Haydn-Studien* 1 (1965–67): 49–114.

———. "Studien zu Haydns Tanzmusik." *Haydn-Studien* 3 (1973–74): 5–28.

Toorn, Pieter C. van den. *Stravinsky and "The Rite of Spring": The Beginnings of a Musical Language*. Berkeley: University of California Press, 1987.

Tovey, Donald Francis. "Haydn, Franz Joseph, 1732–1809." In *Cobbett's Cyclopedic Survey of Chamber Music*, 2 vols., ed. and comp. Walter Willson Cobbett, 1:514–45. London: Oxford University Press, 1929–30.

———. "Sonata Forms." In Tovey, *Musical Articles from the Encyclopedia Britannica*, ed. Hubert J. Foss, 208–32. 1944. Repr. as *The Forms of Music*. New York: World Publishing, 1956.

Tyson, Alan, and H. C. Robbins Landon. "Who Composed Haydn's Op. 3?" *The Musical Times* 105 (1964): 506–7.

Unverricht, Hubert. "Carl Ditters von Dittersdorf als Quartettkomponist: Ein Konkurrent Haydns, Mozarts und Pleyels?" *Haydn-Studien* 7 (1996–98): 315–27.

———. "Die gesammelten Briefe und Tagebücher Joseph Haydns." *Die Musikforschung* 16 (1963): 53–62.

———. *Geschichte des Streichtrios.* Tutzing: Schneider, 1969.

———. "Romanus Hoffstetters Streichquartette." In *Gedenkschrift Hermann Beck*, ed. Hermann Dechant and Wolfgang Sieber, 107–110. Laaber: Laaber, 1982.

Unverricht, Hubert, in collaboration with Adam Gottron and Alan Tyson. *Die beiden Hoffstetter: Zwei Komponisten-Porträts mit Werkverzeichnissen.* Mainz: B. Schott's Söhne, 1968.

Walter, Horst. "Haydn-Bibliographie 1973–1983." *Haydn-Studien* 5 (1982–85): 205–306.

———. "Haydn-Bibliographie 1984–1990." *Haydn-Studien* 6 (1986–94): 173–238.

———. "Haydns späte Streichquartette: Überlieferung und Textkritik." In *Internationales musikwissenschaftliches Symposium "Haydn & Das Streichquartett,"* 139–67.

———. "Zum Wiener Streichquartett der Jahre 1780 bis 1800." *Haydn-Studien* 7 (1996–98): 289–314.

Walter, Horst, with prep. work by Lars Schmidt-Thieme. "Vorwort" and "Kritischer Bericht." *Joseph Haydn: Streichquartette "Opus 76", "Opus 77" und "Opus 103,"* vii–xvi, 177–227 (JHW, 12/6). Munich: Henle, 2003.

Walts, Anthony A. "The Significance of the Opening in Sonata Form: An Analytical Study of the First Movements from Three Quartets by Joseph Haydn." Ph.D. diss., Yale University, 1985.

Webster, James. "The Bass Part in Haydn's Early String Quartets." *The Musical Quarterly* 63 (1977), 390–424.

———. "The Bass Part in Haydn's Early String Quartets and in Austrian Chamber Music, 1750–1780." Ph.D. diss., Princeton University, 1973.

———. "Binary Variants of Sonata Form in Early Haydn Instrumental Music." In *Joseph Haydn*, 127–35.

———. "The Chronology of Haydn's String Quartets." *The Musical Quarterly* 61 (1975): 17–46.

———. "Did Haydn 'Synthesize' the Classical String Quartet?" In *Haydn Studies* (1981), 336–39.

———. "The Eighteenth Century as a Music-Historical Period?" *Eighteenth-Century Music* 1 (2004): 47–60.

———. "The Falling-out Between Haydn and Beethoven: The Evidence of the Sources." In *Beethoven Essays. Studies in Honor of Elliot Forbes*, ed. Lewis Lockwood and Phyllis Benjamin, 3–45. Cambridge, Mass.: Harvard University Press, 1984.

———. "Freedom of Form in Haydn's Early String Quartets." In *Haydn Studies* (1981), 522–30.

———. *Haydn's "Farewell" Symphony and the Idea of Classical Style: Through-Composition and Cyclic Integration in His Instrumental Music*. Cambridge: Cambridge University Press, 1991.

———. "Haydns Opus 9 und Opus 17: Zur Kritik der Ideologie des 'klassischen' Streichquartetts." In *Internationales musikwissenschaftliches Symposium "Haydn & Das Streichquartett,"* 89–122.

———. "Haydns Salve Regina in g-Moll (1771) und die Entwicklung zum durchkomponierten Zyklus." *Haydn-Studien* 6 (1986–94): 245–60.

———. Review of Ludwig Finscher, *Studien zur Geschichte des Streichquartetts*, vol. 1, in *Journal of the American Musicological Society* 28 (1975): 543–49.

———. "The Scoring of Haydn's Early String Quartets." In *Haydn Studies* (1981), 235–38.

———. "The Significance of Haydn's String Quartet Autographs for Performance Practice." In *The String Quartets of Haydn, Mozart, and Beethoven*, 62–95.

———. "Sonata Form." In *The New Grove Dictionary of Music and Musicians*, 2d ed., ed. Stanley Sadie and John Tyrrell, 23:687–701. London: Macmillan, 2001.

———. "Towards a History of Viennese Chamber Music in the Early Classical Period." *Journal of the American Musicological Society* 27 (1974): 212–47.

———. "Violoncello and Double Bass in the Chamber Music of Haydn and His Viennese Contemporaries, 1750–1780." *Journal of the American Musicological Society* 29 (1976): 413–38.

Webster, James, and Georg Feder. *The New Grove Haydn*. New York: Palgrave, 2002.

Wheelock, Gretchen A. "Engaging Strategies in Haydn's Op. 33 String Quartets." *Eighteenth-Century Studies* 25 (1991): 1–30.

———. *Haydn's Ingenious Jesting with Art: Contexts of Musical Wit and Humor*. New York: Schirmer Books, 1992.

————. "The 'Rhetorical Pause' and Metaphors of Conversation in Haydn's Quartets." In *Internationales musikwissenschaftliches Symposium "Haydn & Das Streichquartett,"* 67–88.

————. "Wit, Humor, and the Instrumental Music of Joseph Haydn." Ph.D. diss., Yale University, 1979.

Wiesel, Siegfried. "Klangfarbendramaturgie in den Streichquartetten von Joseph Haydn." *Haydn-Studien* 5 (1982–85): 16–22.

Willner, Channan. "Chromaticism and the Mediant in Four Late Haydn Works." *Theory and Practice* 13 (1988): 79–114.

Winkler, Gerhard J. "Opus 33/2: Zur Anatomie eines Schlusseffekts." *Haydn-Studien* 6 (1986–94): 288–97.

Woodfield, Ian. "John Bland: London Retailer of the Music of Haydn and Mozart." *Music & Letters* 81 (2000): 210–44.

Yeon, Sang-Chun. *Carl Ditters von Dittersdorf: Die Kammermusik für Streichinstrumente.* Hildesheim: Olms, 1999.

Young, David. "Haydn's Opus 33 Number 4: A Neglected Masterpiece?" In *Internationales musikwissenschaftliches Symposium "Haydn & Das Streichquartett,"* 123–38.

————. "The Slow Movements [of Haydn's String Quartets]." In *Haydn the Innovator,* 57–80.

Zilkens, Udo. *Joseph Haydn: Kaiserhymne und Sonnenaufgang. Die Erdödy-Streichquartette im Spiegel ihrer Interpretationen durch Musiktheoretiker und Musiker.* Cologne: Tonger, 1997.

Index of Haydn's String Quartets

Principal references appear in bold type.

General Index

Printed in the United States
135378LV00002B/63/P